European Union Law

Ter herinnering aan mijn moeder, Johanna van Ling (1908–1997)
and to Isabella, Amelia and especially Jude, Europeans
of the new Millennium

BUTTERWORTHS CORE TEXT SERIES
Series Editor: Nicola Padfield

European Union Law

Third Edition

Margot Horspool
Professor of European and Comparative Law at the
University of Surrey; Fellow of the Centre for the Law of
the European Union, University College London.
Professor at the College of Europe

Mark Attew, BA, DPhil   Fellow of the Centre for the Law of the
European Union at University College London.

Antonio Bavasso, JD (Florence)   Fellow of the Centre for the Law
of the European Union, University College London.

Jennifer Davis, MSc, PhD   Norton Rose Lecturer in Intellectual
Property Law, University of Cambridge, Fellow of Wolfson College.

Siri Harris, Lecturer in European Law, Kingston University.

Nicholas Emliliou, LL B, PhD   Fellow of the Centre for the Law of
the European Union, University College London.

Niamh Moloney, LL B, LL M   Reader in Law, Queen's University,
Belfast, Fellow of the Centre for the Law of the European Union,
University College London.

Richard Penfold, Senior Associate, Harbottle and Lewis, London.

Vera Sacks, BA, LL B, Reader in Law, Kingston University.

United Kingdom	LexisNexis UK, a Division of Reed Elsevier (UK) Ltd, Halsbury House, 35 Chancery Lane, LONDON WC2A 1EL and 4 Hill Street, EDINBURGH EH2 3JZ
Argentina	LexisNexis Argentina, BUENOS AIRES
Australia	LexisNexis Butterworths, CHATSWOOD, New South Wales
Austria	LexisNexis Verlag ARD Orac GmbH & Co KG, VIENNA
Canada	LexisNexis Butterworths, MARKHAM, Ontario
Chile	LexisNexis Chile Ltds, SANTIAGO DE CHILE
Czech Republic	Nakladatelstvi Otac sro, PRAGUE
France	Editions du Juris-Classeur SA, PARIS
Germany	LexisNexis Deutschland GmbH, FRANKFURT and MUNSTER
Hong Kong	LexisNexis Butterworths, HONG KONG
Hungary	HVG-Orac, BUDAPEST
India	LexisNexis Butterworths, NEW DELHI
Ireland	Butterworth (Ireland) Ltd, DUBLIN
Italy	Giuffrè Editore, MILAN
Malaysia	Malayan Law Journal Sdn Bhd, KUALA LUMPUR
New Zealand	LexisNexis Butterworths, WELLINGTON
Poland	Wydawnictwo Prawnicze LexisNexis, WARSAW
Singapore	LexisNexis Butterworths, SINGAPORE
South Africa	LexisNexis Butterworths, DURBAN
Switzerland	Stampfi Verlag AG, BERNE
USA	LexisNexis, DAYTON, OHIO

© Reed Elsevier (UK) Ltd 2003

Reprinted 2004

A CIP Catalogue record for this book is available from the British Library.

ISBN 0 406 95000 8

Printed and bound in Great Britain by William Clowes Ltd, Beccles and London.

Visit LexisNexis UK at www.lexisnexis.co.uk

Foreword to the first edition

The law of the European Union has evolved considerably both in scope and importance since the early days. The rapidly changing legal landscape has made it one of the most interesting fields of law for the student, the teacher, the practitioner and even the legal philosopher. Once perceived as a curiosity of only marginal interest to all but the specialist, it has become of central importance for many aspects of the national legal scene, so that the lawyer who dismisses Community law as an irrelevance does so at his – and his insurer's – peril. This risk is all the greater because much of Community law is hidden behind national legislation.

In the early days, when lawyers asked what EC law was about, one could simply recommend them to read the Treaty. Its structure was straightforward and so, for the most part, were its terms. This is still good advice, for the Treaty remains the primary source of law and it is impossible to understand Community law without knowing one's way round the Treaty. But the treaty structure has been complicated by the addition – without a clear indication of their inter-relationship – of the Single European Act, the EU Treaty and now, increasingly, Third Pillar Conventions. The EC Treaty itself has been radically amended, and there has been an explosion of secondary legislation, much of it highly technical.

Some of the new texts seem designed to paper over political differences rather than to set out in a coherent way the legal rules and institutional relationships that form the basis of the European Union. To an increasing extent, the Court of Justice is called upon to complete or explain legislative uncertainties. So, simply to read the texts would give a very incomplete understanding of their legal effect. They must be set in their historical and political context and the special methods of interpreting multilingual texts must be mastered.

This presents a challenge to the student and the teacher. The contours of the Community legal system change so rapidly that textbooks quickly become out-of-date. The student should, in any event, be exposed to more than one view of how the law has evolved, and how it should be read, understood and applied.

Margot Horspool's new book presents EU law, not as a static body of legal rules, but as a dynamic system, evolving as much through case law and academic discussion as legislative activity. It offers a comprehensive guide to the Union and Community system, looking at the institutional structure and processes as well as the substantive and procedural law. A particular strength of the book is that it encourages the reader to adopt a pro-active, reflective approach through the inclusion, at the end of each chapter, of self-test capsules of questions and points for discussion.

This book is a worthy addition to the valuable contribution that University College London has already made to the study of European law in the United Kingdom.

Judge David Edward
Court of Justice of the European Communities
Luxembourg
3 September 1998

Preface

This book is intended as an introductory text to European Union law. Successive Treaties following the inital ones, the impact of European Union law has expanded even further than before. It is becoming practically impossible for law students, and increasingly difficult for legal practitioners in many areas, to do without at least a basic knowledge of European law. This book hopes to serve as a guide and as a basis for further studies of the subject. For a more extensive knowledge of any of the areas of European law dealt with in this book, reference should be made to:

(a) the original sources of European Union legislation
(b) the case law of the European Court of Justice and the Court of First Instance
(c) textbooks on European law
(d) casebooks on European law
(e) European (and sometimes national) law journals
(f) Internet sources, in particular the Europa website

(a)   Original sources

European Union primary legislation is to be found in the various Treaties. There are original versions of the treaties available in all 12 official languages of the Union, but the most useful texts are those in the collections of statutes, which also contain the most important secondary legislation (published in the 11 working languages of the Union, excluding Irish).

Halsbury's Statutes volumes 51 and 52; N Foster *Blackstone's EC Legislation* (Blackstone, latest edition), Rudden & Wyatt *Basic Community Laws* (OUP, latest edition), Butterworths Student Statutes: Gale: *EC Law* (Butterworths, latest edition).

European Union secondary legislation (Regulations, Directives, Decisions) is published in the Official Journal of the European Communities (L Series). The C Series contains proposals for legislation.

Regulations are numbered giving the number first, followed by the year of publication, eg Regulation 1612/68; Directives indicate the year of publication first, followed by the number, eg Directive 64/221. The same applies to Decisions.

(b)   Case law of the European Courts

European Court cases are referred to by number, followed by the year. After the establishment of the Court of First Instance, cases before it are preceded by a T, and cases before the European Court of Justice are preceded by a C. Appeals are marked P, interim measures are marked R.

There are two sets of court reports published in English. The **European Court Reports (ECR)** is the official reporter of cases before the Court of Justice of the European Communities and publishes all such cases. Reference will usually be made to these reports. The All England Law Reports have published EC law reports since 1995 and reference will be made to them where appropriate. The most widely used unofficial reporter is the **Common Market Law Reports (CMLR)**. This series publishes the principal judgments of the European Court of Justice, competition decisions taken by the Commission of the EC, important judgments on Community law by courts of the Member States and other important communications. Reference will be made to this series particularly in respect of national cases which are not reported in the European Court Reports. Important judgments of the Court are also reported in the **Times Law Reports (TLR)**, the **Independent**, the **Financial Times** and the **Industrial Relations Law Report (IRLR)**.

(c)   Textbooks

There are a number of textbooks which may be referred to for more extensive treatment of the subjects in this book. Those published post-Amsterdam are the most useful, but some of the earlier ones could still be referred to:

Craig & de Burca, *EU Law, Text, Cases and Materials* (3rd edn, 2002), OUP.

Lasok & Bridge, *Law and Institutions of the European Communities* (7th edn, 2001), Butterworths.

Steiner & Woods, *Textbook on EC Law* (7th edn, 2000), Blackstone.

Hartley, *The Foundations of European Community Law* (5th edn, 2003), OUP (very good on institutional and constitutional law only, as is)

Douglas-Scott, *Constitutional Law of the European Union* (2002) Pearson.

Kapteyn & Verloren van Themaat, *Introduction to the Law of the European Communities*, edited by L Gormley (3rd edn, 1998) Kluwer.

Weatherill & Beaumont, *EC Law* (3rd edn, 1999), Penguin.

Andrew Evans, *A Textbook on European Union Law* (1998), Hart Publishing.

J Shaw, *Law of the European Union* (3rd edn, 2000), Macmillan.

Wyatt & Dashwood *European Community Law* (4th edn, 2000), Sweet & Maxwell.

Worthy of special mention is HG Schermers and D Waelbroek, *Judicial Protection in the European Communities* (6th edn, 2001), Kluwer.

A good cases and materials plus textbooks published in the US is: Bermann, Goebel, Davey, Fox, *European Community Law* (2002), West.

A useful amount of detailed information will be found in the Sweet & Maxwell *Encyclopaedia of European Community Law* and in *Halsbury's Laws of England* (4th edn) Vols 51 & 52, *Law of the European Communities* (Vaughan, ed, 1991 and updated addenda). The latter is now being updated in looseleaf as *Law of the European Communities Service* and is an invaluable source, covering the whole field of Community law in detail and clarity.

(d)   Casebooks

Because of the rapid development of EU law, the most recent casebooks are the most useful, such as:

Weatherill, *Cases and Materials on EC Law* (5th edn, 2000), Blackstone.

Rudden & Phelan, *Basic Community Cases* (2nd edn, 1997), OUP.

Tillotson, *European Community Law, Text, Cases and Materials* (3rd edn, 2000) Cavendish.

Plender & Usher, *Cases and Materials on the Law of the European Communities* (3rd edn, 1993), Butterworths.

Pollard & Ross, *European Community Law, Text and Materials* (1994), Butterworths.

(e)   Law journals
The principal English language journals that publish articles on European Community law include:

Common Market Law Review (CMLRev)
European Law Review (ELRev)
European Competition Law Review (ECLRev)
International & Comparative Law Quarterly (ICLQ)
European Journal of International Law (EJIL)
Journal of Common Market Studies (JCMS)
Legal Issues of European Integration (LIEI)
Yearbook of European Law (YEL)

A major headache caused by the Treaty of Amsterdam is the re-numbering of the Articles of the Treaty on European Union and of the European Community Treaty. A table of equivalences of the old and the new articles is included in the book. The book uses the new numbers throughout, but frequently refers to the old numbers in brackets.

(f)   Internet sources

The most useful website is that of the European Union itself: www.europa.eu.int, on which most of the materials referred to in (a) and (b) may be found. In addition, all latest developments are also reported there.

Acknowledgments

Several colleagues contributed chapters to the first edition of this book. I am indebted to Vera Sacks (State Liability), Niamh Moloney (Judicial Review), Antonio Bavasso and Nicholas Emiliou (Free Movement of Goods and Competition) and Mark Attew (Intellectual Property), for their most valuable contributions. My thanks again to Vera Sacks, Niamh Moloney and Antonio Bavasso who were kind enough to review their respective chapters for the second edition, and to Richard Penfold who reviewed and updated the intellectual property chapter. My thanks also to my most efficient and helpful research assistant, Stefanie Kupper, who made many useful suggestions.

For the third edition, my thanks again to Niamh Moloney and Antonio Bavasso, and to Jennifer Davis (intellectual property) and Siri Harris (competition) for their valuable contributions in updating the respective chapters.

My co-director of the UCL Centre for the Law of the European Union, David O'Keeffe, has given me his unstinted support and encouragement throughout this project.

Finally, I would like to thank my family, in particular my son David who applied his editorial experience to his reading of the entire text of the first edition, and my husband Christopher, who put up bravely with my mental and physical absences when working on this book with remarkably few complaints.

London/Esher
July 2003

Contents

xviii

Table of abbreviations

Throughout this book, a number of abbreviations are used to save space and to make the text more concise:

AG	Advocate General
All ER	All England Law Reports
CFSP	Common Foreign and Security Policy
CMLR	Common Market Law Reports
CMLRev	Common Market Law Review
EC	European Community
ECA	European Communities Act
ECB	European Central Bank
ECHR	European Convention on Human Rights
ECJ	European Court of Justice
ECLRev	European Competition Law Review
ECR	European Court Reports
ECSC	European Coal and Steel Community
EEA	European Economic Area
EEC	European Economic Community
EJIL	European Journal of International Law
ELRev	European Law Review
EMU	Economic and Monetary Union
EP	European Parliament
EU	European Union
GATT	General Agreement on Tariffs and Trade
ICLQ	International & Comparative Law Quarterly
IGC	Inter-governemental conference
IP	Intellectual property
IRLR	Industrial Relations Law Reports
JCMS	Journal of Common Market Studies
LIEI	Legal Issues of European Integration
LQR	Law Quarterly Review

MEP	Member of the European Parliament
MLR	Modern Law Review
NATO	North Atlantic Treaty Organisation
OECD	Organisation for Economic Co-operation and Development
OJ	Official Journal of the European Communities
QMV	Qualified majority voting
TEU	Treaty on European Union
TLR	Times Law Reports
WTO	World Trade Organisation
YEL	Yearbook of European Law

Table of statutes

Table of EC legislation

List of cases

I

→ *List of cases* ←

→ *List of cases* ←

→ *List of cases* ←

**National cases
decided by national courts
are listed below
alphabetically**

FRANCE

GERMANY

ITALY

UNITED KINGDOM

CHAPTER ONE

Introduction

1.1 Since its inception in 1952, the European Community has come a long way; it has matured and developed a comprehensive legal system which is beginning to penetrate the national legal systems of member states. However, the Community was set up for sound political reasons which since then have undergone profound changes. As a result, the Community—now the European Union—has developed and is turning into something quite different from the model to which many originally aspired. In the middle of the cold war the founding fathers could have had little idea that the Union would expand in the way it has. From the six original members, the European Union, as it is now called, now counts 15 member states and is set to expand to 25 by the middle of 2004. Ten states, mostly in Central and Eastern Europe, are set to join, having discarded their old Communist regimes and turned into democracies with the qualifications to join the Union. Thus, the Union seems to be on the way to eventually achieving a membership of close to 30 states. The inevitable shift in political base and objectives caused by expansion as well as other factors should always be borne in mind when studying the development of the Community legal system. It will explain why there was a need—and indeed a desire—for creativity in the interpretation of Community law in the early days and at certain levels, interspersed thereafter with periods of caution and reticence at times, as has been apparent more recently in certain fields. The shift can also help to explain some of the interventionist decisions of the European Court of Justice. Community law will, in the end, only work with the co-operation of all the member states and their national institutions, governments and courts.

1.2 Why was the Community set up, and set up in the way it was? The idea of a 'united Europe' has a long history. 'Europe' was already conceived of as an entity in Greek and Roman times. Roman citizenship is often taken as the inspiration for the modern idea of European citizenship. It was Cicero, himself a lawyer, who claimed that the proudest boast of an individual in the Roman Empire was *civis Romanus sum* and the aspiration is that one day the European citizen will regard the accolade of European citizenship with the same respect and pride, as Advocate General Jacobs said in Case C-168/91 *Konstantinidis v Stadt Altensteig* (1993): *civis Europeus sum.* The modern ideal is based on an idea of common civilisation, common origins, such as Christianity, and common ways of thinking. Philosophies and spiritual ideas always transcended national borders, as do science, culture, painting, music, and so on. In Roman times, in the Middle Ages, and subsequently, free movement of persons was something to which at least educated people were accustomed, but others, too, travelled surprisingly widely. Obstacles to such travel, and to the free movement of goods, date from relatively recently. The concept of a unified Europe has been put into practice on several later occasions to a greater or lesser extent, but it has never endured. Before the twentieth century, however, conquest was generally the driving force behind attempts at unification. The Carolingian Empire under Charlemagne fell apart after his death and the peace of Verdun in 743, although, as the Holy Roman Empire, it continued to exist in one form or another until the beginning of the nineteenth century. Napoleon, too, succeeded for a short time in bringing most of Europe under his authority, and in modern times Hitler partially succeeded, but for an even shorter period. However, the contemporary idea of a united Europe is a different one. In the nineteenth century, Europe saw itself as the centre of civilisation and the major European powers were the most powerful in the world. After the Congress of Vienna in 1815, following the final defeat of Napoleon, these great powers regulated European affairs between them, organising grand European conferences to settle particular questions. It was also a period of development of public international law and European law. Legal rules were established in a variety of fields, eg the international status of rivers and the law of the sea, and international public services were developed such as the Universal Postal Union and international conventions on intellectual property. Between the two World Wars a federal movement took root in élite circles, inspired by figures such as Coudenhove-Kalergi who proposed a European federation in which states would give up part of their sovereignty and who founded a movement called the Pan-European Union, with the French statesman Aristide Briand as the Honorary President.

1.3 Developments towards integration were halted by the conflagrations of the two World Wars in the twentieth century. Even before the outbreak of the Second World War in 1939, but in particular towards the end of the war, the realisation came that European states were no longer the great powers they once were, although this took a long time to be accepted, particularly in Britain. World supremacy was shared by the United States and the Soviet Union. Thus, the contemporary European idea came to be based, first of all, on the wish permanently to prevent conflict between European states. At the beginning of the Second World War, in the face of the threat of German invasion, there had been a plan, proposed by Winston Churchill and the French Prime Minister, Paul Reynaud, for a complete union between France and Britain. This proposal was, however, rejected by the French cabinet and, under the pressure of events, it disappeared without trace. Then, in a speech to the University of Zürich on 19 December 1946, Winston Churchill relaunched the idea of European Union, a Union mainly to be founded on a Franco-German base, and at the Hague Congress in May 1948 the European Movement was founded.

1.4 The first concrete achievement was the founding of the Council of Europe in 1949, which has its seat in Strasbourg. This organisation included most Western European countries, including the UK. Turkey also became a member. It has now been joined by many Central and Eastern European countries, including Russia. It has no legislative powers but is a consultative body, with an assembly of national members of Parliament and a Committee of Ministers, which discusses and adopts resolutions, recommendations and conventions in fields such as education, culture, science, penal establishments, social policy and legal affairs. Probably its greatest achievement is the European Convention for the Protection of Human Rights and Fundamental Freedoms, which was administered by a Commission and a Court, which have now been merged into a single Court. This Convention entered into force in 1953 and has been ratified by the majority of the (now 41) member states of the Council of Europe.

1.5 European economic co-operation first took shape with the need to administer Marshall Plan aid from the United States to Europe. This led to the setting up of the Organisation for European Economic Co-operation (OEEC) in 1948. This soon took on a broader role in the co-ordination of European economic development and, after the USA and Canada joined in 1960, it was renamed the Organisation for Economic Co-operation and Development (OECD). The OECD has no legislative powers but its analyses, statistics and forecasts of economic development in Europe are important, highly valued and influential. However, this was still only an inter-governmental organisation in which no member needed to give up any of its sovereign powers.

1.6 In 1950, the European idea was given an enormous advance by the inspiration of the two French statesmen, Jean Monnet, who at the time held no public office, and the French Foreign Minister, Robert Schuman. The Schuman plan was formally submitted by the French government on 9 May 1950. It consisted of three strands: political, military and economic; but only the economic strand was taken up at that stage. It set goals to be achieved by a functionalist approach, that is, by steadily transferring an ever-increasing number of '*fonctions*' or 'spheres of activity' from national to supra-national control. It proposed that the whole of European coal and steel production should be placed under a supra-national High Authority with far-reaching powers. Coal and steel were the industries most involved in the process of waging war, providing the raw material and the energy for the arms industry. If these industries could be pooled it would make it very difficult and eventually impossible for the countries involved in this to go to war against each other. The UK's reaction to this plan was cool, and negotiations soon went ahead without it. Although initially only a Franco-German plan, enthusiastic support was received from Italy and the Benelux countries (Belgium, the Netherlands and Luxembourg). In April 1951, the European Coal and Steel Community (ECSC) was established by the Treaty of Paris. The Community consisted of six member states: France, Germany, Italy and the Benelux countries. The Treaty came into force in July 1952. It was signed for a period of 50 years and expired in July 2002. Its relevant articles and powers have been absorbed into the EC Treaty. The governing body was the High Authority under its first President, Jean Monnet. It was endowed with supra-national powers and could take binding decisions without first obtaining the consent of the member states. A Council of Ministers was created side by side with the High Authority, with the balance of power in favour of the latter, and a Common Assembly was set up for consultation, consisting of representatives of the national parliaments. The Assembly had the power to dismiss the High Authority. There was also a Consultative Committee which advised on impending decisions. The Treaty further instituted a Court of Justice which would ensure the implementation of the Treaty and resulting secondary legislation. The ECSC's supra-national powers were considerable: not only did it rationalise coal and steel production, providing major assistance to the coal industry in decline and the conversion of whole regions and their workers to other occupations, it also promoted free trade by prohibiting government subsidies, obstacles to trade and restrictive practices and imposing fines where appropriate. In addition, it had substantive provisions which are the precursors of those in Community law such as those relating to the free movement of workers. The ECSC represented the high point of supra-nationality. Although ostensibly set up for a limited purpose, it was inspired by the mood of the times towards integration, federation and political union in Europe. The preamble to the ECSC Treaty points towards this, stating that the achievement of world peace can only be achieved by creative efforts to counter impending danger.

1.7 Meanwhile, the first steps had been taken towards military co-operation. NATO, with its transatlantic dominance, was established in 1949. In 1952, a European Defence Community treaty was proposed and signed by France, Germany, Italy and the Benelux countries, but eventually failed to be ratified by the French national assembly. Instead, an organisation with few powers, except advisory ones, was established in Brussels in 1955. This arose out of a Treaty—the Brussels Treaty—designed to continue the alliances formed in the Second World War, signed in 1948, and forming the Western European Union consisting of the six member states of the original European Defence Community, plus the United Kingdom. Spain, Portugal and Greece then joined, as did a large number of associate members and partners throughout Eastern and Western Europe and, after languishing for many years in the shadow of NATO, it was reactivated with new tasks and a European identity. It is now absorbed into the EU as the defence arm of the European Union, providing the institutions for a common defence and security policy.

1.8 The failure of the European Defence Community, and the lack of any progress on the European Political Community, for which a draft statute had been proposed at the same time, led to the realisation that political integration had to be preceded by more sober economic considerations. Thus, aspirations had been scaled down by 1955, when the Messina Conference instructed the Belgian Foreign Minister, Paul-Henri Spaak, to explore possibilities for more comprehensive economic integration. The *Spaak* Report, presented to an inter-governmental conference in 1956, led to the establishment of the European Economic Community (EEC) and the European Atomic Energy Community (Euratom). The Treaties of Rome, setting up both Communities, were signed on 25 March 1957 and came into force on 1 January 1958. The United Kingdom had taken part in the negotiations for only a very short time and thereafter had no further involvement. Thus, the two Communities were established with the same six members as those of the ECSC. The Communities followed the institutional pattern of the ECSC, but this time, significantly, they were set up for an unlimited duration. Two new institutions were set up for each: a Commission and a Council of Ministers, with the Court of Justice and the Assembly serving all three Communities. The powers of the Commission were less than those of the High Authority. The idea of supra-nationality had had its day; the presence of General de Gaulle, a firm opponent of federalism, and his vision of '*l'Europe des patries*' continued to influence and dominate the development of the Communities and contributed to a number of crises in the 1960s, such as that which led to the Luxembourg Compromise in 1966 (see **3.16**).

1.9 After the creation of the EEC, a number of countries which did not wish to, or could not, take part, established the European Free Trade Association (EFTA) under the leadership of the UK. This was set up in 1960 and consisted of Austria, Denmark, Norway, Portugal, Sweden, Switzerland and the UK. They were joined later by Finland, Iceland and Liechtenstein. Most of these countries later joined the European Union, so that the EEA members now consist of Norway, Iceland and Liechtenstein. Switzerland had voted in a referendum in 1992 not to join the EEA (European Economic Area) set up jointly between the EU and EFTA (see further **2.34**).

1.10 It soon proved necessary to rationalise the three Communities and in 1965 the Merger Treaty, which came into force in July 1967, merged the High Authority and the two Commissions into one body, the European Commission, and provided that the Communities were to be served by one Council of Ministers. Finances were rationalised in 1971, when the financial contributions from individual member states were replaced by the 'own resources' system. Under this system agricultural levies, customs duties and each member state's share of the Value Added Tax contribution were paid directly to the Community. The Assembly, which had already called itself the European Parliament since 1958, officially became the European Parliament in 1986 in the Single European Act; the first direct elections of Members (MEPs) in the member states took place in 1979.

1.11 Moves towards political union were never absent for long. A number of reports appeared, such as the *Tindemans* Report in 1975; the report of the 'Three Wise Men' in 1979; and a joint proposal for union by the German and Italian foreign ministers, Genscher and Colombo, which resulted in a Joint Declaration on European Unity, adopted by the European Council at the Stuttgart Summit in 1983. This was followed by the Spinelli Draft Treaty on European Union, adopted by the European Parliament in 1984. These initiatives, followed by the *Dooge* Report on institutional reform, and the *Adonnino* Report on a People's Europe presented by ad hoc Committees set up by the European Council in Fontainebleau in 1984, contributed to the convening of an inter-governmental conference to look at Treaty revision. The result was the proposal for the Single European Act, which was signed in 1986 and came into force on 1 July 1987. Summit meetings of heads of state or government—a term for ad hoc meetings of heads of state and government meeting not in the Council but at separate informal meetings, which later became increasingly formalised—have taken place throughout the life of the Community and the European Council, and became institutionalised in 1974. It was formally recognised by the Single European Act in 1986 and is now the supreme political authority in the Union, albeit without formal decision-making powers. European political co-operation, co-operation in foreign policy, grew out of these meetings and has turned into the inter-governmental pillar on the common foreign and security policy (CFSP) in the Treaty on European Union (see Chapter 3).

1.12 After the Community had gone through periods of stagnation in the 1970s and 1980s and the impetus towards the creation of a common market seemed to have been lost, the Single European Act provided a step towards the revival of the single market project. This had been inspired by Lord Cockfield, the British Commissioner, who drew up a White Paper providing for moves towards a true internal market in 1992. The year 1992 became of focus for market integration and the efforts to comply with the deadline, although not entirely successful, nevertheless constituted considerable progress. In 1989, the European Council decided to hold two inter-governmental conferences, on proposals for Economic and Monetary Union (EMU) and on political union. As a result, the Maastricht Treaty on European Union (TEU) was adopted in 1992, and came into force in 1993. The main achievement of that Treaty is the provision for Economic and Monetary Union which entered its third stage for 11 out of the 15 member states of the Union on 1 January 1999. Its currency, the euro, became legal tender in the 11 member states, joined by Greece a few months later. So far it has received a mixed reception and its real effect on the Union cannot yet be comprehensively assessed, but it constitutes without doubt a momentous development.

7

The Treaty also officially adopted the name 'European Union' for the entity governed by all three pillars. The TEU, in its turn, provided for an inter-governmental conference to be held in 1996. This conference terminated in Amsterdam in June 1997 and resulted in the Treaty of Amsterdam, which was ratified in 1999 and itself provided for enlargement tied to institutional reform. This was to be achieved by the next Treaty, prepared by another inter-governmental conference. This IGC led to the adoption of the Treaty of Nice in December 2001. Its main elements concern enlargement and a profound reform of the two inter-governmental pillars. As Nice could not reach agreement on institutional reform, the Treaty provided that a Convention would be called in order to prepare a Constitution for the European Union. This Convention opened in The Hague in March 2002 under the chairmanship of French former President Valérie Giscard-d'Estaing. A draft constitutional Treaty was presented to the Summit Meeting of the European Council in Greece in June 2003. This is to be studied by the subsequent IGC which should terminate its work before enlargement in in May 2004. Meanwhile, the ratification process had been stalled because of a negative referendum vote on contributions to the Community budget because of enlargement, and about the provisions in the second Pillar on Foreign and Security Policy concerning a European army seen as a threat to Irish nationality. After elections in Ireland which returned the government with an increased majority the decision was taken to have a second referendum on 19 October 2002. The Irish people this time voted yes overwhelmingly by 63% to 37%, thus setting the stage for the start of the enlargement process as the last country to ratify the Treaty. The Nice Treaty duly entered into force on 1 February 2003.

1.13 The undoubted economic success of the EEC has attracted more and more members (see 2.3). After the accession of the UK, Ireland and Denmark in 1972, Greece, Spain and Portugal joined, partly also for political reasons, and this trend is set to continue in the future. Since the collapse of the Soviet Union and Communism after 1989 and the unification of Germany in 1990, a large number of countries in Central and Eastern Europe applied to join the Union. At the Copenhagen summit in December 2002 the member states decided that Poland, the Czech Republic, Slovakia, Hungary, the Baltic States Estonia, Latvia and Lithuania, as well as Slovenia and the islands of Cyprus and Malta would be invited to join in the middle of 2004 and, subject to ratification by referendum, accession will now take place in May 2004. Bulgaria and Romania are aiming at joining later, as they still do not fulfil the criteria for membership. Turkey has been given a provisional date of 2005 for a possible opening of negotiations and thus the Union may grow to nearly 30 members in the next decade.

1.14 The Community has now been in existence for 50 years. It has contributed to peace, stability and prosperity in Europe, and there is no doubt that Europe might look very different today if there had not been a Community its present form. It was born out of the wish never to have war again between major powers in Europe, coupled with the perceived need to achieve self-sufficiency in the provision of food, and these goals must be said to have been attained. War between member states would be truly unthinkable today and the common agricultural policy has certainly achieved the aim of self-sufficiency, although it has many other flaws. However, goals and objectives have changed and it is more difficult today than it was in the 1950s and 1960s to identify what stage the European idea has reached, and in which direction it should be moving. Theories of functionalism, and later of neo-functionalism, have tried to attribute different reasons and motives for the creation of the Community. It is probably true that it is not realistic to aspire to a united Europe along the model of the United States. The consensus has grown that such total unification on a federalist model is not the way forward for Europe. The success of EMU would do much to contribute to further developments. The advent of a considerable number of small countries with economies which are behind those of the wealthier present members of the Community will also serve to transform the Community. This 'widening' of the Community may happen at the expense of the 'deepening' desired by many. It will probably be necessary to allow countries at different stages of development a much greater flexibility within the confines of the Union, whilst adhering to its basic principles. Nevertheless, the momentum of developments will inevitably lead to an 'ever closer union'.

Further reading

François Duchêne, *Jean Monnet: The First Statesman of Interdependence,* (1995) Norton London.

Douglas-Scott, *Constitutional Law of the European Union,* (2002) Longman, Chapter 1.

CHAPTER TWO

The Constitutional Base of the Union

SUMMARY
- The ECSC Treaty (1952)
- The EEC and Euratom Treaties (1957)
- The Merger Treaty (1965)
- The Accession of New Members in 1972, 1980, 1986 and 1995
- The Single European Act (1986)—progress towards the Internal Market and 1992
- The Treaty on European Union (1993)
- The Treaty of Amsterdam (signed 1997, entered into force May 1999)
- The Treaty of Nice, adopted December 2001, entered into force 1 February 2003
- The further enlargement of the Community—towards a Community of up to 25 members by 2004 and at least two more by 2007

2.1 Although, usually, reference is made to 'the EC Treaty', or 'the EU Treaty' there are, in fact, several treaties which together represent the primary law of the European Union, its constitutional base. The Treaty which first founded the Community was inspired by the ideals of Robert Schuman and Jean Monnet, and the wishes of the member states, in particular France and Germany, to do away with the rivalries of the two industries which used the raw materials which produced the weapons of war: coal and steel. The member states were prepared to give up their powers to a great extent to regulate those industries. The Treaty of Paris in 1951 set up the European Coal and Steel Community (ECSC) and gave the Community a number of institutions, in particular a High Authority, which was charged with the task of applying the Treaty, having been endowed with supra-national powers by the Treaty (see also 1.6).

2.2 As the memory of war receded and economic concerns and states' self-interests became more pronounced, the need was felt for further European co-operation in the wider economic field. There were, at that time, those who aspired to greater political union, but the Treaty which was eventually signed in 1957, the Treaty of Rome, established a European Economic Community (the EEC Treaty) which was built on economic objectives. At the same time a Treaty founding a European Atomic Energy Community (Euratom) provided for the pooled control of the peaceful use of nuclear power. Both these Communities were run by a Commission as their administrative body. All three Communities had one European Assembly (later the European Parliament) and one Court of Justice in common. The High Authority and the two Commissions were merged into one European Commission by the Merger Treaty in 1965.

2.3 In 1972, the first enlargement of the Communities took place through the Treaties of Accession of Denmark, Ireland and the United Kingdom. The next enlargement came in 1981, with the accession of Greece, after it had divested itself of the regime of the colonels. This was followed in 1986 by the accession of Spain and Portugal, which had both discarded their dictatorship regimes and, most recently, in 1995, by the accession of Austria, Finland and Sweden. Norway, which had signed a Treaty of Accession in 1972 but was prevented from joining after a negative vote in a referendum, repeated the exercise in 1994, when it again signed a Treaty of Accession but was again barred from joining by a negative referendum vote. Norway had joined with Iceland and Liechtenstein, the remaining members of the European Free Trade Association (EFTA), in forming a European Economic Area (EEA) between the European Union and EFTA. Switzerland, which had been a member of EFTA, decided in a referendum in 1992 that it could not join the EEA. The EEA has its own Court and Surveillance Authority, and gives the opportunity to the former EFTA States to have access to the EC internal market. The price paid is the acceptance of the entire *acquis communautaire* (all the legislation passed and decisions taken by the Community up to the time of accession).

The period up to the Single European Act (SEA) 1986

2.4 Ever since the European Community's beginnings, periods of enthusiasm and frantic activity have alternated with periods of 'coasting', or even sometimes virtual stagnation. After the initial thrust in the years after 1957, disillusionment set in, together with a growth in awareness of national identity and importance. In part, this was because the initial primary aim of the Community, the prevention of war between the partners, appeared to have been achieved, and past rivalries were replaced with the common enemy of the cold war. This made countries aware of a wider global threat and of a need to maintain a close relationship with the United States.

2.5 Although the Customs Union had been completed ahead of the deadline in 1969, gaps existed in the Common Market because of the prevalence of so-called non-tariff barriers which acted as obstacles to trade between member states. At this stage quotas and tariffs had been abolished, but in practice the existence of differing regulatory and fiscal regimes at national levels seriously hampered intra-Community trade. For example, there were physical barriers in the form of frontier posts, and there were technical barriers in the form of differing product standards. Although there were moves in the direction of economic and monetary union, a number of obstacles held up the move to the next stage of political union.

• *Unanimity* The first obstacle was an institutional one. In 1965 the transitional period to allow member states gradually to move towards a customs union was coming to an end and this entailed moves to qualified majority rather than unanimous voting in the Council. Following a disagreement on the financing of the Common Agricultural Policy (CAP), the French government operated an 'empty chair' policy in the Community for a period during which no French representatives attended Community meetings. In 1966 the '*Luxembourg Compromise*' solved this crisis. The compromise, which did not have a definite legal status, has continued to exist and has now been given legitimacy by the Treaty of Amsterdam (see **3.16**). It has rarely been threatened and even more rarely invoked, but it is there and could, theoretically, be used. Drawn up for the benefit of France, it provided that, in cases where a vital interest of a country was involved, even if the Treaty provided for majority voting, in fact unanimous voting should be preferred. France wished any discussions to be continued until such unanimity had been achieved. This resort to unanimity led to repeated delays in progress and to stagnation in decision-making.

In particular, under Article 100 (now Article 94 EC), which deals with the harmonisation of rules, standards of products and services Community-wide, decision-making was to continue to be by unanimity.

- *Oil crisis* In 1973–74 the energy crisis hit the Community hard, and triggered recession in Europe. Member states were more concerned to deal with internal economic conditions than to forge ahead with European Union. A symptom of this protectionism was that many member states used regulatory provisions, eg product standards, to prevent access to national markets by goods from other member states.

- *Enlargement* With the advent of the first three new member states, Denmark, Ireland and the United Kingdom, followed by Greece in 1981 and then by Spain and Portugal in 1986, the Community had to adapt. The accession of new members caused difficulties in terms of achieving unanimity in Council meetings. More member states meant that more diverse interests were at stake.

Internal market proposals

2.6 As a result of German/French proposals in 1985, the Commission sent the Council of Ministers a White Paper on completing the internal market. This had been drawn up by Lord Cockfield, one of the two British Commissioners. The Commission stated that to achieve the internal market, physical, technical and fiscal barriers (ie non-tariff barriers) would have to be abolished within the Community. It set a deadline of 1992 for the removal of a great number of different barriers. It was made clear that institutional changes were needed. The European Council stated in 1985 that 'no important economic development could be achieved unless the way the institutions functioned was changed'. The *Dooge* and *Adonnino* reports were drawn up in response to this (see **1.11**).

The Single European Act (SEA) 1986

2.7 Gradually, growing dissatisfaction among member states with the progress towards the single market, which was one of the main objectives in the Treaty of Rome, created the need for a Treaty revision. The Single European Act, which came into force on 1 July 1987, introduced more specific single market objectives, to be achieved by the increased use of qualified majority voting. A new procedure with greater involvement of the European Parliament was introduced in the form of the co-operation procedure (now Article 252 EC) and it was given a power of veto over accession of new member states and the conclusion of association agreements in Articles 237 (now repealed) and 238 EEC (now Article 310 EC). New areas of competence for the Community were introduced or spelt out in more detail, relating to social policy, economic and monetary policy, research and technology and environmental policy. A Title on inter-governmental co-operation in foreign policy was added. The SEA also provided for the eventual creation of a Court of First Instance (CFI) to take over some of the jurisdiction of the European Court of Justice.

The internal market

2.8 The Community aimed at achieving not just a Common Market, but also an internal market. The concept of the internal market was introduced by the SEA and is described in Article 14 (ex Article 7a) EC as 'an area without internal frontiers in which the free movement of goods, persons, services and capital is ensured in accordance with the provisions of this Treaty'. As set out in Article 14 of the Treaty the deadline for completion of the internal market was 31 December 1992. The SEA supplemented the EEC Treaty by adding Article 100a (now Article 95 EC). This provided that certain measures harmonising or approximating member states' laws affecting the functioning or establishment of the internal market could be passed in Council by a qualified majority rather than by unanimity.

Article 95 EC is a broad provision—it covers all measures which are necessary in order to achieve the 'objectives set out in Article 14'. Under Article 94 (ex Article 100) EC which dealt with the harmonisation throughout the Community of rules, standards of products and services before the SEA, decision-making had been by unanimity. The SEA thus considerably speeded up decision-making. However, Article 94 remains the vehicle for those measures which do not fall within the internal market definition of Article 14. The SEA began a massive programme of approximation of laws by way of harmonisation, and, increasingly, by 'mutual recognition', which constituted a less strict approach than harmonisation of national laws.

2.9 The SEA, in spite of many weaknesses which were rightly criticised, nevertheless provided a fresh push towards mainly economic integration, the primary objective being that the completion of the internal market would bring advantages to the Community in the form of increased trade. It also made some institutional reforms and, most notably, introduced a new co-operation procedure which strengthened the position of the European Parliament (see **4.36**). The deadline of 31 December 1992 for completion of the internal market was not met. The White Paper on the internal market had set 282 proposals—by 1992 95% of these had been adopted by the Community but less than half had been transposed into the national law of the member states. One of the thorniest problems, the abolition of border controls, was not solved until later, and even then not completely. However, the process of harmonisation continued. With the creation of the European Economic Area the internal market experienced great expansion.

The Treaty on European Union (the Maastricht Treaty) 1993

2.10 The SEA was always intended as a step in the process towards further Treaty revision. An inter-governmental conference (IGC) was held in Maastricht, in the Netherlands, which was concluded by the signing of the Treaty on European Union (TEU) in February 1992. Although the intention was that the Treaty should come into force on 1 January 1993, the ratification process proved to be fraught with major difficulties. The people of Denmark at first voted in a referendum against ratification. As a result, the meeting of the European Council of heads of state and government in Edinburgh in 1992 added protocols to the TEU containing concessions to Denmark on economic and monetary union and defence. After a second referendum, Denmark ratified with a narrow majority, as did France. In the UK, the Maastricht Bill survived a number of very close votes in the House of Commons, as well as a constitutional challenge in the High Court (*R v Secretary of State for Foreign and Commonwealth Affairs, ex p Rees-Mogg* (1993)). Germany was the last country to ratify, after a constitutional challenge which was rejected, but which created a much greater awareness in Germany of the problems connected with transfer of powers from the member state to the Community (*Brunner v European Union Treaty* (1993), see also **8.37**). The Maastricht Treaty on European Union thus entered into force in November 1993.

2.11 The TEU was again intended as a stage in the process towards further integration. It provided for an IGC to be held in 1996 'to examine Treaty amendments'. A 'Reflection Group' consisting of representatives of the Council, the Commission and the European Parliament was set up by the European Council at the Corfu summit in 1995 to prepare what was to become the Amsterdam Treaty. The IGC opened in Turin in March 1996 and lasted for over a year. Member states and all the institutions had published various documents indicating their own priorities for the IGC to be held in Amsterdam. The Conference was concerned, in particular, with an institutional revision of the Treaty: the powers of the Council, the Commission, the Parliament and the Court of Justice. Of the larger member states, France and the UK were keen to preserve or extend the Council's powers and to curb those of the Commission. They also did not wish to give more powers to the European Parliament, whereas Germany, in particular, wanted the Parliament to be stronger. The role to be played by national Parliaments was, therefore, also examined.

The Treaty of Amsterdam (signed June 1997, entered into force 1 May 1999)

2.12 The Reflection Group's reports contained the points which the Amsterdam IGC was meant to discuss and on which decisions were meant to be taken:

- The qualified majority voting system. Each member state has a different number of votes in the Council. The number of votes per country was to be reviewed, with the objective of establishing a better balance between large and small countries, taking into account potential new members. However, no agreement was reached in Amsterdam on this (see further Chapter 3).

- The Presidency of the Council. At present each country has the presidency for six months (see Chapter 3).

- The Social Chapter. The UK 'opt-out' from the Social Chapter obtained in the TEU was reversed in Amsterdam and the Agreement on Social Policy was included in the EC Treaty.

- A review of different forms of legislation and an examination of a possible hierarchy of norms. This did not seem to receive much attention or arouse much interest. At present, all legislation of varying importance and types has to go through the same cumbersome legislative process (see Chapter 4). A restructuring of this had become necessary but the balance of power between the institutions also had to be preserved.

2.13 In spite of serious endeavours to come to an agreement in Amsterdam, the question of changing the institutions and procedures was not satisfactorily resolved and had therefore to be re-examined by the post-Amsterdam inter-governmental conference preparing the Nice Treaty (see **2.15**). A Protocol to the Treaty of Amsterdam tied the question of institutional reform, of the number of Commissioners (albeit capped at 20), and of the re-weighting of votes in the qualified majority voting in the Council to the admission of new member states and this had to be resolved at least a year before the admission of new members. The legislative procedures were somewhat simplified and the co-decision procedure, in which the European Parliament has an equal say with the Council and may block the adoption of legislation, was extended and almost entirely replaced the co-operation procedure, which in most cases is less favourable to the European Parliament and now only applies to economic and monetary union questions. The UK had wanted a review of the jurisdiction of the European Court of Justice, but nothing was done in this respect. The 'third pillar' on home affairs and justice now includes Article 35, which enables member states to accept the jurisdiction of the court to give preliminary rulings on the validity and interpretation of framework decisions and on the interpretation of conventions concluded under the Title if a member state signs a declaration showing its acceptance of such jurisdiction, either when the Treaty of Amsterdam was signed or later (see **2.31**). Economic and monetary union was not on the agenda, as its timetable had been established in the TEU at Maastricht. A major topic of discussion was to be the enlargement of the EU to include other member states, particularly those from Central and Eastern Europe. A first group of countries was named in December 1997 by the European Council, for the first negotiations for enlargement. They were Cyprus, Poland, Hungary, the Czech Republic, Slovenia and Estonia, and the first steps towards the negotiations were taken in March 1998 (see further **2.37**).

2.14 Subjects which were not discussed include economic and monetary union (see **2.23**) and the common agricultural policy. The conclusion came in June 1997 in Amsterdam with a summit of heads of state or government. At this meeting the Treaty of Amsterdam was signed.

However, the process of 'simplification' of the Treaty, which involved an overhaul of the structure of the Treaty on European Union and the Treaties establishing the European Communities took several more months to complete. This did not, however, impinge upon the ratification process which was conducted in parallel. The result of the simplification process was purely a change in structure and numbering, but this meant that all the articles, both in the Treaty of European Union and in the Treaty establishing the European Community, with which this book is mainly concerned, were re-numbered and consolidated. After the successive amendments of the Single European Act and the Maastricht Treaty on European Union, the Treaty texts had become unwieldy and difficult to understand. Some of the articles in the original Treaties had become spent and needed to be deleted. The Amsterdam Treaty undertook a re-numbering of the articles both in the Treaty on European Union and in the EC Treaty. The articles in the Maastricht TEU were indicated by letters, which were replaced by numbers. The articles in the EC Treaty were re-numbered and this now means that articles in the TEU and the EC Treaty, as amended by the Amsterdam Treaty, may bear the same number; it is, of course, important to distinguish between the two. The updated and consolidated version is referred to throughout this book, generally giving the new articles agreed upon by Amsterdam first, and indicating the former article numbers of the TEU in brackets. A table of equivalences is included in an appendix at p 483.

The Nice Treaty (adopted December 2001, entered into force 1 February 2003)

2.15 In December 2001 an inter-governmental conference convened in Nice. Its remit was to reach an agreement on institutional issues, as the issue of enlargement had been tied to this by a Protocol annexed to the Amsterdam Treaty (see **3.19**), to prepare for enlargement by determining the numbers of seats in the European Parliament and the number of votes per country under the qualified majority voting (QMV) system. It was also hoped that the number of areas subject to QMV would be increased substantially, thus doing away to a great extent with any issues on which unanimity would still be required. The Treaty of Nice, which was agreed in December 2001, signed by all member states' governments on 26 February 2002, and which came into force on 1 February 2003, does indeed deal with the numbers. A Protocol was attached to the Nice Treaty, making provision for the changing situation after enlargement. This Protocol makes provision for the number of representatives in the European Parliament (Article 2) and for the weighting of votes in the Council (Article 3). The number of seats in the Parliament from the next elections in 2004 has been reduced from 626 to 535 for the present member states. The total number of votes for QMV per member state was increased considerably, but more so for the most populated states, taking account of the fact that most of the new member states will be small or, in some cases, very small countries. Thus, the total number of votes was increased from 87 to 237. A Declaration attached to the Treaty then takes account of the situation after enlargement has been completed. This brings the total number of votes for QMV up to 345. It also provides for the distribution of seats for the new member states in the European Parliament. The total number of seats, which had been capped at 700 in the Treaty of Amsterdam (Article 189 (ex Article 137) EC) will be increased from 535 in 2004 to a total of 737 if and when all 12 candidate member states have acceded. This total of 737 is now set as the new ceiling. The Declaration provides for this arrangement to come into force from January 2005 (see Chapter 3 for more detail).

2.16 The Nice Treaty made a number of other changes. Most of these will be discussed under the relevant subject headings. No major changes were made in the institutional balance but particularly in the case of the European Court of Justice (ECJ) and the Court of First Instance (CFI) considerable changes were made in order to streamline and speed up the functioning of the courts (see also Chapter 5). QMV was extended to more areas, although the more contentious ones, such as those concerning taxation and immigration, were left to unanimous voting.

At Nice, the Charter of Fundamental Rights was welcomed by Proclamation. It had been adopted in November in Biarritz by a joint Proclamation by the Council, the Parliament and the Commission. See further Chapter 6.

The structure and content of the Treaties

2.17 The first major Treaty amendment took place in Maastricht where the Treaty on European Union was adopted in 1992. It entered into force in November 1993. The Treaty of Amsterdam which amended the Maastricht Treaty on European Union was adopted in Amsterdam in 1997 and entered into force in May 1999. The Treaty on European Union concluded in Maastricht in its basic form, consists of general framework articles and of three so-called 'pillars'. The first pillar contains the

European Community Treaties, ie the European Coal and Steel Community (ECSC) Treaty, the Euratom Treaty and the EC Treaty. The Amsterdam and Nice Treaties preserved the basic three pillar structure of the TEU. In the main, it has preserved the inter-governmental nature of in particular the second pillar, and, to a lesser extent, of the third pillar. Our attention will focus primarily on the first pillar, and, within it, on the amended EEC Treaty (the original Treaty of Rome), which was renamed the EC Treaty in Maastricht.

2.18 The second pillar consists of Title V, Articles 11–28 TOA (ex Articles J.1–J.18) containing provisions on a common foreign and security policy; the third pillar consists of Articles 29–45 TOA (ex Title VI, Articles K.1–K.17) containing provisions on co-operation in the field of freedom, security and justice. This pillar was renamed from the original name of justice and home affairs given to it in Maastricht and considerably amended. It is now named provisions on police and judicial co-operation in criminal matters.

2.19 The TEU, as amended by the Treaty of Amsterdam, starts with common or framework provisions, Title I, Articles 1–7 (ex Articles A–F), which define the principles of the Union. They speak of ever closer union among the peoples of Europe (Article 1), as did the Treaty of Rome, and add 'in which decisions are taken as openly as possible and as closely as possible to the citizen'. The objectives set in Article 2 include:

> economic and social progress, a high level of employment and balanced and sustainable development to be achieved through the creation of an area without internal frontiers, ie free movement of goods, persons, services and capital within the territory of the Union, and the establishment of economic and monetary union, 'ultimately including a single currency'; to implement a common foreign and security policy including the (eventual) progressive framing of a defence policy which might (in time) lead to a common defence; a more extensive development of the co-operation in justice and home affairs contained in the Maastricht TEU to make the Union 'an area of freedom, security and justice...'; the Maastricht TEU introduced a citizenship of the Union. The *acquis communautaire* (all that the Community has achieved and decided) will be maintained and built upon. All these objectives are to be achieved whilst having regard to the principle of subsidiarity.

2.20 One change made in Nice concerns Fundamental Rights. Article 7 of the TEU, inserted by the Treaty of Amsterdam, which provided for a declaration by the European Council of a 'serious and persistent breach of fundamental rights' by a member state followed by a possible suspension of that member state, was supplemented in Nice by a preventive clause whereby upon a proposal by one third of the member states, the Commission, or the Parliament the Council, acting by a four-fifth majority and with the assent of the European Parliament may 'declare that a clear *danger* exists of a member state committing a serious breach of fundamental rights'. Recommendations may then be addressed to such a member state.

2.21 With one exception (see Article 6(2) TEU and **6.21**) the first part of the common provisions, like most of the second and third pillars, is not subject to the jurisdiction of the European Court of Justice and thus is not governed by the institutional structure of the EC Treaty. The Nice Treaty is also silent on that point. The Nice Treaty provides in Article 46 that the ECJ will be competent only for disputes involving procedural matters concerning Article 7 and not to judge the substance of any dispute.

2.22 The first 'pillar' of the Treaty on European Union consists of the various Treaties as amended. The EC Treaty is thus itself part of the Treaty on European Union. This book deals mostly only with the EC Treaty and references to 'the Treaty' will therefore always concern the EC Treaty and its amendments. EEC Treaty amendments reflect the objectives set in the common provisions. The epithet 'economic' was removed from the Treaty in Maastricht, reflecting the reality of the gradual widening of the scope of the Treaty beyond economic objectives. Thus, the Treaty became the Treaty establishing the European Community: the EC Treaty. The principle of subsidiarity is given a prominent place in Article 5 (ex Article 3b) EC:

> In areas which do not fall within its exclusive competence, the Community shall take action, in accordance with the principle of subsidiarity, only if and in so far as the objectives of the proposed action cannot be sufficiently achieved by the member states and can therefore, by reason of the scale or effects of the proposed action, be better achieved by the Community.

Article 2 TEU in its last paragraph also states that this principle will be respected in achieving the objectives of the Union. It should be noted that subsidiarity does not apply to areas which fall within the exclusive jurisdiction (or 'competence') of the Community. These areas have grown since the inception of the Treaties and concern such matters as the common agricultural policy (CAP), competition rules and the common commercial policy. As more Community action is taken in fields such as a common transport policy and the environment, these matters too will come increasingly under the exclusive jurisdiction of the Community. Subsidiarity will only apply to areas in which there is a shared or concurrent competence between the Community and the member states.

At the European Council Summit in Edinburgh in December 1992, after the signing of the TEU and the refusal of Denmark after a negative referendum to ratify, the practices and procedures were set out which were intended to ensure that subsidiarity was taken into account at every stage of the legislative process (Commission Report to the European Council on the Application of the Subsidiarity Principle). Regular reports are made to each European Council meeting (summit of Heads of State or Government) on the implementation of the principle of subsidiarity. The Amsterdam Treaty includes Protocol 7 on the application of the principles of subsidiarity and proportionality which sets out to establish the principles more clearly, but does not alter the substance of Article 5 (see further **4.52** and **4.54–4.59**).

Economic and monetary union

2.23 Probably the most important element introduced in the EC Treaty in Maastricht, which was included unaltered in the subsequent Treaties, is the creation of an economic and monetary union (EMU). The achievement of a single currency is stated to be the ultimate aim of EMU. In an implementing decision by the Council, the single currency was named the euro. A timetable was set in Title VII Articles 98–124 (ex Title VI, Articles 102a–109m) EC for the achievement of EMU in three stages by 1 January 1999. Strict convergence criteria were laid down with which member states had to comply before they could proceed to the next stage of EMU. The ratio of total government debt to gross domestic product (GDP) should not exceed 60% and the ratio of annual government deficit to GDP should not exceed 3%. Other criteria concern the achievement of a high degree of price stability, apparent from a low rate of inflation, avoidance of currency fluctuation within the exchange rate mechanism (ERM) for at least two years, and sustainable and durable economic convergence. The third stage was set to start on 1 January 1999 for those countries which 'fulfil the necessary conditions for the adoption of a single currency,' ie those complying with the convergence criteria. The countries which were deemed to comply with the criteria were approved by a summit meeting of heads of state and government on 2 May 1998. Of the 15 member states, 11 were deemed to comply with the criteria. Greece did not comply and the United Kingdom and Denmark had obtained 'opt-outs' in protocols annexed to the Treaty on European Union, which released them from the obligation to enter the third stage, although they could choose to do so. Sweden was also found not to qualify and took the decision not to proceed with its application to join EMU. Thus, on 1 January 1999, 11 member states entered the third stage of the single currency and introduced the euro. Of the four member states which did not join, they were later joined by Greece in January 2001 and a referendum in Denmark in September 2000 decided Denmark would stay out for the time being. In January 2002 the euro was introduced as banknotes and coins in the 12 member states which had joined the euro. National banknotes and coins were withdrawn very quickly in some member states, more gradually in others, but this was completed by the middle of February 2002. The success of a smooth introduction helped to fuel a short rally in the value of the euro, which had fallen steadily since its introduction and languished, particularly in its exchange rate to the dollar, at well below parity. The euro then experienced a revival and rose to parity and above. Hopes that particularly the UK population would change its negative attitude towards the currency over the summer when many would have had experience of it during holidays abroad, did not appear to be realised. In June 2003 the British Chancellor of the Exchequer reported that the five economic tests, which he had set in October 1997 as a condition for considering a referendum on entry, had not all been achieved and that re-assessment would take place in about a year.

2.24 Article 8 (ex Article 4a) EC provides for the establishment of a European System of Central Banks and of a European Central Bank (ECB). This happened after the decision on the third stage had been taken. Before that, preparations for EMU were made by the European Monetary Institute (EMI) (Article 117 (ex Article 109f) EC). Germany, after the judgment of the Federal Constitutional Court in *Brunner v European Union Treaty* (1993) (see **8.37**), needed the consent of its own Parliament before it could proceed to the third stage. The German *Bundestag* had stipulated that Germany's move to the third stage should depend on its own assessment of the attainment or failure of the conditions laid down for that stage. It gave its consent in April 1998 when the Central Bank took over from the EMI and the latter disappeared.

Changes in legislative procedures

2.25 The Maastricht TEU introduced a number of changes in the voting system in the Council of Ministers (renamed 'the Council'). It increased the number of articles subject to QMV. It introduced a new voting procedure, mainly referred to as the co-decision procedure (Article 251 (ex Article 189b) EC). The co-operation procedure introduced by the SEA was preserved in Article 252 (ex Article 189c) EC. The co-decision procedure was intended to strike a more even balance of power between the institutions and, in particular, gives the European Parliament the power ultimately to reject legislation (see **4.37**). There is still, however, no opportunity for the Parliament to introduce legislation on its own or to force through a measure against the wishes of the Council. The Amsterdam Treaty reduced the number of main legislative procedures involving the European Parliament to three: assent, co-decision and consultation. It abolished the co-operation procedure except in relation to the EMU provisions which could not be touched by the Amsterdam Treaty. The co-decision procedure was streamlined and extended to a number of Treaty provisions previously subject to either the assent, co-operation or consultation procedure and introduced into a number of new Treaty provisions. The only exception to this is Article 161 (ex Article 130d) on structural and cohesion funds, which remains subject to the assent procedure. In addition, the co-decision procedure also applies to Article 42 (ex Article 51) on social security for Community migrant workers, but unanimous voting will continue to apply. For changes in the co-decision procedure, see **4.37**. The Amsterdam Treaty further extended the fields to which qualified majority voting rather than unanimous voting applies.

Fields of competence

2.26 A number of new fields of competence for the Community were introduced by the Maastricht TEU and further extended by the Treaty of Amsterdam. These include culture, public health, education, consumer protection, trans-European networks, industry and development co-operation. The Court of Auditors was given institutional status, and a new Committee of the Regions was established. Article 17 (ex Article 8) EC, introduced in Maastricht, establishes a citizenship of the Union. Nationals of member states shall be citizens of the Union and Article 18 (ex Article 8a) provides further that every citizen shall have the right to move freely within the territory of the member states. This provision, however, is 'subject to the limitations and conditions laid down in this Treaty'. The fact that these provisions are included in the EC Treaty and are thus justiciable and within the EC which has legal personality (as against the EU which has not) may, however, point to the fact that they have more than symbolic value and go beyond the provisions in the Treaty of Rome concerning free movement of persons. Although regulations and directives have considerably expanded the scope of the free movement articles, certain categories of persons remained excluded. The articles may well mean that internal restrictions on one's own citizens in a country are no longer valid and that excluded classes, such as those who cannot support themselves financially, are no longer excluded. The ECJ went some way towards this by giving the article a broad interpretation in Case C-85/96 *Maria Martinez Sala v Freistaat Bayern* (1998). The question as to whether Article 18 can have direct effect was finally broached in Case C-413/99 *Baumbast* (2002) (see further Chapter 18).

2.27 The second pillar, the common foreign and security policy (CFSP) grew out of a desire for more effective co-operation in foreign and defence policy. A start had been made by the Single European Act which established European political co-operation (EPC), which was no more than a loose inter-governmental agreement. The CFSP put co-operation on a more organised basis. Title V TEU, Articles 11–28 (ex Articles J.1–J.18) set out the provisions for this co-operation. In the amended Amsterdam Treaty the objective of the Union is:

> ...to assert its identity on the international scene, in particular through the implementation of a common foreign and security policy, including the progressive framing of a common defence policy, which might lead to a common defence in accordance with the provisions of Article 17.

The European Council defines general principles, guidelines and strategies. The Council (of Ministers) takes all the decisions, virtually always unanimously—the Commission must be 'fully associated' with the work of the Council (Article 18 (ex Article J.8)) and the European Parliament must be consulted on the main aspects and the basic choices of the CFSP (Article 21 (ex Article J.11))—but there is no doubt that the Council holds the power largely as an inter-governmental body. The Commission's role was somewhat enhanced by the Amsterdam Treaty in Article 14(4) where the Council may ask the Commission to submit proposals which may ensure the implementation of a 'joint action.' There is no jurisdiction by the ECJ over this pillar.

2.28 Reform of the second pillar was made in Amsterdam against the background of the perceived failure of the EU to respond adequately to the crisis in the former Yugoslavia. Co-ordinated policies concerning the former Yugoslavia were not very successful, although there was some intervention which could not have been achieved without the CFSP, such as the administration of Mostar, one of the enclaves. There are changes in decision-making and generally a more pragmatic approach; although unanimous voting remains the norm the Council may decide under certain circumstances to use QMV, by which all member states will then be bound. The Amsterdam TEU also introduced the idea of flexibility on a case-by-case basis, ie bilateral closer co-operation (Article 17 TEU) or abstention from a decision to take action, which the abstaining member state then would not apply. The possibility of establishing enhanced cooperation was introduced in Nice (in Article 27a and following), but only for the implementation of joint action or a common position. It cannot be used for issues with military implications affecting defence matters. The Council, after receiving the Commission's opinion in particular on the consistency with the Union's policies, will grant authorisation by QMV. However each member state may ask that the matter be referred to the European Council for unanimous decision. This is referred to as the 'emergency brake' in the relevant Commission memorandum (see further **2.37**). However, the basic inter-governmental structure of the pillar has remained unchanged.

2.29 The Western European Union (WEU, see Chapter 1), which deals with European defence matters, was associated with the CFSP by the Maastricht Treaty and has acquired new strength through this association. It turned out to be difficult to integrate the WEU fully into the CFSP structure. Neutral EU member states such as Ireland, Austria and Sweden, as well as Denmark, are not members of the WEU. Nevertheless, provision for the possibility of integration of the WEU into the Union is made in Article 17 TEU. With the changes in NATO making the WEU its new reinforced European pillar, the WEU received greater prominence in the Amsterdam Treaty as the defence arm of the EU, assisting the EU in coping with specifically European challenges such as crisis management, humanitarian intervention and peacekeeping. The head of the Council Secretariat (see Article 207 EC) now also holds the office of Secretary-General of the WEU, thus bringing the two organisations closer together. To all intents and purposes the WEU has now been absorbed into the second pillar.

Further amendments made by Amsterdam concern the strengthening of collective solidarity. In Article 11(2) (ex Article J.1) TEU relating to foreign policy objectives and mutual solidarity, the member states commit themselves to work together to enhance and develop their mutual solidarity

2.30 The third pillar is concerned with home affairs and justice. This was one of the areas in which change was clearly needed after the Maastricht TEU and the inter-governmental conference made considerable progress in this area. This resulted in the Treaty of Amsterdam making some major structural changes, and the pillar was renamed 'provisions on police and judicial co-operation in criminal matters'. Since the Maastricht Treaty co-operation in this area had been divided between:

- Title VI of the TEU concerning inter-governmental co-operation, with minimal involvement of the EC institutions, and agreements taking the form of Conventions.

- The Schengen agreement, which was concluded outside the structure of the EC, under which 13 member states, as well as the non-member states Norway and Iceland, are committed to the gradual abolition of checks at common borders.

- Some articles in the EC Treaty concerning freedom of movement, such as Article 7a describing an internal market for the free movement of persons, and Article 100c on a visa regime for nationals of third countries.

2.31 The Amsterdam Treaty brought about changes affecting the systems of decision-making to be applied, the jurisdiction of the ECJ, the role of the European Parliament and the right of the Commission to play an active part. The changes start with the changes in objective. The objective:

...to develop close co-operation on justice and home affairs,

was replaced by a much fuller definition in Article 2(4) TEU:

...to maintain and develop the Union as an area of freedom, security and justice, in which the free movement of persons is assured in conjunction with appropriate measures with respect to external border controls, asylum, immigration and the prevention and combating of crime.

The third pillar is now divided into two parts.

2.32 The new Title IV of the EC Treaty (Articles 61–69 EC) concerns the free movement of persons, asylum and immigration. It establishes mechanisms for the progressive establishment of an area of freedom, security and justice and is mainly governed by the normal institutional structure of the Community, although the role of the ECJ is a limited one. The Schengen agreement has been incorporated into the Treaty, as indicated in the 'Schengen Protocol' annexed to the Treaty. This provides that the 'Schengen acquis' will be incorporated into the framework of the European Union and that its legal basis will be Title IV EC Treaty or Title VI TEU depending on the issues. However, this applies only to the Schengen signatories, although the non-signatories accept the Protocol's provisions which allow the signatories to make use of the Community institutional framework. Two Protocols concerning the position of the United Kingdom and Ireland, and one concerning the position of Denmark, define and limit the impact of the provisions on those countries. As regards the UK and Ireland, these Protocols keep them out of the Schengen acquis, but with 'opt-in' provisions to specific initiatives, if the countries should so wish. The Schengen Convention on the gradual abolition of checks at the common borders was originally concluded in 1990 between five member states of the Union, (the Benelux countries, France and Germany) and came into force on 26 March 1995 with two additional members, Spain and Portugal. Other member states then joined, plus Iceland and Norway, so that only the United Kingdom, Ireland and Denmark were not members of the Convention. In spite of great difficulties and criticisms, it was nevertheless regarded as a useful model for the development of immigration policies under the third pillar and was given Treaty status. The Convention itself therefore lost its *raison d'être* after incorporation of the Schengen acquis.

2.33 The creation of the new Title IV has necessitated a major overhaul of the inter-governmental third pillar. This is now contained in Title VI (Articles 29–45 (ex Articles K.1–K.17)) of the TEU and is, therefore, not covered by the institutional framework or subject to Community competence. Instead of 'justice and home affairs', the Title is now labelled 'Provisions on police and judicial co-operation in criminal matters'. The policies of common interest concerning asylum, external border controls, immigration, conditions of entry and movement, as well as conditions of residence, access to employment and right to family reunion of third country nationals, have all been moved into the framework of the EC Treaty. Article 29 TEU specifically addresses the following criminal activities:

...racism and xenophobia, organised crime in the form of terrorism, trafficking in persons and offences against children, illicit drug and arms trafficking, corruption and fraud. There are also provisions on judicial co-operation, co-operation between police forces, customs authorities, and others, directly and via Europol (Article 30 TEU). Police co-operation has led to the setting up of Europol, which organises a Union-wide system for exchanging information.

Article 34 TEU provides for a general obligation to inform, consult and co-ordinate action through the Council. Common positions will be established and a new category of 'framework decisions', as well as 'other decisions' is introduced which might in time replace the more cumbersome provisions for the conclusion of conventions, which are subject to ratification by the member states 'in accordance with their respective constitutional requirements' (Article 34(d) TEU). Both the Europol Convention and the draft Convention on the crossing of the external frontiers of the member states, as well as the Dublin Convention, were concluded under this provision. The voting rule is still unanimity, but may be replaced by QMV for the implementation of the 'other decisions' category. Article 35 TEU expands the jurisdiction of the Court of Justice in relation to police and judicial co-operation. The Maastricht Treaty limited this jurisdiction to an optional one over conventions. This was rejected by the UK, for example in relation to Europol. The court will have jurisdiction by way of preliminary ruling where the member states agree to accept this. A member state which accepts the court's jurisdiction will choose whether this jurisdiction may be invoked either 'by a court or tribunal of against whose decisions there is no judicial remedy' (a court of last resort), or by 'any court or tribunal', if such a ruling is necessary for it to give judgment (Article 35 (ex Article K.7) 3(a) and (b) TEU). At the time of writing, the Benelux countries, Germany, Austria and Greece had agreed to this. There is, therefore, no obligation to refer as there is under Article 234 EC. The court will also have jurisdiction in direct actions brought by member states or the Commission reviewing the legality of framework decisions and of decisions. It will further have jurisdiction in disputes between member states concerning acts adopted under the Title, and in disputes between member states and the Commission concerning the interpretation or application of conventions established under the Title. Finally, Article 42 provides a *passerelle* provision as before in Article K.9 in the Maastricht TEU. This enables subjects covered by this pillar to be transferred to Community competence in the EC Treaty. So far, this provision has not been used and it is unlikely that a great deal of use will be made of it. It may well

30

never be used without amendment of its procedure as it involves unanimous approval of the member states in accordance with their constitutional requirements, ie involving referenda in a number of cases and large Parliamentary majorities in others.

Agreements with non-member states

2.34 The European Community is empowered under Article 300 (ex Article 228) EC to conclude agreements with non-member states. There have been many such types of agreement. Association agreements have been concluded with European and non-European states, the former often as a prelude to their joining the Community. Such agreements would often contain provisions similar to those in the EC Treaty. In 1992, an agreement was concluded with the members of EFTA (the European Free Trade Association) to create a European Economic Area (EEA). This agreement gave those countries access to the internal market and required the acceptance of the *acquis communautaire*. However, even before the Agreement was signed, a number of former EFTA States had applied to join the Community. This happened the year following the entry into force of the EEA in 1994 with Austria, Finland and Sweden. However, Norway, as we have seen, voted against joining the Community. Switzerland, an EFTA member, voted in December 1992 against joining the EEA and will, consequently, not join the Community in the foreseeable future, although this remains an open question. A special status for Switzerland has been negotiated. The EEA now consists of Norway, Iceland and Liechtenstein, together with the member states of the European Union.

2.35 A number of agreements were concluded with countries of Central and Eastern Europe; the Europe Agreements. Many of the countries which have entered into these agreements saw this as a first step towards EU membership and 10 of these are now set to join in 2004. Romania and Bulgaria will have to wait but may join in 2007, and Turkey, although invited to apply in December 2000, does not seem to have much prospect of joining at the moment (see **2.13** and further **2.37**).

Enhanced co-operation

2.36 A number of new topics were raised in the Treaty of Amsterdam. On the institutional question very little was achieved, but a new Article 207 provides for a new Deputy Secretary-General to the Council to assist the Secretary-General. This is a result of the decision to allow the Secretary-General of the Council to act as the High Representative of the EU in CFSP matters as well as running the day-to-day business of the Council. 'Enhanced co-operation' allows a group of member states within the European Union to co-operate more closely than is provided for by the rules applying to all member states. Examples of such co-operation have existed for a long time, eg the Benelux agreement, the Social Protocol, EMU, and agreements such as Schengen, completely outside the treaties. Article 11 of the EC Treaty sets out the conditions under which such closer co-operation may be achieved. It would only be possible in areas not subject to exclusive Community competence and cannot concern citizenship or discriminate between nationals of member states nor distort competition. Closer co-operation can also apply to the third pillar under Article 40 if it would 'enable the Union to develop more rapidly into an area of freedom, security and justice.' Under the second pillar, case-by-case flexibility is provided for (see **2.28**) and there is what has been called pre-determined flexibility in the case of the UK and Ireland concerning Immigration and Asylum, ie that those countries may choose to opt in to those provisions of the Treaty in Title IV (see the Protocol on the Position of the UK and Ireland (**2.32**)).

2.37 Substantial changes to enhanced co-operation were agreed at Nice. Its essential characteristics remain largely unchanged. There is now a single provision in Article 43 which lists the conditions necessary for such co-operation. It can only be undertaken as a last resort and must be open to all states. However, the minimum number of states required to establish enhanced co-operation has been set at eight instead of the majority of member states. In the EC Treaty (Article 11), as well as in the third pillar the possibility of veto has been removed and replaced with the possibility for the member state to appeal to the European Council. The European Council may then still act by qualified majority on any proposal for enhanced co-operation. If it concerns an area normally subject to co-decision, the European Parliament's assent is necessary (see **2.28** for the second pillar).

Transparency

2.38 Article 1 of the TEU as amended by the Amsterdam Treaty provides that the new stage in the process towards ever closer union is one:

> ...in which decisions are taken as openly as possible and as closely as possible to the citizen.

Several articles try to counteract the criticism that decision-making in the Community is undemocratic and lacks transparency. Article 255 EC provides for access to documents originating from Community institutions for both Union citizens and other natural or legal persons residing or registered in a member state. Article 207 EC provides for special procedures for the Council when acting in its legislative capacity, to provide greater access to documents in those cases.

Non-discrimination

2.39 A new Article 13 EC provides for enabling powers in the field of discrimination based on sex, racial or ethnic origin, religion and belief, disability, age or sexual orientation (see also Chapter 18). This article is only a legal base for future action, but nevertheless its inclusion in the Treaty is encouraging.

2.40 The Union does not have legal personality, whereas the EC does (see Article 281 EC). Hopes that this could have been changed in Amsterdam were not fulfilled and in Nice the subject was again not addressed. The Convention in Brussels preparing a Constitutional document for Europe is discussing the matter (see **2.42**).

Developments since the ratification of the Treaty of Amsterdam.

2.41 In October 1999, the first 'High Representative of the Council' or 'Mr CFSP' was appointed. This was Xavier Solana, formerly Secretary-General of NATO. Shortly afterwards, he was also appointed as Secretary-General of the Western European Union, a further indication of the desire to integrate European defence and security matters within the framework of the European Union.

The Treaty of Amsterdam entered into force on 1 May 1999. Preparations had already started for another inter-governmental conference in February 2000. Summits of the European Council in 1999 started the preparations for this Conference. The October summit in Tampere (Finland) was concerned in particular with the creation of an area of freedom, security and justice and with the drawing up of a charter of fundamental rights. Far-reaching proposals were made regarding asylum and immigration and the fight against crime. A 'Eurojust' unit will facilitate proper co-ordination of national prosecuting authorities and support criminal investigations in organised crime cases. The December summit in Helsinki focused on the enlargement process. Noting progress made in the negotiations with the first six applicant countries, it provided for the opening of negotiations with a further six: Romania, Slovakia, Latvia, Lithuania, Bulgaria and Malta. Turkey was also invited at the summit to become a candidate and negotiations were said to be conducted with that country on the same footing as with the others. Candidate countries had to complete questionnaires referring to the 'acquis communautaire'. The post-Nice Copenhagen summit in December 2002 decided on the admission of 10 countries (see above 1.13).

2.42 The inter-governmental conference concluded in December 2000 at a summit in Nice in France. It deals with institutional reforms for which proposals had been presented earlier in a report by a Committee of 'Wise Men': Mr Dehaene, Lord Simon and Professor Walter van Gerven. The size and composition of the Commission, the weighting of votes in the Council and the possible extension of majority voting in the Council were to be addressed together with other necessary amendments to the Treaty.

2.43 The Nice Treaty was a disappointment in some ways, but achieved one major purpose. It settled the problem of the re-distribution of votes, both in the Council, thus altering the numbers required for QMV (see further **3.15**) and the numbers of seats in the European Parliament. This, together with discussions about defence, took up most of the time during the negotiations. The major wrangling took place in respect of the votes in the Council, with Belgium threatening at one point to wreck the conference by disagreeing with the Netherlands on the number of votes. These had been equal between the two countries. The final outcome, seen as a compromise and a victory for both sides, was the allocation of 12 votes to Belgium and 13 to the Netherlands.

The question of the membership of the Commission was also settled (**3.19**). However, many questions remained unsettled. This is why Declaration No 23 on the future of the Union was annexed to the Treaty in Nice. It called for a deeper and wider debate on the future of the European Union.

Subsequent to this a European Council meeting in Laeken near Brussels decided to set up a Convention to discuss the future of the Union, to look at the status of the Charter of Fundamental Rights, proclaimed in Nice as a non-binding instrument (see also **6.24**), and to prepare a Constitutional document for the enlarged Europe which settles a 'more precise' delimitation of powers between the Union and the member states, reflecting the principle of subsidiarity. The Convention started its work in March 2002 and submitted its final draft for a constitutional Treaty to a Summit in Thessaloniki (Greece) in June 2003. It was composed of representatives of the heads of state or government, of members of national parliaments and of the European Parliament. It included representatives of all the candidate countries for membership who have observer status but who take a full part in the discussions. The Convention, presided over by the former French President Valérie Giscard d'Estaing, made proposals for a Constitutional document dealing in particular with Institutional reform, the reform of legislative instruments, and the incorporation of the Charter of Fundamental Rights. The draft is to be examined by an inter-governmental conference starting in October 2003. With the final ratification of Nice by Ireland in October 2002 and the entry into force of the Nice Treaty in February 2003, nothing now stands in the way of enlargement. On the present timetable 10 new members will join the European Union in May 2004, seven years after the first negotiations started.

Further reading

Gaja, 'How flexible is flexibility under the Amsterdam Treaty?', [1998] 35 CMLRev 855.

Nugent, 'The deepening and widening of the European Community: recent evolution, Maastricht and beyond', [1993] JCMS 311.

Herdegen, 'Maastricht and the German Constitutional Court', [1994] CMLRev 235–249.

Justus Lipsius, 'The 1996 Inter-governmental Conference', 20 ELRev 3, 235–249.

Self-test questions

1. In what respects does the European Community come closest to being a federation and in what respects is it clearly not a federation?

2. What is meant by the statement that 'the EEC comprises a new legal order'?

35

3. Discuss the reasons for the adoption of subsequent Treaty amendments and their contributions, if any, to the process of European integration.

4. To what extent is the EC legal order compatible with a 'multi-speed Europe'?

CHAPTER THREE

The Institutions of the Community

SUMMARY

This chapter deals with the institutions of the Community and with associated bodies. The institutions of the Community are:

• **The European Parliament**
• **The Commission**
• **The Council**
• **The European Court of Justice and the Court of First Instance**
• **The Court of Auditors**

We also discuss:

• **The European Council**
• **The European Central Bank**
• **The Economic and Social Committee**
• **The Committee of the Regions**
• **The European Investment Bank**

We look at the **Luxembourg Accords** and the **Ioannina Compromise**.

Reference is made to the **Convention on the future of the European Union**

Introduction

3.1 According to Article 7 (ex Article 4) EC the tasks entrusted to the Community are to be carried out by five institutions:

- *The European Parliament* (Articles 189–201 (ex Articles 137–144) EC);

- *The Commission* (Articles 211–219 (ex Articles 155–163) EC);

- *The Council* (Articles 202–210 (ex Articles 145–154) EC);

- *The European Court of Justice and the Court of First Instance* (Articles 220–245 (ex Articles 164–188) EC);

- *The Court of Auditors* (Articles 246–248 (ex Articles 188a–c) EC), elevated to a fully fledged institution by the Maastricht TEU.

Each of these institutions has powers specifically assigned to it by the Treaty and 'shall act within the limits of powers conferred on it by this Treaty'.

There are a number of other bodies established:

- by the Treaties: eg the Economic and Social Committee and the Committee of the Regions (Article 7(2) (ex Article 4(2)) EC), the European Central Bank (Article 8 (ex Article 4a) EC), the European Investment Bank (Article 9 (ex Article 4b) EC), the Economic and Financial Committee (Article 114(2) (ex Article 109c(2)) EC), the European Social Fund (Article 143 (ex Article 123 EC)), the Committee of Permanent Representatives (Article 207(1) (ex Article 151(1)) EC); the Committee of Inquiry (Article 193 (ex Article 138c) EC), the Employment Committee (Article 130 (ex Article 109s) EC) or

- in pursuance of the Treaties: eg the European Environmental Agency (Regulation 1210/90, OJ 1990 L 120/1).

3.2 An institution can 'act', that is take generally binding decisions. The other bodies, on the other hand, operate in specific fields and have either a purely advisory role or take decisions which are not generally binding.

Listed separately under Articles 8 and 9 (ex Articles 4a and 4b) EC are the quasi-institutions designed to administer the monetary union, ie the European System of Central Banks (ECSB) and the European Central Bank (ECB). Article 9 provides for the establishment of the European Investment Bank (EIB) which is the EC's long-term lending and regional development bank (see Articles 266 and 267 (ex Articles 198d and 198e) EC). These three quasi-institutions also act within the powers assigned to them by the Treaty.

3.3 The constitutive Treaties (ECSC, EEC and Euratom) provided that each of the three European Communities would be served by separate institutions. However, the Convention on Certain Institutions Common to the European Communities (1957), which came into force at the same time as the EEC and the Euratom Treaties, provided for a single Assembly and a single Court of Justice for the three Communities. A further step towards rationalisation was taken by the conclusion of the so-called 'Merger Treaty' (1965) which came into force in July 1967. The 'Merger Treaty' established the 'Council of the European Communities' which replaced the Special Council of Ministers of the ECSC, and the EEC and Euratom Councils of Ministers, and the 'Commission of the European Communities' which replaced the ECSC High Authority and the EEC and Euratom Commissions. With regard to each Community, however, the basic provisions regarding the composition, powers and jurisdiction of each of the institutions are provided for by the relevant Treaty; thus, the functions and powers differ to some extent. The ECSC and Euratom Treaty expired in July 2002 and its relevant provisions were absorbed into the EC Treaty. We are here concerned principally with the functions of the institutions under the EC Treaty as amended by the Single European Act, the Treaty on European Union (the Maastricht Treaty) and the Treaties of Amsterdam and Nice.

3.4 The unity of the institutions has been reinforced by the TEU. Article 3(1) (ex Article C(1)) TEU provides that 'the Union shall be served by a single institutional framework'. In other words, the EU will be served by a single set of institutions—those of the European Communities—which will act for the purposes of the other two pillars to the extent that they are given the power to do so by the TEU (see Articles 3 and 5 (ex Articles C and E) TEU)). The single institutional framework aims at providing coherence and continuity between the EU's various activities. This is particularly important in the sphere of external relations (Article 3(2) TEU).

3.5 On the institutional level, the Maastricht TEU gave the Court of Auditors full institutional status (Article 7 (ex Article 4) EC) and created other bodies (eg Committee of the Regions (Article 7 (ex Article 4) EC)), amended the provisions governing existing EC institutions (eg Articles

39

189–201 (ex Articles 137–144) EC with regard to the EP) and re-emphasised the role of the European Council (Article 4 (ex Article D) TEU)).

3.6 After the coming into force of the TEU (1 November 1993) the 'Council of the European Communities' renamed itself 'Council of the European Union'. The 'Commission of the European Communities' renamed itself 'European Commission'. The Court of Justice continues to call itself 'the Court of Justice of the European Communities'.

3.7 The 1996 inter-governmental conference (IGC) preparing the Amsterdam Treaty had intended to propose a comprehensive review of the Treaty provisions concerning the institutions. However, during the negotiations on the Treaty of Amsterdam in June 1997, no agreement was reached concerning this question. As a result, a Protocol was annexed to the Treaty of Amsterdam providing that a comprehensive review of the Treaty provisions on the composition and functioning of the institutions was to take place at least one year before the membership of the European Union exceeded 20. Thus, both the question concerning the number of Commissioners (now capped at 20) and the reweighting of votes in the Council needed to be resolved at the inter-governmental conference before any enlargement could take place. This review was duly prepared during the inter-governmental conference leading up to the Nice Treaty and this is reflected in the Nice Treaty, which was adopted in December 2001 and entered into force 1 February 2003.

The Council of the European Union

3.8 The Council is the legislative arm of the European Union. It was created in the Treaty of Rome as the Council of Ministers and is now 'the Council' of the European Union. It is important to note that it should not be confused with the 'European Council' which is not a Community institution and is not part of the institutional framework of the Community (see **3.69**). The Council has the task of taking the final decision on and of carrying out the proposals submitted to it by the Commission under the EC Treaty and of acting on an inter-governmental basis under the two other 'pillars', the Common Foreign and Security Policy (CFSP), (the 'second pillar') and home affairs and justice, renamed 'provisions on police and judicial co-operation in criminal matters' by the Treaty of Amsterdam, (the 'third pillar'), where it takes initiatives, makes proposals and decides alone, usually by unanimity. Under the second and third pillars the Commission is fully associated with the decision-making process. The European Parliament is consulted *ex post facto*, not on single legislative initiatives, but on broader issues.

3.9 Although legally there is just one Council, its composition and name depend on the subject matter of its deliberations. Thus there is an Agricultural Council, a Council of Ministers of Economic Affairs and Finance, known as 'ECOFIN', a Home Affairs Council, an Environment Council, and so on. The Council which meets most frequently is that of Ministers of Foreign Affairs and is known as the General Affairs Council which deals also with 'political' issues. The Council consists of representatives of member states at ministerial level, one representative per member state, who are authorised to commit their governments (Article 203(1) (ex Article 146(1)) EC). This phrase was added by the TEU amendment to the EC Treaty in order to make decision-making in the Council more effective and to avoid the delays which arise if representatives have to refer back to their home governments before they can take a decision. It also allows federal countries like Germany, Belgium and Spain to be represented by Ministers of the *Länder*, of the three Belgian levels, and of the autonomous Spanish regions. In areas within their competence, the same applies to the devolved UK regions of Scotland and Wales. The meetings of the Council are generally not public, and the secrecy of the deliberations has been the subject of much criticism, viewing this as a contributing factor to the democratic deficit in the Union. Some improvement was achieved with a change in 1993 in the Rules of Procedure, which are set by the Council itself, which now provide that under certain circumstances the Council's voting record must be made public, in particular when the Council is acting as legislator under the co-operation or co-decision procedures (see **4.36** and **4.37**). Article 255 EC added by the Treaty of Amsterdam now provides that:

> Any citizen of the Union, and any natural or legal person residing or having its registered office in a member state, shall have the right of access to European Parliament, Council and Commission documents...

This provision is, however, subject to limitations on grounds of public or private interest. In Case T-174/95 *Svenska Journalistförbundet v Council* (1998) the Court of First Instance annulled a Council Decision refusing the applicant access to certain documents. The Council put forward arguments based on public interest and on the protection of confidentiality of the Council's proceedings. On the latter argument the CFI said (at para 113 of the judgment) that the Council must:

> strike a genuine balance between ... the interest of the citizen in obtaining access to the documents and ... any interest of its own in maintaining the confidentiality of its deliberations.

Organisation

The Presidency

3.10 The office of President of the Council is held in turn by each member state for a term of six months. This means that all Councils will be chaired by a representative of the member state which holds the Presidency during that period.

The Presidency was held originally in alphabetical order (based on the name of the country in its own language), but the order is now reversed in pairs. This order will have to be adjusted upon each subsequent accession of new members (see Council Decision 95/2 of 1 January 1995 determining the order in which the office of the President of the Council shall be held (OJ 1995, No L1/220)). The Presidency has no function attributed to it in the EC Treaty; its original tasks were to convene and chair Council meetings and sign legislation and other acts, such as international treaties, on behalf of the Council, but it has gained far greater importance as the Community has developed and now has specific tasks under the second and third pillars. In particular under the second pillar, the Presidency is charged with representing the Union in matters coming within the foreign and security policy (Article 18(1) (ex Article J.8(1)) TEU). The President of the Council represents the Community on many important occasions in the international arena. Use was increasingly made of the Troika (named after the Russian three-horse sleigh), which consists of the President of the Council, his immediate predecessor and his immediate successor. This arrangement is seen as giving added weight to any Union representation. It is used in particular in matters concerned with the common foreign and security policy.

Any country holding the Presidency is intent on achieving special objectives which it usually announces at one of the Summit meetings of the European Council before the beginning of its Presidency and presents to the European Parliament after having consulted the Commission. Particular emphasis will be laid on some aspect of Community policy and the Presidency will endeavour particularly to push through Community measures concerned with such objectives. The Convention in Brussels has proposed an elected President of the Council who would work in tandem with the President of the Commission. It is being argued that, with the advent of 10 new member states, it is no longer practical to have a revolving Presidency which changes every six months.

The Council Secretariat

3.11 Article 207 (ex Article 151) EC, inserted by the Maastricht TEU, gave recognition to the General Secretariat of the Council under the responsibility of a Secretary-General. The Treaty of Amsterdam added a Deputy Secretary-General, both to be appointed unanimously by the Council. The Secretary-General oversees the day-to-day work of the Council, but now also acts as the Council's High Representative in the common foreign and security policy. In October 1999, the first High Representative, 'Mr CFSP', appointed to the newly-restructured office was Xavier Solana, up to then Secretary-General of NATO, who soon afterwards was also appointed Secretary-General of the Western European Union (see **2.41**).

The Committee of Permanent Representatives (COREPER, after its French acronym)

3.12 The work of the representatives on the Council is prepared by this Committee, which consists of Ambassadors from the member states to the EC. There are two levels on this Committee. COREPER I prepares the more technical questions and is composed of deputy permanent representatives. COREPER II deals with political and controversial matters on which it has to advise the Council and which may give rise to debate there. It is composed of permanent representatives who are Ambassadors to the EU. Commission officials attend COREPER meetings and participate in its work.

In urgent cases, acts of the Council may be adopted by a written vote provided all Council members agree to that procedure. If any members disagree, this procedure may not be used, as happened in Case **68/86** *United Kingdom v Council (Agricultural Hormones)* (1988) where the UK and Denmark opposed adoption of the Directive concerned and the procedure should, therefore, not have been used.

COREPER prepares Council deliberations by drawing up two lists, the A List and the B list. The A list contains uncontroversial items which are adopted by the Council without debate. The B list contains items which do need debate within the Council before it can reach a decision.

The work of COREPER in turn is prepared by working groups of representatives of the member states.

After COREPER had been given recognition in the TEU an amendment by the Treaty of Amsterdam now empowers COREPER to adopt procedural decisions provided for in the Committee's Rules of Procedure, thus further easing the burden on the Council (see Article 207 (ex Article 151) EC).

Voting procedures

Simple majority voting

3.13 Simple majority voting is prescribed as the usual rule, 'save as otherwise provided by this Treaty' (Article 205(1) (ex Article 148(1)) EC). In the original Community of the Six, this was sometimes used, but the Treaty often provided otherwise and the instances of simple majority voting are now extremely rare. Its use has now been further whittled away by provisions in the Treaties of Amsterdam and Nice, increasing the use of qualified majority voting. Simple majority voting is still used, eg for the adoption of the Council's rules of procedure (Article 207(3) (ex Article 151) EC), the adoption of the agenda and requests to the Commission to undertake studies and submit proposals (Article 208 (ex Article 152) EC).

Unanimity voting

3.14 Unanimity voting was used frequently until the end of 1965, when the transitional period came to an end and *qualified majority voting* replaced unanimity voting in many instances. In the Europe of the Six, notwithstanding the problems described below (at **3.16**), unanimity was more easily achieved than is the case now. It is clear that it is more difficult to achieve unanimity among 15 member states and that in many cases it may prove impossible to attain. If too many matters have to be decided this way, this will inevitably lead to stagnation in the progress of the Union. A further extension of the Union to 25 members and more will naturally emphasise the practical difficulty, if not impossibility, of using unanimity voting in many instances. The Single European Act and the Treaties of Maastricht, Amsterdam and Nice extended the field of qualified majority voting very much further. Thus, QMV has now become the most frequently used method of voting. This, however, applies only to the EC Treaty part of the TEU. The inter-governmental 'pillars' set up by the

TEU, the Chapters on Common Foreign and Security Policy and on Police and Judicial Co-operation in Criminal Matters use unanimity voting, in most cases in the CFSP and to a slightly lesser extent in the third pillar. Some countries, the UK prominent among them, are reluctant to give up unanimity voting rules, or 'the veto' in matters which they consider vital and which should be dealt with on an inter-governmental level. The Treaty of Amsterdam intended to introduce still more qualified majority voting, but succeeded in doing so only to a limited extent. The Nice Treaty added another 27 areas in which QMV will be used. This includes matters concerning free movement of citizens (Article 18 EC), industrial policy, economic, financial and technical co-operation with third countries and elements of visa, asylum and immigration policies (albeit with conditions attached and to come into force after five years from the entry into force of the Treaty of Amsterdam), but it does not concern taxation, social policy or the central elements of policies on asylum or immigration, subjects which are considered by different member states as too sensitive to be subject to QMV.

Qualified majority voting

3.15 In this procedure the votes are weighted per country as prescribed by Article 205(2) (ex Article 148(2)) EC. The IGC leading up to the Amsterdam Treaty was meant to reform the weighting system. It can readily be seen that the number of votes per country is not necessarily representative of its importance in terms of population. Larger countries considered themselves at a disadvantage and wanted change. They proposed a redistribution of the votes which would have given a greater weight to them and would, in their view, have constituted a more equitable distribution, proportionate to the size of their populations. However, this decision required a unanimous vote in the Council and this was blocked by the smaller countries. It was agreed that the question would be looked at again and that the problem must be solved before the first accession of any new member. This indeed happened in Nice and a redistribution of votes took place (see also **2.15** and **2.43**). A Protocol was attached to the Treaty, making provision for the changing situation before and after enlargement. This increases the total number of votes for QMV per member state considerably, taking account of the fact that most of the new member states will be small or, in some cases, very small countries. The larger countries, in particular those with a large population, have been given more weighting. Thus, the total number of votes was increased from 87 to 237. A Declaration attached to the Treaty then takes account of the situation after enlargement has been completed. This brings the total number of votes for QMV up to 345. The Declaration provides for this arrangement to come into force from January 2005. The qualified majority will have been achieved if two conditions have been fulfilled:

(a) the threshold for the qualified majority, a specified number of votes, must be achieved. This threshold will rise from 169 out of 237 for the present Union to eventually 258 out of 345 for the Union enlarged to 27 member states;

(b) the decision must also be approved by a majority of member states in cases where the Treaty requires it to be adopted on a proposal by the Commission, the usual situation.

Furthermore, the Treaty also provides for the possibility for a member of the Council to request verification that the qualified majority is constituted by at least 62% of the total population of the Union. This is a further element in favour of the larger member states, as three of them would constitute such a majority.

The Luxembourg Accords and the Ioannina Compromise

3.16 In 1966 the 'Luxembourg Accords', also referred to as the 'Luxembourg Compromise' provided that, even where the Treaty had not provided for unanimous voting, if 'very important interests' of one or more member states were at stake, discussions should continue until agreement was reached. France, which had been at the origin of the problem (concerning farm price proposals) which the accords tried to solve, and which had practised an 'empty chair' policy, refusing to send its representatives to meetings, added its own view, stating that discussions should continue until unanimity had been attained.

The Accords are one of the earliest examples of a Community instrument the legal effect of which has never been comprehensively tested. It was a political compromise which was needed in order to avoid total stagnation in the Community. If one of the most important, if not *the* most important, members of a club of six decides not to co-operate, it is difficult for the club to function at all.

Circumstances have changed, however. One large country in a Community of six holds great political power, but in a Community of 15, or 25, or more, it is much more difficult, if not impossible, to make use of an instrument like the Luxembourg Accords. When the UK tried to use political means at Council level in 1996 to try to force through a solution to the BSE beef crisis, it had little effect and the tactic eventually failed.

3.17 The Accords have never been officially revoked. There were often hopes or views that it was no longer relevant, but the threat of the Accords continued to be invoked periodically, eg in connection with the common agricultural policy (the UK in 1981) or concerning a permanent seat for the European Parliament. Indeed, Article 11(2) of the EC Treaty as amended in Amsterdam provides that, if a member of the Council declares that, for important and stated reasons of national policy, it intends to oppose the granting of an authorisation by qualified majority to certain member states to establish closer co-operation, a vote shall not be taken; the Council may, by a qualified majority, request that the matter be referred to the European Council for decision by unanimity. This gives new legitimacy to the Accords and includes them for the first time in the Treaty. As the editorial comment in the August 1997 CMLRev put it:

> ... predictions of demise of the Luxembourg Compromise were thus distinctly premature: it has been given a new lease of life, no longer in the *demi-monde* of political deals but as part of the legal machinery of the EC Treaty. True, the goodwill costs of invoking the rule will be high, and it will seldom, perhaps never, be resorted to: the worry is that, once legally baptized, the Luxembourg Compromise may start popping up in other places. Indeed, its reception into the EC Treaty may have been facilitated by the acceptance, at an earlier stage of the IGC, of a similar rule in the context of the common foreign and security policy. It would have been less subversive of the Community order to have stuck to the unanimity rule.

In the Treaty of Amsterdam, the Luxembourg Compromise was also 'allowed to creep into the new Article 23 TEU, second sub-paragraph' (the first sub-paragraph having provided for unanimous voting, but any abstentions should not prevent the adoption of a decision).

Article 23(2) TEU provides for action in the second pillar, the Common Foreign and Security Policy, by qualified majority in adopting joint actions and in taking decisions implementing joint action. However:

> If a member of the Council declares that, for important and stated reasons of national policy, it intends to oppose the adoption of a decision to be taken by qualified majority, a vote shall not be taken.

The Council may, acting by a qualified majority, request that the matter be referred to the European Council for decision by unanimity.

The 'Ioannina Compromise' on enlargement

3.18 In March, 1994, an 'informal' European Council meeting in Ioannina in Greece, under the Greek Presidency of the Council, had been convened to mark the end of the negotiations for accession with four aspirant member states: Austria, Finland, Norway and Sweden. An issue which had already arisen at the previous summit meeting in Brussels in December 1993 now came to a head and threatened to endanger the accession process. As we have seen, qualified majority voting is now the most common method of adoption of Community legislation, and has been further extended by the Amsterdam and Nice Treaties, reducing the sphere of unanimity voting. The proposal was that on accession of the new member states the number of votes required for a 'blocking minority' would rise from 23 votes to 27 votes. This proposal met with opposition from the UK, initially supported by Spain. It advocated the retention of the present system, which would mean that two large member states could block a decision with the support of just one small member state. Raising this number, as had been done previously upon the accession of other countries, would mean that at least one other country's votes would be needed to obtain a blocking minority. In Ioannina, Spain soon dropped its opposition to the proposal, leaving the UK exposed. Eventually, a compromise was reached which was acceptable to the UK and negotiations for new membership could proceed. The relevant part of the European Council's *Decision* (para c) was as follows:

> If Members of the Council (of Ministers) representing a total of 23 to 26 votes indicate their intention to oppose the adoption by the Council of a decision by qualified majority, the Council will do all in its power to reach, within a reasonable time and without prejudice to obligatory time limits laid down by the Treaties and by secondary legislation, such as in Articles 189b and 189c (now Articles 251 and 252) of the EC Treaty, a satisfactory solution which could be adopted by at least 68 votes. During this period, and always respecting the Rules of Procedure of the Council, the President takes, with the assistance of the Commission, any initiative necessary to facilitate a wider basis of agreement in the Council.

After three, rather than four, countries had joined in January 1995 (as Norway eventually could not join because of a negative vote in its referendum) the number of 26 votes was amended by a Council decision to 25 and the number of 68 votes to 65 votes.

At Ioannina it had been agreed that the whole question should be re-examined by the 1996 inter-governmental conference (IGC). However, agreement could not be reached there and the Treaty of Amsterdam in a 'Declaration to the Final Act' states that the Compromise shall stay in place until the entry into force of the first enlargement, thus confirming the binding nature of the agreement. Unlike the Luxembourg Accords, it is not limited to 'very important interests', so it could be used on any matter and this makes it potentially more open to abuse than the Luxembourg Accords. Whether the Agreement was justiciable has never been tested by the ECJ. The court has held that any Community act which creates legal effects, irrespective of its nature, is an act *sui generis* which is subject to the court's jurisdiction. See Case 22/70 *Commission v Council (ERTA)* (1971).

Thus, two agreements concluded under pressure mostly from one particular country in each case, were given legitimacy by incorporation into the Amsterdam Treaty. The Nice Treaty has now effectively repealed the Ioannina Compromise in its Protocol and Declaration, but this episode has shown again how important the 'numbers game' is in the eyes of the member states. Indeed, during the Nice negotiations there was again a threat of the conference breaking down caused by a 'numbers' dispute between Belgium and the Netherlands which was resolved at the eleventh hour (see **2.43**).

The Commission

3.19 The Commission is often described as the Executive of the Community's policies. Although it is true that the Commission carries out Community decisions and policies, that is not all it does; it also proposes legislation and is, in many cases, instrumental in shaping the decision which is finally taken. Much of the Community's legislative rules are structured in such a way that the Commission has a say at the various stages when legislation is made. The Commission also has its own legislative powers under Article 86 (ex Article 90) EC on state aid and under Articles 81 and 82 (ex Articles 85 and 86) EC on competition. It is also given delegated legislative power by the Council (see **4.28–4.32**).

At present, there are 20 Commissioners, two for the major countries (Germany, France, Italy, Spain and the UK) and one for each of the other countries. The inter-governmental conference which prepared the Amsterdam Treaty made proposals for a change in this situation. It was considered that the number of Commissioners should be reduced, probably to just one per member state, or even to rotating appointments for groups of the smaller states. With the envisaged enlargement of the Union, this will become even more necessary, as there simply will not be enough worthwhile portfolios for all the Commissioners. The appointment of Junior Commissioners was also considered. However, the Amsterdam Treaty did not achieve a solution. It agreed a Protocol (Protocol on the institutions with the prospect of enlargement of the European Union, *CONF/4001/97 EN 114*) which provided upon the first enlargement that the Commission should comprise one national per member state and that a conference of member states should be convened to deal with these problems at least one year before membership of the Union exceeded twenty. This Protocol has now been repealed by the Nice Treaty and comprehensive arrangements have been put in its place in the Protocol and Declaration attached to that Treaty.

The Nice Treaty now limits membership of the Commission to one per member state as from 2005, but imposes a ceiling of 27 once enlargement takes place. This, therefore, means that the when this limit is reached, some countries will be without a Commissioner for a period.

In view of the fact that Commissioners are supposed to be completely impartial and not to have any allegiance to the country from which they come, this should, perhaps, not matter as much as it still clearly appears to.

Nomination and appointment procedure

3.20 According to Article 214(2) (ex Article 158(2)) EC as amended by the Nice Treaty the President of the Commission is to be elected by qualified majority vote by the Council in the composition of the heads of state and/or government of the member states. This replaces the nomination 'by common accord' which had been the case up till then. This nomination is then approved by the European Parliament, a right it acquired under the Treaty of Amsterdam. Under the Treaty of Maastricht, the Parliament was consulted about the Presidency and only had the right to approve or reject the Commission as a whole. Second, the member states, by common accord with the nominee for President, nominate the other persons whom they intend to appoint as Commissioners (Article 214(2) EC), again by qualified majority and not by common accord as under the Amsterdam Treaty. The appointment is made from a list drawn up in accordance with the proposals made by member states. Thus, the Council cannot appoint anyone who has not been proposed by his/her own member state. The President, before agreeing to the list, will undertake political soundings with each member state in order to ensure a balanced composition of the Commission. Third, all the nominees are subject, as a body, to a vote of approval by the European Parliament (Article 214(2) EC). Finally, the new Commission is appointed by the Council acting by a qualified majority (Article 214(2) EC).

3.21 When Jacques Santer was appointed President of the Commission in June 1994 after the British Prime Minister had earlier disagreed with and, in effect vetoed, the appointment of the Belgian Prime Minister, he addressed the European Parliament before his endorsement as President and the European Parliament voted on this nomination as a political act, as it had no real power to approve or reject the President. In a close vote his nomination was endorsed. It was quite clear that, if the Parliament had rejected the appointment, although this would not have had any legal force, M Santer would probably have considered it impossible to take up the post. The Treaty of Amsterdam acknowledged this *de facto* situation by amending Article 214(2) to read that the nomination has to be approved by the European Parliament.

3.22 Members of the Commission are appointed according to the procedure laid down in Article 214. Commissioners are appointed for a five-year term which is renewable (Article 214(1) EC). The approval by the European Parliament is only of the Commission as a body. However, in 1994 and in 1999, after the new members of the Commission had been nominated, hearings took place in the European Parliament, where each individual candidate was questioned. Although criticisms were expressed both times, the Parliament eventually approved the appointment of the Commission as a whole on both occasions. This should be contrasted with the Court of Auditors, where hearings are held for each member and two have actually been rejected by the European Parliament.

3.23 The President of the Commission has a special position. Much depends on his/her personality. Roy Jenkins, for example, achieved the acceptance of the membership of the Commission President at the European Council sessions. Jacques Delors, President from 1985 to 1994, achieved enormous prestige for the Commission and for the Community as well as a fair amount of controversy, particularly in the UK, with his vision of and dedication to Europe. Commissioners all have their own portfolio, ultimately decided upon by the President.

Status of the Commissioners

3.24 The members of the Commission have the duty and the right to perform their tasks with complete independence in the general interest of the Communities. They are forbidden to seek or take instructions from any government or other body and must refrain from any action incompatible with the nature of their duties. The member states have undertaken to respect this principle and not to seek to influence the members of the Commission in the performance of their tasks. During their term of office, Commissioners may not engage in any other occupation, and even after they have ceased to hold office they are required to behave with integrity and discretion as regards the acceptance of certain appointments or benefits (Article 213(2) (ex Article 157(2)) EC).

3.25 Privileges and immunities ensure undisturbed performance of their duties. The member states appoint the members of the Commission, but they cannot discharge them during their term of office. The Court of Justice, on the application of the Council or the Commission, may compulsorily retire an individual member of the Commission from office if he no longer fulfils the conditions required for the performance of his duties or if he has been guilty of serious misconduct (Articles 213(2) and 216 EC). The Commission President may also request a Commission member to resign. Only the European Parliament can compel the Commission to resign as a body, by means of a motion of censure on its activities (Article 201 (ex Article 144) EC).

3.26 In 1999 the Commission's prestige had suffered a grave blow. After a 'whistle-blower', Paul van Buitenen, an official within the Commission, had handed a dossier setting out details of serious mis-management by some Commissioners, and in particular the French Commissioner, Mme Edith Cresson, the European Parliament, instead of proceeding to a vote of censure, appointed a Committee of 'Wise Men' to investigate the matter. The Commission reported in March 1999 and was highly critical, stopping short of accusing any individual Commission of fraud, but pointing out that it was difficult to find anyone with the slightest sense of responsibility. Jacques Santer saw this as his cue to prevail upon his Commissioners to resign as a body. Thus, although the European Parliament did not actually dismiss the Commission, it was nevertheless instrumental in the Commission's eventual resignation. The next President appointed was Romano Prodi, a former Italian Prime Minister. One of the few Commissioners from the old Commission to return, Neil Kinnock, one of the British Commissioners, was instructed to start on a 'clean-up' campaign of the Commission and has achieved some success in this respect. The Nice Treaty takes account of these events in strengthening the role of the President and giving the President, in an amended Article 217, authority to allocate the Commissioners' responsibilities and to re-allocate them where necessary. It also provides (in Article 217(4)) that a member of the Commission should resign at the request of the President, after obtaining the approval of the College.

The Organisation of the Commission

3.27 The Commission has a President and Vice-Presidents whose number is no longer specified in the Nice Treaty. The latter are now appointed by the President from among its members (Article 217(3) (ex Article 161(3)) EC).

The Commission is required to act collectively and is generally governed by the principle of *collegiate responsibility* which, as the ECJ said in Case 5/85 *AKZO Chemie BV v Commission* (1986):

> ... is founded on the equal participation of the members of the Commission in the adoption of decisions and it follows from that principle, in particular, that decisions should be the subject of collective deliberation and that all members of the college of Commissioners bear collective responsibility on the political level for all decisions adopted.

3.28 Each member of the Commission has a personal staff—his/her *cabinet*—which assists him/her. *Cabinets* consist of a number of personally appointed political and administrative advisers whose principal functions are to tender advice and brief their Commissioners about the activities of the Commission as a whole, to speak for their Commissioners in meetings of officials and to co-ordinate their administrative responsibilities which may cover a number of Directorates; to provide liaison between their Commissioners and other EC institutions and his/her home member state. The role of the *Chef de Cabinet* has now become institutionalised and a meeting of the *Chefs de Cabinet* precedes and prepares every Commission meeting.

3.29 The administrative services of the Commission consist of Directorates-General (DGs) which are divided into Directorates which in turn are subdivided into divisions. There are 36 Directorates-General at present, each being responsible for a defined area of the Communities' activities. These Directorates used to have numbers, but Commission President Prodi abolished the numbers of the Directorates (there were 24 before that) and rearranged some of them. The ones for Agriculture, Competition, Economic and Financial Affairs, Employment and Social Affairs, Enterprise, Environment, Fisheries, Health and Consumer Protection, Information, Internal Market, Regional Policy, Research, Taxation and Customs Union, Budget, Development, and Personnel and Administration have largely remained the same. The former DGs for Energy and Transport are now just one DG, as are the ones for Education and Culture and for External Relations. There are three new DGs: Enlargement, Trade, Justice and Home Affairs. Each DG is headed by a Director-General who is responsible to the particular Commissioner to whom the same portfolio has been assigned by the President of the Commission. In addition, there are certain general and auxiliary services, such as the Secretariat-General, Legal Service, Spokesman's Service, Security, Statistical and Publications Offices. The Commission employs about 22,000 permanent staff (including more than 4,000 research staff in a number of centres throughout the Community and a large number of interpreters and translators). This bureaucracy is less than one might think; it is less than an individual UK government department.

Functions and powers

3.30 The Commission's functions and powers are defined in various Treaty provisions. The main responsibilities of the Commission are provided for by Article 211 (ex Article 155) EC and consist of ensuring 'the proper functioning and development of the common market'. To enable it to carry out this task, Article 211 confers on the Commission certain powers and entrusts to it certain specific functions. These are as follows:

(a) To 'ensure that the provisions of this Treaty and the measures taken by the institutions pursuant thereto are applied'. This function has two aspects. First, the function of the Commission as the guardian of the Treaties, ensuring that member states, other Community institutions as well as natural and legal persons who are subject to it, apply the Treaty. Article 226 (ex Article 169) EC provides the instrument for this supervisory task (see Chapter 10). The Commission has the power to take legal and administrative measures against a member state which has violated Community law, and it can impose fines on the offending member state (Article 228 (ex

Article 171) EC). The threat of such sanctions alone is often sufficient to make the member state comply.

The Commission also has supervisory powers over other institutions (see Articles 230 (ex Article 173) and 232 (ex Article 175) EC and Chapter 11) and over natural and legal persons, as for example in the field of competition law.

The second function of the Commission is to act as the executive arm of the Communities. It plays a key role in the day-to-day implementation of Community law in a number of different areas such as the administration of the customs union, the common agricultural policy, competition policy and state aids and the common commercial policy. It has significant powers with regard to transport, taxation and application of the various safeguard clauses. It is required to draft and implement the Community budget and to administer the special funds which form part of it (the structural funds such as the European Social Fund, the European Regional Development Fund and the European Agricultural Guidance and Guarantee Fund, as well as the Cohesion Fund).

(b)   The second paragraph of Article 211 deals with the advisory function of the Commission.

(c)   The third paragraph of Article 211 deals with the decision-making powers of the Commission. This provision again has two distinct aspects. First, it confers on the Commission a decision-making power of its own in Article 85(2) (ex Article 89(2)) EC and Article 86 (ex Article 90) EC. Second, the Commission plays a vital role in the Community law-making process by virtue of its power to initiate legislation. Apart from a few exceptional situations where the Council, or the Council and the European Parliament together, may act upon their own initiative, in most cases the EC Treaty provides that the Council shall act 'on a proposal from the Commission'. In these cases the Commission has an exclusive right of initiative, which it may have to exercise within a specified time limit. However, the Council may request the Commission to submit to it any appropriate proposals (Article 208 (ex Article 152) EC). An important feature of the right of initiative is the right to withdraw proposals for legislation, which can have a considerable effect on legislative progress. In preparing its proposals, the Commission usually consults with representatives of the member states. It may, and where required by the Treaty it must, also consult the Economic and Social

Committee and the Committee of the Regions (Article 262 (ex Article 198) and Article 265 (ex Article 198c) EC). Where the Council acts on a proposal from the Commission, it may amend that proposal only by unanimity (Article 250 (ex Article 189a(1)) EC). As long as the Council has not acted, the Commission may itself alter or withdraw its proposal (Article 250 (ex Article 189a(2)) EC).

(d) Delegated powers: to 'exercise the powers conferred on it by the Council for the implementation of the rules laid down by the latter'. The authorisation for such delegation is given to the Council (since the Single European Act) in Article 202 (ex Article 145) EC.

Decision-making procedure of the Commission

3.31 The decision-making powers delegated by the Council to the Commission are usually subject to the special scrutiny of committees of Council and other national representatives. This process, which is very important to decision-making, is known as '*comitology*'. Comitology involves a range of bodies attached to the Commission. Some are management committees with executive powers, as in agriculture; others are advisory, whether expert or consultative; others are regulatory committees which must concur with the proposed measure before it can be taken. The various types of committee and their procedures are further described in **4.29** to **4.31**.

Two Council Decisions in 1987 and 1999 (87/373 OJ 197 1987 and 1999/468/EC OJ L184 1999) set out detailed provisions for the use and powers of the three different types of Committee. This was inspired by the case brought by the European Parliament in 1987 (Case 302/87) *Parliament v Council*, the *Comitology* case, which, although the Parliament lost on this occasion (see further **4.29**) highlighted the need for greater transparency of the comitology system.

Further powers of the Commission

3.32 In addition to the four important functions listed in Article 211 EC the Commission has other important tasks assigned to it in following areas:

• External relations: Article 133(3) (ex Article 113(3)) EC and Articles 300–304 (ex Articles 228–231) EC provide for the Commission's involvement in opening and conducting negotiations on agreements with international organisations. Such powers are not, however, general powers: see Case C-327/91 *France v Commission* (1994). They are, however, subject to control by the Council.

• Implementation of the Community budget: see Articles 274, 275, 276, 279 (ex Articles 205, 205a, 206 and 209) EC.

• Publication of the General Annual Report (Article 212 (ex Article 156) EC).

The effect of the Maastricht, Amsterdam and Nice Treaties on the Commission

3.33 In addition to making changes as to the appointment of the President and the members of the Commission in both Amsterdam and Nice (see **3.19**) amendments in Amsterdam such as in Articles 99 (ex Article 103), 104 (ex Article 104c), 111 (ex Article 109) and 151–157 (ex Articles 128–130) confer new powers of investigation and initiative in a whole range of policy areas such as EMU and social policy, culture, public health, trans-European networks and industry. The two inter-governmental pillars (common foreign and security policy and judicial and police co-operation in criminal matters, see **2.26–2.33**) provide for involvement and sometimes the submission of proposals by the Commission. The co-decision procedure introduced by the Maastricht Treaty and extended by the Treaty of Amsterdam (Article 251 (ex Article 189b) EC) makes the Commission less independent of the Parliament, and more involved in political management both inside the Council and the Parliament. The Commission is also subject to stricter financial controls and accountability. Under Article 270 (ex Article 201a) EC and Declarations attached to the Maastricht Treaty, it has to establish that the existing budget can finance new activities and that environmental implications are considered. The Commission now operates under stricter policy guidelines which often make it clear that the primary responsibility lies with the member states in certain areas (eg concerning education policy). The Prodi Commission, installed in the autumn of 1999, undertook to carry out investigations and improvements of the internal workings of the Commission. Commissioner Neil Kinnock was instructed to oversee these reforms. The reforms include the adoption of codes of conduct for Commissioners and departments as well as the reorganisation of the Commission's administrative structures. A task force for administrative reform was set up to implement and monitor the reform process within the Commission (White Paper on Reforming the Commission: http:/europa.eu.int/comm/reform/index en.htm).

The European Parliament (EP)

Membership, organisation and procedure

3.34 The European Parliament (EP), previously called the Assembly in the constitutive Treaties, consists of 'representatives of the peoples of the states brought together in the Community' (Article 189 (ex Article 137) EC) who are referred to as 'Members of the European Parliament' (MEPs). Until 1979, MEPs were not directly elected but appointed from among the members of the respective national Parliaments. Direct universal elections were held for the first time in 1979. Elections are held every five years. There is still no uniform electoral procedure even though Article 138(3) EC calls for one. Article 190(3), amending Article 138(3) in the Maastricht Treaty, provides that the European Parliament shall draw up a proposal for elections by direct universal suffrage 'in accordance with a uniform procedure in all member states' or, an addition in the Treaty of Amsterdam, 'in accordance with principles common to all member states'. The intention in the Maastricht TEU was clearly that the uniform electoral system should be some form of proportional representation. A system of proportional representation exists in a variety of forms in the vast majority of member states. The addition 'in accordance with principles common to all member states' provided a let-out for the UK to retain its 'first past the post' system. A variation of this system has now been adopted in Italy for national elections, where it was thought to be capable of providing more political stability. This system is based partly on 'first past the post', partly on proportional representation. In the UK, however, the European elections in 1999 were held based on proportional representation. This was not very successful as the turnout of the electorate was the lowest it has ever been. This could perhaps be blamed on the political situation but there is no doubt that the appearance of a voting system with which the electorate was totally unfamiliar, was also a contributing factor.

3.35 The distribution of the 626 seats is listed in Article 190(2) (ex Article 138(2)) EC. The main criterion for the allocation of seats is the population of the member states concerned, but it is not mathematically precise. The distribution is at present clearly in favour of the smaller member states and, although Germany received an additional number of seats after unification (German MEPs now number 99), a German MEP still represents about ten times as many people as a Luxembourg MEP. The Amsterdam Treaty provided in Article 189 that the maximum number of MEPs would be 700. Article 189 after Nice sets this number at 732. A Protocol annexed to the Nice Treaty now provides that from the next European elections in 2004 the number of seats for the existing members will be reduced from 626 to 535. Germany, which has the same number of votes as the other big countries in the Council, will have a larger number of MEP's than the others, 99 against 72. A Declaration annexed to the Nice Treaty further provides for the situation after the accession of new member states. The total number of seats, which had been capped at 700 in the Treaty of Amsterdam (Article 189 (ex Article 137) EC) will be increased from 535 to a total of 732 if and when all 12 candidate member states have acceded. This total of 732 is now set as the new ceiling. This ceiling will not be attained for some time as only 10 new members are expected to join in 2004 for the time being. MEPs are elected for a five-year term. Any citizen of the European Union can stand for the European Parliament. The Maastricht Treaty introduced the right for citizens of the Union residing in a member state of which they are not nationals to vote and stand in elections for the EP (Article 19(2) (ex Article 8b(2)) EC). MEPs are required to vote on an individual and personal basis and they are not bound by any instructions. During the sessions of the EP, MEPs enjoy the privileges and immunities accorded to members of national Parliaments when in their own countries, and immunity from detention and legal proceedings when in the territory of another member state. MEPs may not concurrently be members of a national government or hold office in another Community institution but they may serve in their own national Parliaments.

3.36 Article 190 (ex Article 138) EC, which makes provision for regulating the performance of the duties of MEP's, now provides that these rules are adopted by qualified majority rather than unanimity by the Council after having sought the Commission's opinion. Rules concerning taxation of Members or former Members will require Council unanimity. Article 191 (ex Article 138a) EC adds a legal base providing for the adoption of rules governing political parties and, in particular, their funding, to be adopted by the Council according to the co-decision procedure.

3.37 Article 196 (ex Article 139) EC provides that the EP shall hold an annual session. The EP may also meet in extraordinary session at the request of a majority of its members or at the request of the Council or the Commission. The annual session is divided into part sessions which are convened as a rule each month, and are subdivided into daily sittings. Plenary sittings are held for one week of each month (except August), while one week a month is set aside for committee meetings and one week for meetings of political groups.

3.38 The EP does not a have a sole seat of operations. As a rule, it holds plenary sessions in Strasbourg and its committee meetings in Brussels, while its Secretariat is based in Luxembourg. There have been disputes concerning this clearly impractical arrangement, such as in Case 108/83 *Luxembourg v EP* (1984), where the court held that a 1983 resolution was incompatible with the member states' decision concerning the provisional location of the EP places of work and therefore void, and in cases brought by France which jealously guards its right to have plenary sessions in Strasbourg because of its symbolic location on the border between France and Germany: Case 358/85 *France v European Parliament (Re Brussels Meetings)* (1986); Cases 358/85 & 51/86 *France v European Parliament (Re Meetings Facilities in Brussels)* (1988). This is the result of political bargaining when the Community was first established. Many members of the European Parliament would prefer to have its plenary sessions in Brussels, as most Committee meetings take place there and it is also the seat of the Commission and the Council. However, it has so far proved politically unacceptable to make a change and the situation is now enshrined in a special Protocol to the Treaty of Amsterdam, which provides that the seat of the Parliament shall be in Strasbourg and at least 12 of its plenary sessions, including the all-important budget session, will be held in Strasbourg. Any additional plenaries may take place in Brussels; the Committees will meet in Brussels and the General Secretariat will remain in Luxembourg.

3.39 MEPs sit in multinational political groups. These groups are a kaleidoscope of European politics. There are groupings of Socialists (currently the largest group), the European People's Party, the Liberal Democratic and Reformist Group, the Greens, the European Democratic Alliance, the United Left, the Rainbow Group, *et al*, as well as non-affiliated MEPs who themselves constitute a group. Even these groupings fail to capture the full picture of diversity. Since it frequently takes an absolute majority of the votes cast in order to act (Article 198(1) (ex Article 141(1)) EC), a degree of consensus is essential. The detailed work of the Parliament is done in the committees, which include committees for Foreign Affairs and Security, Legal Affairs, Institutional Affairs, Agriculture, Budget,

Economic and Monetary Affairs and Industrial Policy, Civil Liberties, Employment and Work Environment. The committees prepare resolutions which are adopted by the EP in plenary session. Where the Parliament is involved in the legislative process (see Articles 250–252 (ex Articles 189a, b and c) EC) the proposal is examined by the relevant Committee(s), which includes its findings and recommendations in a Report drawn up by a *Rapporteur*.

3.40 The EP elects its President (Article 197(1) (ex Article 140(1)) EC) and Vice-Presidents, one per country, who together form the 'Bureau', the executive body. The EP is assisted by a Secretary-General who is appointed by the Bureau and is the head of the Secretariat. At the end of 1994 the Secretariat comprised approximately 3,800 permanent and temporary posts. Members of the Commission may (and do) attend all meetings and the Council is represented in plenary sessions. Members of the Commission and the Council must, at their request, be heard on behalf of their institutions (Article 197 (ex Article 140) EC). Debates are public unless the EP decides otherwise. The minutes of the meetings are published in the Official Journal and the full debates in an annex thereto (Article 199(2) (ex Article 142(2)) EC).

3.41 Except for the adoption of a motion of censure on the activities of the Commission (Article 201 (ex Article 144) EC; see above **3.20**) and certain decisions within the co-operation, co-decision and budgetary procedures, the EP acts by an absolute majority of the votes cast (Article 198(1) (ex Article 141(1)) EC). There is a quorum when one-third of current MEPs are present in the Chamber. However, unless there is a request to do so, the number of MEPs present is not ascertained.

Powers and functions

3.42 *Participation in the Community legislative process.* Although the EP still has no right of legislative initiative, its participation in the legislative process has grown considerably since the original Treaties. It takes part in four procedures: assent, co-decision, co-operation and consultation. The use of the co-operation procedure has been abolished except in relation to the EMU provisions which could not be touched upon in Amsterdam. Co-decision now applies to most of the provisions to which co-operation applied before. This procedure has been simplified by the Treaty of Amsterdam (see Articles 250–252 (ex Articles 189a–c) EC). These procedures are described in more detail in **4.35–4.38**.

3.43 The third pillar of the TEU as amended by the Treaty of Amsterdam increases the right of the European Parliament to be consulted in a number of cases, such as Article 39, and Article 42, the *passerelle* provision under which action in areas under the third pillar may be transferred to Title IV of the EC Treaty and thus be governed by the institutional framework.

3.44 It should be pointed out that the EP can 'request the Commission to submit any appropriate proposal on matters on which it considers that a Community act is required for the purpose of implementing the Treaty' (Article 192(2) (ex Article 138b(2)) EC).

3.45 Article 255 inserted in the Treaty of Amsterdam provides that, like the Commission and the Council, the EP elaborates the rules for access to its documents under its own rules of procedure. This was done to ensure greater transparency of the legislative process and making it more 'citizen-friendly.'

3.46 The EP's supervisory role includes the following:

- setting up a temporary Committee of Inquiry (Article 193 (ex Article 138c) EC);

- the right of petition, handled by a special Petitions Committee (Article 194 (ex Article 138d) EC);

- the appointment of an Ombudsman (Article 195 (ex Article 138e) EC);

- submitting oral or written questions to the Commission and to the Council (Article 197 (ex Article 140) EC);

- the submission of an annual General Report by the Commission, to be discussed in open session (Article 200 (ex Article 143) EC);

- voting a motion of censure against the Commission (Article 201 (ex Article 144) EC);

- participation in proceedings before the ECJ. When the Community was founded, the EP was an unelected assembly with only limited powers of consultation. It was, therefore, not considered necessary for the EP to have legal standing under the Treaty to be a party in proceedings before the ECJ. However, after the EP began to be directly elected and increasingly gained legislative powers under the SEA and the TEU, it needed to have *locus standi* in cases concerning its prerogatives. In a series of cases which were much criticised by those who thought the court was going beyond its jurisdiction, the court gradually allowed the EP increased standing. The EP may intervene in cases before the courts: Case 138/79 *Roquette Frères SA v Council* (1980); the EP may bring an action under Article 230 (ex Article 173) EC: Case C-65/90 *European Parliament v Council* (1992); Case C-70/88 *European Parliament v Council* (1990), noted by Bradley [1991] ELRev 245; also in [1991] CMLRev 663. Cf Case 302/87 *European Parliament v Council* (1988); the EP may also bring an action under Article 232 (ex Article 175) EC: Case 13/83 *European Parliament v Council* (1985); cf Case 377/87 *European Parliament v Council* (1988); see also Case 383/87 *Commission v Council* (1988). The changes brought about by the court's judgments were acknowledged by the revision of Article 173 (now Article 230 EC) in the Maastricht Treaty (see **11.10–11.12**). The Treaty of Nice has now given the EP unlimited standing under Article 230, para 3;

- approval of the President and Members of the Commission (Article 214(2) and (3) (ex Article 158(2) and (3)) EC);

- participation in the Budgetary Procedure (Articles 272–276 (ex Articles 203–206) EC). This was first provided for in the Second Budgetary Treaty 1975. The budgetary procedure is further described in **4.40**.

Petitions

3.47 Any citizen of the Union or any natural or legal person residing or having its registered office in a member state is entitled under Article 194 (ex Article 138d) EC to address petitions on matters within the fields of activity of the Community and which concern them to the EP.

The Parliamentary Commissioner (Ombudsman)

3.48 The Maastricht Treaty introduced the power in Article 195 (ex Article 138e) EC for the European Parliament to appoint an Ombudsman. This official may receive complaints concerning instances of maladministration by Community institutions from European citizens but also from 'any natural or legal person residing or having its registered office in a member state', either directly or through a member of the EP on acts by the institutions. He may investigate such complaints if they are not or have not been the subject of legal proceedings. If he establishes there has been maladministration, he informs the institution which has three months to reply. Thereupon the Ombudsman will forward a report to the EP and the institution concerned. The person lodging the complaint must be informed of the outcome.

Although, as we have seen, a number of positive changes were achieved by the Maastricht and Amsterdam Treaties, the European Parliament is still far short of a being a Parliament in the proper sense of the word. It has practically no legislative initiative and a limited right to reject legislation. In spite of being the only directly elected body in the Union, it still has difficulty in presenting itself as an effective representative of the people of Europe and this is reflected in the extremely low voter turn-out at European Parliament elections.

The European Court of Justice and the Court of First Instance

The changes made by the Nice Treaty

3.49 One of the major changes made in Nice concerned the structure and jurisdiction of the European Court of Justice and of the Court of First Instance. The Treaty introduced greater flexibility in order to prepare the legal system for the future. The Treaty articles concerning the two courts have been substantially changed

The ECJ retains jurisdiction for all other proceedings but the CFI may be entrusted by the Statute with other categories of proceedings than those listed under Article 225 EC which set out the jurisdiction for the CFI. The intention is to keep jurisdiction over essential Community issues within the ECJ and the Nice IGC asked the Court and the Commission to review the distribution of responsibilities as soon as possible so that appropriate proposals may be examined. Preliminary rulings remain reserved for the ECJ, unless the statute gives the CFI the responsibility under Article 225 EC.

The judicial system of the Community was, until Nice, a two-tier system. It consists of the ECJ, which was established by the ECSC Treaty of Paris in 1952, and of the CFI, created in 1989 in order to relieve the growing case load of the ECJ. These courts derive their fundamental task from Article 220 (ex Article 164) EC (following Article 31 ECSC) which provides that 'the Court of Justice and the Court of First Instance, each within its jurisdiction, shall ensure that in the interpretation and application of the Treaty the law is observed'. The Nice Treaty adds a clause to this effectively providing for a third tier of jurisdiction in the form of judicial panels to be attached to the Court of First Instance. We shall here discuss mainly the technical functions of the two courts and how their functions have changed since Nice. How they have dealt with their functions and interpreted their tasks under Article 220 is discussed more extensively in Chapters 5, 6, 7, 8 and 9.

The European Court of Justice

3.50 This is the main court of the European Community. It consists at present of 15 judges, one from each member state, although there is no nationality requirement. The court sits in a 'grand chamber' of 11 judges, replacing the plenary session, and sometimes still in plenary according with the rules in the Court's Statute (Article 221 (ex Article 165) EC). In all other cases it sits in chambers of three, five or seven judges.

3.51 The ECJ is assisted by eight Advocates General whose task is to deliver reasoned opinions on cases brought before the court. This number may be increased by the Council, acting unanimously, at the request of the Court of Justice. Both Judges and Advocates General are appointed for a period of six years. The President of the ECJ is elected every three years by its judges, who are chosen from those with the proper qualifications for the highest judicial appointments in their home country or who are jurisconsults of recognised competence, by 'Common Accord' of the governments of the member states. They act independently of the member states (Article 223(1) (ex Article 167(1)) EC).

3.52 Each member of the court has three 'legal secretaries' (or *référendaires*) who are their legal assistants. They undertake preliminary research and draft essential documents, including draft judgments and opinions, but may not take part in the court's deliberations as these are secret and result in a single collegiate judgment.

3.53 The court's procedure consists of a written phase, which ends in a report by the *'Judge-rapporteur'*, an oral hearing, which is usually very brief, followed by the Opinion rendered by the Advocate General. The final judgment is then given, usually after a number of months has elapsed.

The written procedure and the oral hearings, as well as the delivery of the Advocate General's opinion, are translated into the official languages of the court (11 at the present time, or 12 if one includes the Irish language, which is officially a procedural language). The court's deliberations are subject to the principle of secrecy and are held in the absence of interpreters. Only the French language is usually used in these deliberations, although some chambers have occasionally worked in other languages such as German and English. A single collegiate judgment is delivered. This often represents a compromise of differing views and this may account for some of the difficulties when reading a judgment, which sometimes appears to have an absence of reasoning on certain points.

3.54 The Court of First Instance does not have any Advocates General, but may appoint a judge as an ad hoc Advocate General who does not take part in the judgment. The Advocate Generals' duty is to give reasoned opinions on the cases brought before the court, in open court and with complete impartiality and independence. They indicate to the court how it should decide and give it the arguments it needs to do so. Often the Advocate General presents more extensive reasoning than the court does in its collegiate decision. It may provide a pointer towards future decisions by the court. See Slynn A-G's opinion in Cases 60 & 61/84 *Cinéthèque SA v Fédération Nationale des Cinémas Français* (1985), which, although not followed by the court on that occasion, pointed the way towards its judgment in Cases C-267 & 268/91 *Criminal Proceedings against Keck and Mithouard* (1993). However, the court is not bound to follow the Advocate General and does not always do so. Often the media in the UK report an Advocate General's Opinion as if it were a judgment by the ECJ, which may well turn out to be different. This was the case, for example in Case C-91/92 *Faccini Dori v Recreb Srl* (1994), where the court ruled out the possibility of finding that directives could have horizontal direct effect, ie between individuals, something to which Lenz AG had pointed the way. Sometimes the Advocate General's Opinion is immensely influential, as was the case for Lenz AG's Opinion in Case C-415/93 *Bosman* (see **18.14**), Jacobs AG's opinion in Case C-10/89 *Hag II* (changing the previous case law—see **15.17**), Tesauro AG's opinion in Case C-267/91 *Keck and Mithouard* (see **13.24**) and Elmer AG's opinion in Case C-249/96 *Grant v South-West Trains Ltd* (1998), although in this case the court also declined to follow his lead (see **19.2**).

Jurisdiction of the Court

3.55 The court has the following forms of jurisdiction:

(a) infringement actions against member states. These actions may be brought under Article 226 (ex Article 169) EC, Article 227 (ex Article 170) EC, Article 228 (ex Article 171) EC, and Article 288 (ex Article 215) EC (see Chapters 10 and 11); these actions fall under the plenary jurisdiction of the court;

(b) direct actions under Articles 230 and 232 (ex Articles 173 and 175) EC as well as under Article 235 (ex Article 178) EC are, since Nice, mainly in the competence of the Court of First Instance (see **3.62** and Chapter 11);

(c) preliminary rulings (Article 234 (ex Article 177) EC; see Chapter 5).

3.56 Article 234 of the EC Treaty provides for references to be made by national courts to the ECJ in cases concerning the *interpretation* of the Treaty as well as concerning the *validity* and *interpretation* of acts of the Community institutions as well as those of the European Central Bank. A further paragraph provides for the interpretation of statutes of 'bodies established by the Council where those statutes so provide'.

References are different from appeals in the hierarchy of national courts. In contrast to appeals, references are always made *in the course of proceedings before a national court* and cannot be made after the case has been decided. When dealing with preliminary references, the ECJ does not decide the case concerned, it simply renders a decision concerning the interpretation of a point of Community law which is essential to the outcome of the case. Once this decision is given, the case returns to the national court which takes into account the ECJ interpretation in order to come to its decision. This is why after each judgment in an Article 234 reference the ECJ will say that: 'since the proceedings are a step in the action pending before the national court, the decision on costs is a matter for that court.'

3.57 The national court will apply the ECJ's decision, but in doing so has discretion as to how to apply it. For example in Case 41/74 *van Duyn v Home Office* (1974) the ECJ had ruled that Directive 64/221 had direct effect and that Ms van Duyn could, therefore, rely on the directive before the English court. The English court decided that, having looked at the application of the directive, it was justified in ruling that Ms van Duyn should be excluded from the UK (see **7.8**).

Inherent jurisdiction

3.58 Article 220 (ex Article 164) EC provides 'the Court of Justice and the Court of First Instance, each within its jurisdiction, shall ensure that in the interpretation and application of this Treaty the law is observed'. The court has held that in order to achieve this purpose, in exceptional cases it has inherent jurisdiction which is not expressly provided for elsewhere in the Treaty. Thus, in Case C-70/88 *European Parliament v Council (Chernobyl)* (1990) it allowed the European Parliament to bring proceedings for the annulment of an act adopted by the Council, as this was necessary to protect its own prerogatives. In the Maastricht TEU, this right was incorporated in Article 230 (ex Article 173) EC and the EP's standing was made unlimited by the Treaty of Nice (see Chapter 11).

Interim measures

3.59 Both courts have the power to award interim measures in direct actions, including infringement proceedings (see Articles 242 and 243 (ex Articles 185 and 186) EC). The ECJ has not been called upon to decide whether it may grant interim measures in preliminary references under Article 234 EC. It is generally assumed there is no such power. The interlocutory powers of the national courts making references will generally be sufficient, and this now includes the power to suspend the application of a national measure based on a Community measure. See Joined Cases C-143/88 and C-92/89 *Zuckerfabrik Süderdithmarschen und Zuckerfabrik Soest* (1991); discussed further in Chapter 9.

Enforcement of judgments

3.60 If a member state fails to comply with a judgment, infringement proceedings may be brought against it by the Commission before the court under Article 228 (ex Article 171) EC. By the end of 1994, the ECJ had found against member states on 23 occasions. Thus, the burden of ensuring that a judgment is complied with seems to fall mainly on the Commission, which succeeds in most cases in persuading the member states to comply without court proceedings.

Article 228(2) (ex Article 171(2)) EC, inserted by the Maastricht Treaty, provides for the possibility for the court to impose a financial penalty on the offending member state if it fails to comply.

Miscellaneous powers

3.61

(a) The court may impose penalties under Article 229 (ex Article 171) EC in respect of Regulations adopted jointly by the European Parliament and the Council; this power is mainly used in competition cases.

(b) The ECJ has jurisdiction in disputes involving the European Investment Bank, on arbitration clauses contained in a contract concluded by or on behalf of the Community (Article 238 (ex Article 181) EC), in disputes submitted under special agreements (Article 239 (ex Article 182) EC), in respect of international agreements (Article 300(6) (ex Article 228(6)) EC), Community conventions and with regard to the Euratom Treaty.

The ECJ acts both as a Court of First Instance and as an Appeal Court for cases from the CFI.

The Court of First Instance (CFI)

3.62 The CFI was created in 1989 as a means of relieving the ECJ of its growing case load. This had increased from a few dozen cases in the 1960s to well over one hundred in the 1970s and to more than four hundred in 1995. As early as 1974 the ECJ had already suggested the creation of a separate tribunal to hear staff cases. The SEA in 1986 finally provided for the creation of such a court in Article 225 (ex Article 168a).

3.63 Under Article 225 as amended by Nice the CFI will have at least one judge per member state (at the moment 15 judges determined by the statute). This number may be changed and COREPER has already agreed a possible increase by six judges. The CFI has now become the judge for all direct actions under Articles 230, 232 (ex Articles 173 and 175 EC): (actions and failure to act, Article 235 (ex Article 178) EC: action for damages, Article 236 (ex Article 179) EC: staff cases, and 238 (ex Article 181) EC: arbitration clauses, with the exception of those which will be assigned to a judicial panel and those the statute reserves for the main court. There are no Advocates General, but for certain cases which may involve substantial investigations into facts a judge may be appointed to carry out a similar function to that of an Advocate General. This judge will then not take part in the deliberations or the judgment. Although the Court of Justice itself will retain competence to give preliminary rulings, the statute may entrust such responsibility to the Court of First Instance in specific cases.

Judicial panels

3.64 Specialised chambers, also known as judicial panels, may be set up by the Council to deal with specific matters at first instance, such as in the field of intellectual property. A new Article 229a allows the Council acting unanimously to attribute to the ECJ the responsibility of settling intellectual property disputes between private parties, particularly concerning the Community patent. The Nice IGC has also asked in a declaration for a draft decision to be prepared to set up such a panel for the settling of disputes in staff cases (Article 236 (ex Article 179) EC) which is at present still within the remit of the CFI. An appeal from the decisions of judicial panels may be made to the Court of First Instance.

Other changes made by the Amsterdam and Nice Treaties

3.65 Apart from the changes in composition and jurisdiction made in the Nice Treaty described above, other changes to the original functions of the two courts had already been made in Amsterdam, which extended the remit of the Court of Justice. Before that Treaty, the court had no jurisdiction over the second and third inter-governmental pillars. It was now given competence under the third pillar, Title VI of the TEU, the former home affairs and justice pillar, now renamed provisions on police and judicial co-operation in criminal matters. Whereas previously the jurisdiction of the court was optional, it now has automatic jurisdiction under Article 35 (ex Article K.7) relating to police and judicial co-operation to rule on disputes between the member states over future conventions and with respect to framework and other decisions if the dispute is not settled in the Council within six months. Furthermore, the court may acquire power to give preliminary rulings on questions referred to it by member states' courts under the same title, but this arises only if the member states opt, either at the time of signing of the Treaty, or later, to accept this form of jurisdiction. Only six have done so: Germany, Austria, Greece and the Benelux countries. Article 35 of the TEU provides for an alternative: either a court of last resort in a member state or any court or tribunal in a member state may make references when it considers that a ruling by the ECJ is necessary to enable the national court to give judgment. Lastly, the court may acquire jurisdiction over the parts of the third pillar which have been transferred to Community competence (see Title IV of the EC Treaty, entitled Visa, Asylum, Immigration and other Policies related to Free Movement of Persons). The provisions on closer co-operation in Title VII of the TEU provide for the possible use of the institutional framework, including the court, as do the provision on closer co-operation in the third pillar (Article 40(1) TEU) (see also **2.33**).

Rules of procedure

3.66 The court had wanted the Amsterdam IGC to approve an amendment to the TEU so that it, and not the Council, could draft its own rules of procedure. This power was not granted in the Treaty of Amsterdam. Nevertheless, important changes were made in July 2000 and February 2001 which, in particular, provide for a simplified procedure in making preliminary references (see further Chapter 5). This enables the court to decide by reasoned order that a matter is identical to one previously decided, thus saving a great deal of time. This procedure has been used to good effect by the court. The amendments further enable the judge-rapporteur and/or the Advocate General to request from the parties any information they consider relevant. Other amendments concern accelerated procedures and the possibility for the court to issue Practice Directions for both preliminary references and for direct actions. The Nice Treaty now provides that the court shall establish its own Rules of Procedure which require the approval of the Council acting by a qualified majority.

Judicial activism

3.67 When the first Community, the European Coal and Steel Community, was established in 1952, the Treaty and the institutions of the Community were to a large extent based on, and inspired by, the civil law systems of the six original founder members. The European Court of Justice, too, was probably based on the model of the French *Conseil d'Etat*, the highest French administrative court. Its jurisdiction under Articles 169, 170, 173 and 175 was that of a supreme administrative court reviewing acts by member states and the institutions and entertaining direct actions by individuals against the institutions only under strictly defined, limited conditions. Although the court showed some signs of early action (for example in Case 4/73 *Nold v Commission* (1974), see **6.8**), its real development into a true, supreme court for the

Community, started after the two later Communities, Euratom and the
European Economic Community, had been founded in 1957.

3.68 Case 26/62 *Van Gend en Loos v Nederlandse Administratie der
Belastingen* (1963) established the principle that individuals could rely
on Community law before their national courts, the principle of direct
effect, and Case 6/64 *Flaminio Costa v ENEL* (1964) established the principle
of supremacy of Community law over national law. The court did this
by interpreting the Treaty as to its 'spirit and general scheme' (for a
more extensive discussion of the two cases, see Chapters 7 and 8). In
both cases, the court made it clear that the Treaties should be viewed
as constituting a 'new legal order'. After these judgments, the court has
shown many examples of what critics might call judicial activism, but
which could, on another reading, be considered a filling in of the gaps
in a 'framework treaty', ie a text which is couched in general terms and
which indicates general objectives, to be interpreted purposively, thus
filling in the gaps left in the Treaty articles. The court, fulfilling its task in
exercising its inherent jurisdiction (see **3.58**), thus proceeded to give an
interpretation of Articles 173 and 175 (now Articles 230 and 232 EC)
which gave the European Parliament *locus standi* to bring cases and have
cases brought against it by member states and the other institutions (see
Chapter 11). The invention of state liability for breaches of Community
law is another example (see Chapter 9).

The European Council

3.69 During various periods of stagnation and difficulty in the
Community, heads of state or government have met at summit conferences
in order to reset the political agenda. These meetings became a regular
feature in 1974, when it was decided that regular summit meetings of
heads of state or government and their foreign ministers would be held,
although without any legal basis in the Treaty. Initially, these meetings
did not include the President of the Commission, but this soon changed,
and in 1986 the Single European Act enshrined the European Council
in Article 2. Article 4 (ex Article D) of the TEU expands upon this and
states that the European Council shall provide the Community with the
necessary impetus for development and define general political guidelines.
It also confirmed that the President of the Commission is a member and
that one other Commissioner is entitled to attend. The European Council
is not included in the Institutional structure of the Community and is
not an Institution as such. It does not have general decision-making power,

although notable decisions include the decision to set up the European Monetary System (EMS) and the decision concerning Denmark taken at the 1992 Edinburgh summit. Political decisions taken by the European Council are generally followed up in the form of Community legislation which follows the institutional procedures. However, the political power of the European Council is clearly considerable, and its summit meetings are widely reported and publicised. From the legal point of view, however, it is important *not* to confuse the European Council with the Council (of Ministers), which *is* a European institution.

3.70 Amendments made by the Amsterdam Treaty give a somewhat more concrete definition of the tasks of the European Council. Article 13(1) and (2) first subparagraph (Amsterdam amendments in italics) reads:

1. The European Council shall define the principles of and general guidelines for the common foreign and security policy, *including for matters with defence implications.*

2. *The European Council shall decide on common strategies to be implemented by the Union in areas where the member states have important interests in common.*

Common strategies shall set out their objectives, duration and the means to be made available by the Union and the member states.

3. The Council shall take the decisions necessary for defining and implementing the common foreign and security policy on the basis of the general guidelines *defined* by the European Council.

The Council shall recommend common strategies to the European Council and shall implement them, in particular by adopting joint actions and common positions.

The Council shall ensure the unity, consistency and effectiveness of action by the Union.

3.71 Normally, the European Council meets twice a year. In Lisbon in 2000 it was decided that a third meeting dealing with employment and economic matters would be held in addition each Spring. A Declaration attached to the Treaty of Nice (No 22) specified that as from 2002 one European Council meeting per Presidency will be held in Brussels. Once the Union comprises 18 members (after the next enlargement), all meetings will be held in Brussels. This is an attempt to make these 'summits' more efficient and to avoid difficulties in respect of changing venues which had increasingly dogged recent summit meetings.

The Court of Auditors

3.72 The Maastricht Treaty amended Article 7 (ex Article 4) EC by inserting the Court of Auditors as one of the institutions of the Community. Originally, auditing of accounts was carried out within each Community. Subsequently, the Merger Treaty established a single Audit Board for all three Communities. The Board, however, had an unhappy co-existence with the Commission. It complained that its critical comments were not heeded and it experienced delays and difficulties in obtaining information from the Commission. Its reports were not published, but sent by the Commission together with the accounts for the year, to the Council and the EP, as part of its procedure of giving discharge to the Commission.

3.73 In response to pressure from the EP which called for a European Audit Office (1973) and from the new member states which had different traditions with respect to public sector audit, the Court of Auditors was established by the Treaty establishing a single Commission of the EC signed in 1977. The court attained institutional status only when the Maastricht Treaty came into force. It is governed by Articles 246–248 (ex Articles 188a–c) EC. The Nice Treaty provides that the Court of Auditors will consist of one national from each member state (Article 247(1) (ex Article 188b) EC). It sits in Luxembourg and its structure and status are in many ways similar to those of the European Court. However, unlike some national courts of auditors, it does not have a disciplinary function. Under an important change inserted by the Maastricht TEU the court 'approves' the accounts and may withhold this approval. The present 15 members are chosen from among persons who belong, or have belonged, in their respective countries, to external audit bodies or who are specially qualified for such an office. Their function is to examine the accounts of revenue and expenditure of the Community. It acts by a majority of its members. Fraud and financial mismanagement are serious problems in the Community. The importance of these problems was recognised by the member states when they gave the court the status of a Community institution. This means, therefore, that acts of the Court of Auditors which have legal effects will be subject to the jurisdiction of the ECJ. In Case C-315/99 P *Ismeri Europa v Court of Auditors* (2001) the company Ismeri Europa appealed a judgment by the CFI in Case T-277/97 in which it had claimed damages for loss suffered as a result of criticisms of the company made by the Court of Auditors in a special report. The ECJ upheld the CFI's judgment.

The Economic and Social Committee (ECOSOC)

3.74 Article 7(2) (ex Article 4(2)) EC provides that the Council and Commission are to be assisted by an Economic and Social Committee. This is an advisory body intended to represent various sectional interests. According to Article 257 (ex Article 193) EC it consists of representatives of the various economic and social components of organised civil society, among others, producers, farmers, carriers, workers, dealers, craftsmen, the professions, consumers, and the general public. In practice it consists of three groups: employers, workers (largely represented by the trade unions) and 'others'. The last group includes spokesmen for farmers, consumers and the professions. Its 189 members are appointed by the Council for renewable four-year terms on the basis of national allocations; the largest (UK and other large countries) is 24, the smallest (Luxembourg) is six. The number and distribution per member state was not altered in Nice but the ceiling may not exceed 350. This number, however, will not yet be achieved after the accession of the new member states (344 in a Union of 27 member states). The members, though intended to represent particular groups, may not be bound by any 'mandatory instructions' (Article 258 (ex Article 194) EC). In certain cases the Committee has the right to be consulted by the Council or Commission. Then, however, the Council or the Commission may set a time limit (of at least one month) and, if no opinion is given within that period, go ahead without it. Article 262 (ex Article 198) EC as amended by the Treaty of Amsterdam provides that the Committee may also be consulted by the European Parliament. The Treaty of Amsterdam extends the areas on which the Committee may be consulted to include guidelines and incentives in employment, legislation on social matters and application of the principle of equal opportunities and equal treatment, and public health. Failure to consult the Committee when required to do so would lead to invalidity of legislation for breach of an essential procedural requirement (Article 230 (ex Article 173) EC).

Committee of the Regions (COR)

3.75 This Committee was established by the Maastricht Treaty in Articles 263–265 (ex Articles 198a–c) EC and represents regional and local bodies within the Community. The Treaty of Nice added to this that members must hold either a regional or local authority mandate or are politically accountable to an elected assembly. Like ECOSOC, its role is to advise the Council and the Commission, and membership is divided in very much the same way. The numbers are the same as for ECOSOC and the Nice Treaty again sets a ceiling of 350 for membership. It has been given greater autonomy by the Amsterdam amendments and no longer has a common organisational structure with ECOSOC. Article 263 now specifies that no member of the Committee may also be a member of the European Parliament. The Committee may be consulted by the European Parliament and the areas on which it may be consulted have been extended to include guidelines and incentives in employment, legislation on social matters, public health, environment, implementing decisions in the social fund, measures relating to vocational training and transport.

The European Investment Bank

3.76 Article 9 (ex Article 4b) EC establishes a European Investment Bank (EIB). Articles 266 and 267 (ex Articles 198d and 198e) EC provide for the bank's tasks, which consist of granting loans and giving guarantees on a non-profit-making basis to projects in the Community which contribute to 'a balanced and steady development of the common market'. The bank facilitates the financing of investment programmes together with the structural funds and other Community financial instruments.

The European Central Bank

3.77 Article 8 (ex Article 4a) EC provides for the establishment of a European System of Central Banks (ESCB) and of a European Central Bank (ECB) (Articles 105–115 (ex Articles 105–109d) EC). These were set up for when European and Monetary Union entered the third stage. This occurred on 1 January 2002. At the beginning of the second stage in 1994 a European Monetary Institute had been established as the precursor of the ECB (see Article 117 (ex Article 109f) EC). This has now been replaced by the ECB, which is an independent body determining policy for the single currency.

Further reading

Douglas-Scott, *Constitutional Law of the European Union*, (2002) Longman, Chapter 2.

M Westlake, *A Modern Guide to the EP, the Parliament and the Commission: Partners and Rivals in the European Policy-Making Process* (1994) Butterworths.

Horspool, Buckley, 'Robinson, Law of the European Union', [1995] 48 Current Legal Problems, pp 151–157, 161–164.

COREPER

Hayes-Renshaw, Lequesne & Lopez, 'The permanent representation of the member states to the European Communities', [1989] JCMS 119 (December).

European Council

Bulmer and Wessels, *The European Council* (1987) Macmillan.

D Curtin, 'The constitutional structure of the Union: a Europe of bits and pieces', [1993] 30 CMLRev 17.

Hartley, *The Foundations of European Community Law*, (5th edn, 2003) Clarendon Press, Chapters 1 and 2.

Editorial Comments, [1997] 34 CMLRev 767–772.

O'Keeffe and Twomey, *Legal Issues of the Maastricht Treaty*, (1994) Chancery.

O'Keefe and Twomey, *Legal Issues of the Amsterdam Treaty* (1999) Hart.

The European Court of Justice

The European Court of Justice: A Case Study in Judicial Activism, Sir Patrick Neill QC, Warden, All Souls' College, Oxford – August 1995 European Policy Forum.

Trevor Hartley, 'Judicial objectivity and the constitution of the European Union', [1996] 112 LQR 95, Sweet & Maxwell and contributors.

Anthony Arnull, 'The European Court and judicial objectivity: a reply to Professor Hartley', (1996) 112 LQR 411, Sweet & Maxwell and contributors.

For a comprehensive report on the ECJ and CFI, see: The Role and Future of the European Court of Justice—A report by the EC Advisory Board of the British Institute of International and Comparative Law, 1996.

Anthony Arnull, 'Does the Court of Justice have inherent jurisdiction?', [1990] 27 CMLRev 683.

Self-test questions

1. Discuss the legislative powers of the Commission under the EC Treaty, both original and delegated.

2. 'Where member states' vital interests are at stake, it is the Community practice to proceed only by unanimity.' Discuss the history of this practice and its status in the light of the relevant Treaty provisions.

3. 'The European Parliament has enhanced its role in the political process of the Community by intelligently exploiting the role it has been given in the judicial process.' Discuss, examining the role of the Parliament in proceedings before the European Court and the circumstances in which the Parliament can appear as a party in cases before the European Court.

4. What is meant by the expression 'institutional balance' as it has been developed in European Community law? To what extent is it useful in helping us to understand the relationships among the principal European institutions?

CHAPTER FOUR

The Community Legal System

SUMMARY

- Sources of law and types of acts
- Primary legislation: Treaties, Conventions, acts by member states
- Secondary legislation: Regulations, Directives, Decisions, Recommendations, Opinions
- Other sources of law
- 'Soft law'
- Legislative procedures: consultation, co-operation, co-decision, assent
- Legislative powers: express and implied powers; exclusive and concurrent powers
- The application of the principle of subsidiarity

4.1 The Community legal system is based on several sources of law. Community law is not universal, nor can the Community enact any legislation it pleases; its competence is limited to the powers attributed to the Community by the legal texts adopted by the member states (see Article 5 (ex Article 3b) EC). These powers have grown considerably in strength and extent since the inception of the Community; the field of application of Community law has been widened by each successive Treaty and the Community institutions have received more powers through these Treaties. There is little doubt that through the interpretation of the Community powers by the European Court of Justice, further extension of their application has occurred. General principles of law which are recognised and applied by the member states have been used by the ECJ to underpin the Community legal system.

The sources of Community law are:

Primary legislation: The Constitutive Treaties, subsidiary Conventions, acts by the member states;

Secondary legislation: Regulations, Directives and Decisions; the status of Recommendations and Opinions;

Other sources of law: international agreements, general principles of law (see Chapter 6), case law of the European Court of Justice (see Chapters 3 and 5), 'soft law'—memoranda, circulars, statements, resolutions.

Primary legislation

4.2 The primary legislation of the Community may be divided into three categories: the Constitutive Treaties, subsidiary Conventions, and acts by the representatives of the member states.

4.3 The *Constitutive Treaties* are: the Treaty establishing the European Coal and Steel Community (ECSC) 1951 (now expired and, insofar as necessary, absorbed into the EC Treaty); the Treaty establishing the European Economic Community (EEC) 1957, the Treaty establishing the European Atomic Energy Community (Euratom) 1957; the Convention on Certain Institutions Common to the European Communities, signed at the same time as the EEC and Euratom Treaties in 1957 and providing for a single Parliamentary Assembly and a single European Court of Justice to serve all three Communities; the Merger Treaty 1965, establishing a single Council of Ministers and a single Commission for the three Communities; the Budgetary Treaties, the First Treaty of Accession 1972 (Denmark, Ireland, UK), the Second Treaty of Accession 1981 (Greece), the Third Treaty of Accession 1986 (Spain and Portugal), the Fourth Treaty of Accession 1995 (Austria, Finland and Sweden), the Single European Act 1986, Treaty on European Union 1993 (TEU or Maastricht Treaty), Agreement on the European Economic Area and the Treaty of Amsterdam 1999 (TOA), the Treaty of Nice 2003. The amendment procedure is now governed by Article 48 (ex Article N) TEU. The initiative for a Treaty amendment may come from a member state or from the Commission. The proposal is then submitted to the Council which decides whether to convene an inter-governmental conference. The European Parliament and, where appropriate, the Commission, must be consulted. In the event of institutional changes in the monetary area the European Central Bank must also be consulted. Ratification then takes place by the member states in accordance with their respective constitutional requirements. A special form of amendment procedure applies when new member states join the Community. Any European state may apply for admission (it has to be democratic and to respect human rights: Copenhagen European Council of 7 and 8 April 1978). Such a Treaty of Accession must be ratified by the contracting states in accordance with their constitutional requirements (Article 49(2) (ex Article O(2)) TEU); they must also accept the *acquis communautaire* (see 2.3).

There are numerous Protocols annexed to the various Treaties as well as large numbers of Declarations. The Protocols have the same legal force as the Treaties themselves, but the value of Declarations is mainly political, unless they are unanimous and referred to in the Treaty itself.

Subsidiary Conventions

4.4 Article 293 (ex Article 220) EC provides that member states shall, so far as necessary, enter into negotiations with each other with a view to securing various rights for the benefit of their nationals: the protection of rights of nationals of other member states, the abolition of double taxation, the mutual recognition of companies and the retention of their legal personality if they move to another member state, the possibility of mergers between companies from different countries, the simplification of formalities governing the recognition and enforcement of judgments and of arbitration awards. The Brussels Convention on Jurisdiction and the Enforcement of Judgments in Civil and Commercial Matters 1968, was concluded to attain one of the objectives in the original Treaty. Article 293 imposes an obligation on the member states rather than on the Community, but it is clear that the conclusion of such conventions is relevant to the attainment of Treaty objectives. Conventions under Article 293 therefore probably form part of the Community legal system. Thus, when new member states join, they have to accede to the conventions as part of the *acquis communautaire*. Another example is the Rome Convention on the law applicable to Contractual Obligations (1980), which, like the Brussels Convention, gives the ECJ jurisdiction to interpret its provisions. When new member states join the Community they are expected to become parties to it. Even if conventions concluded between member states do not fall within the areas covered by Article 293, they might qualify. The Schengen Agreements on the gradual abolition of checks at common borders were integrated by a Protocol to the Treaty of Amsterdam into the Treaty on European Union. Schengen consisted of two agreements which were not covered by Article 293. The status of the agreements was the subject of much debate, as it was never certain to what extent they were subject to Community law, although they provided for the supremacy of Community law in case of conflict. The Protocol attached to the Treaty of Amsterdam now provides that Schengen as well as related agreements and rules adopted on the basis of the agreements are to be incorporated into the framework of the European Union. The Schengen acquis is to apply to the 13 member states which have signed up to it. The United Kingdom and Ireland are not bound by the agreements but may elect to take part in some areas of co-operation.

In the event of conflict, the constitutive treaties have superior status in the Community legal system. In the event of a conflict between a subsidiary convention and a Community act such as a regulation or directive which is directly derived from the Treaty, the Community act will prevail.

Acts of representatives of member states

4.5 The member states sometimes act outside the scope of the institutions, often during summit meetings of the European Council. An example is the decision taken by the heads of state or government meeting within the European Council in December 1992 to accommodate some of Denmark's problems which had caused a negative vote in the referendum to ratify the Maastricht Treaty. Before the existence of the European Council, such decisions or declarations were made during meetings of the Council of Ministers but were considered as acts of the member states. Such acts sometimes have legal force, but sometimes their legal effect is not clear, as in eg the Luxembourg Compromise (see **3.16**), the Ioannina Compromise (see **3.18**), which has been now been given legal force by the Amsterdam Treaty, and the Act on Direct Elections to the European Parliament.

International agreements—powers of the Community

4.6 Community law may prevent member states from acting independently in the case of international agreements. Apart from the treaty-making powers expressly given to the Community by the Treaty provisions, essentially as regards the common commercial policy and association agreements, the Community has powers to conclude agreements in areas covered by the Treaties where it has internal powers. How much authority the Community has to negotiate or conclude agreements instead of member states depends on the interpretation of these powers. In a line of decisions the ECJ indicates how far powers can be implied from the express powers given in the Treaties. Express powers exist in the whole field of the common commercial policy, for example. Implied powers can, in the theory of parallelism until recently increasingly favoured by the ECJ, be derived from the express, internal powers. This extends the competence of the Community to conclude agreements to any of its objectives which are concerned with internal as well as external relations.

4.7 If the Community has exclusive power to act, the member state will be precluded from acting itself. Therefore, each time the Community adopts provisions to attain a common objective, the member states no longer have the right, individually or collectively, to adopt measures inconsistent with those rules. There are a number of areas where the Community has exclusive power. As the Community legislates, more areas will fall under this exclusive power. The Community has exclusive powers in the area of agriculture as well as the common commercial policy. In a number of cases the ECJ has held that existence of Community power to enter into international agreements with a non-member state in a certain area can preclude member states from acting independently in that area. The common transport policy called for in Article 70 (ex Article 74) EC provides a good example. In Case 22/70 *Commission v Council (ERTA)* (1971) the court considered whether the Community could enter into agreements with non-member states and stated that the authority of the Community to do so should be viewed in the light of the whole scheme of the Treaty. If such an implied power exists and has been exercised by the Community, it will be able to conclude such agreements. In the field of transport covered by Title V (ex Title IV) EC the Community had been slow in legislating. Although it was accepted that the Community had taken over from the member states where it had legislated, the member states were still accepted as parties to the agreement, as these powers had not yet been exercised when the new agreement was negotiated and it was a renegotiation of an existing agreement. There was a concurrent power between the Community and the member states. In *Opinion 1/75 on an OECD local cost standard* (1975), the ECJ recognised that power was expressly given to the Community by Article 231 (now Article 304 EC). Such express power would lead to the exclusion of concurrent powers by the member states unless member states had been expressly authorised by the Community to act. In *Opinion 1/76 on a Laying-*

up Fund for Inland Waterway Vessels (1977) which again concerned Title V, as in *ERTA*, it was accepted that the Community had legislated and that the implied power which had been the subject of debate in *ERTA* was to be exercised by the Community as an exclusive power. In Opinion 1/91 *Opinion on the Draft Agreement on a European Economic Area* (1991) the court held that the proposed EEA Court was incompatible with the Treaty as it would have jurisdiction to decide on the competence to be attributed to the Community and to the member states, while this is for the ECJ to decide under Article 219 (now Article 292 EC). In its Opinion on the powers of the Community in respect of the World Trade Organisation (WTO) (*Opinion 1/94 Re WTO Agreement* (1994)) the court considered the extent of the powers of the Community. It decided that the Community had exclusive competence in the field of the common commercial policy under Article 113 (now Article 133 EC). This applied to goods, including agricultural products. However, the Community shared authority with the member states in the other parts of the agreement. The part of the agreement concerning services (GATS) fell partly inside, partly outside Article 113. The cross-border provision of services, where neither the provider nor the recipient of the service moves fell inside Article 113, but all other agreements concerning service provision, as well as the part of the agreement concerning intellectual property rights fell outside Article 113. The court ruled out any application of the implied powers doctrine as given in *ERTA* and in *Opinion 1/76* to either GATS or TRIPS (trade-related aspects of intellectual property). The latter agreement concerned intellectual property and was held by the court to fall within the exclusive competence of the member states.

4.8 There are three types of international agreements:

• agreements between the Community and one or more non-member states;

• agreements between the Community and member states acting jointly, and one or more non-member states;

• agreements between member states and non-member states.

4.9 Agreements of the first two types are considered an integral part of Community law; agreements of the third type are generally not part of Community law. Thus, association agreements with the Community are part of Community law, as specifically provided for by Article 300 (ex

Article 228) EC. This was confirmed in Case 181/73 *Haegeman v Belgium* (1974), which concerned the association agreement between the Community and Greece, in Case 12/86 *Demirel v Stadt Schwäbisch Gmünd* (1987) which concerned the association agreement between the Community and Turkey and Case 270/80 *Polydor Ltd v Harlequin Record Shops* which concerned the agreement between the Community and Portugal. Case 87/75 *Bresciani v Amministrazione Italiana delle Finanze* (1976) concerned the Yaounde Convention and in Cases 21–24/72 *International Fruit* (1972) the court held it was competent to review the provisions of the GATT agreement (the General Agreement on Tariffs and Trade). Can such agreements have direct effect? In Case 104/81 *Kupferberg* (1982) the court was asked this question concerning tł ₋ association agreement with Portugal. In a lengthy ruling the court found that they can; the provisions of such an agreement would have to be given uniform effect throughout the Community. However, those agreements which pursue different aims from those of the Community will not be directly effective. In *International Fruit* the GATT, which was concluded before the Treaty of Rome, was held by the court not to be capable of direct effect, even though the Community had succeeded to the obligations of the member states within the framework of the GATT. More recently, however, the question has arisen again, since the conclusion of the World Trade Agreement (WTO) in 1994, of which the GATT is an integral part. The new GATT provisions contain a clear mechanism for the settlement of disputes, including a court by whose decisions member states have undertaken to abide. In some specific cases, the ECJ has accepted that the GATT rules may now take precedence over Community law under certain conditions. In Case C-280/93 *Germany v Council* (1994) the court said it is not generally possible to rely on GATT rules to challenge the legality of a Community act. There are, however, exceptions to this rule:

> ... It is only if the Community intended to implement a particular obligation entered into within the framework of GATT, or if the Community act expressly refers to specific provisions of GATT that the court must review the lawfulness of the Community act in question from the point of view of the GATT rules (para 11 of the judgment).

This last point was repeated in Case C-352/96 *Italy v Council* (1998) (para 19). In Case T-256/97 *BEU v Commission* (2000) the CFI said with reference to the GATT anti-dumping code:

> The Community legislature has signalled that where words are carried over from the GATT agreement into the Regulation, they

should have the same meaning in Community law as they do in the agreement.

Secondary Community legislation

4.10 Secondary Community legislation is provided for by Articles 249 (ex Article 189) and 250 (ex Article 189a) EC. The binding Community acts are Regulations, Directives and Decisions. There are also non-binding acts: recommendations or opinions, which nevertheless are persuasive.

Regulations

4.11 Article 249 (ex Article 189) EC provides that a regulation shall have general application and be 'directly applicable' in all member states (see also Chapter 6). A regulation, therefore, will apply directly in all member states without having to be incorporated by national legislation. The ECJ has stated that regulations should not be subjected to further incorporation as this could endanger the uniform application of Community law if member states made any changes which they might argue were necessary and thus obscure the source and nature of the right. The doctrine that national measures are improper was first laid down in Case 39/72 *Commission v Italy (Re Slaughtered Cows)* (1973). A regulation provided for premiums to be paid for slaughter to counter over-production. The Italian government passed a decree stating that the provisions of relevant regulation were 'deemed to be included in it'. The ECJ said:

> By following this procedure, the Italian government has brought into doubt both the legal nature of the applicable provisions and the date of their coming into force.

According to the terms of Articles 189 and 191 (now Articles 249 and 254 EC) of the Treaty, regulations were, as such, directly applicable in all member states and came into force solely by virtue of their publication in the Official Journal of the Communities, and from the date specified in them, or in the absence thereof, as from the date provided in the Treaty. Consequently, all methods of implementation were contrary to the Treaty which would have the result of creating an obstacle to the direct effect of Community law and of jeopardising their simultaneous and uniform application in the whole of the Community. The court went on to point out that in one respect the Italian decree had departed from the terms of Community law (it set a time limit for implementation). Therefore:

> ... the default of the Italian Republic has thus been established by reason not only of the delay in putting the system into effect, but also of the manner of giving effect to it provided by the decree.

4.12 Although the original Treaty of Rome provided that regulations only must be published in the Official Journal, since the Maastricht Treaty Article 254 (ex Article 191) EC now provides that regulations, as well as directives and decisions, must be published in the Official Journal and enter into force on the date specified in them or, in the absence thereof, on the twentieth day following that of their publication. In Case 34/73 *Variola* (1973) the court said that national implementation could prejudice the ECJ's jurisdiction to give a ruling on the interpretation and validity of the measure under a preliminary reference.

4.13 Regulations do not necessarily always have direct effect (see Chapter 7). Sometimes, it is necessary for national measures to be taken. In Case 128/78 *Commission v United Kingdom (Re Tachographs)* (1979) a regulation required implementing measures, and the UK was asked by the Court to take such measures. If the terms of a regulation are vague and further detailed provisions are advisable the court might accept that such measures are taken, provided that they are not incompatible with the regulation (see Case 31/78 *Bussone* (1978)).

4.14 The type of act is determined, not by its form, but by its content and object (see Cases 16 and 17/62 *Confédération Nationale des Producteurs de Fruits et Légumes v Council* (1962)). If a measure is of general application, it will be considered as to its effect. In Case 92/78 *Simmenthal v Commission* (1979) the court stated that acts, even if not in the form of a regulation, but nevertheless normative in substance, should be treated as a regulation. Cases 41–44/70 *International Fruit* (1971) concerned the procedure for importing apples from non-member states. The importers had to apply ahead of time for a licence. Each week national authorities would collate applications made during the previous week and pass the details to the Commission. The Commission would then enact the measure in the form of a regulation. However, the court held it was a really a 'bundle of decisions' concerning a 'closed category of persons', ie those who had made an application in the previous week (see also 11.20).

Directives

4.15 Article 249 provides that directives are *binding* as to the *effect* to be achieved but leaves the choice as to form and method to the member states. Directives therefore need to be incorporated into national law and are a more flexible instrument of Community law than regulations, which leave no discretion for any consideration of national differences and needs. By their very nature, however, directives may give rise to problems when they are implemented. Without doing so intentionally, a member state may misinterpret the directive or the amount of discretion it has been given by the directive. The member state may be of the opinion that its existing legislation already covers the provisions of the directive when this may not be the case. Examples of these difficulties will be encountered throughout this book, see in particular Chapters 7 and 8.

4.16 Directives are binding on those member states to whom they are addressed. In this they also differ from regulations which are always of general application. This allows directives to be applied to some member states and not necessarily to others. However, the large majority of directives are addressed to all member states and, like regulations, most directives now (since the Maastricht Treaty) have to be published in the Official Journal and enter into force either on the date specified in the directive or on the twentieth day after publication (Article 254 (ex Article 191) EC).

4.17 After the ECJ had found that directives could have (vertical) direct effect in Case 41/74 *van Duyn* (see further **7.8**) it was thought that the difference between regulations and directives could become blurred and perhaps disappear altogether. It has also been suggested that in order to achieve the uniform application of Community law, directives should be incorporated into national law without changing their wording. The inter-governmental conference leading up to the Treaty of Amsterdam was to have considered a hierarchy of Community legislation and possibly a change in the form of legislation. However, this did not happen at that time. The Convention in Brussels has proposed a hierarchy in the legislation, so that secondary legislation does not necessarily have to pass through all the complicated legislative phases.

Decisions

4.18 Decisions are specific measures issued by the Community which are binding on those to whom they are addressed. The Commission makes extensive use of such decisions, particularly in the field of competition.

Under Article 253 (ex Article 190) EC, regulations, directives and decisions must state the reasons on which they are based. Failure to do this may entail annulment (see Chapter 11).

Recommendations and opinions

4.19 Recommendations and opinions are not legally binding. Nevertheless they are of importance and may be persuasive; recommendations must be taken into account when the achievement of Community objectives is concerned. In Case 322/88 *Grimaldi* (1989) the ECJ stated that national courts had to take recommendations into consideration when interpreting national law adopted in implementation of Community law.

Decisions of the ECJ and general principles of law

4.20 Although there is no system of binding precedent in the Treaty, the decisions of the ECJ are generally considered to be a source of Community law. A number of decisions by the court have led directly to Treaty amendments, as, for example, in Articles 230 and 232 (ex Articles 173 and 175) EC where the changes in the European Parliament's position arising from court rulings were embodied in the Maastricht Treaty on European Union (see **3.35**). It is also largely due to the ECJ's decisions granting limited standing to Parliament that the Nice Treaty now provides for full standing for the Parliament, on an equal footing with the other Institutions (see Article 230, paras 2 and 3).

General principles of law originating in the member states are considered by the court to be an inherent part of the Treaty (see further Chapter 6).

Acts sui generis

4.21 This subject is discussed in Chapter 11. There are cases where it is not possible to classify an act under any of the above categories. The list of acts given has been held by the ECJ to be non-exhaustive. There are acts in different forms which will create legal effects and which are often referred to as being *sui generis*: they have their own particular features. Case 22/70 *Commission v Council* (the *ERTA* case, see **4.7**) dealt with a Council resolution which was held by the court to have legal effects and could, therefore, be reviewed by the court. Acts of the European Parliament, acting alone are only reviewable under Article 230 (ex Article 173) EC if they are 'intended to produce legal effects *vis-à-vis* third parties'. This amendment of the article in the Maastricht Treaty was the direct result of the court's judgment in Case 294/83 *Les Verts* (1986) (see Chapter 11).

4.22 The court has also accepted in Case 34/86 *Council v European Parliament* (1986) that the act of the President of the Parliament by which he declares that the Community Budget is finally adopted pursuant to the Treaty is an act susceptible to judicial review. In Joined Cases C-181 and C-248/91 *European Parliament v Council and Commission* (*Bangladesh* case) (1993) the Parliament sought the annulment of a decision taken by the member states meeting in the Council to provide humanitarian aid to Bangladesh following a natural disaster. The European Parliament alleged that the contested decision was in reality an act of the Council which had budgetary implications and which should have been adopted under Article 203 (now Article 272 EC) of the Treaty. The Council's failure to do so allegedly infringed the European Parliament's prerogatives. The Council said the case was inadmissible on the ground that the contested decision was not an act of the Council but of the member states, as described in a press release after the meeting of the Council where it was adopted, and therefore it was beyond the scope of Article 173. The court said (judgment para 922):

> ... it is true that if the member states adopted a collective decision in breach of Community law it would be open to the Commission to initiate enforcement proceedings against the member states under Article 169 (now Article 226 EC) of the Treaty.

This would not be likely in the instant case, however, as the Commission and the member states were in agreement. But in Case C-70/88 *European Parliament v Council (Chernobyl)* (1990) the court said (at para 19):

> ... while the Commission is required to ensure that the Parliament's prerogatives are respected, that duty cannot go as far as to oblige it to adopt the Parliament's position and bring an action for annulment which the Commission itself considers unfounded.

The court had to maintain the institutional balance and ensure the protection of Parliament's prerogatives:

> ... by means of a legal remedy which is suited to the purpose which the Parliament seeks to achieve.

4.23 What does 'legal effect' mean? In Cases 8–11/66 *Noordwijks Cement Accoord* (1967), cement-making companies received immunity from fines imposed under the competition law rules of Article 85 (now Article 81 EC) and EEC Council Regulation 17/62 from the time when the agreement was notified until the Commission reached its decision. As this was thought to be too favourable to the firms, regulation 17 also provided that immunity shall cease to apply once the Commission has informed the firms, *after a preliminary examination* that the agreement appears to violate Article 81(1).

The Commission sent a letter to the firms stating that the Commission subjected the agreement to a provisional examination and concluded that Article 81(1) applied and that there was no exemption. Immunity would therefore cease. The firms brought cases contesting this decision. The Commission argued there was no act which could be quashed and that the letter was a mere expression of opinion. The ECJ rejected this. The effect of the decision was to remove immunity:

> This measure deprived them of a legal situation which Regulation 17 attached to the notification of the agreement and exposed them to a grave financial risk ... bringing about a distinct change in their legal position. It is unequivocally a measure which produces legal effects touching the interests of the undertakings concerned and which is binding on them. It thus constitutes not a mere opinion but a decision.

If an act only concerns the internal operation of an institution it has only internal effects. In *Les Verts* (see above) this argument was advanced but in that case there was an effect *vis-à-vis* a third party.

4.24 In the absence of actions for a declaration, the ECJ has ruled that a statement of intention can be a reviewable act. Letters by the Commission have been so held (Case 8/55 *Fédération Charbonniere de Belgigue v High Authority* (1956) and Cases 7/56, 3-7/57 *Algera v Common Assembly* (1957)). In fact, the ECJ has adopted a doctrine that any statement by a Community institution as to the action it intends to take in given circumstances is a reviewable act provided it is definite and unequivocal. The fact that the institution is not legally bound by such an act appears to be immaterial.

4.25 What if there are a number of steps, each being in itself a preliminary decision (by different bodies)? Case 78/63 *Huber v Commission* (1964) concerned the permanent appointment of a Commission official. The rules were that he could only be 'established' if the relevant review Board gave a favourable report. The Board's opinion was unfavourable. The Advocate General said the report was a reviewable act as the report meant that the appointing authority was legally precluded from establishing the official. The ECJ disagreed: the report was not separable from the final decision and it was, therefore, not reviewable on its own.

4.26 Letters, too, may be reviewable. Case 60/81 *IBM v Commission* (1981) concerned a letter written by the Commission inviting IBM to state its case and enclosing a statement of objections. IBM objected to doing this on procedural grounds: the statement of objections was not clear, the decision to proceed had been taken by an official, not a Commissioner; the proceedings were contrary to national law as the Commission was trying to apply EC law extraterritorially. The ECJ ruled that these were not reviewable acts, they were merely preliminary decisions which could be challenged only in the course of a review of the final decision. This meant for IBM, unfortunately, that it had to bring a case on the merits first before it could raise these preliminary objections. In Case 53/85 *AKZO v Commission* (1986) documents had been shown by the Commission to the complainant, not AKZO. AKZO claimed commercial secrecy and brought proceedings to annul the decision by the Commission to show documents. The ECJ ruled this was admissible as it directly affected AKZO's right to confidentiality, irrespective of the final decision.

4.27 If an act is reviewable it will generally continue to have legal effect until it is annulled. However, if an act is tainted with particular serious illegality, it may be held to be void ab initio. In Cases T-79, 84–86, 89, 91, 94, 96, 98, 102, 104/89 *BASF v Commission* (1992) the CFI held Commission proceedings against a cartel to be so tainted with procedural defect that they were non-existent. The Rules of Procedure's requirements as to the signing of a decision imposing fines had not been complied with. The ECJ, however, took a different view and held that this defect was not so serious as to justify non-existence, but it was serious enough for the act to be annulled.

Legislative procedures

4.28 The adoption of legislation in the Community is governed by Article 249 (ex Article 189) EC. This may be done by the European Parliament acting jointly with the Council, the Council acting alone, and the Commission. The Treaty confers legislative power on the Commission only to a very limited extent, but the Council frequently delegates powers to the Commission in order to allow it to fulfil its executive function.

Decision-making procedure of the Commission

4.29 The Commission meets in closed session and decides by simple majority vote. Often the 'written procedure' is used. Special procedures are followed where powers are delegated by the Council to the Commission under the provision of Article 202, third indent. In order to retain some measure of control, the Council usually provides for the establishment of a committee to which the Commission must submit drafts of measures it intends to adopt under the delegated power. These committees are composed of representatives of the national governments under the chairmanship of a Commission official. The system of comitology, as it became known, became highly complex and lacked transparency. The delegation of power by the Council to the Commission was questioned in Case 25/70 *Köster* (1970) challenging the legality of the system. The court ruled that the principle of delegation was valid and that the authorisation to the Council in Article 145 (now Article 202 EC as amended) to delegate power to the Commission meant (1) that it was sufficient if general principles concerning the procedure were set out, and (2) that the management committee procedure did not constitute an unwarranted restriction on the decision-making power of the Commission as it did not, in fact, take decisions itself but simply obliged the Commission to communicate the measure to the Council. However, the system did not provide for any information of or input by the European Parliament which, after the adoption of the Single European Act and the establishment of the co-operation procedure, became more and more frustrated. This is evidenced by the *Comitology* case (Case 302/87 *European Parliament v Council* (1988) where the Parliament complained about this but was refused standing by the ECJ because it was not directly connected with its prerogatives and a remedy could be obtained by different means. The SEA tried to put the system on a more regular footing by making provision for a framework-decision establishing the principles and rules to be followed (Article 10 SEA amending Article 145, now Article 202

EC). The first such decision was adopted by the Council in 1987 (Decision 87/373). This Decision proved to be unsatisfactory, particularly in the view of the European Parliament which had no involvement. The Decision has, therefore, now been replaced by Council Decision 1999/468 which sets out the type of committee and the procedures in different instances of delegated power. It is followed by Declarations by the Commission and the Council concerned with achieving greater efficiency for the system and an agreement in October 2000 between the Parliament and the Commission on procedures for implementing the Decision, providing for regular information of the Parliament of the proceedings of the committees. The decision sets out four objectives it wishes to achieve:

(1) it aims to achieve greater consistency in the choice of the type of committee and in the criteria relating to the choice of committee procedure;

(2) it simplifies the requirements for the exercise of the implementing powers and achieves a greater involvement of the European Parliament;

(3) it wishes to improve information to the European Parliament; and

(4) it wishes to improve information to the public.

4.30 Under the first procedure, known as the advisory committee procedure, the committee's functions are purely advisory; even an unfavourable opinion does not affect the Commission's powers. Nevertheless, the Commission *must* submit draft measures to the committee for an opinion and 'take the utmost account of the opinion of the committee' (Article 3 of Decision 1999/468).

4.31 Under the second procedure, known as the management committee procedure, which is the procedure most used for proposals, eg in the agricultural and fisheries policies sector, the Commission must put a draft before the committee, and the chairman sets a time limit within which it must give its opinion. The committee votes according to the same system of weighted voting as the Council, so a decision will only go through if a qualified majority is obtained. The chairman has no vote. If the Commission follows the committee's opinion (or if the committee gives no opinion within a given time limit), the Commission measure is definitive. Even if the Commission does not follow the committee's opinion, it may still adopt the measure, but in this case it must immediately communicate it to the Council. Then either the Commission may defer application of the measure for a limited time (a maximum of three months) until the Council has adopted a different one or, if a time limit is specified in the measure the Commission must defer it and Council may adopt a different measure provided it acts within the period (see Article 4).

4.32 The third system, which gives the Commission the smallest input, is the regulatory committee procedure. This is used for 'measures of general scope designed to apply essential provisions of basic instruments'. The committee gives its opinion in the same way as under the management committee procedure. However, the Commission may only adopt the measure if it is approved by the committee. Otherwise, it must put a new draft measure before the Council and inform the Parliament. If the Parliament considers that the proposal goes beyond the implementing powers granted by the basic instrument it informs the Council. If the Council does not act within the period specified in the measure under which the power was originally delegated, the Commission may adopt the measure. The Council may, in some circumstances, also simply reject the measure without submitting a draft of its own (see Article 5). In the case of both management and regulatory committees the members vote by qualified majority.

The declaration and agreement following this decision further clarify the procedures and emphasise further the involvement of the European Parliament.

4.33 The Commission also has its own decision-making power under Article 81(3) (ex Article 85(3)) EC on exempt agreements in competition law, under Article 86(3) (ex Article 90(3)) EC in relation to the application of competition policy to public undertakings and under Article 39(3)(d) (ex Article 48(3)(d)) EC it can draw up implementing regulations on certain workers' rights.

4.34 Most of the legislation in the Community is passed by the Council acting on a proposal by the Commission, together with the European Parliament under different types of procedures provided for under Articles 251 and 252 (ex Articles 189b and 189c) EC. There are occasions where the Council may decide alone and may consult the European Parliament, but it does not have to. These, however, have been reduced to a minimum by the Treaty of Amsterdam (eg Article 26 (ex Article 28) EC on the fixing of common customs tariff duties, Article 99 (ex Article 103) EC on broad guidelines of economic policy and Article 104 (ex Article 104c) EC on excessive deficits.

The consultation procedure

4.35 The consultation procedure was the procedure originally provided for in most of the Treaty. It is a fairly straightforward procedure which only involves the Commission and the Council with regard to decision-making. The other institutions, the European Parliament, as well as the Economic and Social Committee and the Committee of the Regions, simply have to be consulted. The Commission makes the proposal, after the European Parliament (and others) have been consulted, and the Council adopts. The procedure is as follows:

- The proposal is submitted to the Council by the Commission. A working group is usually established, made up of persons nominated by national governments, civil servants mostly, sometimes others (academics etc). The group's powers are only advisory, but its views will be taken into account as the members will advise their governments which will vote on the measure. Sometimes, the Commission invites professional groups to agree on proposals themselves before the Commission will act. This happened for example with the Lawyer's Establishment Directive, where the European Association of Bar Councils (CCBE) was invited to agree on a draft before the Commission would proceed (see further Chapter 18).

- The Commission will then draft a final proposal and send it to the EP, and sometimes ECOSOC, for opinion. After receiving these opinions the Commission may amend the proposals in light of the opinions. The proposal is then sent to COREPER (see **3.12**). A working group of national officials is set up within COREPER to prepare a report for the Council. Commission representatives attend meetings of this group. Amendments are usually put forward by national representatives, which may or may not be accepted by the Commission.

- Finally, the proposal, together with the report of the COREPER working group, goes to the Council. If full agreement was reached in COREPER, the Council will adopt without debate. Otherwise the Council debates the issue and votes. If a technical Council cannot decide, it will go higher.

The European Parliament's opinions have no binding force. However, when provided in the Treaty, consultation with the EP constitutes an 'essential procedural requirement' (Article 230 (ex Article 173) EC) and, as the court ruled in Case 138/79 *Roquette Frères SA v Council* (1980), failure to comply with it constitutes ground for annulment of the acts by the ECJ. On the duty of reconsultation see Case C-65/90 *European Parliament v Council* (1992). Whether reconsultation is required will depend on the type of amendments. If they are minor or in accordance with the Parliament's views, reconsultation may not be necessary.

In addition to mandatory consultations provided for by the Treaties, both the Commission and the Council normally seek the EP's opinion on an optional basis on a wide range of measures having a determining effect on policy. In Case 165/87 *Commission v Council* (1988) the ECJ recognised the validity of such optional consultations.

The use of the consultation procedure has been much reduced by subsequent Treaties. It is still present in eg Article 19 (ex Article 8b) EC on conditions concerning the right of European citizens to stand and vote in municipal elections, Article 22(2) (ex Article 8e(2)) EC on the strengthening of citizens' rights; Article 37(2) (ex Article 43(2)) EC on the common agricultural policy (CAP); Article 89 (ex Article 94) EC on state aids.

The co-operation procedure (Article 252 (ex Article 189c) EC)

4.36 This procedure was introduced by the Single European Act (1986) with a view to increasing the influence of the EP in the legislative process but without giving it a real power of co-decision.

• The same process as in the consultation procedure is followed up to the point where the Council would normally be ready to adopt the act. Instead of doing so, it merely adopts a 'common position', acting by a qualified majority. As under Article 250 (ex Article 189a) EC a Commission proposal can be amended only if the Council is unanimous; the common position will therefore correspond to the Commission proposal (including any amendments adopted by the Commission) unless the Council is unanimous.

• The common position is then sent to the EP together with a statement of reasons which led the Council to adopt it and a statement of the Commission's position. This will be the second occasion on which the Parliament considers the matter; the first will have been under the normal consultation procedure. The EP now has three months in which to act: it may accept or reject the common position or propose amendments to it.

97

- If the EP approves or does not take any action, the Council will adopt the act in accordance with the common position.

- If the EP, however, rejects the common position, the Council can only adopt by unanimity. It must act within three months.

- If the EP proposes amendments, the situation is more complex. The Commission re-examines the proposal and may accept some or all of EP's amendments but is not obliged to do so. However, if it does not accept the EP's amendments it must state the reasons for doing so when forwarding the proposal to the Council.

- If the Council then adopts the proposal as amended, a qualified majority is sufficient.

- It may, however, amend the proposal, either accepting the EP's amendments or adding its own, but then unanimity is needed.

- If the Council does not act at all within three months, the proposal will be deemed not to have been adopted.

This procedure has not proved very satisfactory and does not give much power to the EP. The Council can still override any negative vote by the EP, which does not have the power of veto. Following the amendments made in Amsterdam, the procedure now only applies to the Articles concerning economic and monetary union, as the inter-governmental conference in Amsterdam had expressly excluded EMU from its discussions as did the IGC in Nice.

The co-decision procedure (Article 251 (ex Article 189b) EC)

4.37 This procedure was introduced in the Maastricht Treaty but proved to be too complex. The Treaty of Amsterdam simplified the earlier stages and removed the last.

- The same procedure is followed as in the consultation procedure. The Council may then adopt, either with all the amendments proposed by the EP, or if there have been no amendments.

- Otherwise, the Council will adopt a common position and submit the proposal again to the EP, informing it fully of its reasons.

- If within three months of such communication the EP approves the common position or does not take a decision, the proposed act shall be deemed to have been adopted.

- If the EP rejects the common position by an absolute majority of its component members, the act shall be deemed not to have been adopted.

- If the EP proposes amendments to the common position within three months, the text returns to the Council and the Commission for opinion.

- If the Council approves the EP amendments within three months by qualified majority, the act will be deemed to have been adopted in that form. However, if the Commission has delivered a negative opinion on any of the amendments, the Council has to approve those by unanimity.

- If not all the amendments can be agreed by the Council, the proposal will go to a Conciliation Committee.

- This Committee, composed of an equal number of members of the Council or their representatives, and of the EP, will be convened within six weeks by the Council President in agreement with the EP President. The Commission will be represented but does not have a vote. The Conciliation Committee will study the text with the amendments proposed by the EP and endeavour to reach agreement by a qualified majority of Council representatives and a majority of the EP representatives.

- If a joint text is approved within six weeks, the Council and the EP each have a period of six weeks to approve the text by qualified majority in the case of the Council and by an absolute majority of the votes cast for the EP.

- If no joint text can be agreed by the Conciliation Committee or if either body fails to approve after the six-week period, the text shall be deemed not to have been adopted.

- The periods of three months and six weeks referred to may be extended by a maximum of one month and two weeks respectively at the initiative of the EP. However, a Declaration emphasises that such extensions should be considered 'only when strictly necessary' and that at no time should the period between the second reading by the EP and the decision by the Conciliation Committee exceed nine months.

The use of the Conciliation Committee, which could be brought in at an early stage under the Maastricht Treaty, was thus confined to the later stages of the procedure, and the EP has an opportunity to exercise its veto at an early stage.

The complex arrangements at the end of the procedure if the Conciliation Committee does not approve the joint text in the Maastricht Treaty have been done away with so that rejection is simplified.

4.38 The amended procedure clearly gives the EP more real opportunity to take part in the legislative process, although legally its powers have not been greatly increased. The 'democratic deficit' has not been greatly reduced; the EP still has only a negative power and little power to propose its own legislation. The member states are understandably reluctant to give up too much power. Any gain in power by the EP will also have to entail a reduction in the Commission's powers. The Commission still retains most of the power of making proposals, but the Commission gains considerable bargaining power from the rule that the Council must be unanimous in order to amend the Commission's proposals (Article 251(3) EC).

The assent procedure

4.39 This procedure was introduced by the Single European Act and extended by the TEU. It constitutes a veto right, and when assent is required the Council may act only after it has obtained the EP's agreement. It applies to important matters such as admission of new members to the Community and association agreements.

The budgetary procedure

4.40 This procedure, which is complex, is described in Articles 272 and 273 (ex Articles 203 and 204) EC.

All the institutions draw up estimates of expenditure, and send them to the Commission which consolidates them into a preliminary draft budget. The Council then establishes a draft budget by qualified majority. The budget is sent to the EP, which may propose amendments in case of non-compulsory expenditure, ie expenditure which does not necessarily flow directly from the Treaty or other Community legislation. Otherwise it can only propose 'modifications', in which the Council has the last word. When the budget finally comes back to the EP, it no longer has any right to change modifications made by the Council for compulsory expenditure. For non-compulsory expenditure, the EP has the right to reject the Council's modifications by a majority of *Members* of the EP and three-fifths of the *votes* and this rejection is final. If, however, no such action is taken within 15 days, the budget is deemed to have been adopted. The EP also has the power to reject the budget *in toto* if there are 'important reasons' for doing so (Article 272(8) EC). Such a motion must be passed by a majority of all the MEP's and two-thirds of the votes cast. This happened for the first time in December 1979. When this occurs, a new budget must be drawn up by the Council and the procedure followed again. If no budget has been passed at the beginning of the year, a sum equal to one-twelfth of the previous year's budget may be spent each month. The monthly sums available may be increased by the Council provided the consent of the EP is obtained with regard to non-compulsory expenditure. The latter procedure has been threatened often and used from time to time and constitutes a considerable power for the EP as regards non-compulsory expenditure. The limitation on its powers regarding compulsory expenditure which constitutes the major part of the budget has been alleviated by two joint Declarations, giving the EP a say in the enactment of legislation giving rise to compulsory expenditure via a conciliation procedure and by more clearly defining what constitutes compulsory expenditure by restricting it to expenditure which is necessary to meet the Community's legal obligations towards third parties (member states or non-member states). The Constitutional Convention sitting in Brussels in 2002/3 has recommended that the EP's powers should be extended to the control over the whole of the budget.

Changes made by the Amsterdam Treaty

4.41 The legislative procedures, which had become highly complicated through various Treaty amendments, particularly in the SEA and the TEU, were simplified somewhat in the Treaty of Amsterdam. There was no change in the consultation and co-operation procedures, but the co-decision procedure was simplified and now applies to new EC Treaty provisions (Articles 129, 135, 137(2)(iii), 141, 152, 255, 280, 285, 286), as well as to a considerable number of existing Treaty provisions which were subject to the co-operation procedure in most cases (Articles 12, 71(1), 80); Articles resulting from the transposition into the Treaty of the agreement on social policy (Articles 137(2) and (3), 148, 150(4), 156, 162, 172, 175(1), 179); to the assent procedure (Article 18(2)), or to the consultation procedure (Articles 42, 46(2), 47).

4.42 The assent procedure applies to the new provision in the Treaty on European Union Article 7, and to the existing Article 49 (ex Article O) TEU, as well as to the following articles in the EC Treaty: 161, 190(4), and 300(3)(ii). These changes, however, stop far short of giving real power to the EP and eliminating the democratic deficit. This could only come through full legislative and budgetary powers being given to the EP, as well as giving it real control over the Commission. With the widening of the Community and the accession of new members, it is unlikely that this will be achieved in the foreseeable future.

4.43 The Nice Treaty made further changes, moving more areas over to codecision. The procedure will apply to seven provisions which have changed over from unanimity to QMV (Articles 13, 62, 63, 65, 157, 159 and 191 EC). The assent procedure applies to Article 161 EC. Most of the legislative measures requiring QMV are now therefore decided under the co-decision procedure. This procedure was not, however, extended to legislative measures which already come under the QMV rule, such as agriculture and trade policy.

4.44 The balance of powers between the institutions has tended to shift in favour of the Council at the expense of the powers of the Commission. The Council Presidency has acquired real importance and tended to diminish the role of the Commission as the negotiator in the Community. The absence of the use of majority voting for many years, which led indirectly to the establishment of the European Council, has tended to strengthen the inter-governmental element. Only in the 1980s did majority voting return and the Treaties of Maastricht, Amsterdam and Nice have gone only some way to diminish the democratic deficit. The Constitutional Convention in Brussels has made proposals to further reduce the democratic deficit and made a number of changes in the legislative structure.

Legislative powers (see also 4.6)

Express and implied powers of the Community

4.45 The Communities have only the powers assigned to them by the Treaties (*compétence d'attribution*), while all residual powers are left with the member states. This means the Communities must act within the framework of the provisions laid down in their respective statutes. Article 5 (ex Article 3b) EC states that the Community shall act within the limits of the powers conferred upon it by the Treaty and of the objectives assigned to it by the Treaty. It has also been stated by the court in Cases 188-190/80 *France, Italy and United Kingdom v Commission* (1982) that the Community legislative power could not be described in terms of a general proposition but resulted from different Treaty provisions attributing that power for each of the areas entrusted to the Community.

4.46 With few exceptions (Articles 94 (ex Article 100) EC and 308 (ex Article 235) EC) the powers held by the Community are specific. This is significant in two ways:

(a)   where a measure can be validly based on one (or more) specific provision(s) of the Treaty, it may not be based on a non-specific-power; and

(b)   the decision-making procedure differs from one specific power to another.

The decision-making procedures involve various forms of interaction between the Commission which has near-exclusive power to make legislative proposals, the European Parliament (consultation, co-operation, co-decision or assent) and the Council (deciding with a simple majority vote, a qualified majority vote, or unanimously).

4.47 There are no inherent powers: the Community only possesses the powers conferred on it, which are limited in scope. However, this limitation is diminished by a number of factors: the empowering provisions of the Treaty are interpreted widely, in part on the basis of the theory of implied powers. This theory, which was originally developed in the constitutional and administrative law of such countries as the US and the UK, and which is recognised as a principle of international law, may be expressed in both a narrow and a wide formulation. According to the narrow formulation, the existence of a given power also implies the existence of any other power which is reasonably necessary for the exercise of the former; according to the wide formulation, the existence of a given *objective* or *function* implies the existence of any power necessary to attain it. The narrow formulation was adopted by the ECJ as long ago as 1956 (Case 8/55 *Fédération Charbonnière de Belgique v High Authority* (1956)); the wide formulation was applied with regard to the Commission in 1987. This was in Cases 281/85, 283-285/85, 287/85 *Germany v Commission* (1987), which concerned Article 118 of the Treaty of Rome (since deleted) which gave the Commission the task of 'promoting close co-operation between member states in the social field, particularly in matters relating to...'. This gave the Commission a task, but it did not confer any legislative power. The authors of the Treaty probably thought it was not necessary. However, in 1985, the Commission, acting under Article 118, adopted a decision which obliged the member states to consult with the Commission regarding certain matters and to inform it of draft measures and agreements concerning the topic in question. The decision was challenged by some of the member states, but it was upheld by the ECJ, which held that whenever a provision of the EC Treaty conferred a specific task on the Commission, it must also be regarded as impliedly conferring on the Commission 'the powers which are indispensable in order to carry out that task'. Since the EC Treaty confers many tasks on the Commission including such wide-ranging functions as that of ensuring that the provisions of the Treaty are applied (Article 211 (ex Article 155) EC), this judgment is potentially very significant. Thus, wide provisions such as Article 94 (ex Article 100) EC which empowers the Council to issue directives for the 'approximation' of such laws or other provisions of the member states as 'directly affect the establishment or functioning of the common market' have been used to issue directives to unify the laws of member states on a wide variety of subjects. Article 94 might still be regarded as granting a specific power, but Article 308 goes clearly beyond this: it provides for the Community to take action necessary to attain the objectives of the Common Market if the Treaty has not provided the necessary powers. The requirements are thus that:

- the power must be used to attain one of the objectives of the Community. There are numerous objectives, those set out in Articles 2 and 3 of the Treaty, but also in many other parts of the Treaty;

- action by the Community must be necessary for the purpose, involving a judgement of what is necessary by the Community institutions, mainly the Commission and the Council;

- the Article may only be used if the Treaty has not provided specific powers elsewhere.

The Article provides a general power subject to the limitations described above.

4.48 An illustration of the respective roles of implied powers on the one hand and the residual powers of the institutions by Article 308 (ex Article 235) EC on the other is provided in the ECJ's judgment in Case C-295/90 *European Parliament v Council (Students' Residence Rights Directive)* (1992). The Council had relied on Article 235 (now Article 308 EC) for the adoption of the Directive as in its view the other Treaty articles did not provide for the necessary powers. The use of the Article was challenged by the Parliament. The court used the doctrine of implied powers to interpret Article 6(2) (now Article 12(2) EC), concluding that the general principle of non-discrimination as to nationality could only be applied subject to special provisions of the Treaty. The object of the Article was to enable the Council:

> ... to take necessary measures ... for the effective elimination of discrimination on grounds of nationality where its power has no foundation in one of the special provisions governing the different spheres of application of the Treaty. However, measures adopted under Article 6(2) of the Treaty should not necessarily be limited to regulating rights deriving from the first paragraph of the same article, but they may also deal with aspects the regulation of which appears necessary for the effective exercise of those rights.

4.49 Article 308 grants the power to act where none yet exists if it is necessary to attain one of the objectives of the Community; a new, independent power of action is created alongside the existing ones. This has been very controversial and the court has indicated many times that the Article should only be used if no other, more specific, legal base, can be found in the Treaty (see eg Case C-295/90 *European Parliament v Council (Student Residence Directive)* (1992) further discussed at **11.35**). Implied powers, on the other hand, are those which already exist and may be used to supplement a specific power specifically conferred on the Community if there is a need for this in order to comply with the 'principle of effectiveness' (*effet utile*) frequently referred to by the Court of Justice.

The problem of the legal base

4.50 It has become more and more important to determine the choice of legal base for legislation. The Single European Act and the Treaties of Maastricht and Amsterdam set up new legislative procedures and the importance of the role of one or the other of the institutions in the legislation depends on the legislative procedure which is effectively chosen by the Commission when submitting its proposal. The problem may be illustrated by Case C-300/89 *Commission v Council (Titanium Dioxide)* (1991). This concerned an adoption of a directive setting titanium dioxide levels. It had two objectives: to protect the environment and (because it laid down uniform standards in all member states) to promote fair competition. The former was covered by Article 130s (now Article 175 EC), which then required unanimous voting in the Council and was subject to the consultation procedure with the European Parliament. The latter fell within the scope of Article 100a (now Article 95 EC) which was then subject to qualified majority voting and the co-operation procedure. The Commission had selected Article 100a as the base but the Council had substituted Article 130s. The court ruled that the more general objective of Article 100a providing measures promoting the establishment of the internal market prevailed over the more specific environmental concerns of Article 130s and ruled, therefore, that 100a was the correct legal base. The concern here was undoubtedly that Parliament should be given the opportunity to use its rights under the co-operation procedure.

4.51 One of the few cases where a challenge succeeded was Case C-376/98 *Germany v Parliament and Council* (2000) where the court annulled the Tobacco Advertising Directive 1998 which was based on ex Articles 57(2) (now Article 47(2) EC), 66 (now Article 55 EC) and 100a (now Article 95 EC). The court said that Article 100a was the wrong legal base as the objectives pursued by the directive could not be seen as genuinely aimed at the improvement of the conditions for the establishment and functioning of the internal market.

Exclusive and concurrent powers and the doctrine of pre-emption

4.52 Exclusive Community competence may be derived from:

(1)   express provisions in the primary legislation, eg the common agricultural policy and the common commercial policy;

(2) the scope of internal measures adopted by the Community institution: at internal level within the Community this is described as pre-emption; at the external level it leads to exclusive external competence for the Community, as in some parts of the WTO;

(3) express provisions in internal Community measures; and

(4) situations where internal powers can only be effectively exercised at the same time as external powers.

Article 5 (ex Article 3b) EC implicitly distinguishes between exclusive and concurrent competence. Subsidiarity can only apply to the latter. Every federal or quasi-federal system is based on a distribution of legislative and administrative powers among the federation and its members. As in the case of exclusive powers, concurrent powers are conferred upon the Communities and upon the Communities alone. The EC cannot share the exercise of such powers with the member states. But while the powers defined as exclusive competences by the Treaty are to be exercised by the EC from their entry into force, the exercise of its concurrent powers is postponed and made subject to compliance with certain conditions. Until those conditions are satisfied, the member states will retain the right to legislate, and will lose that right only when the EC decides to exercise its power in the area in question.

4.53 In *Opinion 1/75* (1975) (see also **4.7**) the ECJ recognised, in the field of the common commercial policy, that the EC's powers must lead to the exclusion of concurrent powers exercisable by the member states, other than in specific areas, as where the EC specifically authorised them to act: Case 41/76 *Donckerwolcke* (1976); or where existing obligations necessarily had to be carried out by the member states: Case 174/84 *Bulk Oil* (1986). In Case 50/76 *Amsterdam Bulb* (1977) the ECJ recognised that even where EC institutions have failed to act when powers were given to them, member states cannot act unilaterally. They must at the least co-operate with and consult the Commission since the failure to act may be a deliberate choice of economic policy in an area attributed by the member states to the EC. See also Case 31/74 *Galli* (1975). Once the EC has used its legislative powers to set up a common agricultural market organisation, national powers to regulate the distribution stages covered by that market organisation are pre-empted. Case 14/68 *Walt Wilhelm v Bundeskartellamt* (1969) highlighted the difficulties in respecting the demarcation between national and Community competition law.

Subsidiarity and proportionality as a limit on Community powers

4.54 Article 5 (ex Article 3b) EC embodies the principle of subsidiarity. Its three paragraphs deal with three separate matters.

- Does the Community have a legal base for its actions in the Treaty?

- Should the Community act or can the objective be sufficiently achieved by the member states? If not, can it be better achieved by the Community?

- How much should the Community do? It should use the least onerous form of legislation, leaving as much as possible to the member states.

4.55 The principle of subsidiarity is not a new one. It was first given its formulation in a Papal Encyclical of 1931 entitled *Quadragesimo Anno*:

> It is an injustice, grave evil and a disturbance of right order for a larger and higher association to arrogate to itself functions which can be performed efficiently by smaller and lower societies.

It is also contained in the Constitutions of federal states, in particular those of the US and Germany (Article 72 Basic Law in Germany).

4.56 The principle first appeared in the Community in 1975 in a report on Economic Union by the Commission. It said that an expansion of Community powers should only occur where the member states could not effectively accomplish the desired tasks. In 1984, the Draft Treaty establishing the European Union drawn up by the Italian statesman Altiero Spinelli referred to subsidiarity in the preamble. This draft was adopted by the European Parliament, but never progressed as it was regarded as far too federalist. Subsidiarity and the environment then both came into Community law in the Single European Act in 1986. Article 130r(4) of the pre-Maastricht EEC Treaty (now replaced by a re-worded Article 174) stated:

> The Community shall take action relating to the environment to the extent to which the objectives referred to in paragraph 1 can be attained better at Community level than at the level of the individual member states.

4.57 Finally, subsidiarity was formally introduced as a general principle of Community law in the Maastricht Treaty on European Union in 1992. It is referred to in the preamble, in the framework articles and, finally and most importantly, in Article 3b (now Article 5) of the EC Treaty. It was preserved unaltered by the Treaty of Amsterdam. The Commission issued a communication shortly thereafter setting out its views on the application of the principle.

The text of the subsidiarity article was not altered in Amsterdam, but a binding Protocol lays out the principles of subsidiarity and proportionality more extensively. It obliges the Commission to 'consult widely before proposing legislation and, wherever appropriate, publish consultation documents' and to justify the relevance of its proposals with regard to the principle of subsidiarity. Separate justification is required for the financing of Community action in whole or in part from the Community budget. The Commission is also required to submit annual reports to the European Council, the Council and the European Parliament on the application of Article 5, a requirement since 1993. The Protocol further requires the reasons for concluding that a Community objective can be better achieved by the Community to be substantiated by qualitative or, wherever possible, quantitative indicators. It states that the subsidiarity principle does not affect the primacy of Community law nor call into question the powers conferred on the Community by the Treaty, as interpreted by the ECJ, and that it shall relate to areas where the Community does not have exclusive competence. The legislative process is inevitably lengthened by the various conditions requiring justification and checking in the Protocol. Most preambles to new legislation now contain a reference to the principle which is gaining general acceptance.

4.58 What are the tests to be applied to see if the principle of subsidiarity is complied with?

* The *sufficient attainment* test. Article 5(2) states that the Community shall act 'only if and in so far as the objectives of the proposed action cannot be sufficiently achieved by the member states and can therefore, by reason of the scale or effects of the proposed action be better achieved by the Community'. When is the action sufficient at member state level to achieve the objectives of the Community? This is a negative test which seems to say that if the member state cannot achieve the aim, it should be achieved by the Community. The Commission calls this test 'the comparative efficiency test' but this may be misleading.

- The second test is the positive *better attainment* test. As Dashwood points out in [1996] 21 ELRev 211, Community action should only be preferred to member state action if this will bring demonstrable advantages.

4.59 The Court of Justice has given some guidance as to how the principle should be interpreted but it has been reluctant to interfere with Community action. In Case C-84/94 *United Kingdom v Council* (1996) where the UK objected to the Working Time Directive on a whole number of grounds, the UK argument that the subsidiarity principle had not been complied with was rejected. Community action was necessary in order to achieve the health and safety objectives set in the directive. Other points concerning the legal base (see **4.47**) and the requirement to give reasons (see Article 253 (ex Article 190) EC) were also rejected by the court. The court also rejected similar arguments raised in Case C-377/98 *Netherlands v Parliament and Council* (2001) against the biotechnology patents directive.

Further reading

Douglas-Scott, *Constitutional Law of the European Union*, (2002) Longman, Chapter 3.

T Hervey, 'Up in smoke? Community (anti) tobacco law and policy' (2001) ELRev 101.

Cremona, 'External relations and the Amsterdam Treaty' in D O'Keeffe and P Twomey (eds), *Legal Issues of the Amsterdam Treaty* (1999) Hart Publishing, pp 225–247.

Cremona, 'External relations and external competence: the emergence of an integrated policy' in P Craig and G de Burca (eds), *The Evolution of EU Law* (1999) OUP.

D McGoldrick, *International Relations Law of the European Union* (1997) Longman.

D O'Keeffe, 'Community and member state competence in external relations agreements of the EU', (1999) 4 European Foreign Affairs Review.

The European Union after Amsterdam, Kluwer Law International.

Weatherill, 'Beyond pre-emption? shared competence and constitutional change in the European Community' in D O'Keeffe and P Twomey (eds), *Legal Issues of the Maastricht Treaty* (1994) Chancery, pp 13–33.

Emiliou, 'Implied powers and the legal basis of Community measures', [1993] 18 ELRev 138–144.

Barents, 'The internal market unlimited: some observations on the legal basis of Community legislation', [1993] 30 CMLRev 85.

Emiliou, 'Subsidiarity: an effective barrier against "the enterprises of ambition"?', [1992] 17 ELRev 383.

Toth, 'The principle of subsidiarity in the Maastricht Treaty', [1992] 29 CMLRev 1079.

O'Keeffe, 'External, concurrent and shared competence' in A Dashwood (ed), *Foreign Policy after Amsterdam* (1998) Sweet & Maxwell.

Dashwood, 'The limits of Community competence', [1996] 21 ELRev 211.

Emiliou, 'The internal legislative powers of the European Union' in N Emiliou and D O'Keeffe (eds), *Legal Aspects of Integration in the European Union* (1997) Kluwer Law International.

London Boroughs Transport Committee v Freight Transport Association Ltd [1992] 1 CMLR 5 (implicit application of the principle of subsidiarity by the House of Lords in the field of the environment).

Self-test questions

1. What effects are the Treaties of Amsterdam and Nice likely to have on the Community legislative process?

2. How adequate, in your view, is the Community legislative process? What improvements do you consider desirable?

3. What are the main types of legislative process in the European Community? What role do the different institutions play in each?

4. 'Under Article 308 of the EC Treaty the Community has virtually unlimited legislative powers within the area of the Treaty.'

Is this true and are there any restrictions on the use of this provision? What are the advantages and disadvantages of using the Article? Have the various amendments to the Treaty of Rome made any difference as regards its use?

5. What is meant by the legal base of a legislative measure, and why is it important?

6. 'While Article 249 of the EC Treaty envisages considerable differences between regulations and directives, the practice of the Council and the Commission and the case law of the Court of Justice have substantially eliminated those differences.' Discuss.

CHAPTER FIVE

The Jurisdiction of the Court of Justice: Preliminary Rulings

SUMMARY
Function of preliminary rulings
- **Relationship between national and Community courts:**
  (a) **co-operation**
  (b) **division of competence**
  (c) **refusal to render a ruling**
- **Referable provisions and issues:**
  (a) **relevance**
  (b) **interpretation, not application of Community law**
- **The exercise of the national court's discretion to refer (ECJ's guidelines)**
- **Jurisdiction to refer for a preliminary ruling:**
  (a) **jurisdiction attributed by the Treaty**
  (b) **qualification as a court**
- **Obligation to refer for a preliminary ruling:**
  (a) *acte clair*
  (b) **previous rulings (*acte éclairé*)**
- **Appeals against the order to refer**
- **Interim measures**
- **Effects of preliminary rulings:**
  (a) **interpretation**
  (b) **validity**

Function of preliminary rulings

5.1 The European Court of Justice has different types of jurisdiction. It has plenary jurisdiction in infringement actions against member states under Articles 226, 227, 228, 235 and 288 (ex Articles 169, 170, 171, 178 and 215) EC. Its jurisdiction in judicial review of legality of acts of the Community under Article 230 (ex Article 173) EC and failure to act under Article 232 (ex Article 175) EC has now largely been moved by the Treaty of Nice to the Court of First Instance (see **3.52** and Chapters 10 and 11). For its jurisdiction under the second and third pillars, see **3.53**.

5.2 The majority of cases decided by the ECJ are in response to preliminary references by national courts under Article 234 EC. Here the court gives an interpretation but is not the final arbiter and does not render a definitive judgment. It gives an interpretation of Community law as a step in proceedings before the national court. In contrast to the appeals procedure where the parties to a dispute take the initiative to request an appeal, in the case of a reference the court decides itself whether a reference to the ECJ is necessary. According to the ECJ, Article 234

> ... is essential for the preservation of the Community character of the law established by the Treaty and has the object of ensuring that in all circumstances this law is the same in all States of the Community (see Case 166/73 Rheinmühlen (1974)).

5.3 The article is 'based on co-operation which entails a division of duties between the national courts and the Court of Justice in the interest of the proper application and uniform interpretation of Community law throughout all the member states' (Case 244/80 Foglia v Novello (No 2) (1981)). When a question of interpretation of a Community act is raised in a national court, the ECJ may or sometimes must be requested to give a ruling by the national court. This ruling indicates to the national court what its decision on the point should be, but it is the national court which makes the final decision. It is not an appeal procedure. It is an example of shared jurisdiction, depending for its success on mutual co-operation. The national court retains the final word in its application of the ECJ's interpretation. Case 41/74 van Duyn v Home Office is one example of how such application may differ from the intentions of the ECJ in giving its ruling (see **7.8**). The preliminary reference procedure has proved to be a major contributor to the development of Community law. This development began when the court ruled in 1962 in Case 26/62 van Gend en Loos that individuals could also rely on Community law under certain conditions before their national courts in order to assert their Community rights. Thus, the doctrine of direct effect of Community law has opened the possibility to individuals to have access to the ECJ via their national court in cases where they would not have standing to have direct access to the ECJ. Thus, an individual may indirectly challenge action by member states or by Community institutions before the ECJ and obtain a ruling from the court which will give him/her the possibility to obtain an appropriate remedy from the national court.

Jurisdiction of the ECJ

5.4 The court has jurisdiction to give preliminary rulings concerning the interpretation, and the validity of Community law.

The ECJ may give an interpretation of the Treaty, of acts of the institutions and the ECB, and of statutes of bodies established by an act of the Council where those statutes so provide (Article 307(1) (ex Article 234(1)) EC).

5.5 'Interpretation of the Treaty' includes the EC Treaty and all treaties amending or supplementing it. However, international agreements which are not based on the Treaties do not fall within the scope of Article 234 (see Case 44/84 *Hurd v Jones* (1986), which concerned the Statute of the European School).

5.6 'Acts of the institutions' cover binding acts in the form of regulations, directives and decisions, as well as 'soft law' such as recommendations and opinions if the use of such instruments is necessary to aid the interpretation of national law adopted to implement Community law. See Case 322/88 *Grimaldi* (1989) which concerned a recommendation issued by the Commission. The court said that, although a recommendation is not binding, it must nevertheless be taken into consideration by national courts when it is relevant to the interpretation of a national measure taken on the basis of the recommendation or where it is designed to supplement binding Community provisions.

5.7 In the same way the ECJ has held that an act need not be directly effective to be subject to interpretation under Article 234. See Case 111/75 *Mazzalai* (1976).

5.8 The ECJ has also accepted jurisdiction for the interpretation of international treaties which the Community has concluded, on the basis that these constitute 'acts of the institutions'.

5.9 The ECJ cannot, in Article 234 proceedings, rule on the compatibility of a provision of national law with Community law. The ECJ can, however, provide national courts with all those elements, by way of interpretation of Community law, which may enable national courts to assess that compatibility. See Case C-241/89 *SARPP* (1990). In Cases C-143/88 and C-92/89 *Zuckerfabrik Süderdithmarschen AG v Hauptzollamt Itzehoe* (1991) the validity of a national measure implementing Community legislation was challenged on the basis that the Community measure itself was invalid. The court developed principles on the basis of which interim relief should be granted by the national court (see also **9.23** and **9.24**). Moreover, in order to ensure the uniform interpretation of Community law, the ECJ has jurisdiction to give a preliminary ruling on the interpretation of a provision of Community law in the particular case where the national law of a member state referred to the content of that Community provision, in order to determine the rules applicable to a purely internal situation in that member state. See Cases C-297/88 & C-197/89 *Dzodzi v Belgian State* (1990). In such a case the court said that it would not look into the circumstances which had prompted the reference, since the questions submitted by the national court concerned the interpretation of a Community law provision. See also Case C-231/89 *Gmurzynska* (1990) and Case C-28/95 *Leur-Bloem v Inspecteur der Belastingdienst/Ondernemingen Amsterdam 2* (1997): the court has jurisdiction where the situation in question is not governed directly by Community law, but where the national legislature, in implementing a Community directive, has decided to apply the same treatment to internal situations and to those governed by the directive, so it has aligned its domestic situation to Community legislation. In this case, the court assumed jurisdiction in spite of a contrary Opinion given by Jacobs AG.

5.10 Under the preliminary reference procedure the court will, in principle, only give an interpretation of Community law and not advise a national court on the application of Community law, nor will it order a national court to declare its national law invalid. However, it is sometimes obvious that the court will go beyond the mere interpretation of Community law. Having declared in Case 106/77 *Simmenthal* (see **8.3**) that a national court must apply Community law in its entirety within its jurisdiction and set aside any national law, whether prior or subsequent, which may conflict with it, the court held in Cases C-10/97 to C-22/97 *Ministero delle Finanze v INCOGE* (1990) that this did not mean that the incompatibility of a national rule adopted subsequently to a Community rule did not have the effect of rendering that rule non-existent (see also

Case 283/81 *CILFIT*, **5.22**). In Case C-206/01 *Arsenal v Reed* (2002), the court stated in interpreting Directive 89/104/EEC that the use of the word 'Arsenal' on sports goods by a third party created the impression that there was a connection between the goods and the proprietor of the trade mark. It therefore found an infringement. When the case returned to the national court for a ruling, the judge, Laddie J in *Arsenal Football Club v Reed* (2002), held that in making findings of fact the ECJ had exceeded its duty of interpretation. The national court, therefore, did not consider itself bound by the finding of the ECJ and decided that the goods did not indicate a trade origin and that, therefore, there was no infringement. The case was reversed on appeal. The English Court of Appeal ruled the ECJ's judgments are binding as to interpretation, but this does show the difficulty of finding the exact limits to the concept of interpretation and to the respective competences of the European Court and the national court.

Jurisdiction of national courts

5.11 Under Article 234(2) EC only a 'court or tribunal of a member state' may refer questions to the ECJ. The meaning of the expression 'court or tribunal' is not confined to the central judicial arms of the State but extends also to other tribunals which are authorised to give rulings of a judicial nature. On the other hand, the expression does not cover a body which has before it a request for a declaration relating to a dispute which it is under no legal obligation to resolve.

5.12 In Case 246/80 *Broekmeulen* (1981), the ECJ defined the essential characteristics of a 'court or tribunal'.

Dr Broekmeulen was a GP who wished to register with the relevant Registration Committee in order to be entitled to practise as a GP in the Netherlands. He took his case to an Appeals Committee which, although a private body, exercised great control over medical practice in the Netherlands; it was not possible to practise without its approval. It was composed of medical practitioners, representatives of university medical faculties and government representatives. Although the Committee was not a court or tribunal under Dutch law, the ECJ nevertheless accepted the reference. It said that the expression 'court or tribunal' referred to:

> ... [a body which] performs its duties with the approval of the public authorities and operates with their assistance, and whose decisions

are accepted following contentious proceedings and are in fact recognised as final, must be deemed to be a court of a member state for the purpose of Article 177.

5.13 Case 61/65 *Widow Vaassen* (1966) concerned an arbitral tribunal which dealt with disputes regarding pension funds. The ECJ ruled this constituted a court within the meaning of Article 234 EC, as it was a permanent judicial body founded in the national law, it members were officially appointed by the government and were obliged to apply the rules of the law. In Case 150/85 *Drake v Chief Adjudication Officer* (1986) the UK Chief Social Security Officer constituted a court or tribunal within the meaning of Article 234. However, in Case 102/81 *Nordsee* (1982) an arbitration tribunal established under a contract between private individuals did not constitute a court or tribunal within the meaning of Article 234; this was also applied in Case 318/85 *Criminal Proceedings Against Unterweger* (1986) where a reference was held to be inadmissible because the function of the referring body was not to resolve disputes but to submit opinions in administrative proceedings.

In Case C-24/92 *Corbiau v Administration des Contributions* (1993), the ECJ ruled that 'court or tribunal' could only refer to an authority which was a third party in relation to the body or person which had adopted the decision subject to the proceedings. The reference was refused on the grounds that a director of taxes acting in an administrative capacity was not a court or tribunal. It seems clear, therefore, that the criteria are that the body must be an established, permanent, compulsory jurisdiction, that it must apply rules of law and that it must also be independent of the parties in the dispute. In Case C-54/96 *Dorsch Consult Ingenieursgesellschaft v Bundesbaugesellschaft Berlin* (1997) the court took the opportunity to give a clear re-statement of the criteria; the factors to be taken into account are whether the body is established by law, whether it is permanent, whether its jurisdiction is compulsory, whether its procedure is inter partes, whether it applies rules of law, and whether it is independent. In Cases C-110/98–C-147/98 *Gabalfrisa* (2000) and Case C-407/98 *Abrahamsson* (2000), on the other hand, the Spanish Economic and Administrative Court held there was a separation of the judicial and the administrative function as the tribunal ruled on tax complaints against decisions by the Spanish tax administration without having received any instructions from the tax authority.

See also Case C-17/00 *de Coster* (2001) where AG Colomer criticised the *Vaassen* criteria as being vague and uncertain; and court orders of 26 November 1999 in Case C-192/98 *Azienda Nazionale Autonoma delle Strade (ANASD)* and in Case C-440/98 *Radiotelevisione Italiana (RAI)* which concerned the status of the Italian Court of Audit (Corte dei Conti): a body may be considered a court or tribunal when exercising a judicial function, but cannot be treated as such when it exercises other functions, including administrative ones. Thus, the Court of Audit was not a body which could refer when exercising a function of *ex post facto* review of an administrative activity. This did not constitute a judicial function.

'Of a member state'

5.14 The body should be in a member state, or at least part of the judicial system of a member state. See Case C-355/89 *Barr and Montrose Holdings Ltd* (1991), where the court held that its jurisdiction applied to the Isle of Man, which is not covered by the entire EC Treaty, but to which a special Protocol annexed to the Treaty applies. Protocols have the same legal force as the Treaty itself. The court also accepted jurisdiction in Case C-100, 101/89 *Kaefer and Procacci* (1990), which concerned French Polynesia, a French overseas territory which is part of the French judicial system. Case C-321/97 *Andersson v Svenska Staten* (1999) concerned the potential liability of an EFTA State, as Sweden then was, for damage caused to individuals by incorrect implementation of a directive referred to in the EEA Agreement (see Chapter 9). The court declined jurisdiction. Although at the time of the ruling Sweden had become a member state, the EEA Agreement had not given it jurisdiction to interpret that agreement in respect of its application to situations which did not come within the Community legal order. The court took the same view in Case C-140/97 *Rechberger v Republic of Austria* (1999) (see further Chapter 9).

Discretionary and mandatory references

5.15 Any court or tribunal may ask the ECJ for a preliminary ruling if it considers it necessary to enable it to give judgment (Article 234(2) EC). There is no obligation for the national court to make a reference to the ECJ ('permissive' jurisdiction) unless a question is raised before a court or tribunal 'against whose decisions there is no judicial remedy under national law' (Article 234(3) EC—'mandatory' jurisdiction). In the latter case a reference must be made to the ECJ provided the question will affect the outcome of the case (see Case 283/81 *CILFIT* (1982)).

5.16 The purpose of Article 234(3) EC must be seen in the light of the function of Article 234 EC as a whole, that is, to prevent a body of national case law not in accordance with the rules of Community law from coming into existence in any member state (see Case 107/76 *Hoffmann-La Roche* (1977)).

5.17 The scope of Article 234(3) EC is not entirely clear. While it clearly applies to the courts or tribunals whose decisions are never subject to appeal (the 'abstract theory'), it is less clear whether it applies also to courts whose decisions in the case in question are not subject to appeal (the 'concrete theory'). It has been argued that although the wording of Article 234(3) EC may indicate that the abstract theory should be preferred, on the whole the case law of the ECJ (see Case 6/64 *Costa v ENEL* (1964)) seems to support the concrete theory. If one bears in mind the way in which the court has interpreted Article 234(3) to give the greatest possible access to the court to the individual, the concrete theory would seem to be preferable.

When should a national court refer?

5.18 Article 234(2) provides that:

> ... where such a question is raised before any court or tribunal of a member state, that court or tribunal may, if it considers that a decision on the question is necessary to enable it to give judgment, request the Court of Justice to give a ruling thereon.

The national court, therefore, must consider that a decision on the question is necessary to enable it to give judgment. It follows that a national court may equally decide that the point of European law is not relevant to its decision, so that it is entitled not to make a reference.

5.19 In the early English case of *Bulmer and Bollinger* (1974) Lord Denning gave his interpretation of 'necessary' expressed in four guidelines. These were:

- the decision on the Community law point must be conclusive of the case;

- the national court may follow a previous ECJ ruling, but is free to refer the same point again if it wishes to obtain a different ruling;

- it may apply the doctrine of *acte clair* (see **5.22**);

- 'in general it is better to decide the facts first' before deciding whether a reference is necessary.

Courts should bear in mind factors such as length and extra cost of proceedings, and the importance of not unnecessarily adding to the workload of the ECJ. These guidelines have been cited many times by English courts, but they have also been the subject of much criticism and the courts in later cases have endeavoured to refine and qualify these arguments.

5.20 Questions as to whether a decision is necessary and whether the court has a duty to refer were considered recently in two cases: *Chiron Corpn v Murex Diagnostics Ltd* (1995) and *R v International Stock Exchange of the United Kingdom and the Republic of Ireland, ex p Else (1982) Ltd* (1993). In *Chiron v Murex*, which concerned proceedings for infringement of a patent, a High Court judge struck out certain paragraphs of the defendant's defence and refused leave to add others. There was an unsuccessful appeal to the Court of Appeal, after which the defendant requested the Court of Appeal to refer certain questions to the ECJ for interpretation and applied for leave to appeal to the House of Lords. Leave to appeal was refused and the request for a reference was adjourned until the time for petitioning the House of Lords for leave to appeal had expired, or until after the petition had been made and refused. After the petition had been refused by the House of Lords the application for a reference to the ECJ was renewed. Balcombe LJ, giving judgment, had pointed out in *Magnavision (SA) v General Optical Council (No 2)* (1987) that, once a domestic court has given judgment and its order has been drawn up, it is functus officio and has no power to make a reference under Article 177. 'This is so both as a matter of domestic law and as a matter of European law.' Staughton LJ, giving a concurring judgment, considered, however, that, although this is undoubtedly true in domestic law, it:

> ... must yield to European law if there is a conflict. If an English court is by European law obliged to make a reference it is no answer that by our domestic law its powers are exhausted.

The reference was not made and the problem remains unresolved.

5.21 The problem would not arise if the Community law point, whether it is decisive to the outcome, or might become so, were to be referred first to the ECJ. It would be in the spirit of Article 234(3) to regard that court as a court of last resort from whose decisions no appeal lies as of right. From a practical point of view, however, this would incur extra delay, and the lower court may feel it should first decide the facts, which might then make a reference unnecessary.

Should national courts always make a reference?

Acte clair and acte éclairé

5.22 Article 234(3) EC does not imply that every time a question of Community law arises the final court must refer it to the ECJ. A reference may not be necessary under the *CILFIT* rules (Case 283/81 (1982)) which include the *acte clair* doctrine. There is no obligation to refer where the point has been decided by a previous court ruling, where:

> ... the correct application of Community law may be so obvious as
> to leave no scope for any reasonable doubt as to the manner in which
> the question raised is to be resolved.

However, before it reaches this conclusion the national court or tribunal must be convinced that the matter is equally clear to the courts of the other member states which have different legal systems and different techniques of interpretation, and to the ECJ bearing in mind the peculiar characteristics of Community law, the different language versions, the Community terminology and the contextual understanding of Community law.

5.23 This decision was applied by the Court of Appeal in *R v Stock Exchange, ex p Else* (1993) where Sir Thomas Bingham said:

> ... if the facts have been found and the Community law issue is critical
> to the court's final decision, the appropriate course is ordinarily to
> refer the issue to the ECJ unless the national court can with complete
> confidence resolve the issue itself ... If the national court has any
> doubt it should ordinarily refer.

In this case the Court of Appeal decided it could resolve the issue itself and that it was *acte clair*, although upon a reading of the case it does not appear that the issues involved are entirely simple and straightforward.

Acte éclairé

5.24 Even if the highest court in the case considers a decision on a question raised before it necessary to enable it to settle a dispute, it need not always be obliged to refer. The ECJ referred to an exception to this obligation in Cases 28–30/62 *Da Costa en Schaake* (1963) where the court said:

> ... the authority of an interpretation under Article 177 already given by the court may deprive this obligation of its purpose and thus empty it of its substance. Such is the case especially when the question raised is materially identical with a question which has already been the subject of a preliminary ruling in a similar case.

The court nevertheless then went on to give a ruling in the case. It should, however, be pointed out that *Da Costa* was decided on the same day as *Van Gend en Loos* and served to emphasise one of the most important and seminal judgments of the ECJ.

5.25 The amendments made to the Rules of Procedure of the court in 2000 and 2001 now enable the court to refuse a preliminary reference by reasoned order in cases where an identical point has already been decided (see **3.55**). In Case C-256/99 *Hung* (not reported in the ECR), which was a 'test' case concerning citizenship which was identical to *Kaur*, the court had not given a reply to questions which had been asked more than two years ago, because it was waiting to give a ruling in Case C-192/99 *Kaur* (2001) (see further **18.46**). The national court did not withdraw its questions after the ruling in *Kaur* had been given and the court then made an order which had the same content as that ruling.

5.26 A number of orders have been made by the court where it considered that the answer to the questions submitted could clearly be found in the existing case law. This was the case in Case C-307/99 *OGT Fruchthandelsgesellschaft* (2001) where the court stated that, as it had previously found the agreement on trade-related aspects of intellectual property rights (TRIPS), annexed to the WTO Agreement, not to have direct effect, the same applied for the same reasons to the GATT Agreement which was also annexed to the WTO Agreement (see also **4.9**).

5.27 The application of the *CILFIT* rules needs to take account of the balance to be maintained between the obligation to refer which is essential for the uniform application of Community law and the need to avoid adding an unnecessary burden to the already excessive workload of the ECJ if a case concerns a genuine *acte clair*. The difficulty of this may be seen in the cases described above as well as in others, such as the well-known refusal of the French Conseil d'Etat, the highest administrative court, to refer the *Cohn-Bendit* case to the ECJ (see further **8.26**).

5.28 In Case 314/85 *Foto-Frost* (1987), the ECJ ruled that while national courts have a discretion whether or not to make a reference requesting a ruling on the validity of a Community act, they do not have power to make a finding of invalidity of an act of Community institutions. The ECJ said that national courts could reject an argument based on invalidity of a Community measure, but they could not declare a measure invalid. This decision was justified mainly on the basis that the uniform application of Community law should be safeguarded throughout the Community.

5.29 Where a judicial body has the right to make a reference under Community law, it cannot be deprived of that right by national law. See Case 166/73 *Rheinmühlen* (1974).

5.30 In Case C-415/93 *Bosman* (1996) the court's jurisdiction to give a preliminary ruling was challenged by the Belgian Football Association on the grounds that the questions asked by the Belgian court bore no relation to the actual facts of the case or their purpose. The court asserted (at 59) that:

> ... in the context of the co-operation between the Court of Justice and the national courts provided for by Article 177 of the Treaty, it is solely for the national court before which the dispute has been brought, and which must assume responsibility for the subsequent judicial decision, to determine in the light of the particular circumstances of the case ...

both the need for such a ruling and the relevance of the question which it submits to the court.

Appeals against the order to refer

5.31 An order referring a question to the ECJ can be appealed if national law permits an appeal from a decision of the referring court or tribunal. See Case 146/73 *Rheinmühlen* (1974).

Appeals against a refusal to refer

5.32 The fact that an appeal or application for judicial review is made does not, however, of itself suspend the reference. See Case 13/61 *De Geus* (1962).

Can a reference be stayed or withdrawn?

5.33 It is the practice of the ECJ to continue with the reference unless it is informed by the referring court that the reference is withdrawn or the effect of appealing in national law suspends the order for reference, or if the ECJ is asked by the national court to suspend the reference (see Case 13/61 *De Geus* (1962); Case 127/73 *BRT v SABAM* (1974)). In Case 31/68 *Chanel v Cepeha* (1970) the Court was informed that the case which had been referred to it had been quashed on appeal to a superior national court. It removed the case from the register and gave no ruling.

5.34 It is, however, only the ECJ which can make an order staying the reference once it is seised of it. It will do so where the order for reference is quashed on appeal by a superior court (see Case 106/77 *Simmenthal* (1978)). In *R v Secretary of State for the Home Department, ex p Adams* (1995) the English Court of Appeal had referred a number of questions to the ECJ, including one concerning the potential direct effect of Article 8a (now Article 18 EC) on the rights of free movement of European citizens. The case was subsequently taken off the register when political circumstances in the UK had changed and an order excluding Mr Adams from mainland Britain had been lifted. The withdrawal of that reference is to be regretted as it denied the ECJ the chance to rule on critically important issues raised in the reference (see further Chapter 18).

Interim measures

5.35 A national court may be requested to order interim measures pending a ruling from the ECJ under Article 234. Cases referred to the ECJ take a long time, up to two years, before judgment. In some cases, this may cause major harm to the plaintiffs. In Case 314/85 *Foto-Frost v Hauptzollamt Lübeck-Ost* (1987), the ECJ suggested that a national court might grant such relief even pending a ruling on validity. In Case C-213/89 *Factortame* (1990), the ECJ held that the full effectiveness of Community law would be impaired if a rule of national law could prevent a court seised of a dispute governed by Community law from granting interim relief in order to ensure the full effectiveness of the judicial decision to be given on the existence of the rights claimed under Community law. The ECJ concluded that a court which in those circumstances considered that the only obstacle which precluded it from granting such relief was a rule of national law must set that rule aside.

Effects of preliminary rulings

5.36 The ruling is binding upon the referring court or tribunal as the interpretation or the decision on the validity of Community law by the ECJ is authoritative (see Case 69/85 *Wünsche* (1986)).

The ruling (on interpretation or validity) may operate as a precedent for all national courts (*erga omnes*) in subsequent cases involving the same Community provision. In exceptional cases where the interest of legal certainty so demands, the ECJ has been prepared to limit the general retrospective (*ex tunc*) effect of its ruling by analogy to Article 231 (ex Article 174) EC, despite the absence of an express provision as to the consequences of a declaration of invalidity under Article 234.

5.37 In Case 43/75 *Defrenne* (1976) which involved the interpretation of Article 119 (now Article 141 EC) on the principle of equal pay for men and women the court, by analogy to Article 174 (now Article 231 EC), restricted the temporal effect of its ruling to cases already pending before its judgment, as otherwise the judgment would have been very difficult for member states to apply and would have entailed excessively high expenditure for them.

5.38 In Case 145/79 *Roquette* (1980), the ECJ, using Article 231 EC by analogy, said that it was entitled to limit the effects in time of a judicial declaration of invalidity under Article 177 (now Article 234 EC) despite the absence of any express provision as to the consequences of a declaration of invalidity under Article 177 (now Article 234 EC).

As a result, it can be concluded that generally the court considers that its judgments take effect ex tunc except where it limits the temporal effects of its ruling.

The future of preliminary rulings

5.39 It was inevitable that the role of the court had to change in respect of preliminary references. In the early years the court encouraged member states to bring preliminary references in the interest of the uniform interpretation of Community law. Gradually, the workload of the court grew, the questions put to it by the national courts became more complicated and sophisticated, prompting the court to change its attitude. It started to rewrite the questions referred, irrespective of which court made the reference (see eg Case C-213/89 *Factortame*). Second, it declined jurisdiction in some references. The first case where the court did this was in Case 104/79 *Foglia v Novello* (1980) where the parties wanted to obtain a ruling on the validity of the French tax system and on whether it violated Article 90 (ex Article 95) EC by way of a contrived use of a contractual clause to induce an Italian court to request a ruling. The contract between Foglia and Novello, a wine importer and a wine exporter, contained a clause which provided that Foglia should not bear the cost of any import duties levied by the French authorities in breach of Community law. An action was brought by Foglia before the Italian court seeking to recover the duty paid from Mrs Novello. The Italian court referred the question of the legality of the duty under Community law to the ECJ. The ECJ pointed out that it was only prepared to give a ruling on genuine disputes and refused a ruling. It said these proceedings had been brought simply to seek an answer to the question of legality of the French law. The court again refused to give a ruling in Case 244/80 *Foglia v Novello (No 2)* (1981) which concerned the same point (see also Case C-83/91 *Meilicke*, below, at **5.42**).

The *acte clair* doctrine (see **5.22**) further qualified the unlimited acceptance of preliminary rulings by the court.

5.40 The period leading up to, and beyond, the signing of the Maastricht Treaty on European Union saw the court declining to accept jurisdiction in a growing number of cases. Some of these refusals were due to the fact that the court had no jurisdiction over the second and third pillars of the TEU, a situation which has seen some improvement in the Treaty of Amsterdam (see Article 35 TEU).

Nevertheless, although the limits of its jurisdiction are more closely defined, jurisdiction will still be generally accepted.

5.41 In Case C-130/95 *Bernd Giloy v Hauptzollamt Frankfurt am Main-Ost* (1997) the court referred to cases in which, it said, it had:

> ... repeatedly held that it has jurisdiction to give preliminary rulings
> on questions concerning Community provisions in situations where
> the facts of the cases being considered by the national courts were
> outside the scope of Community law but where those provisions

had been rendered applicable either by domestic law or merely by virtue of terms in a contract (the *Dodzi* line of cases).

It said it was for the national court alone to assess the precise scope of a reference to Community law and that consideration of the limits which the national legislature may have placed on the application of Community law to internal situations is a matter for domestic law, and thus within the jurisdiction of national courts. It decided it had jurisdiction in the present case. This was confirmed by the court in Case C-1/99 *Kofisa Italia* (2001) where Community law was not directly concerned but its application arose from an internal matter which had to be resolved under national legislation which conformed to Community law.

5.42 The case of *Meilicke* may well be one where the court would have declined jurisdiction even in earlier years. In Case C-83/91 *Meilicke v ADV/ORGA* (1992) a professor of company law sued a company as a small shareholder as it refused to disclose information on 'disguised contributions' to the company and a reference was made to the ECJ. He had written a book about the subject, and the questions referred to the ECJ appeared in the book. The court pointed out that it was essential to define the legal context in which the interpretation requested should be placed. The questions raised did not directly relate to the problem of the right of shareholders to receive information from the company's management but sought a clarification of the problem of the compatibility of a judgment of a national court with Community legislation, in casu a judgment of the German supreme civil court (the *Bundesgerichtshof*) and the second company law directive. The court refused to answer the questions as it lacked the necessary basis in fact and law to do so.

5.43 Although the above case may be regarded as unusual and to be judged on its peculiar facts, other cases arose where the ECJ again emphasised that the national court must establish the facts of the case before making the reference. In Joined Cases C-320–322/90 *Telemarsicabruzzo* (1993) two questions on the competition articles of the Treaty were referred to the court, which the court described as 'particularly laconic', providing so few details of law and fact as to make it impossible to identify the purpose of the questions referred. The court declined jurisdiction and made no attempt to reformulate the questions. It sternly told the Italian court that:

> ... the need to provide an interpretation of Community law which will be of use to the national court makes it necessary that the national

court define the factual and legislative content of the questions it is asking or, at the very least, explain the factual circumstances on which those questions are based.

This was particularly necessary in the complex field of competition law. In Case C-157/92 *Banchero* (1993) and Case C-387/93 *Banchero (No 2)* (1995) the court pointed out that the Italian court had failed to define the legal or factual circumstances of the questions or at least explain the assumptions of fact on which they were based. The first case concerned the Italian tobacco monopoly and the national rules applicable to imported tobacco. The Italian court referred to the monopoly without describing any details: what was the content of the national law, what were its reasons for thinking the national law was incompatible with Community law and making a reference? Nearly a year after the reference was made, during which time no clarification was obtained, the case was declared manifestly inadmissible by the ECJ in an Order. In the second case, the court finally gave a ruling but still could not give an interpretation with regard to Articles 81 and 87 (ex Articles 85 and 92) EC. These cases undoubtedly show a tougher approach by the court in its acceptance of jurisdiction, which has been criticised by commentators. However, in many cases it will still accept jurisdiction although not all the conditions described above have been met. This is shown for example in Case C-316/93 *Vaneetveld v le Foyer* (1994). Again, there was little information, but this case concerned a technical point and, in the view of the court, the need was therefore less pressing and it could nevertheless give a useful reply even if the national court had not fully described the legal and factual situation. AG Jacobs emphasised that the court had not altered its fundamental approach to Article 234 and the principle of cooperation and stressed that formalism should be avoided.

5.44 Probably partly as a result of this case law the court issued a note for guidance on references by national courts (Proceedings of the Court of Justice and of the Court of First Instance of the European Communities No 34/97; (1997) 22 ELRev 55). This emphasises the need for:

(a)   a statement of facts;

(b)   an exposition of the applicable law;

(c)   a statement of reasons for the reference;

(d)   where appropriate, a summary of the arguments of the parties.

Submissions may be made by member states and by the Commission. The note emphasises the need for clear and precise drafting.

Further reading

Hartley, *The Foundations of European Community Law*, (5th edn, 2003) Clarendon, Chapter 9.

D O'Keeffe, 'Is the spirit of Article 177 under attack?', [1998] 23 ELRev 6.

C Barnard and E Sharpston, 'The changing face of Article 177 references', [1997] 34 CMLRev 1113.

G Bebr, 'The Existence of a genuine dispute, an indispensable pre-condition for the jurisdiction of the court under Article 177 EEC Treaty', [1980] 17 CMLRev 525.

G Bebr, 'The possible implications of *Foglia v Novello II*', [1982] 19 CMLRev 421.

T Tridimas, 'The role of the Advocate General in the development of Community law: some reflections', [1997] 34 CMLRev 1349.

H Rasmussen, 'The European Court's acte clair strategy in *CILFIT*', (1984) ELRev 242.

G F Mancini and D T Keeling, 'From *CILFIT* to *ERT*: the constitutional challenge facing the European Court', [1991] 11 YEL 1 (see useful extracts in Craig & de Burca, Chapter 10).

Self-test questions

1. In what circumstances will it not be proper for the Court of Justice to answer a question referred to it for a preliminary ruling?

2. What is meant by 'court or tribunal of a member state' in Article 234 EC?

3. In the course of proceedings before an English court between John Brown (a private individual) and the British Government, it is argued that certain provisions of a British statute, the Immigration Act 1971, are contrary to the European Convention on Human Rights. Brown goes on to argue as follows:

(a) the Convention is binding on the Community and therefore binding on the United Kingdom as a matter of Community law;

(b) it is directly effective;

(c) therefore, the Immigration Act should not be applied if it conflicts with the Convention.

The English court then makes a preliminary reference to the European Court, requesting that is should interpret the relevant provision of the Convention and rule whether arguments (a), (b) and (c) are correct. Before the European Court, the United Kingdom Government argues that the European Court has no jurisdiction to interpret the Convention because it does not fall within the list of instruments in the first paragraph of Article 234 of the EC Treaty; it also rejects the arguments put forward by Brown. You have recently been appointed Advocate-General at the European Court. Outline your opinion.

4. 'Many national courts, the British courts included, accept fairly widely the doctrine of *acte clair*. This shows an insular attitude which is incompatible with the meaning and the spirit of Article 234 and should thus be used sparingly. Even then, in order to decide whether or not the answer is obvious one should approach the matter from a thoroughly Community point of view'. Discuss.

5. To what extent is it true to say that the use made in practice of Article 234 EC has gone far beyond the objectives envisaged for it in the EC Treaty?

CHAPTER SIX

General Principles of Law

SUMMARY
The principles to be discussed include:
- **Fundamental human rights**
- **Equality or non-discrimination**
- **Proportionality**
- **Legal certainty, finding its application in**
- **Non-retroactivity and legitimate expectations**
- **The right to be heard**
- **Legal professional privilege**
- **Natural justice**

6.1 The sources of Community law are contained in the texts of the Treaties and derived legislation. The European Court of Justice, as the 'Guardian of the Treaties' has to ensure that in the interpretation and application of the Treaties 'the law is observed' (Article 220 (ex Article 164) EC). In order to carry out this task, the court is concerned to ensure maximum effectiveness (*effet utile*) for the objectives of the Community. It has taken the view that there are general principles of law which, although they are not expressly referred to in the Treaties, nevertheless underlie their provisions and as such bind the institutions in the performance of their duties. These principles may either be derived from principles applying in the member states, or they may be Community law principles as developed by the ECJ (for example direct effect, discussed in Chapter 7; supremacy, discussed in Chapter 8; subsidiarity, although a principle with non-Community origins (see **4.50–4.55**), and, as asserted by the court in Case C-184/99 *Grzelczyck* (2001) and Case C-192/99 *Kaur* (2001) the Community principle of citizenship (see further **18.46**)). Usually, the reference to 'general principles of law' is concerned with the principles which have originated in the member states.

6.2 The references to 'any rule of law' relating to the application of the Treaty in Article 230(2) (ex Article 173(2)) EC and to 'general principles common to the laws of the member states' in Article 288(2) (ex Article 215(2)) EC indicate clearly that from the outset it was envisaged that the Treaty would be operated in accordance with certain principles recognised by the member states.

A principle has a wider scope than a rule. A rule of law is adopted with a view to a specific legal situation while a principle of law is general and may have infinite applications in law.

6.3 The ECJ has applied principles which may be common to some or all of the member states. It appears to be sufficient that one member state applies such a principle. In Case 155/79 *AM & S Europe Ltd v Commission* (1982), the principle of legal professional privilege was considered by the ECJ. Although generally the right of everyone to defend himself when charged with a criminal offence includes the right to confidentiality of documents in the hands of his lawyer, the principle is much more extensive in some countries, eg the UK, than in others. The court drew on this experience and did not choose the lowest common denominator. In applying these principles, the court has generally developed its own interpretation. This can be clearly seen, for example, in the development of the principle of non-discrimination (see Article 12 (ex Article 6) EC and Article 141 (ex Article 119) EC) and of fundamental human rights (see **6.5**).

6.4 General principles of Community law are invoked to assist in the interpretation of Treaty provisions and secondary legislation, to provide guidance for the exercise of powers granted by the founding Treaties or secondary legislation, to provide additional criteria under Article 230 (ex Article 173) EC for determining the legality of acts of the Community institutions and the member states. Where it is necessary for the court to fill gaps in Community law so that existence of a lacuna will not lead to a denial of justice, it will also make use of general principles.

Although the court has applied the main principles of law which exist in the member states, as Community law develops further and covers a wider field of activities, further principles will be applied.

Fundamental human rights

6.5 Unlike, for example, the German Constitution, the Community Treaties contain no catalogue of basic rights which could constitute a check on the exercise of power by Community institutions. It may be thought surprising that the original Treaties contained no reference to fundamental rights. It should be borne in mind, however, that the original objectives of the Community were nearly entirely contained in the economic sphere and that the Treaty provisions concerned economic matters only or matters directly related to them. Thus it was not thought necessary to include any reference to fundamental rights which were considered to be sufficiently guaranteed by the national laws of member states.

However, it was soon seen that the interests of the Community spread so wide that it was not possible to disregard these rights and that it was necessary to develop a Community approach. Since recourse to purely national guarantees of fundamental human rights could jeopardise the existence and further development of Community law, the approach adopted by the ECJ was that the absence of written provisions relating to fundamental rights did not mean that the Community and its organs were not bound by fundamental rights. The position was rather that Community law needed to be supplemented by unwritten legal principles, including basic rights, which have equal status with primary Community law.

Thus, it is not surprising that, despite some initial reluctance to pronounce on such matters, most probably as a result of the insistence of the courts in some member states, in particular those in Germany and, to some extent, Italy, the ECJ has acknowledged the existence and relevance of unwritten principles of law, including protection for certain fundamental rights, as an element of the Community legal order.

In 1989 Mancini J of the ECJ said:

> ... reading an unwritten Bill of Rights into Community law is indeed the most striking contribution the court made to the development of a Constitution for Europe.

6.6 The ECJ adopted a gradual approach. Early attempts to read fundamental rights into Community law were not successful, but in Case 29/69 *Stauder v City of Ulm* (1969) the court took a more positive attitude. The case concerned a Commission Decision providing for cheap butter for pensioners. This was introduced to get rid of the 'butter mountain' which had been created as a result of the common agricultural policy. In some, but not all, language versions of the Decision, an applicant had to present a form bearing his name and address. The applicant argued this was a violation of his fundamental human rights. The ECJ, in reviewing the legality of the Decision, held that properly interpreted, ie opting for the interpretation most favourable to the recipient, using the language version which simply required the form to be 'individualised' the contested measure contained 'nothing capable of prejudicing the fundamental human rights enshrined in the general principles of Community law and protected by the court'. Thus the court indicated early on a recognition of fundamental rights as a general principle of Community law.

6.7 In Case 11/70 *Internationale Handelsgesellschaft* (1970) (see also **8.31**), the ECJ held that:

> ... the protection of [fundamental] rights, whilst inspired by the constitutional traditions common to the member states must be ensured within the framework of the structure and objectives of the Community.

Thus, the court reaffirmed its view that these rights, although based on national constitutions, were part of the Community general principles. The case concerned the common agricultural policy, under which a maize export licensing scheme required the payment of a large deposit before the licence was granted. The German applicant forfeited part of the deposit when he failed to export all the maize before a certain date. He complained that the deposit system infringed the principle of proportionality, which is enshrined in the German Constitution (Basic Law) as a fundamental right. The German courts found a violation but the ECJ did not. It stated that the validity of Community measures cannot be tested against the concepts of national law, including those of a member state's constitution and must be judged only in the light of Community law. The court then examined the deposit system to ascertain whether an 'analogous guarantee inherent in Community law' had been disregarded. It concluded, however, that this was not the case. When the case had been returned to the German Constitutional Court, major problems arose when this court insisted on conducting its own examination and concluded that there had been a violation of the constitutional principle of proportionality. The potential conflict this created appeared to be laid to rest with the application of the ECJ's judgment in Case 345/82 *Wünsche Handelsgesellschaft v Germany* (1984) (see, for a discussion of these cases, **8.31** and **8.36**).

6.8 In Case 4/73 *Nold* (1974) the ECJ declared a further source of inspiration for fundamental rights, that is, 'international treaties for the protection of human rights on which member states have collaborated or of which they are signatories'.

The ECJ observed, however, that such rights were subject to limitations 'justified by the overall objectives pursued by the Community'.

6.9 In Case 36/75 *Rutili* (1975) (see **18.6**) the ECJ held that various rights invoked by the applicant and contained in express provisions of Community secondary legislation were specific manifestations of more general principles enshrined in the European Convention on Human Rights (ECHR). Further references to specific provisions of the ECHR were made by the ECJ in Case 222/84 *Johnston v Chief Constable of the RUC* (1986) where the court said that the requirement of judicial control reflected a general principle of law common to the member states as laid down in Articles 6 and 13 of the ECHR. Article 6 of the Equal Treatment Directive 76/207 had to be interpreted 'in the light of the general principle'. On other occasions, the ECJ has also referred to the European Social Charter and a Convention of the International Labour Organisation concerning discrimination in respect of employment and occupation (see Case 149/77 *Defrenne* (1978)).

6.10 Case 44/79 *Hauer* (1979) offers an excellent example of the ECJ's comparative approach to the sources of Community fundamental rights. In this case, reference was made by the ECJ not just to the ECHR, but also to specific constitutional provisions of particular national constitutions. Thus, the right to make use of one's own property, in this case in order to plant it with vines, had to be weighed against the Community interest which had led to a Regulation restricting the use of property for the purpose of planting vines in order to avoid overproduction of wine. In this case, the Community interest prevailed.

Extension from jurisdiction over Community acts to acts by the member states

6.11 The earlier cases concerned the application of general principles to Community rules. It has been seen, however, that the interpretation of these principles may also apply to acts of the member states. In Case 36/75 *Rutili* the court said that French measures, ie a discretionary act by a member state implementing a provision of Community law, restricting M Rutili's movement in France, had to be examined as to their compliance with Directive 64/221 which sets out the limitations on the right of free movement of workers under Article 39(3) (ex Article 48(3)) EC) in the light of provisions of the ECHR.

6.12 It was only in 1989 that the court clearly examined the validity of an act of a member state on the basis of fundamental rights considerations. In Case 5/88 *Wachauf* (1989), the member state was in a sense acting as the agent for the Community in implementing a milk quota scheme. The plaintiff was a tenant farmer. During the term of his lease he built up a dairy herd to devote his farm exclusively to dairy production. In the process he obtained a milk quota. A Community Regulation provided these quotas should be transferred on the sale, lease or inheritance of the land to the person taking over the running of the farm until the quota was surrendered. If the quota was surrendered to the state, compensation was to be paid to the milk producer. According to the German Order implementing the Community compensation scheme, the tenant farmer was unable to surrender the quota and claim compensation without the consent of the landlord. In this case such consent was withdrawn. The ECJ held that such deprivation of the fruits of his labour would be incompatible with his fundamental rights: 'expropriation without compensation'. The court said:

> It must be observed that Community rules which, upon the expiry of the lease, had the effect of depriving the lessee, without compensation, of the fruits of his labour and of his investments in the tenanted holding would be incompatible with the requirements of the protection of fundamental rights in the Community legal order. Since those rights are also binding on the member states when they implement Community rules, the member states must, as far as possible, apply those rules in accordance with those requirements.

Nevertheless, in that case, the Community regulation itself was held to be in broad enough terms to allow for compensation to be granted, thereby allowing fundamental rights to be respected. The problem was, therefore, not with the regulation itself, which was not declared invalid, but with the German implementing order. The German court was invited to look again at the implementing order and decided that it could be applied to award compensation.

The ECJ stated that Community measures which are incompatible with fundamental rights recognised by the constitutions of the member states 'may not find acceptance in the Community'. The ECJ also pointed out that protection of fundamental rights in the Community is not absolute but must be considered in relation to their social function. However, restrictions on such rights should be in accordance with the principle of proportionality (see **6.26**).

6.13 It seems that national legislative provisions which lie outside the field of application of Community law cannot at present be reviewed by the ECJ for compliance with Community fundamental rights and the ECHR. In Cases 60 and 61/84 *Cinéthèque* (1985), the ECJ held that it had 'no power to examine the compatibility with the European Convention [on Human Rights] of national law which concerns, as in this case, an area which falls within the jurisdiction of the national legislator'. The ECJ confirmed this approach in Case 12/86 *Demirel* (1987). Case C-168/91 *Konstantinidis v Stadt Altensteig* (1993) concerned a claim by a Greek national that the way in which his name had been transcribed from Greek (with a different alphabet) into German constituted discrimination. Advocate General Jacobs concluded that there was discrimination which could not be objectively justified. He reasoned that there was a fundamental right for any citizen of the Union to move freely anywhere in the Community and to be treated 'in accordance with a common code of fundamental values' which included the right to have the correct transcription of the spelling of his name. However, the court did not follow him and held that the transcription rules were only to be regarded as incompatible with Article 52 (now Article 43 EC) on establishment in so far as its application would cause a Greek national such a degree of inconvenience so as to interfere with his freedom of establishment. This would only occur if the transcription would expose him to a risk of confusion with other persons. The court took the same approach in Case C-299/95 *Kremzow v Austria* (1997). Mr Kremzow had won in the ECHR on the right to a fair trial (Article 6 of the ECHR). He now sought compensation in the domestic court and a reference was made to the ECJ asking whether the ECHR was part of Community law and whether the ECJ could give preliminary rulings on its interpretation. Kremzow argued he was within the scope of EC law under Article 18 (ex Article 8a) EC, as his right to free movement had been infringed by the unlawful detention. The court refused to be drawn and said that the national (criminal) legislation in the main proceedings related to a situation which did not fall within the field of application of Community law.

> (para 12) A purely hypothetical prospect of exercising the right of free movement for persons does not establish a sufficient connection with Community law to justify the application of Community provisions. (see also Chapter 18)

See also Case C-144/95 *Maurin* (1996) where the court said again that the offence with which Mr Maurin was charged involved national legislation and thus fell outside the scope of Community law. However, in Case C-260/89 *ERT* (1991), which concerned the public policy exception under Article 66 (now Article 55 EC) invoked by the Greek state monopoly over broadcasting which was challenged by a private company, the ECJ, referring to its decisions in *Cinéthèque* and *Demirel*, said that where national legislation did fall within the field of application of Community law the court, when requested to give a preliminary ruling, must provide the national court with all the elements of interpretation which are necessary in order to enable it to assess the compatibility of that legislation with fundamental rights – as laid down in particular in the ECHR – the observance of which the court ensures. In particular, when a member state invoked Treaty provisions justifying a rule which restricted a basic Community freedom (Articles 56 (now Article 46 EC) and 66 (now Article 55 EC) in casu), this restriction, provided for by Community law, should be interpreted in the light of the general principles of law and fundamental rights in particular. It was for the national court and, if necessary, the European Court, to appraise the application of the provisions, and the limitations imposed on the power of member states to apply these provisions must, therefore, be judged in the light of the ECHR. Thus, this decision clearly shows the court's concern to ensure compliance with fundamental rights by member states when they apply derogations from fundamental Treaty rules, in casu important Treaty articles. The court extends its jurisdiction in concerning itself with the protection of fundamental rights and other general principles within the member states. Where the application of such principles varies from one member state to another, as will almost always be the case, the court will define its own scope of protection of the right involved.

6.14 Case C-159/90 *SPUC v Grogan* (1991) concerned the advertising by a students' union in Ireland of legal abortion clinics in the UK. The information was provided free of charge. Abortion was contrary to the Irish constitution. The court did not adopt van Gerven AG's formulation suggesting the following approach: the measure represented a ban on a service which would be void but for the fact that it met an important requirement of public interest. The measure should therefore be addressed in the light of:

- whether it was compatible with the fundamental rule of the Treaty (ie that it was actually intended to discriminate);

- whether it was reasonably necessary to meet the requirement of public interest;

- whether it was proportionate;

- whether it was contrary to a fundamental human right;

- whether it was contrary to the ECHR.

The court contented itself with reiterating:

> In *Cinéthèque* it was stated that the Court's power of review did not extend to an area which falls within the jurisdiction of the national legislator ...

yet, once a national rule is involved which has effects in an area covered by Community law and which, in order to be permissible, must be able to be justified under Community law:

> ... then the appraisal of that rule falls no longer under the exclusive jurisdiction of the national legislator.

The court said it was competent to pronounce on fundamental rights issues 'where national legislation falls within the field of application of Community law ...', but the court had no such jurisdiction with regard to national legislation outside the scope of Community law. It considered that this case did not concern an economic activity, as the service was provided free of charge and it therefore fell outside the scope of Community law. It should be noted that the case was also pending before the European Court of Human Rights in Strasbourg, and there could have been a possibility that the two courts might have rendered divergent judgments.

Rights against Community institutions or agents

6.15 Whereas the measures discussed above can be scrutinised for human rights compliance either at the national level or at the Court of Human Rights in Strasbourg under the ECHR, action taken by Community organs can only be reviewed by the ECJ. The European Commission of Human Rights has rejected applications against Community bodies simply stating that the Community is not a party to the ECHR. This means that the only protection available to victims is to be found at the ECJ. The ECJ has examined the action of Community organs for compliance with the rights contained in the ECHR.

The ECJ has accepted, inter alia, the following rights and freedoms:

- freedom of religion (see Case 130/75 *Prais* (1976));

- respect for private life (see Case C-404/92P *X v Commission* (1994));

- the inviolability of the home (see eg, Cases 46/87 & 227/88 *Hoechst* (1989)); there was a general right to the inviolability of private dwellings, but commercial premises would only be protected against arbitrary or disproportionate intervention by public authorities;

- freedom of expression (see Case C-100/88 *Oyowe and Traore* (1989));

- the right to a fair hearing (see eg, Case C-49/88 *Al-Jubail* (1991)). In Case C-462/98 P *Mediocurso v Commission* (2000) the court recalled that respect for the rights of defence must be guaranteed even in the absence of any rules governing the proceedings in question. That principle requires that the addressees of decisions which significantly affect their interests should be placed in a position in which they may effectively make known their views. The case concerned an action for annulment of two Commission decisions reducing funding of training programmes by the European Social Fund for training programmes which had been funded, where the company alleged that its right to a prior hearing had not been observed. On appeal from a rejection of its claim by the CFI, the Court of Justice ruled that the appellant had not been asked to counter the Commission's criticisms, which had therefore not enabled it to counter the accusations made against it effectively. Taking the view that therefore his rights to a fair hearing had not been observed, the Court of Justice set aside the judgment of the Court of First Instance and annulled the Commission decisions;

- the right to a fair trial; see eg, Case 374/87 *Orkem* (1989) and Case 27/88 *Solvay v Commission* (1989). Here the right to refuse self-incrimination was denied by the court as a principle in an economic context, in this case the context of competition law Regulation 17/62. Nevertheless, the court held that national provisions which protect individuals against self-incrimination should also apply to the payment of EEC fines. However, the ruling by the European Court of Human Rights in *Funke v France* (1993) ruled that this right existed under Article 6 of the ECHR. Now the UK has passed the

Human Rights Act, in November 1998, this requires the public authorities including the courts to interpret legislation in a manner which is not incompatible with the terms of the Convention in 'so far as it is possible to do so'. It may well turn out to be difficult for the English courts to reconcile *Solvay* and *Orkem* with *Funke* and a change in the view of the European Courts may be needed. In Joined Cases C-174/98 P and C-189/98 P *Netherlands and van der Wal v Commission* (2000), the court dealt with the relationship between the right to a fair trial, the principle of access to Commission documents, and the exception to that principle based on the protection of the public interest in the context of court proceedings contained in a Decision on public access to Commission documents. Mr van der Wal asked the Commission for copies of letters replying to questions from national courts within the framework of the co-operation between the latter and the Commission in applying Articles 85 and 86 of the EC Treaty (now Articles 81 EC and 82 EC). The Commission took the view that disclosure could be against the public interest and hamper the sound administration of justice and adopted a decision refusing Mr van der Wal access. His action before the Court of First Instance, for annulment of that decision, was dismissed. On appeal the ECJ took the view that the general principle of Community law, under which every person has a right to a fair trial, inspired by Article 6 ECHR, comprises the right to a tribunal that is independent of the executive in particular, but that it is not possible to deduce from that right or from the constitutional traditions common to the member states that the court hearing a dispute is necessarily the only body empowered to grant access to the documents in the proceedings in question. Thus, it would depend on the way in which the obligation of co-operation with national courts incumbent upon the Commission works in practice, whether there is an obligation on the Commission to refuse access to documents on the grounds of protection of the public interest. This obligation would depend on the nature of such documentation. The Commission should ensure that disclosure does not constitute an infringement of national legal procedural rules. If in doubt, it must consult the national court and refuse access only if that court objects to disclosure of the documents. In this case, the documents in question had been drafted by the Commission solely for the purpose of such court proceedings, and the Court of Justice therefore set aside the judgment of the Court of First Instance and annulled the Commission decision;

- legal professional privilege (see Case 155/79 *AM & S Europe Ltd* (1982) applying the principle of confidentiality of written communications between lawyers and their clients and see further refinement of this in Case T-30/89 *Hilti v Commission* (1991) where internal documents reporting the contents of legal advice obtained by an undertaking from external lawyers was held by the court to be entitled to the benefit of the confidentiality granted to the original information);

- the right to property (see eg Case 44/79 Hauer (1979));

- the right to form trade unions (see eg Case 175/73 *Union Syndicale* (1974)).

Non-judicial protection of fundamental rights

6.16 Although the ECJ has declared that it will ensure that Community action conforms with fundamental rights, it may be that judicial protection after the event is not the best form of protection. The inevitable delays and cost involved in obtaining such protection, particularly if a reference to the ECJ has to be made, often deter parties from mounting a challenge. For these reasons it is not particularly appropriate that protection should be left in the hands of the ECJ alone.

A 'catalogue of human rights'?

6.17 On several occasions it has been proposed to codify the human rights to which the Community should be bound and thus give them a stronger basis than that of general principles of law. The German Federal Constitutional Court made this suggestion in the *Internationale Handelsgesellschaft* case for the purpose of ensuring greater legal certainty.

The possibility of acceding to the European Convention on Human Rights was suggested several times by the European Commission. Article 300(6) (ex Article 228(6)) of the EC Treaty provides for the possibility of the Commission, the Council or a member state to obtain an opinion from the ECJ concerning a proposal to join an international organisation. If this opinion is adverse the agreement may enter into force only by Treaty amendment. The latest proposal by the Commission for the Community to accede to the European Convention on Human Rights was submitted to the court but in *Opinion 2/94* (1996) the court concluded that it was not possible under the present Treaty provisions for the Community to accede to the ECHR. The court emphasised the importance attributed to fundamental rights by member states and Community institutions in declarations and in various provisions in the Treaties (see below). The court repeated that it was well settled that fundamental rights formed an integral part of the principles of law whose observance the court ensures. However, the Community only has competence which is attributed to it by the Treaty and no Treaty provision conferred on the Community any general power to enact rules on human rights. Such rights could also not be implied. Article 235 (now Article 308 EC) could not be used to confer exclusive competence where none existed. Thus, an accession to the Convention could only be brought about by Treaty amendment. (On conferred, express and implied powers, see Chapter 4.)

Institutional and legislative action

6.18 In their Joint Declaration of 5 April 1977 (OJ 1977 C 103/1), the European Parliament, the Council and the Commission underlined the importance they attach to the protection of fundamental rights, as derived in particular from the constitutions of the member states and the ECHR. This declaration was probably inspired by the difficult constitutional cases, such as *Internationale Handelsgesellschaft*, which the court had had to cope with recently, and the court has since referred many times to this Declaration. It was followed by several others, eg several declarations and resolutions on racism and xenophobia by the European Council and a Declaration on Fundamental Rights and Freedoms by the EP in 1989.

6.19 In the preamble to the Single European Act, the member states declared their resolution:

> ... to work together to promote democracy on the basis of the fundamental human rights recognized in the constitutions and laws of the member states, in the Convention for the Protection of Human Rights and Fundamental Freedoms and the European Social Charter, notably freedom, equality and social justice.

6.20 The first time that human rights were explicitly referred to was in the Maastricht Treaty on European Union (TEU) (see Article F (now Article 6) TEU). The Amsterdam Treaty amended this article in order to strengthen the fundamental rights commitment of the European Union. Reference is made to them in the preamble, in the Common Foreign and Security Policy (CFSP) chapter (in the fifth indent of Article 11 (ex Article J.1(2) TEU)), and in Article 177(2) (ex Article 130u(2)) EC on development co-operation.

6.21 Amendments were made by the Treaty of Amsterdam. Article 6(1) (ex Article F(1)) expands on the previous text in the TEU and declares that:

> (1) The Union is founded on the principles of liberty, democracy, respect for human rights and fundamental freedoms, and the rule of law, principles which are common to the member states.

Article 6(2) contains the unchanged text from Article F(2) of the TEU:

> (2) The Union shall respect fundamental rights, as guaranteed by the European Convention for the Protection of Human Rights and Fundamental Freedoms signed in Rome on 4 November 1950 and as they result from the constitutional traditions common to the member states, as general principles of Community law.

These provisions were included in the Treaties mainly as a result of the case law of the ECJ.

6.22 The Amsterdam TEU in Article 7 introduced a procedure for determining instances of a serious and persistent breach of the fundamental principles referred to in Article 6 and allows for a suspension of certain rights, including voting rights, of a member state, found to be in breach. The Nice Treaty amended this article to read that if the Council determines there is a *clear risk* of a serious breach a suspension of rights may follow. This safeguard was originally introduced in view of the impending enlargement of the Union to Central and Eastern European countries, where human rights, the rule of law and democracy are often relatively new. There is also a corresponding article in the EC Treaty as amended in Amsterdam, which provides in Article 309 (ex Article 236) EC for the suspension of voting rights and other, unspecified rights:

> ... certain of the rights deriving from the application of this Treaty to the State in question.

Amendments to Article 49 (ex Article O) of the TEU introduce specific conditions for membership of the European Union which include the respect of the principles set out in Article 6(1).

6.23 The first time that the possible invocation of Articles 6 and 7 TEU was referred to, however, was in relation to Austria in January 2000 when at the European Council summit meeting in Portugal 14 member states (all but Austria) expressed concern about the participation in government of the ultra-right Austrian People's Party, whose leader was Jörg Haider. The governments of the 14 member states said that they would no longer promote any bilateral contacts with Austria, nor would they support Austrian candidates seeking positions in international organisations. Fears were expressed that there could be a violation of Article 6 TEU. As it happens, there probably was no such violation, merely the eventuality of one taking place in the future. As a result of these events, the Nice Treaty was amended to include a risk of serious breach (see **6.22**).

6.24 At the Cologne summit in June 1999 the European Council decided to set up a 'body' to study the drafting of a European Charter of Human Rights. In February 2000 this body was named the 'Convention'. It consisted of 15 representatives of the heads of state or government of the member states, of 16 MEPs, of one representative of the President of the European Commission and of 30 representatives of national parliaments. It was chaired by the former German Federal President, Roman Herzog, who previously was a judge at the German Constitutional Court. The formula for this Convention proved successful and it is, therefore, not surprising that the Convention in Brussels preparing a Constitutional Treaty for the Union under the chairmanship of former French President, Valérie Giscard d'Estaing, has a similar composition. The basis for the Charter was drawn mainly from the ECHR, the Declaration on Fundamental Rights drawn up by the EP in 1989 and, of course, the Treaties. The Charter was not intended to duplicate the European Convention, but to form a Constitutional basis for the Union and be tailored to the specific powers of the European Union and its institutions. The Convention completed its work in less than the two years set for it and the Charter was proclaimed at the summit which adopted the Nice Treaty in December 2001. It includes not only the rights contained in the ECHR, but also a catalogue of economic and social rights. It was not the intention that these should be new rights, but rather that the Charter should draw together existing rights under the EC and EU Treaties and make them more visible as a result. The Charter is not a binding instrument, but, as was inevitable, its very existence has had an impact. Several Advocates General have already alluded to it in their Opinions. The Convention in Brussels which has prepared a

Constitutional Treaty includes the Charter in the new Treaty, so that it will become binding. Only minor amendments were made.

Other general principles of Community law

6.25 The dividing line between fundamental human rights and other general principles of Community law is not always clear. There are some general principles, such as natural justice, which some might classify under the heading of fundamental human rights while others would characterise them as administrative law principles.

Proportionality

6.26 In Case C-331/88 *Fedesa* (1990), the ECJ defined proportionality as follows:

> The principle of proportionality ... requires that measures adopted by Community institutions do not exceed the limits of what is appropriate and necessary in order to attain the objectives legitimately pursued by the legislation in question; when there is a choice between several appropriate measures recourse must be had to the least onerous, and the disadvantages caused are not to be disproportionate to the aims pursued.

It is clear that this definition contains the three subsidiary principles that constitute the principle of proportionality in Germany (suitability, necessity and proportionality stricto sensu).

Proportionality appears in the Treaty in relation to the Community principle of subsidiarity, where Article 5(3) (ex Article 3b(3)) EC states:

> Any action by the Community shall not go beyond what is necessary to achieve the objectives of this Treaty. (see **4.50**)

The principle of proportionality has been used to challenge both Community action and member state action in the Community sphere. It has been invoked in many cases, eg in Case 11/70 *Internationale Handelsgesellschaft* (1970); Case 181/84 *ED & F Man (Sugar) Ltd* (1985).

Equality

6.27 The principle of equality means, in its broadest sense, that persons in similar situations are not to be treated differently unless difference in treatment is objectively justified. The EC Treaty expressly prohibits discrimination on the grounds of nationality (Article 12 (ex Article 6) EC) and, to a limited extent, sex (Article 141 (ex Article 119) EC) provides for equal pay for men and women for equal work). In the field of agricultural policy, Article 34(2) (ex Article 40(2)) EC prohibits 'discrimination between producers or consumers within the Community'. The EC Treaty as amended by Treaty of Amsterdam contains an enabling clause in Article 13 which allows the Council to take measures by unanimity and 'without prejudice to the other provisions of the Treaty' in respect of discrimination based on sex, racial or ethnic origin, religion or belief, disability, age or sexual orientation. This moves much further in the direction of a general principle of equality than the limited heads of equality contained in the previous treaties, but the clause is very weak. Nevertheless, as the court had recognised already, the general principle of equality is clearly wider in scope than the provisions in the previous Treaty. See, inter alia, Cases 103 & 145/77 *Royal Scholten-Honig (Holdings) Ltd* (1978); Case 117/76 *Ruckdeschel* (1977). It has applied the wider principle in cases which at the time were not covered by specific provisions of Community law, eg in Case 21/74 *Airola* (1975) (discrimination other than pay on grounds of sex) and in Case 130/75 *Prais* (1976) (discrimination on the grounds of religion).

Legal certainty

6.28 The principle, which is a very wide one, has been applied in more specific terms as:

- the principle of legitimate expectations;

- the principle of non-retroactivity.

6.29 The principle of legitimate expectations means that, in the absence of an overriding matter of public interest, Community measures must not violate the legitimate expectations of the parties concerned. See eg Case 112/77 *Töpfer* (1978). However, this expectation must be a reasonable one. If the Commission adopts a decision in order to bring an end to a speculative situation which brings windfall profits this could not be objected to on the principle of legitimate expectation: see Case 2/75 *EVGF v Mackprang* (1975).

6.30 The principle of non-retroactivity, applied to Community secondary legislation, precludes a measure from taking effect before its publication. In Case 63/83 *R v Kirk* (1984) this principle was applied to criminal proceedings arising out of the application of a regulation. Case 80/86 *Officier van Justitie v Kolpinghuis Nijmegen* (1987) concerned a criminal prosecution where the authorities sought to rely on provisions detrimental to the defendant in a directive which was not yet implemented. The court repeated that a member state cannot rely on an unimplemented directive if the time for implementation has not yet elapsed. Nevertheless, there was an obligation on the national court to interpret national law as far as possible in the light of Community law. This obligation is, however, limited by general principles of law and, in particular, the principles of legal certainty and non-retroactivity. Thus, as the court ruled in Case 14/86 *Pretore di Salò v X* (1987) a national court's interpretation of the directive cannot have the effect of determining or aggravating criminal liability.

Legal certainty sometimes requires judgments of the ECJ to be limited in time. The court normally states the law as it is and this applies back to the time the law came into force. However, in Case 43/75 *Defrenne* (1976) the court ruled that Article 119 (now Article 141 EC) could not be relied upon to support claims prior to the date of the judgment unless legal proceedings had already been brought; the court concluded the same in Case C-262/88 *Barber v Guardian Royal Exchange* (1990). However, these rulings are exceptional and are perhaps inspired more by realistic considerations of not causing undue financial hardship to member states. The normal practice is affirmed by the court, eg in Case 811/79 *Ariete* (1980); Cases 66, 127 and 128/79 *Salumi* (1980); Case 309/85 *Barra* (1988) and Case 24/86 *Blaizot* (1988).

Procedural rights (rights of defence)

6.31 Procedural rights are often just as important as substantive rights in safeguarding a person's interests. Community law often provides procedural safeguards. See eg Directive 64/221, Articles 8 and 9. In Case C-175/94 *R v Secretary of State for the Home Department, ex p John Gallagher* (1995) Mr Gallagher invoked the procedural safeguards of Article 9 of the Directive against a decision to expel him from the British mainland. In the absence of such provisions, however, the court may invoke general procedural principles to fill any gaps. See also Case C-462/98 P *Mediocurso v Commission* (see **6.15**).

Natural justice (audi alteram partem)

6.32 A person whose interests are perceptibly affected by a decision taken by a public authority must be given the opportunity to make his views known: see Case 17/74 *Transocean Marine Paint Association* (1974).

The duty to give reasons

6.33 A person whose rights under Community law are adversely affected by a decision must be informed of the reasons upon which the decision was based: see Case 222/86 *UNECTEF v Heylens* (1987).

The right to due process

6.34 As a corollary to the right to be informed of the reasons for a decision is the right, alluded to in *UNECTEF v Heylens*, to legal redress to enable such decisions and reasons to be challenged: see Case 222/84 *Johnston v Chief Constable of the Royal Ulster Constabulary* (1986).

6.35 The right not to be proceeded against more than once for the same act (*non bis in idem*) has been accepted as a general principle to a certain extent by the court: see Cases 18 and 35/65 *Gutmann* (1966). However, if the proceedings are by Community authorities and by national authorities, or if the proceedings are instituted by a non-member state and a Community institution (Case 45/69 *the First Boehringer Case* (1970) and Case 7/72 *the Second Boehringer Case* (1972)), the rule probably does not apply.

Nulla poena sine lege

6.36 A penalty, even of a non-criminal nature, may not be imposed unless it has a clear and unambiguous legal basis (Case 117/83 *the Third Könecke Case* (1984)). Measures which have the effect of constituting ex post facto sanctions may also breach the principle (Case 14/81 *the Alpha Steel Case* (1982)) that in the absence of Community rules national procedural rules and remedies must continue to be used. However, the use of these rules for the enforcement of Community norms must be on a comparable basis to the enforcement of equivalent national norms. Furthermore, such national procedural rules must not make the enforcement of Community rules impossible or excessively difficult: see Joined Cases C-430/93 and

431/93 *van Schijndel* (1996) and Case C-312/93 *Peterbroeck* (1996), discussed at **9.10** to **9.15**.

Further reading

Henry G Schermers and Denis Waelbroeck, *Judicial Protection in the European Communities* (6th edn, 2001) Kluwer, Chapter 1.

Coppel and O'Neill, 'The Court of Justice: taking rights seriously?', [1992] 29 CMLRev 669.

Weiler and Lockhart, ' "Taking rights seriously" seriously: The European Court and its fundamental rights jurisprudence', [1995] 32 CMLRev 51 (part I) and 579 (part II).

Sharpston, 'Legitimate expectations and economic reality', [1990] 15 ELRev 103.

A Toth, 'The European Union and human rights: the way forward', [1997] 34 CMLRev 491.

Self-test question

'As the Community legal system develops, the role of general principles of law, derived from the laws of the member states, is unlikely to diminish as a source of Community law, but on some occasions some further general principles may emerge.' Discuss.

CHAPTER SEVEN

Direct Effect of Community Law

SUMMARY
This chapter deals with one of the main principles of Community law: direct effect. It covers the following:
- Direct applicability and direct effect: the distinction
- Direct effect of Treaty articles
- Direct effect of International Agreements
- Direct effect of Directives
- Horizontal and vertical direct effect
- Indirect effect
- Other ways of giving maximum effect to Community law

Direct applicability and direct effect

7.1 Article 249 (ex Article 189) of the EC Treaty provides that regulations are 'directly applicable in all member states'. Thus, regulations become automatically part of national legislation and do not require, or indeed allow, any further implementation. See Case 34/73 *Variola SpA v Amministrazione Italiana delle Finanze* (1973). The early view in the Community was that all Community legislation should apply uniformly in all member states and, once made, should not be further interfered with by the different member states. This was perfectly possible and acceptable to all member states, and still is, in fields such as, for example, agriculture and customs.

7.2 Article 249 then goes on to state that directives are 'binding as to the result to be achieved', but the member states are left to choose how they implement them. The EC Treaty is silent on the subject of Treaty articles. If the situation had been left at that, and the Community rules had simply been regarded as falling within orthodox international law, this would have meant that the only way in which individuals could challenge European law was where it had been incorporated into national law in the form of regulations. Regulations are automatically valid in the member states, but not necessarily always directly effective if they need further legislation. See Case 39/72 *Commission v Italy (Slaughtered Cows)* (1973) and Case 128/78 *Commission v United Kingdom (Tachographs)* (1979).

Direct effect of Treaty articles

7.3 However, the ECJ changed matters. In Case 26/62 *NV Algemene Transport-en Expeditie Onderneming van Gend en Loos v Nederlandse Belastingadministratie* (1963) the Advocate General advised the Court to follow the orthodox line of interpretation of international law. The case concerned a re-classification for purposes of customs duties of a product (ureaformaldehyde) imported into the Netherlands. This resulted in a higher level of duty being applied to the product. Article 12 of the EEC Treaty (the Treaty of Rome) (now Article 25 EC) provides that existing customs duties must be dismantled and no new ones must be imposed, a so-called 'stand-still' clause. There was clearly a conflict between the national customs regulation and the Treaty article. Under Article 177 of the EEC Treaty (now Article 234 EC), the national court made a reference to the ECJ, asking two questions:

- did Article 12 have direct application within the territory of a member state...meaning...could nationals of such a member state on the basis of the Article lay claim to individual rights which the court must protect?

- whether the changed duty was an unlawful increase?

We are concerned here with the answer to the first question only.

7.4 Having dismissed objections as to admissibility of the case, the court continued by saying that the Treaty's objective is more than simply to set up an international agreement between states. The preamble refers not only to governments, but to peoples. Article 234 gives the task to the court to secure uniform interpretation of the Treaty and confirms that the States have acknowledged that Community law has an authority which can be invoked by nationals before their own courts. The court went on to say:

> The conclusion to be drawn from this is that the Community constitutes a new legal order of international law for the benefit of which the states have limited their sovereign rights, albeit within limited fields, and the subjects of which comprise not only member states but also their nationals. Independently of the legislation of member states, Community law therefore not only imposes obligations on individuals but is also intended to confer upon them rights which become part of their legal heritage ...

Article 12 contained clear wording and a negative objection. The prohibition was clear and unconditional and did not require a legislative implementing measure on the part of the state. The very nature of the prohibition, therefore, made it ideally adapted to produce direct effects in the legal relationships between member states and their subjects. The Court concluded, therefore, that:

> ... according to the spirit, the general scheme and the wording of the Treaty, Article 12 must be interpreted as producing direct effects and creating individual rights which national courts must protect.

This judgment set out the criteria for the direct effect of Treaty articles: they had to be clear, unconditional and not subject to further implementation. What were the limits to the doctrine? Did it only concern negative objections? Subsequently, Case 57/65 *Alfons Lütticke GmbH v Hauptzollamt Saarelouis* (1966), which concerned Article 95(1) and (3) EEC (now Article 90(1) and (3) EC), found that Article 95(3), which imposed a positive obligation to abolish any discriminatory taxation by the beginning of the second stage, was directly effective. Individuals could, therefore, rely on this provision before their national courts from that time.

7.5 These cases all concerned actions by individuals against official authorities, ie involving vertical direct effect. What of actions between one individual against another, based on a Treaty article, involving horizontal direct effect? In Case 43/75 *Defrenne v Sabena* (1976) Ms Defrenne, a Belgian air hostess, claimed she received less pay than male stewards who did the same work. This was in conflict with the 'equal pay for equal work' provision contained in Article 119 (now Article 141

EC). The court dismissed arguments that Treaty articles addressed to the member states could only be vertically effective and held that this provision, too, should be considered in the light of the principle (of equal pay), the aim of the provision and its place in the scheme of the Treaty. The court said that:

> ... the fact that certain provisions of the Treaty are formally addressed to member states does not prevent rights from being conferred at the same time on any individual who has an interest in the performance of the duties thus laid down ...

Despite the fact that there could be circumstances where the words 'pay' and 'equal work' needed further interpretation and, for example in cases of indirect discrimination (see Chapter 19), further implementing criteria, the fundamental principle still conferred a right on which individuals should be able to rely.

7.6 Many Treaty articles have since been held to have direct effect. Although the court has held that Articles 28, 29, 30 concerning free movement of goods and Article 31(2) on state monopolies (ex Articles 30, 34, 36 and 37(2)) EC have direct effect but may only be relied upon as against the state (see **13.2**), Articles 39, 43 and 49 (ex Articles 48, 52 and 59) EC on the free movement of persons, as well as the 'Competition Articles' 81 and 82 (ex Articles 85 and 86) EC have been held by the court to be both horizontally and vertically directly effective. For a more complete list, see Laurence Collins *European Community Law in the United Kingdom* (4th edn, 1990), Butterworths, at pp 122–126. The discrimination as to nationality Article 12 (ex Article 6) EC has been held by the court as being capable of direct effect, at first mainly used in conjunction with other Treaty articles on, for example, free movement of persons: Case 293/83 *Gravier v City of Liège* and Case 186/87 *Cowan v French Treasury*, corollary of right to receive services. More recently, in Case C-415/93 *Union Royale Belge des Sociétés de Football Association ASBL v Jean Marc Bosman* (1996) the direct effect of Article 6 (now Article 12 EC) in conjunction with Articles 52 and 59 (now Articles 43 and 49 EC) on establishment and services was confirmed and professional sport was drawn more firmly into the ambit of the Treaty. See also Case 36/74 *Walrave and Koch v Association Union Cycliste Internationale* (1974) (see further Chapter 18). In Cases C-92/92 and C-326/92 *Phil Collins v Imtrat Handelsgesellschaft mbH* (1993) the Court ruled that Article 6 (now Article 12 EC) could be used on its own as a basis for claiming discrimination without the need to link it to any other Treaty provision.

Direct effect of international agreements

7.7 The question of direct effect of international agreements has come up many times, and more frequently recently. In Cases 21–24/72 *International Fruit Company v Produktschap voor Groenten en Fruit* (1972) the question was posed whether the GATT (General Agreement on Tariffs and Trade) provisions could have direct effect. The Court concluded that 'the spirit, the general scheme and the terms' of the provisions were different from those in the EEC Treaty. It was true that the GATT agreement intended to bind the Community but, on the other hand, the flexibility of the provisions and the fact that Members to the Agreement could vary or even withdraw from it made the provisions not sufficiently precise and unconditional for direct effect to apply. Free trade agreements were also held not to be capable of creating direct effect as their aim was not to create a single market (Case 270/80 *Polydor and RSO Records Inc v Harlequin Record Shops and Simons Records Ltd* (1982)). However in Case 104/81 *Haupzollamt Mainz v Kupferberg* (1982) another provision of the same agreement was found to have direct effect, as it did fulfil the conditions and fell within the purpose of the agreement. It is true that this concerned a country, Portugal, which at the time was not yet a member state but was a potential member. However, after the new WTO agreement had come into being in 1994, including a new GATT agreement with more binding provisions, and the existence of a court, the ECJ ruled in Case C-280/93 *Germany v Council* (1994) that under very limited circumstances a GATT provision could prevail over an EC provision only if the relevant EC provision expressly referred to the GATT provision. The question of direct effect was also raised in Case C-149/96 *Portugal v Council* (1999). Portugal asked for annulment of a Council decision, arguing it was in breach of WTO rules, including GATT provisions. The Court ruled that, although the provisions of the WTO were strengthened and more effective, they were still based on the principle of mutually advantageous negotiations, there was a lack of reciprocity in applying the agreements and the dispute settlement procedure still did not 'determine the appropriate legal means of ensuring that [the agreements] are applied in good faith in the legal order of the contracting parties'. The Court therefore declined to rule that the agreements could have direct effect in this case. This emphasises the much greater reluctance of the Court to find direct effect in respect of international agreements.

Direct effect of directives

7.8 According to Article 249, directives must be implemented by member states, the *result* to be binding on the member states, but leaving a choice as to *form* and *method* to the member states. By their very nature, therefore, they are not directly applicable, as Regulations are. Directives also could not have direct effect under the same conditions as Treaty Articles, as they could not fulfil the condition of 'no further enactment necessary by the member state'. However, in Case 9/70 *Grad v Finanzamt Traunstein* (1970) the Court stated that decisions could have direct effect and implied that this also applied to directives. Confirmation of this came in Case 41/74 *Van Duyn v Home Office* (1974). Ms van Duyn wanted to enter the United Kingdom to take up a job with the Church of Scientology, an organisation which was considered to be socially harmful by the UK government but which was not banned. She was refused entry and she brought an action against the Home Office. The High Court referred three questions to the ECJ.

- Was Article 48 directly effective? The ECJ said it was.

- Did EEC Directive 64/221 have direct effect?

- How should the term 'personal conduct' be interpreted? (see 18.3).

Article 48(3) (now Article 39(3) EC) permits limitations to the free movement principle of Article 48(1). The objective of Directive 64/221, adopted on the basis of Article 48, is to co-ordinate the measures to limit movement by foreign nationals which member states may take on grounds of public policy, public security or public health. The Directive provides in Article 3(1) that such measures should be based exclusively on the personal conduct of the individual concerned, thus removing 'guilt by association'.

The Court said that the obligation thus imposed on member states was 'not subject to any exception or condition' and did not require the intervention of any act by Community institutions or by member states. As the clause derogated from the fundamental free movement principle of the Treaty, legal certainty for the persons concerned required that they should be able to rely on this obligation. The Directive did, therefore, have direct effect. Although the scope of 'personal conduct' might give rise to questions of interpretation, this is a question which the courts (national or the ECJ under Article 177 (now Article 234 EC)) could resolve and direct effect was possible as long as the wording was 'sufficiently precise'. These words were repeated in subsequent cases, most clearly for example in Case 8/81 *Becker v Finanzamt Münster-Innenstadt* (1982), where the Court said (at para 25):

> Thus whenever the provisions of a Directive appear, as far as their subject matter is concerned to be unconditional and sufficiently precise, those provisions may, in the absence of implementing measures prescribed within the prescribed period, be relied upon against any national provision which is incompatible with the Directive or in so far as the provisions define rights which individuals are able to assert against the State.

See also van Gerven AG in Case C-271/91 *Marshall (No 2)* (1993) and Jacobs AG in Case C-316/93 *Vaneetveld* (1994).

7.9 As the court indicated in *Becker*, directives have to be implemented. The date of implementation is usually contained in the Directive itself but a new provision was inserted in the Maastricht TEU that otherwise implementation must take place within 20 days from publication of the directive in the Official Journal (Article 254 (ex Article 191) EC). In Case 148/78 *Pubblico Ministero v Ratti* (1979) the Court reaffirmed that directives could have direct effect, and then went on to say (at 1642) that a member state which had not implemented a directive within the prescribed period 'may not rely, as against individuals, on its own failure to perform the obligations which the directive entails'. At the same time, it was clear that an individual would have to wait until the date for implementation had passed, and thus in *Ratti*, where two directives were involved, the defence was only available in respect of the one for which the implementation date had passed. In *Becker* Ms Becker could rely on the provisions of an unimplemented directive after the implementation date had passed in order to bring proceedings against the state. Thus, the argument may be used as an offensive, as well as a defensive, weapon. In Case C-208/90 *Emmott* (1991) the Court stated that where an individual could not have initiated proceedings earlier, thus exceeding a national procedural time limit, due to the member state's defective implementation of a directive, the national time limit should not start to run before the directive has been properly transposed. However, it seems that, although this applies to mandatory time limits for bringing proceedings, it does not apply to a rule restricting retroactivity of claims, which served to ensure sound administration. In Case C-338/91 *Steenhorst-Neerings v Bestuur van de Bedrijfsvereniging voor Detailhandel, Ambachten en Huisvrouwen* (1993) such a rule restricting the retroactive effect of claims for benefits for incapacity for work was judged by the Court not to be affected by the non-implementation of Council Directive 79/7/EEC on the progressive implementation of the principle of equal treatment for men and women in matters of social security. This is clearly, therefore, not an absolute rule and, as always, the Court will have to strike a balance between Community interests, the interests of individuals, which often coincide with those, and the interests of member states concerning eg finance and proper administration. When the Court decided that the making of prescription charges to men for longer than to women was in violation of Community equal treatment principles, the UK government's action in restricting retroactive claims to six months may be seen to be justifiable on the basis of its reasoning in eg *Steenhorst-Neerings.* In Case C-188/95 *Fantask A/S v Industrieministeriet (Erhvervsministeriet)* (1998) the broad wording of *Emmott* was critised by Jacobs AG and the Court stated that the solution adopted in *Emmott* was justified by the special circumstances of the case, where the time limit meant that the applicant was deprived of any opportunity to rely on her right to equal treatment under a Community directive. It ruled that Community law did not prevent a member state which has not properly transposed a directive from relying on a national limitation period:

> ... provided that such a period is not less favourable for actions based on Community law than for actions based on national law and does not render virtually impossible or excessively difficult the exercise of rights conferred by Community law.

Horizontal and vertical direct effect

7.10 Having established that Treaty articles can have horizontal as well as vertical direct effect, ie they can be relied upon not only against the state, but also against an individual (see Case 43/75 *Defrenne v Sabena* (1976)) the question then arose whether the same could apply to directives. Directives, however, are addressed to the member state, and must be implemented by them. In Case 152/84 *Marshall v Southampton Area Health Authority* (1986), the Court pointed out that directives are only binding on the member state to whom they are addressed and that, therefore, '... a directive may not of itself, impose obligations on an individual ...' and 'may not be relied upon as such against such a person'. Miss Marshall had brought a case against the Southampton Area Health Authority which had a policy of compelling women to retire earlier than men (women at 60, men at 65). This policy linked retirement to the payment of the state pension. The latter was an exception under Directive 79/7 (Directive 79/7 EEC, OJ 1979 8/24) which excludes 'the determination of old age for the purposes of granting old-age and retirement pensions' from the application of the equal treatment principle under Article 141 (ex Article 119) EC. The ECJ had to find, first, whether the Directive had direct effect and, if so, whether this could be horizontal as well as vertical. However, the Court found that the Area Health Authority could be regarded as 'the state' and that this applied to the state as employer, not just as a public authority. The ECJ confirmed that the authority was, in the words of the Court of Appeal when submitting questions for interpretation to the court, an 'emanation of the state'. This included all organs of the administration, including authorities such as municipalities.

7.11 It is not a satisfactory situation that two individuals with exactly the same grievances should be treated differently according to whether their employer is a public authority or a private employer. One line of decisions pursued by the court tried, therefore, to interpret the concept of public authority as widely as possible in order to minimise the difficulty, while nevertheless maintaining the principle of vertical direct effect. The highwater mark was probably in Case C-188/89 *Foster v British Gas plc* (1990). Again, this case concerned different retirement ages for men and women and the 1976 Equal Treatment Directive (Directive 76/207 EEC OJ 1976 39/40). Could its provisions apply in the case of British Gas, which had been privatised by the time the case was brought, but was still a nationalised industry at the time the alleged discrimination occurred? The Court cited its previous case law where it had held that tax authorities (Case 8/81 *Becker v Finanzamt Münster Innenstadt* (1982)); local or regional authorities (Case 103/88 *Fratelli Costanzo SpA v Commune di Milano* (1989)); a constitutionally-independent police authority (Case 222/84 *Johnston v Chief Constable of the RUC* (1986)) and a health authority were to be regarded as representing the state. It concluded that a body, whatever its legal form, which provided 'a public service' under the control of the state and had 'for that purpose special powers...' should be included among bodies against which (vertical) direct effect could be invoked. However, in *Doughty v Rolls-Royce plc* (1992) the Court of Appeal held that, although the company was wholly owned by the state and was, therefore, under state control, this was not sufficient, and that *Foster* indicated other criteria should also be present, in particular, the special provision of a public service and the exercise of special powers, which was not the case here. The interpretation of what is 'the state' is a matter for the national courts, but it is clear that such an interpretation should, as a matter of Community law, be as wide as possible. Are universities to be regarded as public authorities? In Continental Europe they are mainly under state control, and the answer is probably yes; with British universities there is more of a problem.

7.12 As the European Community developed, the distinction between regulations and directives became more blurred. Member states tended sometimes to incorporate directives into their legislation using the same wording, thus making them resemble regulations. It has been suggested that, after the Maastricht TEU made publication of directives in the Official Journal obligatory in Article 191 (now Article 254 EC), the arguments for equating directives with regulations have become even stronger. In fact, directives applying to all member states were always published in the Official Journal even before it was made obligatory. Lenz AG put forward a strong argument in favour of giving horizontal effect to directives in Case C-91/92 *Faccini Dori v Recreb Srl* (1994), repeating the above arguments. He added that the introduction of a European citizenship in Article 8(a) of the Maastricht TEU (now Article 18 EC) 'raises the expectation that citizens of the Union will enjoy equality, at least before Community law'. In spite of the many objections against such a route, such as those of legal certainty and legitimate expectations, he nevertheless concluded that directives adopted after the TEU should be capable of having effect *erga omnes* for the future. The Court, however, repeated the well-rehearsed arguments against horizontal direct effect and declined to follow the Advocate General. It emphasised that extending the direct effect doctrine to individuals would 'be to recognise a power in the Community to enact obligations with immediate effect', a power which at present it holds only with regard to regulations. Thus, the distinction between regulations and directives would be blurred further. This appears to be the end of that line for the time being.

Indirect effect

7.13 The European Court is first and foremost concerned to give as much as possible useful effect (usually the term *effet utile* is used untranslated) to Community law. It tried, therefore, to circumvent the difficulties as to direct effect described above by pursuing another line of reasoning. This first became apparent in Case 14/83 *Von Colson and Kamann v Land Nordrhein-Westfalen* (1984). Two female applicants for posts as social workers in a German prison complained about sex discrimination. The 1976 Equal Treatment Directive had been implemented in such a way that all they would receive by way of compensation was some minimal travelling expenses. They would not be able to claim appointment to the post or, in the alternative, six months' salary in lieu if the directive could not be held to be directly effective. The Court recognised that the directive did not include any unconditional and sufficiently precise obligation as regards sanctions for discrimination, but went on to say that member states had a duty under Article 5 of the EEC Treaty (now Article 10 EC) to '... interpret their national law in the light of the wording and the purpose of the Directive in order to achieve the result referred to in Article 189(3)' (now Article 249(3) EC). The national court had an obligation to interpret its own legislation in conformity with the requirements of Community law. Subsequent cases refined this principle. In Case 80/86 *Officier van Justitie v Kolpinghuis Nijmegen BV* (1987) the obligation was expressly made subject to general principles of law such as legal certainty and non-retroactivity and the effect of interpreting national legislation 'in the light of the wording and purpose of the directive'. Criminal liability should, therefore, not be determined or aggravated as a result of the directive. In *Von Colson*, the Court said that the obligation extended only in so far as the national court is given discretion to do so under national law.

7.14 In Case C-106/89 *Marleasing SA v La Comercial Internacional de Alimentación SA* (1990), which, it must be remembered, followed the Court's ruling in *Marshall* which outlawed horizontal direct effect, the Court clarified the position. It referred to *Von Colson* and repeated the national court's obligation to interpret national legislation whether adopted before or after the directive, as far as possible in the light of the wording and the purpose of the directive. This case was brought by one company against another, ie two non-state entities. Marleasing alleged that La Comercial's articles of association should be declared void for 'lack of cause', a ground for nullity under the Spanish Commercial Code, but not in Council Directive 68/151 (the First Company Directive) which should have been implemented by Spain. However, Spain viewed its existing Commercial Code as sufficiently implementing the directive. The Court said that this interpretative obligation arose from the duty of member states under Article 5 (now Article 10 EC) to take all appropriate measures, whether general or particular, to fulfil their obligations under the Treaty and to 'abstain from any measure which could jeopardise the attainment ...' of Treaty objectives. In two later cases: Case C-456/98 *Centrosteel v Adipol* (2000) and Cases C-240-244/98 *Oceano Grupo Editorial v Rocio Murciano Quintero* (2000) the Court reiterated that a national court is obliged when applying provisions of national law predating or postdating the Community legislation (directives in both cases) to interpret those provisions, so far as possible in the light of the wording and purpose of the Community law instrument. As in *Marleasing* , the court in *Oceano Grupo* should do so of its own motion (see also **9.13**). We shall see later (in Chapter 8) how courts in member states, and in particular the UK, have interpreted this obligation. It is clearly not absolute, however. In Case C-334/92 *Wagner Miret* (1993) the Court accepted that Spanish legislation could not be interpreted to give effect to the directive concerned. This case concerned the same point as the earlier case of *Francovich* (see Chapter 9). The Court was looking for ways in which to solve the difficulties raised by the direct effect doctrine. It therefore accepted the suggested solution in the question raised by the Spanish court of its own motion in *Marleasing*, which concerned non-directly effective legislation. This route, as we have already seen, is not an entirely satisfactory one either. The limitations of the interpretive method were further emphasised by the court in Case C-168/95 *Criminal Proceedings against Luciano Arcaro* (1996). The Court said (at 42) that the interpretive obligation reached a limit when such interpretation would mean the imposition of an obligation on an individual which would determine or aggravate the individual's criminal liability as a result.

Incidental horizontal direct effect; triangular situations

7.15 In a number of more recent cases, the Court seems to hint at the possibility of what Craig and de Burca have termed 'incidental horizontal direct effect' where private parties were concerned on both sides, but where no particular obligation was put on the defendants. This was the case in Case C-194/94 *CIA Security International v Signalson and Securitel* (1996) where effectively a non-implementation by the state of a directive in not notifying certain technical regulations to the European Commission was pleaded by the plaintiff in horizontal proceedings to relieve him of an obligation without it imposing an obligation on the defendants under the directive (see also Chapter 13). In Case C-129/94 *Criminal Proceedings against Rafael Ruiz Bernáldez* (1996) compulsory motor insurance in Spain relieved the insurance company from the obligation to compensate a third party victim of a drunk driver. The ECJ nevertheless held that the unimplemented directive which imposed such an obligation should apply. This imposed indirectly an obligation on a private insurance company. The situation still seems to be far from clear, and the court seems still to be taking a case-by-case approach, although not going so far as to admit horizontal direct effect of directives. The last word on this has clearly not yet been spoken.

7.16 The Court turned in a different direction first indicated in Cases C-6/90 and C-9/90 *Francovich and Bonifaci v Italy* (1991). Should there be remedies available for breaches of all Community law? We will discuss this further in Chapter 9.

Further reading

J Coppel, 'Horizontal direct effect of directives?', [1997] 26 ILJ 69.

'Case C-194/94, CIA International SA v Signalson SA and Securitel SPRL', annotation by PJ Slot [1996] 33 CMLRev 1035.

H Schermers, 'No direct effect for directives', [1997] 4 EPL 529.

De Burca, 'Giving effect to European Community directives', [1992] 55 MLR 215.

Pescatore, 'Direct effect: an infant disease of Community law', [1983] 8 ELRev.

Winter, 'Direct applicability and direct effect: two distinct and different concepts in Community law', [1972] CMLRev 425.

Case C-188/89 *Foster and Others v British Gas plc*, annotation by E Szyszczak, [1990] 27 CMLRev 859.

Self-test questions

1. Do you agree that direct effect is one of the greatest achievements of the European Court of Justice?

2. To what extent is it possible to distinguish between direct applicability and direct effect?

3. Was the European Court of Justice right in not accepting the horizontal direct effect of directives in *Faccini Dori*? Do you agree that the recognition by the European Court of the horizontal direct effect of directives would blur irretrievably the distinction between directives and regulations?

4. Consider the purpose of the doctrine of indirect effect in relation to *Marleasing*. What are the difficulties with this doctrine?

CHAPTER EIGHT

Supremacy of Community Law

SUMMARY
This chapter discusses:
- **The doctrine of supremacy (primacy) as developed by the ECJ**
- **Application of Community law in the United Kingdom**
- **Application of Community law in other member states**
- **The interpretation of Community law; need for a reference**

The doctrine of supremacy

8.1 After the ECJ had set out the doctrine of direct effect in Case 26/62 *van Gend en Loos* (1963), giving rights to individuals to invoke Community law in their national courts, and thus providing for member states the possibility of making Community law as effective as possible, it next moved to the question of what happens in a situation of conflict between national law and Community law. The development of the doctrine of supremacy of Community law over national law is the reverse side of the coin and a logical sequel to the doctrine of direct effect. As was the case with direct effect, the Treaty does not expressly provide for supremacy and it therefore does not specify how it should be applied in the member states.

8.2 A first indication of what was to happen was given in *van Gend en Loos*, when the Court spoke of the new legal order constituted by the Community for whose benefit the member states had limited their sovereign rights. In Case 6/64 *Costa v ENEL* (1964) the Court then spoke out far more clearly and stated:

By creating a Community of unlimited duration, having its own institutions, its own personality, its own legal capacity and capacity of representation on the international plane and, more particularly, real powers stemming from a limitation of sovereignty or transfer of powers from the State to the Community, the member states have *limited their sovereign rights* , albeit within limited fields, and have thus created a body of law which binds both their nationals and themselves.

The integration into the laws of each member state of provisions which derive from the Community, and more generally the terms and the spirit of the Treaty, *make it impossible for the States*, as a corollary, *to accord precedence to a unilateral and subsequent measure over a legal system accepted by them* ... [my emphasis]

In order to attain the objectives of the Treaty set out in Article 10 (ex Article 5) EC it was necessary for Community law not to vary from one state to another 'in deference to subsequent domestic laws'.

8.3 In Case 106/77 *Simmenthal* (1978) the precedence of Community law was referred to by the Court as a 'principle'; a national court was under a duty to give full effect to provisions of Community law:

... if necessary refusing of its own motion to apply any conflicting provision of national legislation, even if adopted subsequently.

The national court should not wait for a national provision to be set aside before doing so. The Court held that the legislator could not introduce any legislation contrary to Community law.

8.4 In Case 11/70 *Internationale Handelsgesellschaft* (1970) the court stated (at para 3):

Recourse to the legal rules or concepts of national law in order to judge the validity of measures adopted by the institutions of the Community would have an adverse effect on the uniformity and efficacy of Community law. The validity of such measures can only be judged in the light of Community law. In fact, the law stemming from the Treaty, an independent source of law, cannot because of its very nature be overridden by rules of national law, however framed, without being deprived of its character as Community law ...

This was true even in the face of arguments that a Community measure might run counter to a fundamental right or a constitutional principle.

As we shall see below, this case caused difficulties in the Federal Republic of Germany.

In Case C-213/89 *Factortame (No 2)* (1990) (see further below) the Court replied to a question posed by the House of Lords:

> Community law must be interpreted as meaning that a national court which, in a case before it concerning Community law, considers that the sole obstacle which precludes it from granting interim relief is a rule of national law, must set aside that rule.

8.5 The acceptance of supremacy of Community law has resulted in difficulties in different member states. The difficulties have concerned, in particular, the acceptance of primacy tested against a member state's constitutional principles, or the acceptance of secondary Community legislation (such as directives) as superior over a member state's own law. In Case C-213/89 *Factortame (No 2)* the UK had to accept that it should grant interim relief to suspend an Act of Parliament, thus showing the limitation on sovereignty it had accepted when joining the Community; Germany had to accept that Community law should not be tested against the basic rights enshrined in its own Constitution; Italy, too, needed to give up the rights of its Constitutional Court to test the compatibility of Community law against the Italian Constitution; France had to accept the supremacy of secondary legislation, in particular directives, over its own laws ranking at the top of its hierarchy of laws. Denmark also had difficulties testing Community law against its Constitution. Have all these problems now been resolved? (See below.)

8.6 Member states have shown diverse attitudes to the place of Community law in their legal orders. Even within a single member state, the doctrines of direct effect and supremacy of Community law have sometimes evoked different responses from different courts. Moreover, national attitudes have changed significantly over time.

8.7 In dealing with the question of the reception of Community law in the member states, one should always bear in mind that the constitutive Treaties are in their origins basically international treaties. Thus, national attitudes towards Community law depend to a considerable extent on more general understandings about the position of international law in the domestic legal systems. Member states follow one of two doctrines which govern the relationship between international and national law: monism and dualism.

8.8 Under the monist doctrine, domestic and international law constitute a single integrated legal system. As a result, in monist states international law is automatically incorporated into national law without the need for further transposition. In addition, while monism does not logically imply the precedence of international over domestic law in the event of conflict, it is commonly associated with that principle. France and Italy are examples of monist states; the Netherlands also has a monist system, albeit a qualified one. Thus, it is generally considered to be easier for monist states to accept the supremacy of Community law, although this is not necessarily always the case.

8.9 Dualism presupposes the existence of two separate systems of law: international law and national law. These two systems of law have different purposes and occupy different spheres. Under dualism, international law does not become part of national law until, and to the extent that, appropriate national measures so provide. What legislative or administrative form these measures take does not matter, provided the one selected does provide for the proper transposition of the international legal measure.

A dualist member state may still, of course, recognise privileged status to Community law within its domestic legal order. Thus, both primary and secondary Community law may be entrenched in national law through an express constitutional amendment or other special enactment to that effect. Depending on the instrument and language used, the direct applicability, direct effect and supremacy of Community law may be safeguarded. Ireland and the UK are examples of dualist states.

The fact that the Court chose to assert the doctrine of supremacy in *Costa v ENEL*, a case from Italy, which is a monist country, was a matter of Community law, not of national law.

Community law in the UK

8.10 In the UK, the incorporation of Community law presented two specific problems:

(i)   dualism is followed strictly; and

(ii)   there is the doctrine of parliamentary supremacy. In other words, Acts of Parliament and not a Constitution are the highest form of law.

To some extent, the doctrine of Parliamentary sovereignty has been altered recently by the Human Rights Act 1998, which permits UK courts to make declarations of incompatibility where an Act of Parliament is found to violate the European Convention of Human Rights. However, courts cannot disapply Acts of Parliament on this ground, in contrast to challenges on the ground of violation of Community law.

Moreover, the Scotland Act 1998 devolves power to a new Scottish Parliament to enact primary legislation. Such legislation, however, like that of the UK Parliament, must not be in conflict with Community law.

8.11 There is no single constitutional document in the UK which could provide for UK accession to the Community. International treaties are ratified by the government exercising powers derived from the prerogative (the residual powers of the Crown, which are not conferred by Act of Parliament). Generally, the government does not need to seek prior parliamentary approval before ratifying a treaty. Treaties entered into by the UK government do not affect the law applied by the domestic courts and are only binding in international law. A treaty will only have effect in the domestic legal system if an Act of Parliament incorporates it. Thus, in order to incorporate the Community treaties into domestic law, an Act of Parliament was necessary – the European Communities Act 1972. This Act enabled the UK to comply with all of the obligations of membership. The ECA 1972 has been amended to incorporate the Single European Act, Maastricht, Amsterdam and Nice Treaties, in so far as they modify the EC Treaty.

Scheme of the ECA 1972

8.12 Section 1 enables other treaties signed by the EC to become part of the UK law by order-in-council (a type of delegated legislation). The order-in-council must be laid in Parliament according to UK procedures for statutory instruments. Section 2 of the ECA 1972 provides for the constitutive Treaties, secondary legislation and the case law of the ECJ to be applied in the British courts. Without using the terms, sub-s 2(1) provides for the direct applicability and the direct effect of Community law, whenever it is appropriate, as determined by Community law. Both existing and future Community law are included.

The wording of s 2(1) has had the effect of making all Treaty rights, powers, liabilities, obligations and restrictions, without further enactment, legally enforceable in the UK.

Section 2(2) and (4), with Sch 2 to the Act, gives the government powers to make delegated legislation for the implementation of Community law, when action of that kind is necessary or desirable. However, such legislation has to be approved by the Houses of Parliament, and there are some matters which cannot be dealt with by those means; these are set out in Sch 2 to the ECA (see **8.13** below).

Section 2(4) was interpreted in the *Factortame* case by the House of Lords (para 13):

> The words 'is to be construed and take effect subject to directly enforceable community rights' are to be understood as having the same effect as if a section were incorporated into the Merchant Shipping Act 1988 which enacted that the provisions with regard to the registration of British fishing vessels were to be 'without prejudice to the directly enforceable Community rights of national of any member state of the EC' (see further **8.17**).

Understood in a broader context this leads to the conclusion that all UK law (whether in any enactment or other form) must always be read subject to directly enforceable EC rights (whether directly effective or not). In other words it secures the supremacy of EC law in accordance with *Costa v ENEL*.

Schedule 2 exceptions to the power conferred under s 2(2)

8.13 A statutory instrument (SI) cannot be used:

- when taxation is to be imposed;

- to make any provision taking effect from a date earlier than that of the making of the instrument containing the provision;

- to confer power to legislate to others (ie no sub-delegation possible by SI);

- when a new crime is being created which carries the possibility of imprisonment for more than two years or is punishable on summary conviction with imprisonment for more than three months or with a fine of more than level 5 on the standard scale.

Statutory instruments enacting EC law are made according to the positive resolution procedure; that is they must be laid in draft and then approved by Parliament.

Section 3 of the ECA 1972 provides that judicial notice will be taken of Community law, and that it will be treated as law in British courts (unlike foreign law, which has to be proved as fact). It also provides, in furtherance of the aim of ensuring the uniform application of Community law, that any question as to the meaning or effect of the Treaties, or the meaning, effect or validity of Community legislation, if not referred to the ECJ, shall be decided by the courts in the UK in accordance with any relevant principles laid down by the ECJ. A statutory instrument made in 1972 under s 2(2) of the Act provided for the enforcement in the UK of judgments of the ECJ and fines imposed by Community institutions.

The interpretation of Community law; need for a reference

8.14 The effect of the ECA 1972 (as amended) is to make all EC law (whether contained in primary, secondary legislation or in case law) part of UK law. This means that it can be pleaded in any relevant proceedings, ie concerning those matters which fall within the scope of Community law. There may be doubt as to whether there is an arguable Community law point. If in doubt, the matter may or must be referred to the ECJ (see Article 234(2) and (3) EC and Chapter 5). For example, the *Freight Transport* case (*Freight Transport Association Ltd (FTA) v London Boroughs Transport Committee (LBTC)* (1991)), raises questions of: (a) the proper approach to the interpretation of directives; and (b) the duties of a court from which there is no appeal to refer matters of Community law to the Court of Justice. Two European Directives regulating the condition of heavy vehicles were involved: the Brake Directive and the Sound Level Directive.

8.15 The question concerned the fitting of noise suppressors in heavy duty vehicles. In the view of the English courts, this matter concerned environmental protection and safety measures, whereas in the view of the Community, vehicle control was involved. In the field of vehicle control, the Community had legislated and had exclusive competence (see **4.52**) whereas in environmental and health and safety matters, the member states still had the power to legislate. The House of Lords considered that there was no question of referring the matter to the ECJ as it fell within national competence. However, both the High Court and the Court of Appeal had interpreted the question as falling under the two directives and, therefore, being a matter of Community law. The House of Lords would have been able to interpret Community law so as to allow the measure. However, the reasoning followed by Lord Templeman denied that Community law applied at all and developed arguments on the principle of subsidiarity and shared competence between the Community and the member states. The refusal of the House of Lords to refer the question to the ECJ, something it is bound to do under the provision of Article 177(3), especially in a case where its decision is a reversal of the decisions of both the High Court and the Court of Appeal, is suspect from a point of view of Community law. Such reference may not be necessary under the *CILFIT* rules (Case 283/81 (1982)) which include the acte clair doctrine (see **5.22**). There is no obligation to refer where the point has been decided by a previous court ruling, where 'the correct application of Community law may be so obvious as to leave no scope for any reasonable doubt as to the manner in which the question raised is to be resolved'. This rule is then qualified by a number of precautions: 'the matter must be equally obvious to the courts of the other member states and to the Court of Justice'. However, even without taking into account the different interpretation techniques of common law and civil law countries and comparing different language versions, this point of interpretation of Community law was far from clear, nor had it already been decided by the ECJ. In other cases such as *Chiron Corpn v Murex Diagnostics Ltd* (1995), *R v International Stock Exchange of the United Kingdom and the Republic of Ireland, ex p Else (1982) Ltd* (1993), and *Magnavision (SA) v General Optical Council (No 2)* (1987) (see **5.20**) it would also seem that the need to make a reference is not interpreted uniformly by the British courts.

8.16 It is clear, therefore, that the case law under the ECA 1972 is not always consistent, although more recent cases seem to confirm the willingness of English courts to avoid creating difficulties in the application of Community law.

In *Bulmer v Bollinger* (1974) Lord Denning had said: 'Parliament has decreed that the Treaty is henceforward to be part of our law. It is equal in force to any statute'. The crucial constitutional question is, however, not whether Community law has the same force as a statute, but whether it has greater force than a statute, by being able to prevail over subsequent Acts which may be in conflict with it. (For further discussion of the case and the guidelines as to whether a national court should make a reference, see Chapter 5.)

This was recognised by Lord Denning in Case 129/79 *McCarthys Ltd v Smith* (1980) when he said:

> In construing our statute, we are entitled to look to the Treaty as an aid to its construction: and even more, not only as an aid but as an overriding force. If on close investigation it should appear that our legislation is deficient – or is inconsistent with Community law – by some oversight of our draftsmen – then it is our bounden duty to give priority to Community law. Such is the result of section 2(1) and (4) of the European Communities Act of 1972 ...

However, he added:

> Thus far I have assumed that our Parliament, whenever it passes legislation, intends to fulfil its obligations under the Treaty. If the time should come when our Parliament deliberately passes an Act – with the intention of repudiating the Treaty or any provision in it – or intentionally of acting inconsistently with it – and says so in express terms – then I should have thought that it would be the duty of our courts to follow the statute of our Parliament... *Unless there is such an intentional repudiation of the Treaty, it is our duty to give priority to the Treaty.* [my emphasis]

8.17 The supremacy question was confirmed in the UK in *Factortame*. In *Factortame* (1990), the national court, following a preliminary ruling by the ECJ in Case C-213/89 *Factortame (No 2)*, granted for the first time interim relief by way of an order suspending the operation of a statute pending a determination of its validity by the ECJ. On the wider issue of sovereignty the grant of interim relief by the House of Lords reaffirmed the primacy of Community law in areas covered by the Treaties as asserted by the ECJ in *Factortame I*. The British Parliament accepted the obligations arising from membership of the European Community, including that of refraining from making laws incompatible with Community law. The long-running *Factortame* saga started with a complaint made by Spanish fishermen. The common fisheries policy had decided fishing quotas to be allocated to different member states. Spanish nationals purchased British fishing vessels in order to be allowed to fish in British waters. Parliament then brought in the amended Merchant Shipping Act 1988 which, inter alia, provided that the majority (75%) of directors of any company owning a British fishing vessel had to possess British nationality. This would, in effect, drive Factortame, which was largely Spanish-owned, out of business. Factortame therefore brought a case by way of judicial review against the British government alleging breach of Community law and, in particular, breach of the then Article 6 (now Article 12 EC) concerning non-discrimination on grounds of nationality. In interim proceedings, Factortame requested a suspension of the operation of the Merchant Shipping Act. If there had been no such suspension, Factortame would have gone out of business before the ECJ had time to rule on the main case. Under English law, it was not possible for a court to grant an interim injunction against the Crown and suspend an Act of Parliament. Parliament's sovereignty meant that only Parliament itself could amend or repeal an Act. The House of Lords referred the case to the ECJ for a preliminary ruling. The ECJ replied that a rule of national law should be set aside if that was the sole obstacle to the granting of interim relief (see **8.4**). When the case returned to the House of Lords, Lord Bridge pointed out that it had always been clear that it was the duty of a British court under the ECA 1972, when delivering a final judgment, to override any rule of national law found to be in conflict with any directly enforceable rule of Community law. He also stressed the fact that when decisions of the ECJ exposed areas of British statute law which failed to implement directives, Parliament had always loyally accepted the obligation to make appropriate and prompt amendments.

8.18 A UK court or tribunal can deal with Community law as follows:

1   It can apply the EC rule and disapply the UK rule (*Factortame, R v Secretary of State for Employment, ex p EOC*) (see **8.21**).

2   It can interpret UK law in accordance with EC law where possible. In *Pickstone v Freemans plc* (1988), the House of Lords gave effect to Community law by adopting a novel method of interpreting national law. It was held that British courts must apply a purposive construction to legislation affecting obligations under the EC Treaty, and in so doing could rely upon parliamentary debates (Hansard) on the relevant national legislation. Although this type of interpretation, and the reliance on Hansard, was initially confined to cases concerning EC law, this changed in the English tax case of *Pepper v Hart* (1993) where reference to parliamentary materials was deemed permissible, albeit under strictly limited circumstances. This is an example, as there are others in several fields and in several countries, of the 'spill-over' effect of Community law into national law. In *M v Home Office* (1994) the House of Lords for the first time awarded an interlocutory injunction against the Crown in domestic proceedings, a remedy which under the Crown Proceedings Act 1947 had been previously considered to be unavailable until in *Factortame* it had been accepted for a European case.

3   If the UK law was passed in order to implement a directive, UK courts will interpret it in accordance with the Directive (*Litster v Forth Dry Dock and Engineering Co Ltd* (1990) following *Von Colson*). *Litster* concerned a claim against a private employer (based on a directive, so the question of direct effect did not arise). The claim was based on the 'Transfer of Takeovers' Directive (Directive 77/187). The domestic Regulation in question had been introduced in order to implement the directive. Therefore, the House of Lords was prepared to interpret the regulation contrary to its prima facie meaning in order to comply with the directive in the interpretation of the ECJ.

This was explained in *Garland v British Rail* as applying the doctrine of implied repeal and the ECA 1972, s 2(4). In *Garland* (1983) Lord Diplock suggested the possibility that, unless Parliament expressly said otherwise, 'it is a principle of construction...' that the courts would always interpret a statute to comply with a Community obligation, however much this violates the language of the statute. For example, a court could 'read into' any statute the words 'except where Community law applies'.

8.19 However, a more satisfactory interpretation seems to be that in the Spanish Case C-106/89 *Marleasing* (1990), where the ECJ took a purposive or teleological approach requiring national statutes to be interpreted in the light of EC law, whether passed before or after the EC law if possible (see **7.14**). This approach is preferable as it enables the English courts to give effect to the ECA 1972, ss 3(1) and 2(4). In *Marleasing*, the Spanish law predated the Community directive. However, in *Duke v GEC Reliance Ltd* (1988), although Lord Templeman said: 'The British courts will always be anxious to conclude that the UK law is consistent with Community law,' the case concerned the Sex Discrimination Act (SDA) 1972 which antedated and thus was not passed to give effect to the Equal Treatment Directive 76/207 and he refused to distort the meaning of the English statute.

The House of Lords, therefore, held that the duty arising under Community law to interpret British legislation in a manner securing consistency with Community law is confined to legislation that was passed to give effect to Community obligations. The question arose again in Case C-32/93 *Webb v EMO Cargo (UK) Ltd* (1994) (see **19.49**). Without overruling *Duke*, Lord Keith of Kinkel was somehow able to construe *Dekker* (Case C-177/88 *Dekker v Stichting Vormingscentrum voor Jonge Volwassenen* (1990)) in accordance with the ECA 1972, s 3(1). Lord Keith noted that the ECJ in *Marleasing* had required national courts to construe domestic law to accord with the Directive 'only if it was possible to do so'. He referred to his own remarks in *Duke* suggesting that this would only be possible if it could be done without 'distorting' the meaning of the domestic legislation, ie where a domestic law was 'open to an interpretation consistent with the Directive, whether or not it is also open to an interpretation inconsistent with it.' Now s 99 of the Employment Rights Act 1996 provides that dismissal is unlawful if the reason (or if more than one, the principal reason) for the dismissal is that an employee is pregnant or any other reason connected with her pregnancy. Whether this will end the confusion remains to be seen. It will require a UK court to disapply the SDA 1975 or to interpret s 99 (above) in the light of *Dekker*. So far, UK case law (before s 99 came into force) is very ambivalent. Article 10 (ex Article 5) EC in effect directs the courts to do this by instructing member states to give the best possible effect to Community law. This was doubted by Slynn AG (as he then was) in the first *Marshall* case, but this can no longer be true. Whether *Duke* is correctly decided depends on the interpretation of *Marleasing*. According to the ECJ in Case C-334/92 *Wagner Miret v Fondo de Garantia Salaria* (1993), putting a further gloss on *Marleasing*, in order to interpret national law in conformity with EC law it must be presumed that the state intended to achieve the result pursued by the directive. If this is not possible, as was the case in *Wagner Miret*, the state's liability under the *Francovich* principles may arise (see further Chapter 9).

8.20 In Case C-9/91 *R v Secretary of State for Social Security, ex p Equal Opportunities Commission* (1992) (the *EOC* case) the court made a declaration that the Employment Protection Act (EPA) 1978 was not in accordance with EC law. The House of Lords did not direct the Minister to change the law and in fact said it could not do so:

> The question is whether judicial review is available for the purpose of securing a declaration that certain UK primary legislation is incompatible with Community law ... In my opinion it is, although there is no need for a declaration that the Secretary of State is in breach of obligations under Community law. A declaration that the threshold provisions of the 1978 Act are incompatible with Community law would suffice for the purpose ... This does not involve any attempt by the EOC to enforce the international treaty obligations of the UK.

The House of Lords then made a declaration that the EPA 1978 was incompatible with Article 119 (now Article 141 EC), Directive 75/117 and Directive 76/207.

178

8.21 There are a number of different ways in which EC law can be raised in English courts:

- application for judicial review, eg *EOC* case (see above);

- by way of a defence to a claim, as happened in *Marleasing*;

- to found a claim, either free standing or in conjunction with a claim based on English law (*Rankin v British Coal Corpn* (1993); *Factortame*). If the Community rule is different from the national rule then the EC rule must prevail;

- as a guide to the interpretation of English law implementing Community law (as above). However, it is not possible for a UK court to declare a Community legal measure unlawful. If the plaintiff or defendant wishes to raise that as a defence then the UK court must stay the proceedings and ask for a reference. If it is sufficiently convinced of the possible outcome, it could grant interim relief (*Factortame*).

8.22 The case of the 'metric martyrs' raised the question of supremacy once again. *Thoburn v Sunderland County Council, Hunt v London Borough of Hackney, Harman and Dove v Cornwall County Council* and *Collins v London Borough of Sutton* (2002). Mr Thoburn was a market trader who refused to use scales for weighing vegetables in metric weights as well as in imperial weights. He was convicted in the magistrates' court of breaching the Weights and Measures Act 1985. The others were convicted for similar offences under other similar statutory instruments. The various orders amended legislation under the power to amend primary legislation contained in the ECA 1972, s 2(2). Laws LJ dismissed the appeals. He stated that the ECA 1972 is a constitutional statute which means, in the proper interpretation of s 2(2) read together with s 2(4), that it cannot be impliedly repealed by a later inconsistent statute and would prevail over such a later statute. The respondents' argument that Community law has supremacy over domestic legislation and that the ECA 1972 was, in effect, entrenched legislation, until Parliament repealed that Act, was false, but the common law has come to recognise that there are particular fundamental or constitutional rights. Such rights contained in a constitutional statute could not be the subject of an implied repeal and the statute could only be repealed by express words in a constitutional statute such as the ECA 1972. (See also **5.10** Case C-206/01 *Arsenal v Reed* (2002) and *Arsenal Football Club v Reed* (2002)).

Community law in other member states

Community law in France

8.23 There are two main separate court systems in France. The judicial courts deal with civil and criminal matters while administrative courts under a separate system review the legality of administrative action. Administrative courts may also annul legislative measures enacted by the executive. The highest court in the judicial order is the *Cour de Cassation* while the *Conseil d'Etat* is the supreme administrative court. There is also the *Conseil Constitutionnel* which by virtue of its power of review under Article 61 of the Constitution of 1958 may examine the constitutionality of legislation before it comes into force.

8.24 The two court systems, the judicial and the administrative, have very different traditions and the most notable feature of the French attitude towards Community law has been the different approach adopted by the judicial courts and the administrative courts, and, in particular, by the two supreme courts: the *Cour de Cassation* and the *Conseil d'Etat*. While the former has sought ways of resolving the legal problems raised by French membership in the Community, the latter has, if anything, been determined to exaggerate them, until fairly recently at least. Article 55 of the Constitution of 1958 provides that:

> Treaties or agreements which have been duly ratified or approved shall, on publication, have higher authority than that of statutes, provided that the agreement or treaty in question is applied by the other party.

This provision therefore implies that the constitutive Treaties prevail over national law without further enactment.

In the judicial system, this was confirmed by the *Cour de Cassation* in *Vabre and Weigel* (1975). Vabre, a coffee importer, claimed violation of Article 95 (now Article 90 EC) of the Treaty. A customs law of 1966, subsequent to the Treaty, was in conflict with the Treaty provision. The court stated that:

> The EEC Treaty prevails over subsequent national statutes; it establishes a new special legal order which forms a constitutive part of the national legal orders and is directly valid for the subjects of the member states and binding for their judicial institutions.

The court based its decision on Article 55 of the Constitution as well as on the specific nature of Community law.

8.25 The highest administrative court, the *Conseil d'Etat* (CE) avoided a clear position on the matter of supremacy of Community law for much longer, and for a time did not make a reference to the ECJ under Article 177 (now Article 234 EC), on the grounds that the points of Community law which were occasionally raised before it were clear. In practice, this theory offered a wide scope for subjective and controversial rulings on matters of Community law on the part of national courts in general and the CE in particular. In *Chemins de Fer Français* (1962), the CE ruled that, on the basis of Article 55, the EC Treaty had similar status to that of French laws (lois), but this did not resolve the problem of supremacy of Community law. In *Shell-Berre* (1964), the CE refused to make a reference to the ECJ under Article 177 (now Article 234 EC) for the interpretation of Article 37(1) (now Article 31(1) EC: state monopolies of commercial character) despite the fact that the meaning of that provision was subject to serious controversy. Later, in the *Semoules de France* case (1970) the CE applied a French statute despite the existence of a conflicting EC regulation enacted before that statute. Shortly afterwards, in *Synacomex*, the CE made its first reference to the ECJ under Article 177 (now Article 234 EC).

8.26 The CE reaffirmed its negative attitude towards EC law in the celebrated case of *Cohn-Bendit* (1980). Daniel Cohn-Bendit, a German citizen born in France, was one of the leaders in the May 1968 student revolt. He had been deported after that, but when he tried to enter France in 1975 in order to take up an offer of employment, his request was refused. He challenged the decision, relying on Article 48 (now Article 39 EC) and Council Directive 64/221 (see Chapter 18). In its decision the CE held that directives could not be invoked by individuals in national courts in order to challenge an individual administrative decision. The *Commissaire du Gouvernement*, who has a similar function to that of the Advocate-General in the ECJ, had cited all the relevant cases decided by the ECJ and had come to a directly divergent conclusion. In spite of this, the CE ignored the doctrine of the direct effect of directives which had been firmly established before Cohn-Bendit (since van Duyn). Other, similar judgments followed. However, the CE gradually recognised that legislation adopted by the French executive (as opposed to statutes passed by the legislature) could be annulled if it conflicted with the result to be achieved under a directive. See, inter alia, *Compagnie Alitalia* (1990).

8.27 The CE adopted a more positive attitude towards the doctrine of supremacy of Community law in its decision in *Nicolo* (1990), which concerned a challenge by two French citizens of legislation giving the right to vote and stand for European Parliament elections to non-European French citizens of the overseas departments and territories. In its judgment, the CE impliedly recognised that the EC Treaty would prevail over a French statute in case of conflict. The CE took a further step in *Boisdet* (1991) where, for the first time, it recognised the primacy of EC regulations over a French statute, even when the statute was enacted after the EC regulation concerned. Subsequently, in several cases concerning directives: *Rothmans and Philip Morris* (1993) and in *Arizona Tobacco* (1992) the Conseil d'Etat acknowledged that a directive would prevail over a subsequently adopted statute.

8.28 However, the lack of any clear statement of principle in the above decisions means that there are still doubts regarding the CE's attitude towards Community law in general, especially directives. On the other hand, it should be borne in mind that CE judgments often consist of one or two lines and that very little reasoning is given. Therefore, indications of attitudes to Community law come from the opinions of the *Commissaire du Gouvernement* or from extra-judicial writings of the members of the CE.

8.29 The position of Community law in France took on a new dimension by amendments to the French Constitution adopted in order to make possible the ratification of the Maastricht TEU by France. These amendments were made necessary by a decision of the *Conseil Constitutionnel* (1993), which declared the provisions of the TEU concerning the right of EC citizens to vote in municipal elections, the EMU, and common visa policy to be incompatible with the French constitution. The most important amendment was the introduction to the Constitution of Title XIV (Article 88), which makes provision for French membership of the European Communities and the EU. Previously, there was no mention of the Community in the Constitution. Even though it is still too early to assess the impact of the new constitutional provisions on French judicial attitudes towards Community law, one should expect that their effect would be favourable. It should be noted, however, that the reciprocity clause 'provided that the agreement or treaty is applied by the other party' appears in this article as it does in Article 55 of the Constitution.

Community law in Germany

8.30 In Germany there are five separate court systems. In addition to the ordinary courts (having jurisdiction in civil and criminal law), there are specialised courts dealing with administrative, labour, social security and fiscal matters. Each of these court systems is headed by a federal supreme court. Each system is independent of the other. On constitutional issues, however, all courts are subject to the rulings of the Federal Constitutional Court (the *Bundesverfassungsgericht* – *BVerfGe*) hereafter referred to as the FCC.

8.31 Germany, which has a mitigated dualist system, recognised the special position of the Community legal order as distinct from traditional international law. In *Internationale Handelsgesellschaft* (1974), which followed the ECJ ruling in Case 11/70 *Internationale Handelsgesellschaft* (1970) which upheld the annulment of the Community's export licence regulations, the FCC held:

> This court – in this respect in agreement with the law developed by the European Court of Justice – adheres to its settled view that Community law is neither a component part of the national legal system nor international law, but forms an independent system of law flowing from an autonomous legal source ...

> In principle, the two legal spheres stand independent of and side by side one another in their validity, and, in particular the competent Community organs, including the European Court of Justice, have to rule on the binding force, construction and observance of Community law, and the competent national organs on the binding force, construction and observance of the constitutional law of the Federal Republic of Germany.

8.32 In Germany, the existing Article in the Basic Law (Article 24 GG) which provided that sovereign powers may be transferred to international organisations was considered to be an insufficient basis for Germany's accession to the Maastricht Treaty in 1993. Consequently, the Constitution was amended in December 1992 to authorise a further transfer of powers to the European Community. The new Article 23 GG enabled Germany 'with a view to establishing a united Europe' to participate in the development of the European Union, which is committed to democracy, the rule of law, social and federal principles as well as the principle of subsidiarity. It ensures protection of basic rights comparable in substance to the protection afforded by the Basic Law.

8.33 See also the FCC's judgment in *Lütticke* (1971) to the effect that, in Germany, Community law is applied directly and cannot be set aside by subsequent national laws. In Germany every court is entitled not to apply national laws which are contrary to EC law.

8.34 As a rule, German courts loyally apply Community law. But there are exceptions. One branch of one of the German supreme courts (the 5th Senate of the *Bundesfinanzhof*, the Federal Tax Court) in July 1981 wrongly applied an EC directive without prior request for a preliminary ruling. It referred to the French *Cohn-Bendit* case and decided on the same grounds that an EC directive could not be applied within the national legal order.

Following a preliminary ruling given by the ECJ in the *Kloppenburg* case (Case 70/83 (1984)), the 5th Senate of the Federal Tax Court took the opportunity to question the whole case law of the ECJ concerning the direct effect of directives. The thrust of the argument was that the ECJ had transgressed the proper limits of interpretation of Article 189(3) (now Article 249(3) EC) and thereby extended the effect of directives in a way that was not covered by the German Acts of Accession to the Treaties.

On appeal, the FCC held that the ruling of the ECJ was binding on the Federal Tax Court and that the question of the direct effect of directives was a proper matter for the ECJ to decide under Article 177 (now Article 234 EC). In its judgment, the FCC viewed the ruling by the ECJ as an act of judicial law-making which, however, did not transgress the proper bounds of the inherent limits of the judiciary.

8.35 One of the most difficult points is the question of constitutional review. The key question is whether Community law can be set aside if it violates the Basic Law. In *Internationale Handelsgesellschaft (Solange I)* (1974), the FCC considered that the protection of fundamental human rights was an essential element of the Basic Law, an element which could not automatically be restricted by transferring sovereignty to a supranational organisation under Article 24 GG. In the opinion of the FCC, the fundamental rights guaranteed by the Basic Law were insufficiently protected under Community law, as the Community lacked a democratically legitimated and directly elected parliament as well as a codified catalogue of human rights. The protection of fundamental rights by the ECJ was considered insufficient as the case law of courts could not fully guarantee legal certainty. It could be changed in any future decision. The FCC confirmed that it would not rule on the validity or invalidity of a rule of Community law, but it held that the German authorities or courts should not apply rules of Community law which infringed a rule of the Basic Law relating to basic rights as long as (in German: *solange*) the EC did not itself provide adequate protection of fundamental rights. In cases of doubt the FCC would rule on the existence of such an infringement.

8.36 It was not until 1986 that the FCC revised its position *in Application of Wünsche Handelsgesellschaft (Solange II)* (1987). The FCC referred to various developments in the Community concerning the protection of basic rights and held that the protection of fundamental rights in the Community had reached a degree essentially comparable to the standard set by the Basic Law. On this basis, the FCC ruled that it would no longer exercise its jurisdiction to review secondary Community law by the standards of the fundamental rights guaranteed by the Basic Law. The FCC, however, pointed out that a transfer of sovereign rights may not impinge on the basic constitutional structure of the Federal Republic which encompassed the 'federal order' set up by the Basic Law.

It is clear from this judgment that the FCC had not given up its former interpretation of Article 24 GG with regard to the implicit limitations of the transferral of rights to a supranational organisation. The judgment expressly linked the question of non-exercise of jurisdiction concerning basic rights by the FCC to the state of Community law. The FCC will be content not to exercise this jurisdiction only 'as long as' the Community, and in particular the case law of the ECJ, generally ensures an effective protection of fundamental rights as against the sovereign powers of the Communities (see also Chapter 6).

8.37 In *Brunner v European Union Treaty* (1994) the FCC used the opportunity of a constitutional challenge of the Maastricht Treaty to conduct an analysis of the Treaty and outline the limits of competence of the Community vis-à-vis the Federal Republic. A number of constitutional complaints (*Verfassungsbeschwerden*) were lodged with the Federal Constitutional Court by four Green MEPs and by Manfred Brunner, a former EEC official. The judgment, rendered on 12 October 1993, declared the Greens' complaint inadmissible, but dealt at length with the Brunner application. It concluded that the transfer of powers to the Union, and in particular those concerning Economic and Monetary Union, fell within the acceptable limits of the democratic principle guaranteed by the Basic Law (Article 38 GG) which precludes such transfer if it leaves the Parliament devoid of sufficient sovereign powers. With what *Die Zeit* called 'judicial self-restraint' (in English) the court held that the decisive factor was that the democratic foundations of the

Union should be extended in step with further integration. The Union remains a Confederation (*Staaten(ver)bund*) rather than a Federation (*Bundesstaat*). It states, however, that the German Federal government has a constitutional obligation to submit any decision on entry into the third stage of Economic and Monetary Union to the Bundestag and that any decision on the 'softening' of the convergence criteria should be approved by Parliament. The court clearly restricts integration in its statement on a 'dynamic interpretation of Community law'. The judgment states that if any judgment of the Court of Justice in its interpretation of Community law 'is tantamount to an extension of the Treaty' such a decision could not be considered as binding and the Constitutional Court reserves the ultimate right of review on the model of its decision in *Solange I*. The court does, however, stress its 'relationship of co-operation' with the European Court of Justice. A similar constitutional challenge in 1998, heard just before the decision taken by the Council as to which member states would qualify to join EMU, was rejected by the FCC.

8.38 Further difficulties have arisen in the so-called banana cases: Case C-280/93 *Germany v Council* (1994) and Cases C-465/93 and C-466/93 *Atlanta Fruchthandelsgesellschaft v Bundesamt für Ernährung* (1995), where German administrative and tax courts ruled on constitutional questions of proportionality and the right to private property and on whether the banana Regulation (Council Regulation 404/93) violated the provisions of the GATT. The FCC, however, ruled in a Decision of July 2000 that in previous cases it had declared itself satisfied with the standard of protection of fundamental rights, that there was no evidence of these standards having declined since and that the present cases were therefore inadmissible.

Community law in Italy

8.39 In Italy, too, there have been problems, mainly with the Italian Constitutional Court. In Case 6/64 *Costa v ENEL* (1965) the ECJ ruled that Community law prevailed over national law, including a member state's Constitution (see **8.2**). The Italian court had also referred the case to the Italian Constitutional Court for a ruling, as this is the only court which may declare a statute invalid. The Constitutional Court ruled that, as the then EEC Treaty had been incorporated in Italian law as an ordinary statute, the Treaty was subordinate to subsequent Italian legislation. The ECJ was well aware of this ruling when deciding *Costa*. The Attorney General warned of 'disastrous consequences for the future of the Common Market' and suggested that there were only two ways open to a member state whose Constitution prevented it from giving immediate effect to Community legislation over national law: either to amend the Constitution or to amend the Treaty. As we have seen (in **8.2**), the ECJ ruled that member states had given up some of their sovereign rights by joining the Community and this had made it impossible for them to give effect to a subsequent conflicting measure.

The law stemming from the Treaty could, therefore not be overridden by national law without depriving it of its character as Community law. Consequently, Article 177 (now Article 234 EC) was to be applied irrespective of any domestic law.

8.40 Case 106/77 *Simmenthal* (1978) ascertained that any rights or duties conferred on individuals by the Treaty must be protected, and any prior or posterior national rules, including any legislative, administrative or judicial practice which might impair the effectiveness of Community law, by withholding from the national court having jurisdiction to apply such law the power to set aside national law preventing Community rules from having full effect must be disapplied. The court should not await a ruling from the Constitutional Court in this respect. However, in Joined Cases C-10/97-22/97 *Ministero delle Finanze v IN CO GE '90* (1998) the court reconsidered the judgment in *Simmenthal* recalling that it had, essentially, held that every national court must, in a case within its jurisdiction, apply Community law in its entirety and protect rights which Community law confers on individuals, setting aside any provision of national law which may conflict with it, whether prior or subsequent to the Community rule. The court held that it could not be inferred from that judgment that the incompatibility with Community law of a subsequently adopted rule of national law had the effect of rendering that rule of national law non-existent. Furthermore, Community law did not require that any non-application, following a judgment given by the court, of legislation introducing a levy contrary to Community law should deprive that levy retroactively of its character as a charge and divest the legal relationship, established when the charge in question was levied between the national tax authorities and the parties liable to pay it, of its fiscal nature. Any such reclassification was a matter for national law.

In *Frontini* (1974) the Constitutional Court, while generally recognising the primacy of Community law and holding that any question under the Constitution of incorporating Article 189 (now Article 249 EC) of the Treaty into the Italian Act of ratification 'must be dismissed', nevertheless reserved the right to control the continuing compatibility of the Treaty with fundamental principles guaranteed by the Constitution.

8.41 *Granital* (1984), annotated by Gaja, follows the case law of the Court of Justice. It uses the principle of pre-emption, ie once the Community has competence, the Italian state was no longer competent to legislate. This still left doubt as to non-directly effective legislation (Treaty articles and directives). Later, in cases such as *Fragd* (1990), the Constitutional Court seems to confirm that it considers that a provision of Community law (in this case a rule drawn from Article 234 (ex Article 177) EC), could be held to be inapplicable in Italy if it infringes fundamental human rights, ie that if the ECJ went as far as ruling out that the effects of a declaration of invalidity cover the act or acts of the dispute this would mean that serious doubts would arise about the consistency of a rule that allows this type of judgment with the essential elements of judicial protection.

Community law in Ireland

8.42 Early cases after accession suggested that Community law is part of the Irish legal order and that there are no problems with supremacy. A Constitutional amendment to join the Community gives complete supremacy to Community law over national law, even above the Constitution itself. However, none of the cases concerned basic rights guaranteed by the Irish Constitution; which, however, was the case in Case C-159/90 *Society for the Protection of the Unborn Children Ireland Ltd v Grogan* (1991). The Irish Supreme Court ruled that this constitutional right needed to be protected and that there was no question of a possible or putative right which might exist in European law as a corollary to the right to travel. The High Court had referred the question to the ECJ and the Supreme Court, while allowing the injunction against the students to stop disseminating information on abortion clinics in England, also allowed the reference to the ECJ to go forward. The ECJ, however, established that there was an absence of economic nexus, as the students did not charge for the service and, in effect, did not give a ruling on the point.

A similar problem came up in February 1992 when a pregnant 14-year-old girl was barred from travelling to England for an abortion. However, the Supreme Court finally allowed the abortion to go ahead as there was a real and substantial risk to the mother's life.

Protocol No 17 to the TEU on the Irish Constitution provides:

> Nothing ... (in the Treaties ...) shall affect the application in Ireland of Article 40.3.3 of the Constitution ... (which protects the right to life of unborn children and prohibits abortions).

The legal interpretation of the Protocol on 1 May 1992 by lawyers reporting to the European Council is recorded as follows:

> It shall not limit freedom to travel between member states or, in accordance with conditions which may be laid down, in conformity with Community law, by Irish legislation, to obtain or make available in Ireland information relating to services lawfully available in member states.

Community law in Austria

8.43 With the accession of Austria in 1994 the issue of supremacy arose in a new member state. In Case C-224/97 *Ciola v Land Vorarlberg* (1999) the Court firmly rejected the Austrian State's argument that national law in conflict with EC law should be obeyed as long as the Treaty right had not been established by the national court. An Austrian citizen could be prosecuted for failing to follow an unlawful instruction during the period preceding the national court's finding of such illegality, out of respect for authority. 'If in doubt, obey the state. Treaty rights only take precedence once they are established by the national court.'

New member states

8.44 The accession of 10 new member states is scheduled for the middle or the end of 2004. Most of these states are new democracies, emerged from the Communist era. They have new Constitutions, many of which include an express recognition of supremacy of Community law. However, such supremacy will still be interpreted by the courts, both higher and lower, of the countries themselves, in the context of their own constitutional views. As has been seen, the interpretation of supremacy of EC law over national law depends on the constitutional positions of the respective member states which is not necessarily quite the same as that of the ECJ. A case such as the one above in Austria may be an indication of the kind of difficulty which might rise with the supremacy question. It is perhaps unlikely that the new member states and their respective constitutional courts will not view supremacy of EC law in the light of their own constitutions.

8.45 Matters of procedure are for national law, provided that the procedure does not make it impossible for the plaintiff (or defendant) to rely on directly effective EC law. For example, time limits are matters of procedure and determined by national law subject to principles laid down by the ECJ (see further Chapter 9).

8.46 However, the ECJ has started to make greater inroads into the domain of procedural law. It was assumed that the member states had procedural autonomy, ie that the way in which they dealt with Community law under their procedures was a matter for the national court. In Case C-312/93 *Peterbroeck van Campenhout & Cie SCS v Belgium* and Cases C-430 and C-431/93 *van Schijndel v Stichting Pensioenfonds voor Fysiotherapeuten* there were applications to amend pleadings to include new points of Community law. The two cases were decided differently, but the conclusion seems to be that Community law does not prevent courts from raising Community law points of their own motion, even if their national procedural law does not provide for this, and that this should be done if it is necessary to ensure effective application of Community law (see further Chapter 9).

Further reading

U Everling, 'Will Europe slip on bananas? The bananas judgment of the ECJ and the national courts' [1996] CMLRev 401.

S Peers, 'Taking supremacy seriously' 23 ELRev 146.

W van Gerven, 'Bridging the gap between Community and national laws', [1995] 32 CMLRev 679–702.

Caranta, 'Judicial protection against member states', [1995] 32 CMLRev 703–726.

K Bradley, 'The sovereignty of parliament?', in Jowell and Oliver (eds), *The Changing Constitution*, (4th edn) 2000, OUP, pp 23–58

H Schermers, 'The scales in balance: National Constitutional Court v Court of Justice', [1990] 27 CMLRev 97.

M Herdegen, 'Maastricht and the German Constitutional Court: constitutional restraints for an ever closer Union', [1994] 31 CMLRev 235.

Bruno de Witte, 'Direct effect, supremacy, and the nature of the legal order' in Craig & de Bùrca (eds), *The Evolution of EU Law* (1999) OUP, pp 177–213.

Self-test questions

1. What is meant by the statement that the Community constitutes a new legal order? In what way does it differ from the English legal order?

2. How was the doctrine of supremacy developed by the ECJ?

3. The national courts of member states vary in their recognition of the primacy of Community law over national law. In Germany, the Federal Constitutional Court has changed its position from opposition to support of the Community. In France, on the other hand, the Conseil d' Etat, the highest administrative court, still has difficulties in accepting primacy unreservedly. Discuss.

4. 'There are now few remaining obstacles to the acceptance by national courts of the primacy and direct effect of the Community law.' Discuss, and consider by what means the remaining obstacles could best be removed.

CHAPTER NINE

Remedies in Community Law

SUMMARY

- **Remedies for breach of Community law can be obtained primarily through national courts**

- **The Community has not harmonised remedies or procedural rules, but has over the years built up a body of case law setting out general principles which guide national courts on the approach to the kind of remedies which should be available for breach of Community law**

- **The most important principles are:**
  - **(a) that an *effective* remedy must be available,**
  - **(b) it must be neither *impossible* nor *too difficult* to obtain in practice, and**
  - **(c) it must at least be *comparable* to those available for breach of national law**

- **The relationship between Community and national procedural rules remains problematic, but recent cases have achieved some clarification**

- **Serious breaches of Community law by member states may give rise to liability to the individual who has suffered loss: the creation of a uniform Community remedy**

- **The remedies which must be available include awards of damages and interim relief (injunctions)**

Introduction

9.1 Most of the rules of the EC are enforced through national legal systems. Although the ECJ has made clear that the provisions of Community law, and especially those which have direct effect, must take primacy over national law and that national rules which prevent the effective implementation of Community law must be disapplied, the principle of the autonomy of national procedural rules has been maintained. It can be said that:

> ... an assumption was made by the authors of the EC Treaty that national legal systems based on the rule of law could be relied upon to provide an adequate level of judicial protection; it was therefore sufficient to allow Community law to be enforced by national remedies through national courts in accordance with national procedural rules. (Jacobs *Enforcing Community Rights and Obligations: Striking the Balance in Remedies for Breach of EC Law*)

Harmonisation of remedies and procedures is probably not possible because of the variety of approaches in different jurisdictions, and because procedural rules and remedies are part of a coherent whole legal system with different philosophies, histories and court systems. The consequence of this has been that the enforcement of Community law has been uneven and partial from one member state to another. It has therefore been left to the ECJ to strike the balance between the autonomy of the member states in this area and the need to ensure proper application of Community law.

9.2 Initially, therefore, and until the 1980s the ECJ contented itself with laying down guidelines for national courts to follow when they were considering what would constitute a suitable remedy for breach of EC rules. Drawing on Article 5 (now Article 10 EC) the Court has obliged national courts to take into account two principles or guidelines laid down by the ECJ to ensure the proper application of EC law. These guidelines are contained in two cases:

- Case 33/76 *Rewe-Zentralfinanz v Landwirtschaftskammer* (1976);

- Case 45/76 *Comet BV v Produktschap voor Siergewassen* (1976).

In *Comet* the Court stated:

> It is for the domestic law of each member state to designate the courts having jurisdiction and the procedural conditions governing actions at law intended to ensure the protection of the rights which subjects derive from the direct effects of Community law, it being understood that such conditions cannot be less favourable than those

relating to similar actions of a domestic nature... (non-discrimination principle)

The position would be different only if these rules made it impossible in practice to exercise rights which the national courts have a duty to protect.

In *Rewe* the Court said:

> Although the Treaty has made it possible ... for private persons to bring a direct action (before national courts based on EC law), it was not intended to create new remedies in the national courts to ensure the observance of Community law ... On the other hand ... it must be possible for every kind of action provided for by national law to be available for the purpose of ensuring observance of Community provisions having direct effect, on the same conditions as would apply were it a question of observing national law.

Thus, to sum up, as long as national law provided a remedy similar to that provided for breach of a similar national rule, and did not make it impossible in practice to exercise Community law rights, ie complied with the principles of equivalence and non-discrimination, EC law was satisfied.

9.3 This was illustrated by Case 199/82 *Amministrazione delle Finanze dello Stato v San Giorgio* (1984). Fixed charges on cattle health inspections had been declared unconstitutional by the Italian court. On the basis of that order, San Giorgio brought an action to recover the charges paid and a reference was made to the ECJ. The Court referred to its judgment in Case 68/79 *Hans Just v Danish Ministry for Fiscal Affairs* (1980) where it had ruled that it was for the member states to ensure that repayment of charges in accordance with the rules of their internal law was not subject to less favourable conditions than those in domestic law and must not make it impossible in practice to exercise the rights conferred by the Community legal system. In *San Giorgio* the Court said that Community law did not prevent a national legal system from disallowing the repayment of charges which have been unduly levied where to do so would entail unjust enrichment of the recipients. National law could, therefore, take account of the fact that such charges had been passed on to others by incorporating them in the price of the goods. However, any requirement of proof which had the effect of making it virtually impossible or excessively difficult to secure the repayment of the charges would be contrary to Community law and this was so particularly in the case of presumptions or rules of evidence intended to place upon the taxpayer the burden of establishing that the charges unduly paid had not been passed on to other persons or special limitations as to the form of evidence to be adduced such as the exclusion of any kind of evidence other than documentary evidence. The Court's answer to the Italian court's question was that a member state cannot make repayment of national charges levied contrary to the requirements of Community law conditional upon the production of proof that those charges have not been passed on to other persons if the repayment is subject to rules of evidence which render the exercise of that right virtually impossible, even where the repayment of other charges levied in breach of national law was subject to the same restrictive conditions. *San Giorgio* reinforced the principle that national law must not make the remedy for breach of EC law extremely difficult. In fact, therefore, under *San Giorgio* there could be a better remedy for breach of Community law than for breach of national law. The question of how *effective* the remedy was, or the question of what was to happen when national law provided no remedy, remained unclear for some time.

The principle of effective remedies

9.4 In Case 14/83 *Von Colson v Land Nordrhein-Westfalen* (1984) two German nationals claimed that the provisions of German law implementing Directive 76/207 (the Equal Treatment Directive) were inadequate to ensure that their EC rights were protected. The German law only enabled those wronged by breach of the rights contained in the Directive to recover the actual amount lost. The case is significant because the court pronounced on the nature of the remedy that the national court must provide and ruled that sanctions must be *effective, adequate and act as a deterrent and must be such as to guarantee real and effective protection*. This started a new stage in the development of remedies. *Von Colson* drew on Article 5 (now Article 10 EC): the duty of the member states to take all appropriate measures to ensure the fulfilment of obligations arising under the treaty, *and* to facilitate the achievement of the Community's tasks. It should also be noted that here, as throughout the whole corpus of EC law, the principle of proportionality applies and lies at the heart of the *Von Colson* judgment, ie the means chosen to provide the remedy must be appropriate to the infringement and it must be adequate, *and* act as a deterrent.

9.5 In Case 222/84 *Johnston v Royal Ulster Constabulary* (1986) the Court enlarged upon the general principle of effective judicial protection. In that case the RUC had submitted a ministerial certificate stating that national security required that the issue of arming women police officers in Northern Ireland was one that the Court could not consider. Article 6 of the Equal Treatment Directive (76/207) required that those who consider themselves wronged within the scope of the Directive, must be able 'to pursue their claims by judicial process'. There was no previous indication what 'judicial process' meant and it was assumed that it meant being able to bring the matter before a court. However the ECJ laid down that EC law required that the principle of *effective judicial protection*, first raised in *Von Colson*, meant that the member state must take measures which are sufficiently effective to achieve the aims of the Directive. This principle precluded a minister from relying totally on the certificate, because it would disable the plaintiff from having her case properly considered.

9.6 In the light of *Von Colson* and *Johnston* it could now be said that the concept of effective judicial protection includes a proper hearing and an effective remedy for the applicant and is an aspect of the general effectiveness principle laid down in *Simmenthal* and reinforced in *Factortame* (see Chapter 8). The general effectiveness principle referred to in those cases means that national courts are required to disapply any national measures which would prevent the effective application of Community law.

9.7 Effectiveness was taken a stage further in Case C-271/91 *Marshall v Southampton and South West Hampshire Area Health Authority (No 2)* (1993) where the Court was considering Article 6 of Directive 76/207 again. The Court held that Article 6 was directly effective *and* that the requirement of effective judicial protection meant that the plaintiff who has suffered loss as the result of a breach of EC law (in this case because there was an upper limit for compensation under the Employment Protection Act 1975) must receive full compensation for her loss. Where damages are chosen as the main remedy by the member state, all the financial loss including interest on the award between the date of the breach and the judgment must be made good; the Court said that this was prevented by the application of the upper limit.

Thus the rule laid down in *Rewe* and *Comet* (see **9.2**) that the remedy must be comparable to remedies for breach of national law, ie non-discriminatory, and possible in practice to be relied upon, has been extended. If no remedy or an inadequate remedy exists in national law, it inevitably follows (although the Court did not actually say this), that the national system would have to improve on the one that was available or invent a new one.

9.8 In later cases, such as Case C-338/91 *Steenhorst-Neerings* (see further 7.9 and 19.24) and Case C-66/95 *R v Secretary of State for Social Security, ex p Eunice Sutton* (1997) the Court showed a greater amount of caution in deciding what constitutes an effective remedy. In *Steenhorst-Neerings*, it considered the retroactive limitation of a benefit to be compatible with Community law; in *Eunice Sutton* non-payment of interest on a claim for social security benefit was contrasted with *Marshall II* and distinguished from the finding there on the basis that such benefits did not constitute compensation for loss as suffered in *Marshall*.

The principle of equivalence

9.9 The principle of equivalence, ie that rules for protecting Community rights must not be less favourable than those governing domestic actions, established in *Rewe* and *Comet* has been explained more fully recently, especially in Case C-261/95 *Palmisani v INPS* (1997) [annotated by Odman in 35 CMLRev 1395] and Case C-326/96 *Levez v Jennings (Harlow Pools) Ltd* (1998). Both cases involved the existence of time limits in national law. The ECJ in *Palmisani* explained that to establish that there is no discrimination between domestic and EC remedies in particular cases, it must be shown that the claims must be similar, the procedural rules on which the comparison is based must not be considered in isolation, but in their procedural context, and those procedures must not be chosen at random but must be of a similar kind.

In *Levez* the Court (at para 41) stated that the principle of equivalence requires that the rule at issue be applied without distinction, whether the infringement alleged is of Community law or national law, where the purpose and cause of action are similar. Here the evidence showed that other discrimination claims in UK law were not subject to the same limitation.

In Case C-78/98 *Preston v Wolverhampton Healthcare NHS Trust* (2000), when asked by the House of Lords to provide further explanation, the Court emphasised that the equivalence of national procedural rules should be ascertained by an objective and abstract assessment, taking into account the role, operation and any special features of those rules.

At this point in the developing case law it is clear that national remedies and national procedure available for enforcing or protecting Community rights must comply with the principles of equivalence and effectiveness. It will be seen that the latter principle is often less important than the former.

Procedure

9.10 As with remedies, Community law has adhered to what has been called the principle of procedural autonomy. This means that the procedure followed by national systems for the enforcement of EC law was a matter for each national legal system subject to the principles in *Rewe* and *Comet* (above). It is for the domestic system of each member state to designate the courts having jurisdiction and to determine the procedural conditions for the recovery of damages, *provided that any conditions may not be so framed as to render the recovery of damages impossible in practice or excessively difficult*. However, the implication of this is that national procedural rules can still make a remedy difficult to obtain. For example, in many cases time limits are short, whether the matter is one of purely national law or of EC law, and can lead to making the right in effect impossible to achieve. This is what occurred in *Rewe* and *Comet*. Guidelines in those cases tried to find a balance in demarcating the extent of national autonomy in matters of procedure and the effective enforcement of Community law. In Case C-208/90 *Emmott v Minister for Social Welfare* (1991) the three-month limitation to bring an application for judicial review had led the ECJ to rule that, while reasonable time limits satisfied the principle of procedural autonomy, 'account must nevertheless be taken of the particular nature of directives'. The consequence could be that for wrongly transposed directives, time cannot begin to run until the directive is properly transposed. This has given rise to many criticisms, especially as the *Francovich* principle may expose the state to massive claims. A number of subsequent similar cases have distinguished *Emmott* and it may now be said that the *Emmott* principle will only be applied when the state is seriously in default in failing to implement a directive and obstructing the plaintiff from relying on it. The issue now appears to have been settled by Case C-188/95 *Fantask* (see **7.9**). Time limits appear to be acceptable to the ECJ provided that the principle of equivalence is upheld and despite the fact that they may threaten the effectiveness of the protection offered by EC law. But many other procedural rules can prevent or inhibit the application of EC law and can also threaten the principle of effectiveness. The following cases illustrate this.

9.11 In Cases C-430, 431/93 *Van Schijndel and Van Veen v Stichting Pensioenfonds voor Fysiotherapeuten* (1996) and Case C-312/93 *Peterbroeck, Van Campenhout SCS & Cie v Belgian State* (1996) a more fundamental change to the general principle of procedural autonomy occurred. The issues here involved national courts whose procedural rules disabled

Community law points from being argued when the parties had not argued EC law themselves. In most legal systems, it is the parties themselves who decide which facts and law will be presented to the court, leaving the judge to decide the outcome on the facts and law as presented. But in order to secure the effective implementation of Community law, must the national judge raise EC law of his own motion, despite the principles of procedural autonomy, the passivity of the judge, and even where national law precluded the judge from taking the initiative?

9.12 In *Van Schijndel*, the applicant challenged a national law imposing compulsory membership of an occupational pension scheme. It lost at first instance where its arguments were based solely on national law, but then appealed to the *Hoge Raad*, the Dutch Supreme Civil Court, raising Community law points, on the grounds that the Appeal Court should have considered 'if necessary of its own motion' the question of the compatibility of compulsory Fund membership with EC law, eg, Articles 3(f), 5, 52–58, 59–66, 85, 86 and/or 90 (now Articles 3(1)(f), 10, 43–48, 49–55, 81, 82 and/or 86 EC). This would mean raising new points and procedural rules in the Netherlands provided that parties could only raise new points of law and then only if they did not involve new considerations of fact. The plaintiffs were not able to comply with this rule as raising EC law meant a new investigation of fact. The *Hoge Raad* referred questions to the ECJ as to whether the relevant Dutch procedural rules were compatible with Community law and whether the national court is required to raise points of EC law of its own motion, even where the parties to the proceedings had not relied upon them. In Dutch law there is a limited right for the judge to do this.

This raised the fundamental question of whether the procedural rule under consideration made it excessively difficult or even impossible to rely on Community law, something which is prohibited. The ECJ held that while Community law does not *require* national courts to abandon the passive role generally assigned to them, nor were national judges required to go beyond the ambit of the dispute defined by the parties, these being fundamental principles of the legal systems of most member states, none the less, in considering the compatibility with Community law of national procedural rules, the national court should consider the role and purpose of the provision in question in the legal system. This can be described as permitting a purposive approach to the rule in question.

9.13 In *Peterbroeck*, compatibility of Belgian (tax) law with EC law was considered. Here the claimant only raised the EC law point at the Court of Appeal level (after its claim had been rejected by the Regional Director of taxes) and this new point of law was *time barred* under the relevant national law (60 days from the certified decision of the tax director). The question here was whether EC law must be interpreted as meaning that a national court hearing a dispute concerning Community law must set aside a provision of national law (here time limits) which it considers makes the power of a national court to apply Community law, which it is bound to safeguard, subject to the making of an express application by the plaintiff *within a short time limit*, which is not always applied to national law.

9.14 Both cases were really concerned with, inter alia, the question of whether a national rule which presumptively precluded a national court from considering EC law of its own motion was itself compatible with EC law. Again drawing on Article 5 (now Article 10 EC) and the principle of co-operation the ECJ ruled:

> Each case which raises the question whether a national procedural provision renders application of Community law impossible or excessively difficult must be analysed by reference to the role of that provision in the procedure, its progress and its special features, viewed as a whole, before the various national instances. In the light of that analysis the basic principles of the domestic judicial system, such as protection of the rights of the defence, the principle of legal certainty and the proper conduct of procedure, must, where appropriate, be taken into consideration. (*Peterbroeck* at paras 12–14.)

In *Peterbroeck* the Court held that the Belgian rule had to be disapplied because it made the application of EC law *impossible*. Therefore, pursuant to the obligation of co-operation under Article 5 (now Article 10 EC), and the principles of non-discrimination and equality and *effectiveness*, a national court must, if necessary, apply directly effective Community law *of its own motion if necessary* provided national law permits or obliges the court to do this for national rules. Thus if a rule of national law prevented the application of Community law, then this must be set aside (para 18).

However, in *Van Schijndel* the Court, while reaffirming this principle, took the view that in this case the raising of the new EC point would force the national court to give up its passive role and go beyond what the parties had decided was the dispute, the Belgian rule so disenabled the party from raising the EC point (due to the short time scale) that the rule that made it impossible for the national court to raise the EC point of its own motion could not be justified.

9.15 These cases seem difficult to reconcile. Jacobs AG (whose views had not been followed in *Peterbroeck* but had been followed in *Van Schijndel*) writes:

> The Court was perhaps influenced by the fact that in *Peterbroeck* the Belgian rule was rather restrictive by comparison with equivalent rules in other member states and should be thought of as a 'hard case' and rather exceptional.

What do these cases tell us in relation to the autonomy of procedure principle? The two cases do not seem substantially different but it may be that in a case where the national court would really have to abandon its passive role in relation to the parties, too many important justifications for passivity would have to be jettisoned. On the other hand, where the national rule did not have the same scope, but it would nevertheless make the exercise of Community rights impossible, procedural autonomy must give way to supremacy of EC law. Thus 'in order to determine whether a given national rule renders the exercise of a Community right excessively difficult, the reasons for the application of that general rule in the context of the case should be examined to see whether it is justified. Thus the question of excessive restrictiveness would seem to depend on the precise details and circumstances of the individual case'.

This complicates the role of the national court and makes prediction difficult because each time the national court will be involved in applying a type of proportionality test whereby the rule in question will have to be analysed in order to ascertain its objective, and whether the means adopted can be justified by some fundamental principle of the domestic legal system. The test is vague and can result in an easy justification for any rule. It may be that this shows that a balance is being struck between procedural autonomy and the principle of effectiveness.

9.16 The following cases seem to show a confirmation of the court's concern to strike such a balance:

Case C-126/97 *Eco Swiss China Time v Benetton International* (1999); the Court held that if a national court was required by its domestic rules of procedure to grant an application for the annulment of an arbitration award as national rules of public policy had not been observed, it was also obliged to grant such annulment if there had been failure to comply with the prohibition under Article 85(1). The national rules were subject to strict limits of public policy Although the Court acknowledged that such strict national limits were necessary in order to safeguard the effectiveness of arbitration proceedings, it was in the interest of uniform interpretation of Community law that an application based on Community law should be granted, as the arbitration body, according to the Court's own case law, was not a court or tribunal within the meaning of Article 177 (now Article 234 EC), and therefore could not make a preliminary reference itself.

In Case C-302/97 *Konle v Austria* (1999) the Court ruled that any public body which is responsible for causing a breach should make reparation. There is no need in a federal state like Austria to make changes in the distribution of powers of such bodies, but simply to ensure that national procedural rules do not make it more difficult to protect the rights of individuals derived from the Community legal system.

Conclusion

9.17 It is still for the national court to decide the remedy and to follow its own procedures, but clearer guidance now exists on what that remedy should be as well as the validity of national procedure. The principle of effectiveness is paramount. What 'effectiveness' amounts to will vary from case to case, but it must be appropriate (this may be the same as proportionate), adequate (ie compensate the victim for actual loss) and readily available, ie in practice not excessively difficult. If it is excessively difficult because of procedural rules (as in *Peterbroeck* and in *Eco Swiss China Time*) then the national court is required to raise EC law of its own motion so as to ensure the effective application of EC law. Nevertheless, each case must be considered within its own context and the context includes the procedural rule in question (see above *Peterbroeck* at paras 12–14, set out in **9.14**).

The creation of a uniform Community remedy

9.18 One of the difficulties which those seeking to rely on Community rights may face is that Community law itself inhibits the possibility of a remedy, for example, where as a consequence of the doctrine of horizontal direct effect (see Chapter 7) the plaintiff cannot enforce a Community right against a private party and hence the wronged plaintiff can get no remedy at all. But usually this occurs because of the failure of the member state to implement the Directive. Until Case C-6 & 9/90

Francovich and Bonifaci v Italy (1991), as has been seen, the ECJ had left remedies in the hands of national legal systems, but since that case the Court has departed from this position and laid down a new Community rule of state liability. In *Francovich* Italy had failed to implement Directive 80/987 on the protection of employees in the event of the insolvency of their employer. Although the Directive was held not to be directly effective, the Court held that the protection of Community rights would be weakened if individuals were unable to obtain any effective remedy when their rights were infringed by a breach of Community law for which a member state can be held responsible. The Court, again drawing on Article 5 (now Article 10) of the EC Treaty, ie the obligation of the member state to ensure fulfilment of the obligations arising out of the Treaty, introduced the principle of state liability to the individual, stating that this, a right to a Community remedy, not a national remedy, derives from the Treaty and is inherent in its system. Provided that the plaintiff could show that the right being relied upon was one which could be identified from the Community measure and that a causal link existed between the state's breach of its obligation and the harm suffered by the individual, the state would be liable in damages even if the measure was not directly effective. Thus a successful plaintiff must in principle be able to recover his loss from the state.

9.19 The principle of state liability is known in most of the member states which have a civil law system and this was, therefore, not considered to be as major a development by most states as it was by the common law members of the Community.

Although very important, the case left open a number of questions, principally as to the conditions under which liability would arise.

Conditions for liability

9.20 In the long running Cases C-46/93 and C-48/93 *Brasserie du Pêcheur v Germany*, and *R v Secretary of State for Transport, ex p Factortame (Factortame 3)* (1996) answers to these questions were given by the Court. In those cases Germany and the UK had respectively been in breach of the Treaty by enacting laws which breached Treaty provisions. The ECJ ruled that liability would not arise for all breaches; but in those cases where the breach was sufficiently serious in that the state had manifestly and gravely disregarded the limits of its discretion, liability would arise. Where there was no discretion (as in *Francovich*) and the state had simply failed in its obligation under Article 189 (now Article 249 EC), for example to implement a directive, then, provided that the other *Francovich* conditions were present, that is identifiable individual rights and a causal link, liability would arise. But when the breach occurred in cases where the state had had a wide discretion to make legislative choices, the right to reparation depended not only upon the breach having been sufficiently serious but on a number of other factors. The factors to be considered, with respect to the definition of a serious breach, include: (a) the clarity and precision of the rule breached; (b) the measure of discretion left to the national authorities; (c) the question whether the infringement and damage caused was intentional or involuntary; (d) whether any error of law was excusable; and (e) whether the position of the Community institutions may have contributed towards the member state's breach of Community law.

A breach of Community law will be sufficiently serious if it has persisted despite a judgment that has established the infringement, or a preliminary ruling or settled case law of the Court has made it clear that the conduct constituted an infringement. What was not relevant was whether the measure in question creates direct effect, or whether an Article 169 or 170 (now Articles 226 and 227 EC) action had established the breach.

Case C-140/97 *Rechberger v Austria* (1999) concerned incorrect implementation of the Package Travel Directive 90/314 EEC in two points. Only trips with a departure date of 1 May 1995 or later were protected by the directive and instead of providing for full refunds and repatriation costs in the case of insolvency of the travel company, Austria had only provided for insurance cover or bank guarantee. Austria had acceded to the Union on 1 January 1995, and had no discretion in the duty of full implementation. Such incorrect implementation constituted a sufficiently serious breach. Austria's argument was that there was no direct causal link, only the result of a chain of 'wholly exceptional and unforeseeable events'. The Court answered that even such events would not have presented an obstacle to the refund of money or the repatriation of travellers if the directive had been correctly implemented and found, therefore, that there was a causal link.

The question of damages in relation to state liability under Francovich

9.21 When the Court finds that there has been a serious breach as discussed above, and that the measure in question (whether a Directive or Regulation or Treaty article) creates identifiable rights for the individual seeking to rely on it, and that there is a causal link, the national court must provide a remedy. Where the *right* to damages exists, then it is national law which will determine the nature and extent of damages. The right to full compensation had already been established in *Marshall (No 2)*; exemplary damages for unconstitutional or oppressive conduct must also be available where this is provided for in national law and the total exclusion of profit in the context of economic and commercial litigation is not acceptable, as this would make reparation practically impossible in these circumstances. The ECJ has in effect harmonised the conditions for State liability with that of the conditions for liability of the Community institutions under Article 215 (now Article 288 EC).

The application of state liability

9.22 There have been other cases where the breach has consisted of either non-implementation of Directives (as in *Francovich*) or improper implementation of them (*BT* case below) or improper application of them (*Hedley Lomas* see below). The Court has, in applying the principles laid down in *Francovich* and the *Factortame* and *Brasserie du Pêcheur* cases, provided additional qualifications. For example where the state had a wide discretion as in Case C-392/93 *R v HM Treasury, ex p British Telecommunications plc* (1996) where the issue was concerned with incorrect implementation of a directive. It was claimed that the member state could determine which services were to be excluded from its scope, but the UK had chosen (wrongly as it turned out) to exclude certain services from the operation of the directive. This was held to be improper implementation. The important question was whether the UK had to pay compensation to the injured party. It was urged that a distinction ought to be drawn between non-implementation as in *Francovich* and improper implementation as here. The Court refused to draw this distinction, but reiterated that the only question was whether the breach was sufficiently serious – ie had there been a manifest and grave disregard on the limits on the exercise of its powers. In the instant case the Court found that no such breach had occurred because the wording of Article 8(1) of the directive was imprecise and ambiguous and the construction placed on it by the UK was not manifestly incorrect; furthermore no guidance from the Court existed and the Commission had not raised the matter with the UK when that country had implemented the directive in question. This appears to imply that an element of fault has to be present in order for liability to be established.

9.23 On the other hand in Case C-5/94 *R v Ministry of Agriculture, Fisheries and Food, ex p Hedley Lomas (Ireland) Ltd* (1996) the issue of non-compliance with the requirements of Directive 74/577 led to the plaintiff suing the UK government for loss of profit they had suffered. Hedley Lomas were exporters of live animals destined for slaughter in Spain; the UK government had systematically refused to grant export licences for this purpose on the grounds that the Spanish slaughterhouses did not observe the provisions of the relevant directive. In the action brought by Hedley Lomas claiming damages for their loss during the period of the ban, the Court declared that the export ban was a quantitative restriction on exports within the meaning of Article 34 (now Article 29 EC), and was not covered by Article 36 (now Article 30 EC). The lack of monitoring of slaughterhouses could not excuse the UK from non-compliance with the law:

> In this regard the member states must rely on trust in each other to carry out inspections in their respective territories.

Where the state has completely failed to implement a directive, that will constitute a serious breach per se. In Cases C-178, 179, 189 and 190/94 *Dillenkofer v Germany* (1996) the Court stated that if the member state fails to take any measures to achieve the objectives of the directive, that member state has manifestly and gravely disregarded the limits of its discretion. That gives rise to a right of reparation on the part of the individual, provided that the rights can be identified and a causal link exists as required by *Francovich*.

9.24 In Case C-352/98P *Laboratoires Pharmaceutiques Bergaderm and Goupil v Commission* (2000) the Court said that the concept of a 'sufficiently serious breach' of Community law by an institution must be interpreted in the same way with regard to an institution as it is for a member state. This concerned an action by a pharmaceutical company and its chief executive, seeking compensation for damage allegedly suffered as a result of the preparation and the adoption of a Commission directive relating to cosmetic products. The Court dismissed the appeal against the judgment of the CFI and recalled the principle laid down in Joined Cases C-46/93 and C-48/93 *Brasserie du Pecheur and Factortame* (1996) that the conditions under which the member states may incur liability for damage caused to individuals by a breach of Community law cannot, in the absence of particular justification, differ from those governing the liability of the Community in like circumstances. The protection of the rights which individuals derive from Community law cannot vary depending on whether a national authority or a Community authority is responsible for the damage. As regards non-contractual liability of the

Community as well as that of the member states, the decisive test for finding that a breach of Community law is sufficiently serious is whether the member state or the Community institution concerned manifestly and gravely disregarded the limits on its discretion. Where the member state or the institution has only considerably reduced, or even no, discretion, the mere infringement of Community law may be sufficient to establish the existence of a sufficiently serious breach. Moreover, the general or individual nature of a measure taken by an institution is not a decisive criterion for identifying the limits of such discretion.

9.25 In Case C-424/97 *Haim* (2000), the question as to discretion was also raised. Mr Haim, a dentist, brought an action to obtain compensation for the loss of earnings which he claimed to have suffered as a result of the refusal of an association of dental practitioners, a public body, to register him, in breach of Community law. The Court was asked whether, where a national official had no discretion in applying national law conflicting with or in a manner not conform with Community law the mere fact that he did not have any discretion in taking his decision gives rise to a serious breach of Community law. The Court replied that the existence and scope of the discretion which should be taken into account when establishing whether or not a member state has committed a sufficiently serious breach of Community law must be determined by reference to Community law and not by reference to national law. The question of discretion was, therefore, not relevant. Liability for reparation for loss and damage caused by non-compliance with Community law lies with any public body which caused the damage.

Application of these principles in the UK

9.26 In the national law of some member states, however, state liability for an unlawful act is limited and difficult to establish, and the absence of any judicial remedy is in principle manifestly a breach of the principle of effective protection of EC law. This has created a particular problem for the UK. In the UK the right to damages is a private law action and it is not enough to prove a breach by the defendant of his Community law rights. Damages will only be available if the defendant's action constitutes a tort, a breach of contract or a breach of a statutory right entitling him to damages. This approach does not fulfil British Community obligations.

To meet the problem involving enforcement of Community law in the UK, Lord Denning had, years ago, suggested that we needed a new tort which he suggested should be called 'Breach of Community law', but this was not pursued at the time, and it remained problematic as to how the UK was to meet its obligations to provide an effective judicial remedy for breach of EC law when no cause of action existed in English law. This is especially true in the case of public authorities, who are given considerable latitude by statute and case law as to how they carry out their obligations. The normal action against a public authority is an application for judicial review, and liability of the Crown when exercising its sovereign powers is not possible unless a tort can be proved. In *Bourgoin SA v Ministry of Agriculture, Fisheries and Food* (1986) the Court of Appeal had to face this problem when a French exporter of turkeys who had been excluded from the UK market by an (unlawful) statutory instrument sought compensation for their loss of trade during the period of the ban. As explained above, in English law it is not possible to obtain damages against the Crown unless it could be shown that some tort had been committed. It was suggested there that the tort of misfeasance in public office might be available (as, in an earlier case, the tort of breach of a statutory duty was suggested), but the Crown settled the case and left the matter undecided. In the (perhaps) final stage of the *Factortame* litigation, the House of Lords accepted that there had been a serious breach of Community law by the UK but rejected the tort of misfeasance in public office, at least for this case, and instead ruled that this had been the tort of breach of statutory duty. This had already been promoted in an earlier case, *Garden Cottage Foods Ltd v Milk Marketing Board* (1982), this despite the fact that in non-EC cases this tort has been applied inconsistently by the court. However, it may be that for breach of Community law when based on the *Factortame* criteria, it will be the normal right of action in the UK in actions against public bodies including the Crown.

Interim measures as a remedy

9.27 These are important because the validity of EC law (and sometimes national law) has to be decided by the ECJ and the time lag requires that rights be preserved pending the decision. In Case C-213/89 *R v Secretary of State for Transport, ex p Factortame* (1990) for example, the plaintiff sought an injunction to have the operation of s 14 of the Merchant Shipping Act 1988 disapplied pending the final determination of the legality of that provision by the ECJ. An injunction is a temporary order of the court to maintain a current state of affairs or to prevent the other party doing something which would prejudice the outcome of the case.

The application of the effectiveness principle might require an interim measure to be available to the party seeking to rely on EC law. It is for national courts to uphold rights guaranteed by Community law; thus in the UK, where an injunction could not be granted against the Crown, the court ruled that such a national legal rule must be set aside. The law now is that the national courts are required to grant injunctive relief according to criteria established for national law but taking into account the need to protect Community law rights. Thus the urgency of the matter, the balance of probabilities of success, and the impact on the outcome are the major factors, ie whether there is a substantial risk of irreparable harm if the injunction is not granted.

9.28 When, however, the issue depends either on the validity of a national measure based on the Community regulation, or the validity of the Community measure itself, a different approach to the grant of interim relief has been followed (Cases C-143/88 and C-92/89 *Zuckerfabrik Süderditmarschen AG* (1991)). Here the stress has been on upholding the validity of the Community measure; it is presumed to be valid so long as a competent court has not made a finding of invalidity. Serious doubt as to validity must exist, the national court must make a reference to the ECJ and pending that the suspension of enforcement must retain the character of an interim measure. All national courts must take a uniform approach to this because otherwise the uniform application of Community law would be jeopardised. In Joined Cases C-465/93 and C-466/93 *Atlanta Fruchthandelsgesellschaft mbH v Bundesamt für Ernährung und Forstwirtschaft* (1995) an application for positive interim relief was requested; the applicants wanted the supply of bananas to be continued pending a challenge to the Community measure concerned. The Court upheld its approach in Joined Cases C-143/88 and C-92/89 *Zuckerfabrik Süderdithmarschen and Zuckerfabrik Soest v Hauptzollamt Itzehoe and Hauptzollamt Aachen* (1991) stating that the:

> ... interim protection which national courts must afford to individuals must be the same, whether they seek suspension or enforcement of national administrative measures adopted on the basis of a Community regulation or the grant of interim measures settling or regulating the disputed legal position or relationships for their benefit (at para 28).

The Court also considered the criteria for interim relief in this kind of case. For the urgency test to be satisfied the damage relied upon must materialise before the ECJ can give a ruling on the contested measure, and the national court must take account of the damage which will be caused to the legal regime which the contested measure establishes, including the cumulative effect if other courts adopted similar measures. In particular the national court must respect the balance struck by the ECJ between the Community interest and the interest of the economic sector concerned.

Further reading

T Tridimas, 'Liability for breach of Community law: growing up and mellowing down?' [2001] 38 CMLRev 301.

A Biondi, 'The European Court of Justice and certain national procedural limits: not such a tough relationship', [1999] 36 CMLRev 1271.

Jacobs, 'Enforcing Community rights and obligations', in Lonbay and Biondi (eds), *Remedies for Breach of EC Law* (1997) Wiley.

M Ross, 'Beyond *Francovich*', [1993] 56 MLR 55.

J Steiner, 'From direct effect to *Francovich*', [1993] 18 ELRev 3.

De Burca, 'National procedural rules and remedies', in Lonbay and Biondi (eds), *Remedies for Breach of EC Law* (1997) Wiley.

'Joined Cases C-94 and 95/95, Daniela Bonifaci and Others & Wanda Berto and Others v INPS; Case C-373/95, Federico Maso and Others, Graziana Gazzeta and Others v INPS; and Case C-261/95, Palmisani v INPS', annotation by A Odman [1999] 35 CMLRev 1395.

C Kakouris, 'Do the member states possess judicial procedural 'autonomy'?', [1998] 34 CMLRev 1389.

P Craig, 'Once more unto the breach: the Community, the state and damages liability', [1997] 109 LQR 67.

Self-test questions

1. What principles does the ECJ apply in its assessment of legal remedies?

2. Why was it necessary for the ECJ to develop case law concerning remedies for member state breach of Community law?

3. What were the ECJ's conditions for state liability in *Francovich*? Did the case assist in creating a solution for shortcomings in Community law?

4. What key questions were left unanswered in *Francovich*? Have some answers been found in subsequent cases?

CHAPTER TEN

Enforcement of Community Law by the Institutions

SUMMARY

The efficacy and uniformity of EC law cannot be guaranteed without an effective enforcement mechanism. This chapter examines how the obligation on member states to apply Community law is enforced, first, by the Commission under Article 226 (ex Article 169) EC in its role as guardian of the Treaties and, second, by the member states themselves under Article 227 (ex Article 170) EC. It covers the following:

* the Article 226 procedure
* the administrative stage
* the judicial stage
* consequences of the judicial stage (Article 228 (ex Article 171) EC)
* the Commission's discretion
* Article 227

Article 226 (ex Article 169) EC

Introduction

10.1 Article 226 provides that:

> If the Commission considers that a member state has failed to fulfil an obligation under this Treaty, it shall deliver a reasoned opinion on the matter after giving the State concerned the opportunity to submit its observations.

If the State concerned does not comply with the opinion within the period laid down by the Commission, the latter may bring the matter before the Court of Justice.

The Commission has a duty under Article 211 (ex Article 155) EC to ensure that the provisions of the Treaty are applied. The Article 226 enforcement mechanism is the most significant and wide-ranging of the weapons available to the Commission in ensuring that member states apply Community law. In addition to Article 226, the Treaty grants specific enforcement procedures to the Commission in particular areas of EC law, such as the procedure in Article 88(2) (ex Article 93(2)) EC for supervising breaches of state aid rules. Under Article 237 (ex Article 180) EC, the Board of Directors of the European Central Bank is given equivalent powers to those granted to the Commission under Article 226 in order to ensure that member states comply with their obligations under the Statute of the European Investment Bank. In entrusting the general Article 226 procedure to the Commission, the Treaty places the supervision of breaches of Community law by member states in the hands of a supranational, neutral arbiter and so seeks to secure evenhanded enforcement across the Community. This enforcement power is enthusiastically wielded by the Commission. The Commission issues an annual report on the monitoring of the application of Community law which examines the main infringements committed by member states and provides valuable statistical information on the operation of Article 226 in the relevant year.

10.2 The Article 226 enforcement action is now so widely used that the Commission has stated that Article 226 is not simply a legal device for enforcing EC law, but is also an instrument for achieving policy goals. By choosing to pursue certain breaches of EC law (as we shall see, the Commission has a discretion as to when to take enforcement action), the Commission has significant power to influence the development of EC law and policy. The Commission, may, for example, bring an Article 226 action where there is a genuine difference of opinion between the Commission and the member state as to the interpretation of the relevant Community law obligation in order to clarify the nature of that obligation. It may, of course, also commence proceedings with the specific intention of condemning the member state or delivering a warning about the existence of a violation. A particularly important feature of Article 226, however, is the communication channel it establishes between the Commission and the member states during the pre-litigation phase (see below). The Commission has stressed the importance of establishing co-operation and dialogue with national authorities so that recourse to the full Article 226 procedure, culminating in an action before the Court of Justice, can be avoided. To that end, Commission officials regularly visit member state authorities in order to encourage co-operation and communication on the application of EC law and resolve possible infringements. During these so-called 'package meetings' Commission officials will consider a set of possible infringements and attempt to achieve a non-contentious solution. The Commission views these bilateral meetings as equal in importance to the formal Article 226 enforcement procedure in dealing with infringements of Community law (*Twelfth Annual Report* on Commission Monitoring and Application of Community Law [1995] OJ C254/1) and, indeed, in 1996 the Commission reported that of the 172 infringements discussed at these package meetings, resolution was achieved in 73 cases (*Fourteenth Annual Report* [1997] OJ C322/1). The communication between the Commission and the member state during the pre-litigation phase of Article 226 procedure can serve as a very effective form of alternative dispute resolution. Ultimately, Article 226 operates at the controversial interface between member states' Community obligations and independent supranational enforcement. Consequently, the Commission exercises political sensitivity when employing Article 226.

The application of Article 226

10.3 The enforcement mechanism may be triggered when a member state fails to comply with an obligation under the Treaty. The range of actions by a member state that may provoke an enforcement action under Article 226 therefore include violating a Treaty provision, violating Community legislation, breaching agreements concluded by the EC with a third country, or non-compliance with a judgment of the Court of Justice. The illegal action by the member state can be either an act or an omission. Member states will also be liable for state agencies whose conduct is the cause of the Treaty infringement, even where such institutions are constitutionally independent. In Case 77/69 *Commission v Belgium* (1970) the Belgian government was held responsible for the inaction of the Belgian Parliament which, following a dissolution, had not passed draft measures which were designed to revise a Belgian law which violated the Treaty.

10.4 Certain breaches are more prevalent than others. A typical and increasingly popular ground for action by the Commission is breach by the member state of the Article 10 (ex Article 5) EC co-operation obligation. Inadequate implementation of Community law, in particular, is vigorously pursued by the Commission. In a majority of cases, the member state has failed to implement a directive but failure to bring into force the necessary measures to implement fully a regulation, where implementing measures are necessary, will also be pursued, as in Case 128/78 *Commission v United Kingdom (Re Tachographs)* (1979). In an effort to improve the record of member states in the transposition of directives and to avoid enforcement action, the Commission organises meetings in the member states (called directive missions) to consider how the member state is approaching the implementation of directives and to address any potential problems. Member states appear to be improving with respect to the implementation of directives, however. In its *Eighteenth Annual Report* (COM (2001) 309), the Commission reported a sharp improvement in the transposition rate, with member states achieving the highest rate since 1992. The Commission was particularly encouraged by the fact that the transposition rate was up across all the member states.

10.5 Alleged violations come to the attention of the Commission either through its own investigations or, more often, through complaints from individuals or undertakings. In its *Eighteenth Annual Report*, for example, the Commission referred to the importance of complaints from the public in detecting infringements. It is a matter of some controversy that individuals and lobbying groups who complain to the Commission, and who are in fact encouraged to do so by the Commission, do not, as discussed below, have standing before the Community courts to challenge a subsequent refusal to act by the Commission, and that complainants are, in general, peripheral to the enforcement procedure. There have been difficulties in the past in managing complainants' expectations of the Article 226 procedure. In its *Fourteenth Annual Report* the Commission noted that the number of complaints made fell by 14% from 955 in 1995 to 819 in 1996. While acknowledging that this downward trend (which had started in 1995) was not easy to explain, the Commission noted that, while it did seek to 'construct a people's Europe whose doors are always open to complainants', the objective of the Article 226 procedure was to bring an erring member state back into line and not to provide individual solutions to individual problems. Indeed, in its *Thirteenth Annual Report* the Commission stressed that the main purpose of the Article 226 procedure was to induce member states to comply with their Community obligations and not to protect individuals. Nevertheless, in an effort to stem this decline the Commission issued a new complaint form, which gives a fuller and clearer explanation of the Article 226 procedure, in order to encourage the making of complaints and to render the process more transparent. This movement by the Commission to improve the position of complainants and encourage the flow of complaints has been sustained. In its *Eighteenth Annual Report*, the Commission noted the status and importance of complaints from the public in the Article 226 procedure and referred to the steps which had been taken to formalise the role of complainants, including the registration of complaints, respect for confidentiality, and the possibility of making views known when a decision had been taken on a particular case. It did emphasise, however, that the primary objective of the infringement procedure was to bring offending member states into line with Community law and, in particular, underlined its discretion as to whether or not to initiate proceedings following a complaint. Notably, the Commission acknowledged that the Article 226 procedure can be frustrating for complainants in that it does not offer complainants specific redress for harm caused to them by the actions of the member state in question. It highlighted, however, the role of national courts in providing individuals with redress for damage caused by member states in breach of Community law. In 2000 the number of complaints registered by the Commission was down slightly by 6% on 1999 (*Eighteenth Annual Report*), although in 1999 the number of complaints registered was up by 16% on 1998 (*Seventeenth Annual Report* ([2001] OJ C30/1). The Commission's official attitude towards the place of complainants in the Article 226 procedure is perhaps best illustrated by its comments in the *Sixteenth Annual Report* ([1999] OJ C354/1) to the effect that while it does not regard complainants as being, strictly speaking, interested parties for the purposes of the Article 226 procedure, it nonetheless attaches great importance to informing them properly of the response to their complaints at all stages of the procedure. This conciliatory approach can also be seen in the Commission's policy of transparency. Since January 2001, the Commission has announced decisions to issue letters of formal notice and reasoned opinions (both documents form part of the pre-litigation procedure discussed below), to refer cases to the Court of Justice, and to terminate proceedings on the official EU Europa website (*Eighteenth Annual Report*). This policy of publicity has also had the effect, the Commission noted, of encouraging erring member states to rectify breaches of Community law more quickly, particularly where there is no real room for dispute as to the nature of the member state's violation.

The degree of access which a complainant may gain to internal Commission deliberations concerning Article 226 proceedings was recently discussed by the Court of First Instance in Case T-309/97 *Bavarian Lager Co Ltd v Commission* (1999). The judgment also contains an important indication that the Commission views the Article 226 procedure not simply as an enforcement tool but also as a mechanism for negotiation and compromise. At issue was the 1994 Code of Conduct Concerning Access to Commission Documents which provides for access to internal Commission documents in certain circumstances. Following a decision by the Commission not to issue a reasoned opinion to the UK in respect of certain restrictions on the sale and supply of imported beer to pubs tied to breweries (the Guest Beer Provisions) which the complainants had claimed were in breach of the Treaty, the complainants sought access to the draft reasoned opinion. The Commission refused access. In its defence, it raised the public interest exception contained in the Code of Conduct on the grounds that revealing the draft reasoned opinion would harm the administration of justice, compromise the treatment of infringements and undermine the climate of mutual confidence required for a full and frank discussion between the Commission and the member state with a view to ensuring compliance by the member state. The Court of First Instance found that the disclosure of documents in the investigation stage of an Article 226 procedure, during negotiations between the Commission and the member states, could undermine the proper conduct of the enforcement procedure in that its purpose of enabling the member state to comply or justify its position could be jeopardised.

Notwithstanding the importance of complaints from the public, the Commission appears increasingly to be emphasising its own internal procedures in detecting infringements. In its *Eighteenth Annual Report* it noted that it was becoming less dependent on what it termed the 'unpredictable aspects' of sourcing violations from the public. In particular, the Asmodée II directives database allows it to systematise pre-litigation letters of formal notice to member states in respect of failures to notify the implementation of directives.

Procedure

10.6 The enforcement procedure as set out in Article 226 is a potentially two-pronged action. The initial administrative or pre-litigation stage involves (after certain preliminary negotiations not provided for by the Treaty) the issue by the Commission of a letter of formal notice (see below) informing the member state of the alleged violation. If resolution does not follow at this point, the Commission will issue a reasoned opinion (see below) which will set a time limit for compliance by the member state. If the matter remains unresolved when the time limit expires, the enforcement procedure may move to the judicial stage where the Commission may refer the matter to the Court of Justice. If the

Commission case is made out (the Commission carries the burden of proof), the Court of Justice may declare that the member state has failed to fulfil its Treaty obligations. In its *Fourteenth Annual Report* for 1996 the Commission noted a 'sharp increase' in the number of formal letters and reasoned opinions sent to member states. The number of formal letters sent increased from 1,044 in 1995 to 1,142 in 1996 while the number of reasoned opinions issued rose from 194 in 1995 to 435 in 1996. The Commission did note that it was more difficult to persuade member states to rectify infringements than in earlier years with the number of referrals to the Court of Justice up from 72 in 1995 to 93 in 1996, a rise which the Commission described in the *Fourteenth Annual Report* as an 'historic record'. Prior to 1994, the trend in the number of referrals made to the Court of Justice had, in fact, been largely downwards but in 1994 the number of referrals made rose from 44 in 1993 to 89 (*Twelfth Annual Report*). By 1998 the position had changed somewhat. In its *Sixteenth Annual Report* for 1998 the Commission reported that the number of reasoned opinions issued had reached an all-time high at 675, up 102% on the figure of 334 for 1997. This sharp increase was due to stricter and quicker action by the Commission in the wake of improvements made to Commission working methods during 1998. In particular, the Commission has recently implemented new procedures to speed up the handling of cases, including increasing the number of infringements considered at its fortnightly meetings on the application of Community law by the member states. Previously, infringements were only considered in four periodic reports produced in March, June, October and December. Unlike the position in 1996, however, the number of formal letters had decreased, down from 1461 in 1997 to 1101 in 1998. This decrease reflected a drop in the number of proceedings for failure to implement directives, although the number of formal letters issued in respect of failures to comply with Community law more generally and incorrect applications of Community law rose from 432 in 1997 to 486 in 1998. Overall, the Commission reported somewhat wearily that compliance in general by the member states with Community law remained 'sadly inconsistent' (*Sixteenth Annual Report*). In its Annual Report for 1999 (*Seventeenth Annual Report*), the position remained steady with respect to letters of formal notice, with only a slight increase in the number issued (up to 1,075). The number of reasoned opinions issued fell, however, by 32%, as a result of the 'special effort' made by the Commission to reduce delays in 1998. The number of referrals to the court remained generally low, although it rose to 178 from 123 in 1997, a statistic which was, according to the Commission, proof of the effectiveness of the pre-litigation procedure. By 2000, the number of formal letters of notice issued had increased sharply, up by 22.5% on 1999 to 1317 (*Eighteenth Annual Report*). This rise was explained by the Commission as a consequence of the considerable efforts it is making to check the conformity of member states' implementation measures with Community law. The number of reasoned opinions issued remained static from 1999 at 460; evidence, the Commission noted, of its attempts to catch up on the delays in the system, while the number of referrals to the court continued to remain low in relation to the numbers of letters of formal notice and reasoned opinions issued at 172.

The administrative stage

10.7 The administrative procedure is characterised by dialogue between the Commission and the member state as resolution of the difficulty is sought – it provides an important channel for communication between member states and the Commission. The Court of Justice stated in Case 85/85 *Commission v Belgium* (1986) that the purpose of the administrative phase is to give the member state an opportunity to justify its position or comply with the Treaty requirements of its own accord. It is only when that process fails that the Commission proceeds to demanding compliance.

10.8 The Treaty provides for two stages in the administrative phase; the issuing of a formal letter and, if there is no resolution, the subsequent delivery of a reasoned opinion. Before initiating the formal administrative procedure, however, the Commission will first advise the member state informally of the alleged breach and request an explanation. Resolution will often arise at this point. If this is not the case, a letter of formal notice which defines the subject matter of the dispute is sent to the member state. This letter, which will request the member state to submit its observations within a period of time, usually two months, allows the member state to prepare its defence. The letter must set out the complaint in general terms, but it is not subject to the strict requirements of precision which apply to the reasoned opinion (see below) as, as the Court of Justice has found, it cannot, by necessity, contain anything other than an initial brief summary of the complaint (Case C-191/95 *Commission v Germany* (1998)). As part of the Commission's drive to improve its working practices in relation to Article 226, it is now enforcing the time limit set out in formal letters for responding to the complaint more rigorously. The Commission has also recently set about, in its own terms, 'dedramatising' the letter of formal notice in order to restore its primary function of seeking observations from the member state in question. In its *Seventeenth Annual Report* it noted that the letter of formal notice must be used for its true purpose and only request information from the member state. It must not express the Commission's legal position. The ability of the member state to respond to the Commission's allegations and submit observations on the complaint as set out in the formal letter is seen as an essential procedural guarantee, adherence to which is an essential formal requirement of the Article 226 procedure.

Reasoned opinion

10.9 If the issue remains unresolved and the Commission considers that the member state has failed to fulfil a Treaty obligation, the Commission may then move to the second stage of the administrative phase and deliver a reasoned opinion. Delivery of the reasoned opinion forms a very important part of the Article 226 procedure and ensures that the member state is formally and fully informed of the nature of the charges laid against it. The reasoned opinion will state why, in law and fact, the Commission believes that the member state has violated its Treaty obligations and must be based on the same complaints as are set out in the letter of formal notice. The reasoned opinion will give the member state a reasonable period of time, again, often two months, within which to remedy the alleged breach, failing which the Commission may refer the matter to the Court of Justice. The reasons for the Commission's action must be set out in the reasoned opinion. In Case 274/83 *Commission v Italy* (1985) the Court of Justice interpreted this requirement as an obligation on the Commission to provide a coherent and detailed statement of the reasons leading the Commission to believe that there has been a breach of a Treaty obligation (see also Case 7/61 *Commission v Italy* (1961)). It appears that the reasoned opinion does not have to counter all the arguments made by the member state in response to the formal letter and, as confirmed by the Court of Justice in Case C-247/89 *Commission v Portugal* (1991), that the reasoned opinion need not set out the steps necessary to remedy the breach. The reasoned opinion also serves to limit the scope of any subsequent judicial proceedings, as the Court of Justice has consistently held that the content of the legal arguments ultimately made by the Commission before the Court of Justice (if the action proceeds to the judicial phase) must be largely the same as the content of the reasoned opinion (Case C-52/90 *Commission v Denmark* (1992) and Case C-217/88 *Commission v Germany* (1990)). As a result, the Commission may not raise complaints in its application before the

Court of Justice which have not been covered in the reasoned opinion. It is clear, however, that although the reasoned opinion and the proceedings must be broadly based on the same complaints as are set out in the letter of formal notice, it is not necessary that in every case they are exactly the same as long as the subject-matter of the proceedings has not been extended or altered, just limited.

Weaknesses in the reasoned opinion may, in certain circumstances, be remedied by the Commission's conduct during the informal procedure. This was the case in Case 23/84 *Commission v United Kingdom* (1986), where certain UK milk pricing rules were at issue. During the informal negotiations, the Commission had highlighted the fact that the compatibility of price differentiation criteria in the milk products market with Community rules could be assessed independently of any effects such criteria had on the functioning of the common organisation of the milk market. Neither the letter of formal notice nor the reasoned opinion had explicitly raised this point. Nevertheless, the Court of Justice allowed such an argument to be made as it had been flagged during the informal stage. The application to the Court of Justice must state the specific grounds for the action. It is not sufficient simply to refer to the reasoned opinion (Case C-347/88 *Commission v Greece* (1990)). It is clear from Case 48/65 *Lütticke v Commission* (1966) that the reasoned opinion cannot be challenged as an act of the Commission under Article 230 (ex Article 173) EC as it is not a binding act. The Court of Justice found in that case that no measure taken by the Commission during the administrative stage has any binding force, and that as a result annulment actions by third parties were, in principle, inadmissible. The member state may, however, challenge the legality of the reasoned opinion at the judicial phase of the Article 226 action.

10.10 The nature and purpose of the reasoned opinion was recently examined by the Court of Justice in Case C-191/95 *Commission v Germany* (1998) in the context of the application of the principle of collegiality and collective responsibility to members of the Commission. Germany challenged the issue of a reasoned opinion to it in respect of its alleged failure to implement correctly certain company law directives concerning the disclosure of annual accounts, on the grounds that the members of the Commission did not have sufficient information made available to them when making the decision to issue the reasoned opinion. The Commissioners had not seen the draft reasoned opinion. The Court confirmed that a decision to issue a reasoned opinion (or to commence judicial proceedings) was subject to collegiality and that, accordingly, the information necessary to reach that decision should be available to each Commissioner, although it was not necessary for the Commission to decide on the exact wording. The Court described the decision to issue a reasoned opinion as neither an administrative nor managerial decision but, as the reasoned opinion formally stated the infringement and concluded the pre-litigation procedure, one which was part of the supervisory function entrusted to the Commission under Article 211 (ex Article 155) EC and which could not be delegated. The Court also noted that the issue of a reasoned opinion was a preliminary procedure without binding legal effect for its addressees and was merely a stage which might lead to judicial proceedings. If settlement was not forthcoming after its issue, the reasoned opinion then served to define the subject matter of the dispute.

10.11 If the member state fails to comply with the reasoned opinion, the Commission may then, using the reasoned opinion as the basis for the action, initiate legal proceedings before the Court of Justice. It is under no obligation to bring an action. It is clear from *Lütticke* that the decision to initiate proceedings is a matter entirely for the Commission's discretion.

10.12 The conduct of the Commission during the administrative phase is subject to review. At the judicial stage, the Court of Justice may examine the Commission's actions during the administrative phase for procedural irregularities and declare the action void for infringement of an essential procedural requirement if the Commission does not comply with the procedural guarantees under Article 226. One essential element of the administrative stage is that the member state be given the opportunity to respond to the allegations. In Case 51/83 *Commission v Italy* (1984), where the Commission took an Article 226 action against an alleged violation by Italy of Article 30 (now Article 28 EC), the Court explained that the opportunity for the member state to submit its observations was an essential guarantee required by the Treaty and an essential formal requirement of the Article 226 procedure. In that case, the reasoned opinion raised issues which had not been covered in the letter of formal notice (the letter of formal notice referred to import restrictions imposed by Italy on sweets containing gelatine, while the reasoned opinion referred to import restrictions on confectionery products, preserved meat and ice-cream containing gelatine), and so Italy had not been in a position to offer its observations fully. The member state is not, however, required to offer observations. The member state must also be granted a reasonable time within which to respond to the letter of formal notice and to remedy the breach following the issue of the reasoned opinion. The Court of Justice uses a reasonableness standard in assessing the appropriateness of the time period granted to the defaulting member state. In Case 293/85 *Commission v Belgium* (1988), an Article 226 action by the Commission against Belgium, for not implementing a decision of the Court of Justice in an earlier case, was dismissed as the Belgian authorities had not been given adequate time to respond to the letter of formal notice or comply with the reasoned opinion. The Court of Justice held that in assessing whether the time period granted was reasonable, it would examine all the factors in the case, including whether the action was urgent, although it would take into account whether the urgency arose from a failure by the Commission to take action earlier and whether the member state had been aware of the Commission's position prior to the commencement of the Article 226 procedure. The Commission had been aware of the alleged violation for several months before sending the letter of formal notice, which gave Belgium a mere eight days to respond, and issuing the reasoned opinion, which gave the member state 15 days to respond. The Court of Justice made clear that the Commission could not rely on urgency which had developed through its own failure to take action earlier. In Case 85/85 *Commission v Belgium* (1986), by contrast, the Court of Justice found that allowing less than two months to elapse between the issue of the letter of formal notice and the ultimate issuance of proceedings was, in the circumstances, reasonable. An important factor in that case was that significant communication took place with Belgium during the informal stage. Further, Belgium had not challenged the Commission view at any point during the informal procedure, nor had it in any way attempted to comply with the wishes of the Commission. Conversely, in general the pre-litigation procedure must not be of such excessive duration that the member state's right to a defence is infringed in that the delay makes it more difficult for the member state to rebut the Commission's arguments (Case C-207/97 *Commission v Belgium* (1999)).

10.13 The Commission's actions are also subject to scrutiny by the European Ombudsman (see Article 195 (ex Article 138e) EC). The European Ombudsman is charged with dealing with instances of maladministration by Community institutions and bodies and so may conduct investigations into the conduct of Article 226 proceedings by the Commission. In one instance, the issuing of a press release announcing a decision to terminate infringement proceedings before the complainant was informed was criticised, and the Commission modified its procedures accordingly.

The judicial stage; interim measures

10.14 Once the judicial stage has commenced, but not before, the Commission may apply for interim measures under Article 243 (ex Article 186) EC. Article 243, curiously, gives the Court of Justice wider powers at the interim stage of the judicial procedure than during the full action. The Court of Justice may, under Article 243, suspend the application of any contested act or grant any necessary interim measures. The main action, by contrast, may only result in a declaration that the member state has failed to fulfil a Community law obligation. It is clear, however, from Article 83(2) of the Rules of Procedure of the Court of Justice, that such measures may not be granted unless there are circumstances giving rise to urgency, and factual and legal grounds establishing a prima facie case for the measures to be granted. The grant of interim measures must not prejudge the points of fact or law at issue. In Case C-180/96 *United Kingdom v Commission* (1996) the Court, in the context of an application by the UK to suspend a Commission decision banning the export of British beef to the EC, reiterated that showing the requisite urgency involves establishing that the Article 186 measure sought must be granted to avoid serious and irreparable harm, and that the interests at stake must also be balanced. In Case C-246/89R *Commission v United Kingdom* (1989) the Commission took action against the UK under Article 226 on the basis that the Merchant Shipping Act 1988, which required that vessels registered in the UK be under British ownership, was contrary to the Treaty. The Commission requested that an interim order be made suspending the nationality requirements of the Act. After an examination of the UK interests at stake, the Court of Justice found that the Commission had made out a prima facie case based on the putative directly effective rights of the Spanish fishermen who were prohibited from fishing as a result of the nationality requirement. The issue was also seen as sufficiently urgent, as Spanish firms were suffering serious economic loss as a result of the contested Act.

The main action

10.15 It is clear from Case 240/86 *Commission v Greece* (1988) that the Commission may proceed with the legal action even if the member state remedies the breach after expiry of the time limit set in the reasoned opinion (although it may not if the member state acts within the time limit). In that case Greece claimed that the action by the Commission before the Court of Justice was inadmissible as it had lifted the requirement that cereal importers hold a foreign currency permit approved by the Bank of Greece, which the Commission alleged was in breach of Treaty obligations, before the judicial action commenced. The Court of Justice found that Greece had not complied with the reasoned opinion within the stated time limit and so the action by the Commission was admissible. The Court recently confirmed this point in Case C-355/ 98 *Commission v Belgium* (2000) where it stated that the question of whether a member state had fulfilled its obligations was to be determined by the situation prevailing in the member state at the end of the period set out in the reasoned opinion. Member states will often request that judicial proceedings be stayed in order that the Commission can assess new developments, but the Court of Justice usually looks unkindly on such applications on the ground that it is for the Commission, on expiry of the time limit, to decide whether or not to bring an action and that, accordingly, once it has decided to proceed, it would be inappropriate for the court to stay the proceedings (Case C-212/98 *Commission v Ireland* (2000)). The member state may concede the action before judgment but after the action has commenced, in which case the Commission may ask that the case be removed from the register. Alternatively, it may continue to pursue the action. The Commission may wish to proceed with such moot cases, as it may be important for the Commission to secure a determination that a breach had actually occurred to affirm or clarify the relevant principles of EC law. It may also, as the Court confirmed in *Commission v Greece* (1988), be important to establish a basis for the liability of a defaulting member state, as such a determination may be significant in establishing rights which might accrue to third parties, particularly in the light of *Francovich* liability.

The Court of Justice then examines the merits of the case (together with any breaches of procedural requirements as already outlined) and determines whether a breach of Community law has occurred. An objective finding of failure to comply with Community obligations is sufficient for a successful Article 226 application by the Commission. Further proof of inertia or opposition by the member state is not required (Case 301/81 *Commission v Belgium* (1983)). Equally, the fact that the failure had no adverse effects is not relevant to the finding of an infringement (Case C-150/95 *Portugal v Commission* (1997)).

Defences

10.16 As a general rule, the Court will not look on the various excuses offered by member states in respect of their failure to comply with EC obligations with a kindly eye. In 128/78 *Tachograph*, the excuse offered by the UK that practical difficulties (there was significant resistance to the introduction of the tachograph or 'spy in the cab' among transport trade unions) were behind the failure to implement fully the Tachograph Regulation was given short shrift. The Court held that unilateral breaches of EC law, driven by a member state's own conception of its national interest, brought into doubt the principle of the equality of member states and would not be tolerated. In a similar vein, the defence of necessity has not found favour with the Court. In Case 7/61 *Commission v Italy* (1961) Italy, in breach of the Treaty, suspended the importation of certain pig-meat products claiming that such action was necessary due to a serious crisis in the pig-meat market. The Court rejected the argument as to necessity and urgency, finding that the Treaty itself contained appropriate procedures, at that time, for dealing with emergencies. Similarly, internal legal, constitutional or administrative difficulties will not avail a member state.

10.17 Predictably, the Court of Justice has dispatched in robust terms any contention, based on the public international law principle of reciprocity, that breach by other member states or by a Community institution allows the defaulting member state to withdraw from its Community obligations. In Joined Cases 90 and 91/63 *Commission v Luxembourg and Belgium* (1964) Luxembourg and Belgium maintained duties on import licences for milk in violation of the Treaty. They claimed in their defence that the Council had failed to put in place Community measures on the common organisation of the milk market, as it was required to do. The Court rejected this contention stating that the new Treaty legal order, which included the procedures for the identification and supervision of breaches of EC law, was not limited to reciprocal obligations. Failure by a Community institution to carry out its obligations did not release a member state from its EC obligations. The same analysis applies to excuses based on non-compliance by other member states. In Case C-146/89 *Commission v United Kingdom* (1991) the UK had extended its baseline for fishing purposes in breach of EC rules. In the course of the judicial proceedings the UK pointed out that other member states had made similar adjustments but the Court simply referred to what it termed the well-established principle that implementation of EC law by member states could not be made subject to a condition of reciprocity.

10.18 While it accepts the possibility of *force majeure*, the Court is not usually sympathetic to such claims. In Case 101/84 *Commission v Italy (Transport Statistics)* (1985) Italy had breached a Community directive by not submitting certain statistical information on road transport, but raised *force majeure* as the relevant data-processing centre had been bombed. The subsequent delay of four and a half years, however, was found to be unacceptable, with the Court finding that while *force majeure* might have applied at the time, it only applied for the length of time that an administration exercising a normal degree of diligence would require to replace the equipment and provide the data.

10.19 Finally, another defence raised at times by member states is that while Community law may not be applied as a matter of law, administrative practices are such that, in fact, EC law is actually applied. The court has rejected this contention on the grounds that the very existence of national law which breaches EC obligations gives rise to uncertainty. In Case C-381/92 *Commission v Ireland* (1994) the administrative practices followed by Ireland (it had informally notified the relevant inspectors in the beef industry as to what actions were required to comply with the directives in question, which had not been officially implemented) did not absolve Ireland from its breach of EC law.

10.20 While in the judicial proceedings the Commission may not extend the complaint beyond the scope of the formal letter and reasoned opinion, the member state is not similarly barred from raising defences which it had not previously referred to during the pre-litigation procedure. In Case C-414/97 *Commission v Spain* (1999), in an action concerning an infringement of the Community VAT rules, the Commission sought to prevent Spain from raising pleas which had not been raised during the pre-litigation period. The court found that any requirement to raise all defences in advance during the pre-litigation period would be contrary to the general principle of respect for the rights of the defence. Proper conduct of the pre-litigation procedure was an essential guarantee required by the Treaty, not only to protect the member state, but to clearly define the subject-matter. Once the subject-matter was defined, however, the member state had the right to raise all pleas available to it.

Consequences of the judicial phase: Article 228

10.21 The result of the legal proceedings, should the Court of Justice find that there has been a violation, is a declaration that the member state has failed to fulfil an obligation under the Treaty. Article 228 (ex Article 171) EC provides that the member state must then act to rectify the situation. Under Article 228 the member state must take 'the necessary measures to comply with the judgment of the Court of Justice'.

This declaratory remedy is not, however, completely satisfactory. The Court has often repeated (see for example Case C-291/93 *Commission v Italy* (1994)) that while Article 228 does not itself state a time limit for compliance, on interpretation it does require that the necessary action be undertaken immediately. Member states have, however, on occasion, taken a very long time to comply with the judgment. This behaviour can undermine the uniformity and efficacy of Community law. In such cases the only course of action available to the Commission prior to the TEU was a second Article 226 action for breach of Article 228.

10.22 This inherent weakness in Article 226 has now been addressed, to a certain extent, through the introduction of a fining procedure by the TEU. Article 228(2) now provides that if the member state defies the Article 226 declaration, the Commission may, at its discretion, and after a second administrative procedure which involves giving the erring member state the opportunity to submit observations and the issue of a reasoned opinion, bring an action under Article 228 for the imposition by the Court of Justice of a 'lump sum or penalty payment' if the member state fails to comply with the second reasoned opinion. The Commission is required to specify the amount of the penalty to the Court of Justice. In its *Twelfth Annual Report* the Commission expressed its serious concern at the persistent delays by member states in giving effect to judgments of the European Court and put member states on notice that it intended to make full use of Article 228. In assessing the fine, the Commission has adopted, as set out in its Memorandum on Applying Article 171 (now Article 228) of the EC Treaty ([1996] OJ C242/6) (1) the gravity of the breach, (2) the duration of the breach, and (3) the need to have a dissuasive effect as the criteria for determining the level of the proposed penalty. In January 1997 the Commission also adopted a method for the calculation of penalties ([1997] OJ C63/2) which is based on a uniform flat rate of ECU 500 per day of delay multiplied by two factors which reflect the seriousness of the infringement and its duration. The calculation method also takes into account the ability of the member state to pay (based on its GDP) and the number of votes it can cast in the Council. Penalties may only be imposed in respect of periods of violation after the entry into force of the TEU. The Commission has not been reluctant to use the penalty provisions. In 1998 it took five decisions to apply for penalties when referring cases to the Court of Justice for the second time. Two cases were actually brought before the court in 1998. The penalty provisions appear to be proving effective, with the Commission reporting in its *Sixteenth Annual Report* that most member states respond to penalty decisions by rapidly coming into line with

Community law, either before the case is referred to the court or shortly afterwards. This state of affairs continued in 1999, with the Commission reporting in its *Seventeenth Annual Report* that the penalty system had an effective dissuasive effect with most member states coming into line as soon as the case was referred to the court for the second time. In 2000, however, the first fine was imposed on a member state under Article 228 EC. The Court ordered Greece to pay a penalty payment in respect of its failure to comply with an earlier judgment of the court concerning environmental obligations (Case C-387/97 *Commission v Greece* (2000)). In its ruling, the Court emphasised that the Commission's guidelines on the levying of penalties do not bind the Court, but are a useful point of reference. It found that the penalty must be appropriate to the circumstances and proportionate to the breach and the member state's ability to pay. The Court also found that the degree of urgency that the member state in question should fulfill its obligations could vary, depending on the breach. The basic criteria which should be taken into accounting in setting the penalty were, therefore, the duration of the infringement, its degree of seriousness, and the ability of the member state to pay. The Court imposed a penalty of 20,000 Euro per day (from the date on which the judgment was originally served), down from the Commission's proposal of 24,600 Euro per day.

Further, individuals who suffer harm as a result of a breach of EC law by a member state can now bring an action for damages against the member state under the *Francovich* principle. Significantly, in Case C-46/93 *Brasserie du Pêcheur SA v Germany* (1996) the Court confirmed that a breach of Community law would be considered sufficiently serious (as required by the tests for establishing state liability) if it has persisted despite a ruling finding that an infringement of Community law had been established (see **9.20**). In some respects this is, perhaps, the most effective deterrent of all.

Commission discretion

10.23 The Commission will not pursue every infringement of EC law by a member state under Article 226. While the Commission has a duty under Article 211 (ex Article 155) EC to ensure that the Treaty is applied, it is not under a parallel obligation to take proceedings against a member state at any stage of the Article 226 process. The Commission alone is competent to decide whether it is appropriate to issue the letter of formal notice, issue the reasoned opinion, or sue the member state before the Court of Justice (Case C-207/97 *Commission v Belgium* (1999)). Workload pressures and political considerations each play a part in deciding which infringements to pursue. The Commission is not, therefore, as relentlessly evenhanded as one would expect from a neutral enforcer of Community law. Article 226 EC operates at the level of inter-institutional relations, with the Commission fulfilling a politically-sensitive role in policing the application and implementation of EC law by the member states and it is not mechanically applied to all violations. In its *Eighteenth Annual Report*, for example, the Commission noted that it would give priority to pursuing infringements where there was evidence of a recurring tendency of the member state to breach Community law.

10.24 The Court has respected the larger institutional interests of the Commission in applying the Article 226 procedure and has demonstrated, on a number of occasions, a reluctance to fetter Commission discretion to take action. The Court will not, for example, enquire as to the Commission's motive in bringing an Article 226 action (Case 416/85 *Commission v United Kingdom* (1988)). The UK defended its breach of Community turnover tax rules by alleging that the Commission was using Article 226 judicial proceedings to achieve what was properly the subject of legislation, and so seeking to bypass the procedural requirements for decision-making in the Community. The Court of Justice tersely stated that given the balance of powers between the institutions as established in the Treaty it was not for the court to consider what objectives were being pursued by the Commission. The Commission may also judge the time when best to bring an action before the Court (Case 7/68 *Commission v Italy* (1968)). Indications are appearing, however, that Commission discretion is not entirely unchecked. In Joined Cases C-48/90 and C-66/90 *Netherlands v Commission* (1992) the Court held that excessive duration of the pre-litigation period may infringe the rights of the member state's defence.

10.25 By contrast, the Court has been extremely reluctant to allow private parties to challenge Commission discretion to take an action under Article 226. In Case 247/87 *Star Fruit v Commission* (1989) the applicant had requested the Commission to take action under Article 226 against France with respect to certain French laws concerning the operation of the banana market and subsequently brought an action for failure to act under Article 232 (ex Article 175) EC against the failure of the Commission to take action under Article 226. The Court rejected the application, finding that it was clear from Article 226 that the Commission was not bound to take action but had a discretion. It further pointed out that the Commission had a right but not a duty to initiate proceedings before the Court of Justice following non-compliance with the reasoned opinion. This discretion excluded individuals from requiring the Commission to adopt a particular position. The Court confirmed this position in Case C-87/89 *Société Nationale Interprofessionelle de la Tomate (Sonito) v Commission* (1990) where Sonito brought an annulment action under Article 230 (ex Article 173) EC against the decision of the Commission not to act upon its request that Article 226 action be taken. Reiterating the *Star Fruit* reasoning, the Court found that individuals were also debarred from bringing an Article 230 annulment action against a refusal by the Commission to take action. Isolating Commission discretion to take action from challenge by private parties, who may have initiated the complaint and who may ultimately be adversely affected by the decision of the Commission not to proceed, is now a relatively settled principle. The Court dealt with the issue tersely in Case C-107/95P *Bundesverband der Bilanzbuchhalter eV v Commission* (1997) stating briefly that the jurisprudence of the court provides that individuals may not bring an action against a refusal by the Commission to initiate Article 226 proceedings. The Court of First Instance has also confirmed this position in cases such as Case T-5/94 *J v Commission* (1994) and Case T-182/97 *Smanor SA, Hubert Ségaud and Monique Ségaud v Commission* (1998). The question remains whether this is a legitimate perspective or whether the larger institutional interests which are the focus of Article 226 should defer to the right of the individual to challenge Commission inaction, even though Article 226 is not primarily a vehicle for individual protection, where there has been a grave injustice.

10.26 However, while the Commission may choose not to pursue an infringement it is clear from Joined Cases 142–143/80 *Italian Finance Administration v Essevi* (1981) that it may not authorise unlawful conduct by a member state. The Court held that the Commission was not empowered in the course of Article 226 proceedings to exempt member states from their Community obligations and that, further, it could not prevent individuals from relying on their Treaty rights to challenge measures taken by a member state which might be contrary to Community law.

Article 227 (ex Article 170) EC

10.27 Article 227 largely tracks Article 226. Under Article 227 a member state may take enforcement action against another member state where it considers that the member state has failed to fulfil an EC law obligation. While Article 10 provides that member states have a duty to take all appropriate measures to ensure the fulfilment of obligations under the Treaty, enforcement action by member states is, inevitably, much rarer due to the likely political ramifications.

10.28 The member state who wishes to bring an Article 227 action against another member state before the Court must first bring the matter before the Commission. The Commission then plays a vital role in easing tension between the member states. The Commission is required to deliver a reasoned opinion after each member state involved has been given the opportunity to present its case and submit observations both orally and in writing. If the Commission does not issue a reasoned opinion within three months, the member state may still proceed with a legal action before the Court. The result of such an action, if the case is made out, will be a declaration that the member state failed to fulfil an obligation under EC law. The member state will then be required to take remedial action under Article 228 and may be subject to fines if it does not comply.

10.29 Article 227 actions are extremely rare as, for political reasons, member states are very reluctant to tackle each other directly and usually rely on the Commission to take action where necessary. In one infamous example, France claimed that UK fish conservation measures were contrary to EC law and initiated an Article 227 action (Case 141/78 *France v United Kingdom* (1979)). The Court ultimately found in favour of France.

Further reading

Schermers and Waelbroeck, *Judicial Protection in the European Communities* (5th edn, 1992), Kluwer.

Dashwood and White, 'Enforcement actions under Articles 169 and 170 EEC', [1989] 14 ELRev 388.

Mastroianni, 'The enforcement procedure under Article 169 of the EC Treaty and the powers of the European Commission: *Quis Custodiet Custodes*', [1995] 4 EPL 535.

Commission's Tenth Annual Report on Monitoring the Application of Community Law [1993] OJ C233/1.

Commission's Eleventh Annual Report on Monitoring the Application of Community Law [1994] OJ C154/1.

Commission's Twelfth Annual Report on Monitoring the Application of Community Law [1995] OJ C254/1.

Commission's Thirteenth Annual Report on Monitoring the Application of Community Law [1996] OJ C303/1.

Commission's Fourteenth Annual Report on Monitoring the Application of Community Law [1997] OJ C332/1.

Commission's Fifteenth Annual Report on Monitoring the Application of Community Law [1998] OJ C250/1.

Commission's Sixteenth Annual Report on Monitoring the Application of Community Law [1999] OJ C354/1.

Commission's Seventeenth Annual Report on Monitoring the Application of Community Law [2001] OJ C30/1

Commission's Eighteenth Annual Report on Monitoring the Application of Community Law COM (2001) 309

Self-test questions

1. Discuss how the Treaty allows the Commission to ensure that member states fulfil their Treaty obligations.

2. Examine the extent to which the power given to the Commission to bring an action under Article 226 is a discretionary power. Why is the Commission given such a wide discretion?

3. Does a private party have standing to challenge a refusal by the Commission to bring an enforcement action against a member state which is in breach of EC law?

4. Has the Court of Justice placed any limits on how the Commission manages the Article 226 action in order to protect the member states?

5. What are the consequences of a declaration by the Court of Justice that a member state has failed to fulfil an obligation under the Treaty? How was the position improved by the TEU?

6. Why is the Article 227 power rarely used by member states?

CHAPTER ELEVEN

Judicial Review of Community Action

SUMMARY

This chapter examines how the legality of acts of Community institutions are reviewed by the Community courts. It discusses:

- Article 230 (ex Article 173) EC
- Reviewable acts
- Locus standi
- Privileged, semi-privileged and non-privileged applicants
- Time limitations
- Grounds for annulment
- Effects of an annulment
- Article 232 (ex Article 175) EC
- Locus standi under Article 232
- Indirect challenge and the plea of illegality, Article 241 (ex Article 184) EC
- Contractual and tortious liability: Article 235 (ex Article 178) and Article 288 (ex Article 215) EC

Article 230 (ex Article 173) EC

11.1 Article 230 empowers the ECJ and the Court of First Instance to review the legality of binding institutional acts. Reflected in some form in almost all member states' legal systems, but largely modelled on French administrative law, it constitutes an important safeguard against abuses

237

of authority by Community institutions and is a key element of the Community system of judicial review.

Reviewable acts

11.2 Under Article 230 EC, the ECJ 'shall review the legality of acts adopted jointly by the European Parliament and the Council, of acts of the Council, of the Commission and of the European Central Bank, other than recommendations and opinions, and of acts of the European Parliament intended to produce legal effects vis-à-vis third parties'. The range of acts subject to review has been interpreted broadly by the Court of Justice and covers institutional acts which have binding effects. Article 249 (ex Article 189) EC lists the binding acts which may be adopted by the Community institutions (regulations, directives and decisions), but in determining whether the contested measure is reviewable, and in the light of its often-repeated view that Article 230 not be interpreted restrictively (as expressed in the ERTA case discussed below), the ECJ looks to the nature and effect of the measure and does not simply consider its form.

11.3 In the early Case 22/70 Commission v Council (ERTA) (1971) the ECJ found that a Council resolution which set out the position to be taken by the Council in the preparation of a European road transport agreement, and which, per the Council, was simply a co-ordination of policies among member states, could be challenged under Article 230. Why? The contested resolution was binding and was designed to have legal effects on relations between the Commission and the member states and on inter-institutional relationships. The ECJ stated that:

> ... Article 173 [now Article 230 EC] treats as open to review by the Court all measures adopted by the institutions which are intended to have legal force. An action for annulment must therefore be available in the case of all measures adopted by the institutions, whatever their nature or form, which are intended to have legal effects.

The ERTA approach is echoed in Case C-316/91 European Parliament v Council (1994) where the ECJ found that a development aid regulation adopted by the Council under the Fourth ACP-EEC Convention was subject to review despite its adoption pursuant to an internal Convention agreement rather than pursuant to the Treaty, as:

... annulment must be available in the case of all measures adopted by the institutions, whatever their nature or form, intended to have legal effects. It follows that an action...is admissible irrespective of whether the act was adopted by the institution pursuant to the Treaty provisions.

11.4 The ECJ also held in Case 294/83 *Les Verts v European Parliament* (1986) that acts of the Parliament, although not specifically listed as reviewable in the pre-Maastricht Treaty version of Article 230, were subject to review when such acts produced legal effects *vis-à-vis* third parties. It found that:

... Article 173 [now Article 230 EC] refers only to acts of the Council and Commission. However, the general scheme of the Treaty is to make a direct action available against all measures adopted by the institutions which are intended to have legal effects.

In this case, the allocation by the Parliament of campaign funds for the 1984 elections, which had been based on the existing membership of the Parliament, was challenged by the Greens as discriminating against those seeking election for the first time. The ECJ reasoned that in a Community based on the rule of law, all institutions of the Community must be subject to review and pointed to the fact that Parliament could now adopt binding acts. The contested allocation decision governed the rights and obligation of political groups, produced legal effects *vis-à-vis* third parties, and so was reviewable. In a similar vein, Case 34/86 *Council v European Parliament* (1986) established that a declaration by the President of the Parliament as to the final adoption of the general budget of the EC was reviewable as the budget was an act capable of producing legal effects *vis-à-vis* private parties. By way of contrast, Case 190/84 *Les Verts v European Parliament* (1988) established that measures adopted by Parliament which have purely internal effects within the administration of Parliament and which do not produce legal effects for third parties are not reviewable under Article 230. Equally, a decision by Parliament to set up a committee of enquiry was found by the ECJ not to produce legal effects *vis-à-vis* third parties, and so fell outside the scope of Article 230: Case 78/85 *Group of the European Right v European Parliament* (1986).

11.5 On occasion, the Commission has attempted to prevent review of certain 'soft law' measures. In Case C-325/91 *France v Commission* (1993) a Commission communication which imposed detailed reporting obligations on member states with respect to public funding of public undertakings was reviewable despite the Commission's argument that it was not intended to have legal effects, but simply explained the nature of obligations already established in an earlier directive. The ECJ found that the communication was reviewable as it had added new obligations to those imposed by the directive and so 'was intended to have legal effects of its own distinct from [the directive]'. For further challenges by France to soft law instruments produced by the Commission, see Case C-366/88 *France v Commission* (1990) on the reviewability of internal Commission instructions to officials; Case C-303/90 *France v Commission* (1991) on the reviewability of a code of conduct concerning structural assistance; and Case C-57/95 *France v Commission* (1997) on the reviewability of a Commission communication on the internal market for pension funds, based on an unsuccessful proposed directive, written in imperative language and so producing legal effects rather than merely interpreting Treaty obligations. Given the increasing tendency of Community acts to take the form of what might appear to be 'soft law', the expansive and vigilant approach taken by the ECJ in subjecting their legality to review is to be welcomed.

11.6 Administrative acts taken by the Commission in the area of competition policy are frequently challenged. In Cases 8–11/66 *SA Cimenteries CBR Cementbedrijven NV v Commission* (1967) the administrative act challenged was a registered letter sent by the Commission. The letter was not called a decision, but it produced legal effects for the companies concerned in that it stated that a group of companies no longer had an immunity from fines, brought about a distinct change in their legal position and so was open to challenge under Article 230. That the form of the contested measure is of limited importance is clearly seen in Case T-3/93 *Air France v Commission* (1994) where an oral statement by a Commission official, reported by a press agency, to the effect that a proposed acquisition by British Airways of Dan Air fell outside the scope of the Merger Regulation 4064/89 as it did not have a Community dimension, was found to be reviewable. Despite what it termed the unusual form of the measure, the Court of First Instance found that the statement produced legal effects for the member states, for the parties concerned and for their competitors. The Commission measure must, however, be definitive. In Case 60/81 *IBM v Commission* (1981) a Commission letter notifying IBM of certain alleged abuses of Treaty competition rules was challenged by IBM. The ECJ found that Article 230 was designed for measures which have binding legal effects and affect the interests of the applicant by causing a distinct change to the applicant's legal position. Here, the act challenged was adopted through a specific procedure and so was only open to review if it definitively set out the final position of the Commission or Council and was not a provisional measure (see also Case T-37/92 *BEUC and NCC v Commission* (1994)). In this case, review of the contested measure might have prejudiced the substance of the final decision of the Commission on the alleged violation of the competition rules. Where the preliminary decision concerns the disclosure of confidential documents, however, it will often be subject to review. In Case 53/85 *AKZO Chemie BV v Commission* (1986) the ECJ found that a decision of the Commission, taken while infringement proceedings were still in progress, to disclose confidential information to the party who had originally complained of AKZO's behaviour, could be subject to review even though a final resolution of the proceedings had not been reached. Finally, where appropriate, the court will sever an initial Commission measure which has legal effects from a larger contractual procedure at national level in order to subject the Commission measure to review. In Case C-395/95P *Geotronics SA v Commission* (1997) a Commission decision rejecting a bid by the applicant to be included in a PHARE programme tender was found to be reviewable by the ECJ as it produced legal effects for the applicant (overruling the Court of First Instance), even though the Commission decision was simply part of a larger contractual procedure where the ultimate tender decision would be made at national level.

11.7 Certain acts will not be reviewable. In Joined Cases C-181/91 and C-248/91 *European Parliament v Council and Commission* (1993) the European Parliament challenged both a decision by the member states in Council granting special aid to Bangladesh and the Commission measures taken to implement that decision. The ECJ ruled that although the contested decision was called an act of the Council, it was in fact an act of the member states acting collectively. Equally, the Commission action was the result of a special delegation to it by the member states and was not the result of a Council delegation, so it was not reviewable. In Case T-584/93 *Roujansky v Council* (1994) the Court of First Instance found that a declaration by the European Council that the Maastricht Treaty was to enter into force on a certain date was not subject to review as the European Council was not listed as an institution subject to the annulment action and was not subject to the jurisdiction of the Community courts. The Court of First Instance also found that the Maastricht Treaty was not subject to review under Article 230 as it was not an act of a Community institution. Further, Acts of Accession of new member states will not be reviewed (Cases 31 and 35/86 *LAISA v Council* (1988)).

Nevertheless, while the challenged act must be that of a Community institution, Case C-327/91 *France v Commission* (1994) provides that it does not have to be a *unilateral* act of a Community institution. The ECJ rejected the Commission's argument that Article 230 was restricted to unilateral Community acts and that an agreement entered into between the Commission and the US was not, as a result, subject to Article 230 finding that:

> ...the [e]xercise of powers delegated to the Community institutions in international matters cannot escape judicial review under Article 173 of the Treaty...

Finally, Case **48/65** *Lütticke v Commission* (1966) established that a reasoned opinion delivered by the Commission in the course of Article 226, (ex Article 169) EC proceedings may not be reviewed under Article 230 as it is not a binding act.

Locus standi

Introduction

11.8 The most controversial question raised by Article 230 is who can bring this action for annulment, or, who has locus standi. Locus standi is conferred by the Treaty, as interpreted by the ECJ.

Privileged applicants

11.9 Article 230(2) provides that the Commission, the Council and the member states all have standing by right as they are considered to have a direct interest in any of the acts under review. These privileged applicants do not have to establish a particular interest in the action. See Case 230/81 *Luxembourg v European Parliament* (1983), where Luxembourg brought the equivalent of an Article 230 action under the ECSC Treaty to annul a resolution by the Parliament to hold committee meetings and other plenary sessions outside Luxembourg (the ECJ did not address the admissibility argument under Article 230 once the ECSC Treaty action was declared admissible). Arguably, Luxembourg did have a strong interest to protect, but, in any event, it was not required to demonstrate a particular interest.

Semi-privileged applicants

11.10 The European Parliament, the European Central Bank and the Court of Auditors (the latest added by the Amsterdam Treaty) are semi-privileged applicants, insofar as their right to seek review is more limited. They may take an action only 'for the purpose of protecting their prerogatives'. Prior to the Maastricht Treaty revisions, however, Parliament did not appear, even in this limited fashion, as a potential applicant under Article 230. In a creative series of judgments the ECJ, concerned to redress what it saw as an institutional imbalance, acted as a dynamic agent for change by introducing Parliament as an applicant under Article 230. Case 138/79 *Roquette Frères v Council* (1980) and Case 139/79 *Maizena v Council* (1980) (the isoglucose cases) established that Parliament did, under Article 37 of the Statute of the Court of Justice, have the right to intervene voluntarily in cases before the ECJ. Parliament used this facility to great effect to protect its right to be consulted in decision-making. Being an essentially reactive mechanism, however, intervention alone was of limited use. A significant step towards integrating Parliament fully into the review process was taken in Case 294/83 *Les Verts v Parliament* (1986) where all measures of Parliament having legal effect were found to be subject to review under Article 230. Despite the hint in *Les Verts* that the ECJ was favourably disposed towards the integration of Parliament in the Article 230 procedure, it refused to grant standing to Parliament in Case 302/87 *European Parliament v Council* (1988). Parliament had sought annulment of a Council decision which set out the procedures to be followed in choosing committees to oversee delegations of power from the Council to the Commission but was refused standing on the grounds that other legal remedies were available to protect the Parliament. The Commission could take an Article 230 action or Parliament itself could take an action under Article 232 (ex Article 175) EC. In Case C-70/88 *European Parliament v Council (Re Chernobyl)* (1990), however, the ECJ changed its position and gave Parliament the right to challenge under Article 230 when its own prerogatives (such as its right to participate in the legislative process as laid down in the Treaty) were directly affected. The ECJ found that a grant of standing to Parliament was necessary as other Treaty remedies did not effectively protect Parliament's prerogatives. Employing a classic form of constitutional rhetoric, the ECJ found that these (unenumerated) prerogative powers of Parliament were part of the institutional balance created by the Treaty and the omission of Parliament from Article 230 was a procedural gap which could not prevail over the fundamental interest in maintaining this institutional balance. It followed that:

243

> ... an action for annulment brought by Parliament against an act of the Council or the Commission is admissible provided that the action seeks only to safeguard its prerogatives...

Parliament has been vigorous in asserting this right. See, for example, Case C-295/90 *European Parliament v Council* (1992) where the ECJ accepted that Parliament's prerogatives to participate in decision-making were at stake when Parliament sought to annul Directive 90/366 on vocational training on the basis that it had been erroneously adopted under Article 308 (ex Article 235) EC which merely provided for consultation of Parliament (see further 11.35).

11.11 The restriction of standing to these occasions when a prerogative power is at issue can serve to prevent Parliament from taking an action. In Joined Cases C-181/91 and C-248/91 *European Parliament v Council (Re Aid to Bangladesh)* (1993) the ECJ found that the prerogative powers of Parliament had not been infringed as the Commission action in implementing the aid decision did not involve any changes to the budget of the Community and so did not impinge on a prerogative power of Parliament. It is clear, however, that where the prerogatives of the Parliament are at stake, the ECJ will be robust in granting standing even if in practice Parliament's powers have been respected. In Case C-316/91 *European Parliament v Council (Re Development Aid)* (1994) although the ECJ ultimately found that the act had been correctly adopted, it also stated that:

> ...[t]he right to be consulted in accordance with a Treaty provision is a prerogative of Parliament. Adopting an act on a legal basis which does not provide for such consultation is liable to infringe that prerogative, even if there has been optional consultation.

11.12 This judicial expansion of Article 230 enhanced the powers of Parliament, but problems of perception remained, in that the wording of Article 230 appeared to institutionalise Parliament's traditionally weak position. Article G of the Maastricht Treaty (now Article 8 Amsterdam TEU) amended Article 230 to bring Parliament specifically within its scope as a semi-privileged applicant together with the European Central Bank (and reflected the co-decision procedure by adding 'acts adopted jointly by the European Parliament and the Council' to those acts subject to review). The current article does not, however, give Parliament a general right to challenge and confers standing only for the purpose of protecting Parliament's prerogatives. Given that one of Parliament's main functions is to supervise the Council and Commission, this is an unfortunate lacuna and one which was not addressed by the Amsterdam Treaty.

Non-privileged applicants

11.13 Natural and legal persons may bring an annulment action under Article 230(4), but they are non-privileged applicants and have difficult hurdles to clear in establishing standing. The Court of First Instance has jurisdiction in these actions with an appeal lying to the ECJ. Article 230(4) has been interpreted strictly and restrictively by the court in a line of cases which inevitably raise questions as to the nature of the protection of the individual in the Community legal order. The ECJ has on occasion, however, lowered the hurdles presented by Article 230 when the specific facts of the case seem to call for judicial review. This was the case in *Codorniu*, discussed further below at **11.22**. The Amsterdam Treaty has not relaxed the standing rules.

Under Article 230(4), the act which is being challenged must fit into one of three categories before standing will be granted to the applicant: (1) a decision addressed to the applicant; (2) a decision addressed to another person which is of direct and individual concern to the applicant; or (3) a decision in the form of a regulation which is of direct and individual concern to the applicant.

Decision addressed to the applicant

11.14 A decision, which under Article 249 (ex Article 189) EC is 'binding in its entirety upon those to whom it is addressed', may be challenged by the natural or legal person to whom it is addressed. Commission decisions addressed to companies in the area of competition law are frequently challenged. If the addressee of the contested decision brings the action within the two-month time limit which is set for all Article 230 actions (see below), the claim will be admissible.

Decisions addressed to another person, but of direct and individual concern to the applicant

11.15 The admissibility criteria of Article 230 pose formidable challenges where the contested decision is not addressed to the applicant. A natural or legal person may bring an annulment action under Article 230 where the contested measure is a decision addressed to another person (and so outside the first category) but is, nonetheless, a decision of direct and individual concern to the applicant. There are two elements to this test: (i) individual concern and (ii) direct concern (see below at **11.26**). The application of this deceptively simple formula has been problematic. The approach of the ECJ has been to interpret the concept of individual concern, in particular, restrictively so that, in practice, the applicant challenging a decision addressed to another person faces a formidable obstacle before an action may be brought.

Individual concern

11.16 In the early Case 25/62 *Plaumann & Co v Commission* (1963) the ECJ established the test for determining whether a contested decision, addressed to another person, was of individual concern to the applicant. Following representations from the German government to the Commission, the Commission issued a decision, addressed to the German government, refusing to suspend the import duty imposed on importers of clementines to Germany. One of the importers concerned, Plaumann, challenged this decision on the grounds that, as a large scale importer of clementines, it was individually concerned. The ECJ stated the test for individual concern as follows:

> Persons other than those to whom a decision is addressed may only claim to be individually concerned if that decision affects them by reason of certain attributes which are peculiar to them or by reason of circumstances in which they are differentiated from all other persons, and by virtue of these factors distinguishes them individually just as in the case of the person addressed.

In applying this test for individual concern and assessing whether *Plaumann* was, in fact, distinguished by virtue of certain attributes or circumstances, the ECJ examined whether Plaumann was a member of an open or closed class and so distinguished from all other persons. The court found that Plaumann was affected by the decision simply by reason of engaging in a commercial activity (importing clementines) covered by the decision, which could have been practised at any time by any person. This was not enough to create a closed class and thereby distinguish the applicant in relation to the decision as in the case of the addressee. So, as a member of a general and open class, Plaumann was not individually concerned.

11.17 Subsequent case law has shown that establishing the circumstances or attributes which differentiate the applicant from all other persons presents a troublesome task for the applicant. In Joined Cases 106 and 107/63 *Toepfer v Commission* (1965) the ECJ, in finding individual concern, stressed the fact that the number and identity of the individuals concerned by the decision in question was fixed and ascertainable before the time of the adoption of the decision (see also Case 62/70 *Bock v Commission* (1971)). As long as the class remains potentially open, however, individual concern will not be established merely because it is possible to show that the number and identity of those affected by the contested measure can be determined (Case 123/77 *UNICME v Council* (1978)). The difficulties raised for potential applicants by the Plaumann tests are well-illustrated by Case 11/82 *Piraiki-Patraiki v Commission* (1985). A Commission decision authorised the French government to impose a quota system on the import of Greek yarn. Seven cotton undertakings sought to challenge this decision, including certain firms which had already entered into contracts to export yarn during the quota period. The applicants claimed individual concern since they were the main Greek undertakings in the production and export of yarn to France and were therefore an identifiable group of traders. They argued that they were not an open class (the stumbling block for *Plaumann*) as it was impossible to establish a business in the yarn sector quickly and, in any event, impossible to do so during the term of the decision. The ECJ found that the export of yarn to France could be carried out at any time by any company but did accept, however, that one sub-group of traders had established individual concern. Those exporters that had already entered into contracts to be performed during the period of application of the decision and who could not now carry out their contractual obligations were individually concerned. Their class closed on the date of the adoption of the measure and the ECJ therefore found that:

> ...the fact that, before the adoption of the decision at issue, they had entered into contracts which were to be carried out during the months to which the contracts applied constitutes a circumstance which distinguishes them from any other person concerned by the decision, in so far as the execution of their contracts was wholly or partly prevented by the adoption of the decision.

Nevertheless, the grant of standing to the small group of exporters who had previously entered into contracts does not necessarily show a more relaxed approach to individual concern as there were very particular circumstances in *Piraiki* which may weaken its use as a general principle. Under the terms of the Act of Accession of Greece to the Community, before authorising protective measures, such as the one taken by France in this case, the Commission had a duty to make certain enquiries as to the economic effects of the decision and the undertakings which would be affected by it.

11.18 Individual concern may be shown where the contested decision addressed to another person has been adopted following a specific procedure in which individuals may participate. Regulation 17/62 establishes a procedure for the adoption of decisions and the lodging of complaints on the application of Treaty competition rules. In Case 26/76 *Metro v Commission* (1977), following a complaint by Metro concerning a refusal by SABA to allow it to participate in its distribution network, the Commission, in a decision addressed to SABA, decided that the distribution system was in accordance with Treaty rules. This decision was then challenged by Metro who were granted standing as the decision was adopted partly as a result of a complaint by Metro and '[I]t was in the interests of a satisfactory administration of justice and of the proper application of Articles 85 and 86 (now Articles 81 and 82 EC) that natural or legal persons who are entitled to request the Commission to find an infringement of Articles 85 and 86 should be able, if their request is not complied with either wholly or in part, to institute proceedings in order to protect their legitimate interests'. The importance of procedural guarantees in providing a basis for standing is particularly apparent in the area of state aids, where standing has been granted to individuals who complain of unlawful state aids and submit observations to that effect. Article 88(2) (ex Article 93(2)) EC makes provision for 'parties concerned' by a Commission decision on a state aid measure under Article 88(2) EC to submit comments during the decision-making procedure and this procedural mechanism informs the state aid standing case law. In Case 169/84 *COFAZ v Commission* (1986), for example, the ECJ granted locus standi to the applicant to challenge a Commission decision, taken under Article 88(2) and addressed to the Netherlands, on the lawfulness of a state aid. The grant of standing to COFAZ was based on a number of factors which reflected the role played by the applicant in the decision-making procedure in submitting observations, as well as the fact that COFAZ was, as a competitor of the beneficiary of the grant of state aid, affected by the decision on state aid. Where a decision on a state aid measure has been taken under the preliminary procedure in Article 88(3) EC, which does not make specific provision for 'parties concerned' to be heard, procedural considerations still influence standing decisions. In Case C-198/91 *Cook v Commission* (1993) the ECJ found that individuals, who, as 'parties concerned' could have benefited from the procedural guarantees under Article 88(2) EC and submitted observations, still have standing to challenge decisions taken by the Commission under Article 88(3) EC where the Commission has not adopted the fuller review process under Article 88(2) (see also Case C-225/91 *Matra v Commission* (1993)). A similar approach is taken with respect to undertakings who seek to challenge Commission decisions finding that a merger is compatible with the Common Market, where the undertakings seeking review have submitted observations under the Merger Regulation (Regulation 4064/89) (Case T-2/93 *Air France v Commission* (1995)). These rulings, which are undoubtedly favourable to individual applicants, tend, however, to reflect the existence of a defined procedure for adopting decisions and a defined role for complainants. Where Community law does not provide for such a procedure, concerned individuals who simply complain to the Commission outside a procedural framework face difficulties in establishing standing to challenge the decision ultimately taken. The Court of First Instance found in Case T-32/93 *Ladbroke Racing Ltd v Commission* (1994) that individuals would not be in a position to establish individual concern simply by virtue of having requested, in that case, the Commission to adopt remedial measures under Article 86(3) (ex Article 90(3)) EC. Article 86(3) concerns the regulation of state monopolies and, unlike Article 88 and Articles 81 and 82 (ex Articles 85 and 86) EC, does not have a specific procedure for decision-making or lodging complaints. The same applies to complainants who request that the Commission take action under Article 226 (ex Article 169) EC despite the fact that the Commission is heavily reliant on the information supplied by complainants in policing breaches of the Treaty: Case C-107/95P *Bundesverband der Bilanzbuchhalter eV v Commission* (1997). A change may be in the offing, however. In *Bilanzbuchhalter*, the ECJ hinted that individuals may, in exceptional circumstances, have standing to challenge a decision by the Commission refusing to take action under Article 86(3), but may not compel a state to adopt legislation of general application.

Decision by way of a Regulation, where the applicant is directly and individually concerned

11.19 Generally speaking, individuals cannot challenge regulations due to their abstract and general nature. Where a regulation drops its general character and, in deciding a specific issue, becomes in practice a disguised decision, standing may be granted if direct and individual concern can also be established.

11.20 Initially, the ECJ focused on whether the contested regulation applied to a closed category of persons. In Cases 16 and 17/62 *Confédération Nationale des Producteurs des Fruits et Légumes v Council* (1962) the ECJ found that the essential characteristics of a decision

> arise from the limitation of the persons to whom it is addressed whereas a regulation, being essentially of a legislative nature, is applicable not to a limited number of persons, defined or identifiable, but to categories of persons viewed abstractly and in their entirety. Consequently, in order to determine in doubtful cases whether one is concerned with a decision or a regulation, it is necessary to ascertain whether the measure in question is of individual concern to specific individuals.

Similarly, in Cases 41–44/70 *International Fruit Co v Commission* (1971) the ECJ found that if the 'regulation' applied to a closed group of people and reflected past events it would not have the character of a true regulation. In this case, the regulation set out the quantity of import licences to be issued for a certain period based on applications received during the previous week, applied to a finite group of people and so was actually a bundle of disguised decisions. The ECJ took a different approach and referred to the general legislative character of regulations in Case 789, 790/79 *Calpak v Commission* (1980), where it found that if the contested measure applied to 'objectively determined situations and produces legal effect with regard to categories of persons described in an abstract and generalised manner', then it would be a regulation. The court went on to confirm that, once the measure fulfils this test of its legislative character, the measure will remain a regulation even if it is possible to identify those affected. The ECJ also made the important point in *Calpak* that the inclusion of decisions in the form of regulations in Article 230(4) is

> to prevent the Community institutions from being in a position, merely by choosing the form of a regulation, to exclude an application by an individual against a decision which concerns him directly and individually...

11.21 In Case C-152/88 *Sofrimport v Commission* (1990), however, the ECJ appeared to adopt a more flexible approach to challenging regulations in that the court looked for individual concern without examining whether the regulation was in fact a decision. In that case an action was brought by an importer of Chilean apples against a Commission regulation which suspended the issue of import licences for, and imposed quotas in respect of, Chilean apples. The ECJ held that importers of apples which were in transit at the time the regulation was adopted were a 'sufficiently well-defined' and 'restricted' group as compared to other importers of apples and so could show individual concern. The ECJ did not, however, refer to the general legislative character of the regulation. While this case could be read to show a more flexible approach concerning standing to challenge regulations, it can also be explained by the fact that the court was dealing with the very specific case of goods in transit being affected by the adoption of a regulation. Indeed, the parent Council regulation required the Commission to take into account the position of goods in transit to the Community when adopting protective measures such as the ones taken here.

11.22 More significantly, cases have arisen where the ECJ permits individual challenges to regulations even where the measures do exhibit legislative characteristics and do not seem to apply to a closed and fixed group. This was the case in the very significant ruling in Case C-309/89 *Codorniu SA v Commission* (1994) where the ECJ accepted that a measure was of general legislative character but still allowed a challenge by an individual. The principal Spanish producer of a sparkling wine was allowed to challenge a regulation which provided that the word 'crémant' was to be reserved for certain quality sparkling wines produced in France and Luxembourg only. The applicant had held a trade mark in Spain over 'Gran Cremant' since 1924. The ECJ first found that the legislative character of a measure cannot be doubted simply because it is possible to identify those to whom it applies, so long as the measure applies by virtue of an objective legal or factual situation. The ECJ then made the ground-breaking finding that although:

> ...the contested provision is, by its nature and by virtue of its sphere of application, of a legislative nature in that it applies to the traders concerned in general, that does not prevent it from being of individual concern to some of them.

The contested regulation was of individual concern to the applicant as the applicant used 'crémant' in its trademark. The ECJ found that:

> ...[b]y reserving the right to use the term 'crémant' to French and Luxembourg producers, the contested provision prevents Codorniu from using its graphic trade mark. It follows that Codorniu has established the existence of a situation which from the point of view of the contested provision differentiated it from all other persons.

Codorniu, which was, as the ECJ referred to, the main Community producer of wines which would come under the designation 'crémant', also stood to lose 38% of its turnover as a result of the regulation. The ECJ did not establish that the measure was, in fact, a disguised decision but focused instead on the fact that the regulation was of direct and individual concern to the applicant and so allowed a direct challenge to a general legislative measure. While *Codorniu* might appear to augur well for the position of the individual before the Community courts, the ECJ remains reluctant to grant standing to challenge regulations which have a legislative character. In particular, it has been slow to find that applicants challenging regulations which have general legislative effects are, in some way, differentiated from all other persons by reason of certain attributes or circumstances, as in *Codorniu*. In Case C-209/94P *Buralux v Council* (1996) the applicant and its partners were involved in the management of household waste and sought to annul a regulation on the supervision and control of shipments of household waste within the Community. The ECJ found that the measure produced legal effects on categories of persons in a general and abstract manner and so could not be challenged even though the number and identity of those affected could be determined as Buralux were affected in the same way as every other operator in the waste transfer business. Lenz AG (who also gave the Opinion in *Codorniu* and advised the ECJ that the action by Codorniu was admissible) had found, however, (relying on *Extramet*, see below) that Buralux was the largest importer of waste in France and Germany and would be particularly seriously affected by the import prohibition envisaged by the regulation.

11.23 The Court of First Instance has adopted a similarly restrictive approach to challenges to regulations. In Case T-472/93 *Campo Ebro Industrial SA v Commission* (1995) the applicant isoglucose producers attempted to challenge a regulation aligning the price of sugar in Spain, arguing that they were individually concerned as they were the only producers of sugar in Spain at the time the regulation was adopted, and the only producers to have been adversely affected by the reduction in the price of sugar. Stating that the general application and legislative nature of a measure could not be called into question simply because it was possible to define the number of persons to whom it applied, the Court of First Instance found that even if the applicants were the only producers affected by the regulation, they were affected in their objective capacity as isoglucose producers in the same way as any other traders in the sugar sector who actually or potentially were in an identical situation. In Case T-47/95 *Terres Rouges Consultant SA v Commission* (1997), banana importers into the Community who were responsible for 70% of all bananas exported from the Ivory Coast challenged a regulation which restricted the quantity of bananas which could be exported into the Community from the Ivory Coast. The Court of First Instance characterised the measure as a general legislative act drafted in abstract and general terms. Moving on to the *Codorniu* analysis, it found that the applicants were not individually concerned. The regulation affected every importer wishing to import bananas from the Ivory Coast. Even though the applicants imported a large proportion of bananas from the Ivory Coast, this of itself was not a circumstance differentiating them from all other importers. See also Case T-122/96 *Federolio v Commission* (1997) where, despite the fact that all those subject to the regulation in question could be identified, the Court of First Instance relied on the fact that the regulation imposed a penalty structure based on objective criteria as evidence of its legislative character and non-reviewability. In Case T-109/97 *Molkerei v Commission* (1998), in finding a challenge by the applicant to a regulation, which registered as a protected designation of origin the designation 'Altenburger Ziengenkäse' for a particular type of cheese coming only from a specified geographic area, inadmissible, the Court of First Instance ruled that the mere fact that the Commission had received comments from the applicant on the subject of the geographical area in question and had replied to those comments was not sufficient to distinguish the applicant from all other traders. It found that in the absence of expressly guaranteed procedural rights, it would be contrary to the spirit and wording of Article 173 (now Article 230 EC) to allow any person who had taken part in the preparation of a legislative measure subsequently to bring an action against that measures.

11.24 The cases have not, however, all been in one direction. In Joined Cases T-125/96 and 152/96 *Boehringer v Commission* (1999), the applicant was successful in challenging a regulation. At issue was a regulation which laid down a procedure for setting limits for the quantity of residual veterinary drugs (in particular a chemical called clenbuterol) which could be legally contained in certain foodstuffs, and effectively banned the use of clenbuterol where it might appear in foodstuffs which were not subject to a permitted level of the drug. The applicant was one of only two producers of clenbuterol in the Community and accounted for 97% of sales of the products affected by the regulation. The Court of First Instance found that the measure applied to objectively determined situations and produced legal effects in general and abstract terms for all pharmaceutical firms who produced clenbuterol and for all those who prescribed the drug. It then turned to an examination of whether, nonetheless, the applicant was individually concerned by the regulation. The court ruled that the applicant was individually concerned as the regulation was adopted after a formal request from the applicant that limits be set, the earlier foundation regulation on which the contested regulation was based provided that the applicant be involved in the process of setting limits, and the draft regulation had been notified to the applicant. It appears nonetheless that the Community courts remain concerned to protect general legislative measures from individual challenge.

Decision by way of a Directive

11.25 Challenges to directives by individuals under Article 230 are usually despatched quickly by the Community courts due to the problem of individual concern. In Case T-135/96 *UEAPME v Council* (1998), for example, where a European association representing the interests of small and medium-sized enterprises challenged Directive 96/34 on parental leave, the Court of First Instance found without difficulty that the directive was a legislative measure and could not be characterised as a decision. As in *Codorniu*, however, the Court of First Instance went on to address whether, notwithstanding its general legislative character, the association was individually concerned. It found that the association was not affected by the directive by reason of attributes peculiar to it or by reason of circumstances which differentiated it from all other persons. The Court of First Instance did point out, however, that the mere fact that the contested measure was in the form of a directive was not sufficient, of itself, to render the action inadmissible as Community institutions could not be allowed, through their choice of instrument, to deprive individuals of judicial protection.

Anti-dumping regulations

11.26 The ECJ has taken a less stringent approach to standing and has been quicker to find that a true regulation may be open to challenge (where it can be shown to be of direct and individual concern to the applicant) where the regulation is an anti-dumping measure. Standing may be granted to challenge an anti-dumping measure, where the applicant has participated in the preparation of the measure in question and initiated the complaint (Case 264/82 *Timex Corpn v Council and Commission* (1985)); where the applicants, either as producers or exporters, are affected by the anti-dumping regulation (Joined Cases 239/82 and 275/82 *Allied Corpn v Commission* (1984)); and where the applicant is an independent importer of goods subject to an anti-dumping duty. See Case C-358/89 *Extramet Industrie SA v Council* (1991) where the ECJ highlighted the fact that the importer was seriously affected as it was the largest importer of the goods in question; it was an end-user of the goods; its activities depended to a large extent on the goods which were subject to the duty; and it would face significant difficulties in finding an alternative source of supply. It is also worth noting that the Commission took account of Extramet's figures in formulating the regulation. The anti-dumping cases do not, however, necessarily serve as a solid basis for a more relaxed approach to standing to challenge regulations generally, as anti-dumping measures take the form of regulations and not decisions and, as a result, absent this somewhat modified approach to the standing rules, individuals would always be precluded from challenging anti-dumping measures.

The difficulties raised by individual concern for natural and legal persons: interest groups

11.27 This formulation of the standing rules serves, in effect, to exclude individuals from judicial review of Community acts in all but a few cases. Further, it makes the position of lobbying groups and collective associations particularly difficult. The Community courts have held in a number of cases that associations which protect the collective interests of a group of persons will not be considered directly and individually concerned by measures affecting the general interests of the group and so cannot take an annulment action where the members may not do so on an individual basis: Joined Cases T-447/93, T-448/93 and T-449/93 *AITEC v Commission* (1995). Certain special circumstances, however, such as participation by the association in the procedure which led to adoption of the decision, may confer standing on the association even where the members are not directly and individually concerned: *Federolio v Commission*; Case C-313/90 *CIRFS v Commission* (1993); and Joined Cases 67, 68 and 70/85 *Van der Kooy v Commission* (1988). As an illustration, Case T-585/93 *Greenpeace v Commission* (1995) shows that the test for individual concern does not allow the increasingly high-profile concerns of the environmental lobby with respect to Community measures to be fully reflected in the judicial review process. Greenpeace mounted a valiant attempt to convince the Community courts to re-evaluate the nature of individual concern when seeking annulment of a Commission allocation of funds to Spain for the purposes of building power stations on sites which were considered environmentally sensitive. Greenpeace claimed that '... all individuals who have suffered or potentially will suffer detriment as a result of a Community measure which affects the environment have standing to bring an action under Article 173 (now Article 230 EC)...' and so sought to introduce a wider test. They specifically requested the court to adopt 'a liberal approach' and '...recognise that...locus standi can depend not on a purely economic interest but on their interest in the protection of the environment, abandoning the approach adopted in the past in cases concerning purely economic interests'. The Court of First Instance decided against a relaxation of the rules, rejecting the view that standing could be based on a general interest in environmental protection, and reiterated that the applicant was required to show that it was affected by the measure in such a way that differentiated the applicant from all other persons. In Case C-321/95P *Stichting Greenpeace Council (Greenpeace International) v Commission* (1998), the ECJ confirmed the ruling of the Court of First Instance. It found that where the specific situation of an applicant was not taken into consideration in adopting a measure which concerned the applicant in an abstract and general fashion, and, in fact, like any person in the same situation, the applicant was not individually concerned by the measure. The same analysis applied to associations, such as Greenpeace, which claimed to have locus standi on the grounds that the persons they represented were individually concerned by the measure. Greenpeace had claimed that the approach of the Court of First Instance 'created a legal vacuum' in ensuring compliance with EC environmental law as the interests in the area (and in particular the right to be involved in environmental impact assessment procedures) were, by their nature, common and shared and the rights relating to those interests were liable to be held by a potentially large number of persons. The court ruled that it was the decision to build the power station which was liable to affect EC environmental rights invoked by Greenpeace and not the contested decision, which concerned financing. It also pointed to the possibility of enforcing environmental rights through the national courts and the preliminary reference procedure.

Plaumann and individual concern

11.28 It may appear from a consideration of the case law that there have been a number of cases where the ECJ has been flexible with respect to individual concern. It is worth considering, therefore, whether the original and stringent *Plaumann* test is still good law. Those cases where the ECJ appears to take a more relaxed approach to standing can, however, largely be explained by the particular factors present in those cases. In

Piraiki, the Greek Act of Accession required the Commission to take particular account of those undertakings likely to be affected by protective measures. In *Sofrimport,* the particular situation of goods in transit when the contested regulation was adopted was at issue. In *Codorniu,* the applicant was in a particularly distinctive situation as it held a very large market share in the product affected by the regulation and, further, its legal rights under a prior trademark were extinguished by the regulation. Indeed, the cases which apply the apparently more flexible *Codorniu* test appear to indicate that it is only in exceptional circumstances that an individual will be able to show individual concern in respect of a regulation which has a general legislative character. In *Extramet,* and in the anti-dumping cases generally, a more flexible approach is called for as anti-dumping legislation invariably takes the form of regulations, and not decisions. It would appear that, as a general rule, *Plaumann* will still present significant difficulties for most applicants.

The Court of First Instance champions individuals' access to justice

11.29 The Court of First Instance has recently emerged, however, as a champion of individuals' access to justice under Article 230 EC in an important case decided in May 2002: Case T-177/01 *Jégo-Quére et Cie v Commission,* in which it drastically recasts the law on individual concern. Jégo-Quére was a fishing company which used nets with a mesh of 80mm, which were banned by a Community regulation. It applied to the CFI for an annulment of two provisions of the regulation. The Commission argued that the action was inadmissible as, based on the previous case-law, Jégo-Quére was not individually concerned. While the provisions in question were of direct concern to Jégo-Quére, it was not individually concerned in that the net mesh size rules applied equally to all fishing operators subject to the regulation. In deciding that the action was admissible, and that Jégo-Quére was individually concerned, even though the regulation was of general application, the CFI took a radically different approach to the question of individual concern. It noted that the previous case law prevented a number of individuals from challenging measures of direct application which directly affected their legal position, and that none of the other procedural routes available under the Treaty provided an appropriate vehicle for challenging the legality of a Community measure. The CFI found that access to the courts was a fundamental element of a Community based on the rule of law, as guaranteed by the legal order based on the EC Treaty which had established a system of legal remedies and procedures to permit the ECJ to review the legality of Community measures. It also noted that the ECJ had held that the right to an effective remedy before a court of competent jurisdiction was based on the constitutional traditions common to the member states and the European Convention for the Protection of Human Rights and Fundamental Freedoms. The Charter of Fundamental Rights of the European Union (2000) also affirmed the right to an effective remedy for all persons whose rights and freedoms under EU law have been violated. The CFI found, as a result, that, in order for individuals to be effectively protected by the courts, a natural or legal person was to be regarded as individually concerned by a Community measure of general application that concerns him directly, if the measure in question affects his legal position, in a manner which is both definite and immediate, by restricting his rights or by imposing obligations on him. The number and the position of other persons likewise affected by the measure, or who might be so, would not be relevant. As the regulation on net mesh size imposed obligations on Jégo-Quére, it was both directly and individually concerned and the action was admissible.

This groundbreaking ruling by the CFI reflects the more liberal approach to individual concern called for by Jacobs AG in his Opinion earlier in March 2002 in Case C-50/00P *Unión de Pequeños Agricultores v Council* which concerned a challenge by a trade association to a regulation of general application. He proposed that 'a person is to be regarded as individually concerned by a Community measure where, by reason of his particular circumstances, the measure has, or is liable to have, a substantial adverse effect on his interests.' The ECJ did not adopt the Advocate General's approach, however, in its ruling on the case later in July 2002. In particular, it found that while the condition that individual concern must be shown was to be interpreted in light of the principle of effective judicial protection, by taking into account the various circumstances which may distinguish an applicant individually (it referred to, inter alia, *Codorniu* and *Extramet*), 'such an interpretation cannot have the effect of setting aside the condition in question, expressly laid down in the Treaty, without going beyond the jurisdiction conferred by the Treaty and the Community courts'. It concluded that '[w]hile it is, admittedly, possible to envisage a system of judicial review of the legality of Community measures of general application different from that established by the founding Treaty and never amended as to its principles, it is for the member states, if necessary, in accordance with Article 48 EU to reform the system currently in force'. It seems unlikely that the CFI's approach will survive.

Direct concern

11.30 In the case of both decisions addressed to another person of individual concern to the applicant, and of decisions in the form of regulations of individual concern to the applicant, a second hurdle, additional to individual concern, must be crossed before standing will be granted. The contested measure must also be of direct concern to the applicant. Direct concern will be established where there is a direct causal link between the challenged Community measure and its ultimate impact on the applicant. Where a member state is given a discretion to act by a decision, an applicant may not be directly concerned by the decision due to the lack of a direct link between the Community decision and the impact on the applicant. In Case 69/69 *Alcan v Commission* (1970) the Belgian and Luxembourg governments lobbied the Commission to increase the Belgian allocation of low tariff aluminium. The Commission refused to increase the quota and this decision was challenged by the applicant. The ECJ found that the decision was not of direct concern as, even if the Commission had agreed that the quota could be increased, the decision would not have required the member states to increase the quota. This was so despite the fact that Belgium and Luxembourg had actively lobbied for an increase in the quota. The ECJ now seems to take a more realistic approach in that it accepts that where the implementation of the Community decision is a foregone conclusion, as one would presume where the member state has sought permission or authorisation for the action, the measure will be of direct concern to the applicant. In *Piraiki-Patraiki v Commission* (see above 11.17) a Commission decision authorised the French government to impose a quota system on the import of Greek yarn. The ECJ decided that any possibility that the French government would not impose the quota was purely theoretical, and therefore the decision was of direct concern to the Greek applicant. Direct concern will also be established if the member state indicates in advance how it will exercise the discretion it enjoys under the contested Community measure (Case 62/70 *Bock v Commission* (1971)).

11.31 The ECJ recently looked at the question of direct concern in Case C-403/96P *Glencore Grain Ltd v Commission* (1998). At issue was the implementation of a loan from the EU to certain Republics of the Soviet Union, the benefit of which was directed to individual undertakings by means of the award of a contract to supply wheat. A producer was found to be directly concerned by a decision addressed to the financial agent of the borrowing republic refusing to approve the supply contract due to non-compliance with Community rules, as there was only a theoretical possibility that the agent would, notwithstanding the decision, still proceed to approve the contract between the producer and the agent. The Court found that for a measure to be of direct concern the measure must directly affect the legal situation of the individual and leave no discretion to the addressees of the measure who are entrusted with implementing it.

Time limitations

11.32 An annulment action must be brought within two months of the publication of the measure or its notification to the applicant or, in the absence thereof, within two months of the day on which the contested measure came to the notice of the applicant (Article 230(5) EC). Notification involves communication of a detailed account of the measure's content and the reasons for its adoption. The time period runs from notification of the full text of the decision and not from when a brief summary of the decision's content was notified to the applicant (see Case C-143/95P *Commission v Socurte* (1997)). This time bar is strictly enforced and filters out a number of actions (for example, see Case C-178/95 *Wiljo NV v Belgium* (1997)). The Rules of Procedure of the ECJ do provide for short extensions of the two-month period in certain limited circumstances. The party alleging the existence of a time bar has the responsibility of showing on what date the decision was notified: Joined Cases T-70/92 and T-71/92 *Florimex BV v Commission* (1997) and Case T-94/92 *X v Commission* (1994).

Grounds for annulment

11.33 The grounds for annulment are set out in Article 230(2). A measure may be annulled for lack of competence on the part of the Community institution(s) which has adopted the measure. The ECJ takes a broad teleological approach to the interpretation of the Treaty, however, and has adopted a doctrine of implied powers and this approach, together with the broad law-making power given under Article 308 (ex Article 235) EC, means that this ground for annulment can be difficult to establish (see Cases 281, 283-5 and 287/85 *Germany v Commission* (1987)). Infringement of an essential procedural requirement is another ground for annulment. For a classic example of failure to adopt the correct legislative procedure see Case 138/79 *Roquette Frères v Council*, above (at **11.10**). Compliance with the duty to give reasons is another key procedural requirement. In Case T-105/95 *WWF UK v Commission* (1997) a Commission decision refusing access to Commission documents was annulled for breach of the duty to give reasons. This duty is assuming an ever-greater importance in the Community order. A measure may also be annulled for infringement of the Treaty or any law relating to its application and this ground is very often raised in annulment proceedings. Infringements under this ground include infringements of general principles of Community law. See Case 112/77 *August Töpfer & Co GmbH v Commission* (1978) and Case C-152/88 *Sofrimport v Commission* (1990) on breach of the principles of legal certainty and legitimate expectations and Case 114/76 *Bela-Mühle v Grows-Farm* (1977) on breach of the principle of proportionality. A number of annulment actions have attempted to raise breach of the fundamental human rights which form a part of the general principles of Community law as grounds for review. While the ECJ has created a catalogue of fundamental human rights which form part of the general principles of Community law, it does not often find that there has been a breach of these rights (see Case 4/73 *Nold v Commission* (1974) at **6.8**). Finally, a measure may be annulled for misuse of powers. In Case 105/75 *Giuffrida v Council* (1976) an unsuccessful applicant for a position in the Commission brought an action alleging that the competition was, in reality, a smokescreen as the position in question had already been reserved for another Commission official. The ECJ found that the competition had been held for the sole purpose of appointing a particular Commission official to a higher grade and so was contrary to the aims of the recruitment procedure and a misuse of powers. In addition to recognising the need to review abuses of authority by covering misuses of power and breaches of Treaty rules, the grounds for annulment also reflect the fact that the Community legal order is a formal one, where institutional acts must have a legal basis and follow the relevant procedural requirements.

The effect of an annulment

11.34 If the action is well founded, the measure will be declared void under Article 231 EC. A declaration of nullity will be retroactive and will have effect *erga omnes* and so be of general application. The exact ambit of *erga omnes* effect is not clear. Certain commentators are of the opinion that a declaration of annulment can only affect those persons whose rights or interests could have been affected by the measure annulled, and so it is only those annulments of general measures which affect the public which will have full *erga omnes* effect. Annulments of individual measures, such as decisions, will, by contrast, only have effects with respect to those persons affected by such measures. An alternative view is that declarations of annulment apply to all persons. The ECJ recently addressed this issue in Case C-310/97P *Commission v AssiDomän Kraft Products* (1999). The case concerned a 1984 Commission decision (composed of a number of individual decisions adopted under the same procedure) which had found price-concertation in the wood pulp market and imposed fines on a number of wood pulp producers. It was successfully challenged under Article 230 by a number, but not all, of its addressees and annulled. The remaining producers addressed by the decision, who had not been party to the original Article 230 action, requested the Commission to reimburse the fines they had paid in light of that annulment and, following the Commission's refusal to do so, brought an action under Article 230 for annulment of that refusal. Examining the effect of the original annulment, the court confirmed that the annulment of a decision benefited only the addressees of the decision who had taken the annulment action, and explained that the *erga omnes* effect of an annulment did not include the annulment of an act which had not been challenged before the Community courts, but was alleged to suffer from the same illegality. The court emphasised the connection between the Article 233 obligation and the scope of the underlying annulling judgent, which was limited to the parties who have taken the action.

Under Article 233(1):

> ...the institution whose act has been declared void will be required to take the necessary measures to comply with the judgment of the Court.

Accordingly, it found that while Article 233 required the institution concerned to ensure that any act intended to replace the annulled measure was not affected by the irregularities identified in the annulling judgment, it was not necessary for the institution to re-examine identical or similar decisions which were allegedly affected by the same illegality.

11.35 As permitted by Article 231(2), the ECJ has declared on occasion that certain or all parts of a measure which has been declared void will, nonetheless, continue in force for certain periods of time if it considers such an action necessary. In Case C-295/90 *European Parliament v Council* (1992), although the ECJ annulled Directive 90/366 which concerned the elimination of discrimination with respect to vocational training, it found that outright annulment would undermine the exercise by students of the right of residence for vocational training reasons and, further, that the date for the implementation of the contested directive had passed.

As a result, reasons of legal certainty justified a declaration that the directive would continue to have legal effects until such time as the Council replaced it with a directive which had been correctly adopted. As well as providing an illustration of when the ECJ will limit the temporal effects of an annulment, the case also shows that the court will not restrict this power to regulations, as seems to be suggested by the strict wording of Article 231(2). Similarly, in Case C-21/94 *European Parliament v Council* (1995) the ECJ annulled a regulation on transport policy for breach of an essential procedural requirement, but declared that the measure would remain in effect until the Council had passed a replacement measure in order to avoid any discontinuity in the transport harmonisation programme and to ensure legal certainty. See also Case C-388/92 *European Parliament v Council* (1994) and Case 81/72 *Commission v Council* (1973). In these cases it is worth noting that the ECJ often refers to the fact that the party seeking annulment does not object to the measure remaining in force until a replacement act is passed, or that there is no serious dispute with respect to the content of the measure. An interim order may, of course, suspend the operation of the contested measure until a final ruling is made if the court finds this is necessary. It is also clear from Case C-137/92P *Commission v BASF (PVC)* (1994) that, in certain extreme cases, a measure may be so defective that it will be declared void ab initio, or non-existent. The ECJ overruled a finding by the Court of First Instance that a decision of the Commission that certain companies were in breach of Treaty competition rules was so defective that it was non-existent, but stated that there was a possibility that the irregularities which a measure contained were so grave that it could not be tolerated by the Community legal order and must be regarded as wholly non-existent. In this case, however, the irregularities as to competence and form were not of such obvious gravity that the measure should be treated as legally non-existent.

Article 230 and Article 234 (ex Article 177) EC

11.36 Article 234(1)(b), which allows preliminary references to be made by national courts on the 'validity and interpretation of acts of the institutions of the Community', may, in certain circumstances, provide an indirect alternative for individuals who wish to challenge Community acts. A national court may, in the course of an action by an individual for judicial review of a Community measure and its application to him, or, during an action taken against an individual for non-compliance with a Community act and its national implementing measure, where the validity of the Community act is raised, refer a question to the ECJ on the validity of the Community act in question. This route may be particularly useful with respect to regulations because, as we have seen, individual applicants face particular obstacles in establishing standing to challenge regulations under Article 230.

11.37 In Joined Cases 133-136/85 *Rau v BALM* (1987), the ECJ held that the possibility of bringing an annulment action under Article 232 did not prevent the validity of the Community decision being raised in an action in a national court against a national measure implementing that Community decision. The ECJ has now amplified that basic principle and placed limitations on when the national courts and the preliminary reference procedure may be used to challenge Community measures. In Case C-188/92 *TWD Textilwerke Deggendorf v Germany* (1994), a company tried to raise the legality of a Commission decision (addressed to the German government and finding that aid granted to the company by the German government was unlawful and had to be repaid) in the German national courts. The ECJ held that the invalidity of the Commission decision could not be raised in proceedings against the German authorities' implementing decision before the national courts where the company had not applied under Article 230 for annulment of the contested Commission decision within the prescribed period, and where the company could undoubtedly have done so. The ECJ found that the company:

> ...was fully aware of the Commission decision and of the fact that it could without any doubt have challenged it under Article 173 of the Treaty.

The court referred to the fact that the company had been informed in writing of the Commission decision by the German authorities and had also been informed of the possibility of taking an annulment action. The ECJ took a similar line in Case C-178/95 *Wiljo NV v Belgium* (1997) where the plaintiff sought to challenge the validity of a Commission decision (which stated that a vessel owned by Wiljo did not come within the terms of a particular exemption from certain Community scrapping requirements) in proceedings before the national courts concerning the national measure implementing the Commission's decision. It found that where the Commission decision was addressed to an owner of a vessel and that owner had not brought an action under Article 230 within the time limits, the Commission decision was binding on the national courts and its invalidity could not be raised under Article 234. The ECJ found that the time period within which annulment proceedings could be brought was designed to ensure legal certainty and, as a result, a decision which had not been challenged by its addressee within the time period became final and definitive against him. The court rejected any arguments based on the *Rau* principle, pointing out that in *Rau* the plaintiffs had brought an action for annulment of the decision in question and that the Court of Justice had not, therefore, dealt with the effect of a time bar to an annulment action on subsequently raising the validity of the Community measure in national proceedings. The ECJ noted the *TWD* principle applied where there was a failure to bring an Article 230 action in circumstances where the action could 'undoubtedly' have been brought. As the addressee of the decision, Wiljo was in such a position. It appears from Case C-241/95 *R v Intervention Board for Agricultural Produce, ex p Accrington Beef Co Ltd* (1997), however, that, where it is not clear that the individual would have standing to challenge the contested Community act under Article 230, the validity of the act may be raised in national proceedings and so through a preliminary reference, despite the fact that an annulment action is time barred. The ECJ found that in *TWD* the company was, without doubt, entitled to bring an action and had been notified to that effect, but that here:

> ...since the contested provisions are contained in a Community regulation and are addressed in general terms to categories of persons defined in the abstract and to situations determined objectively, it is not obvious that an action...under Article 173...would have been admissible.

As a result, the reference was admissible despite that fact that the companies in question had failed to bring an annulment action within the time limit. The court took a similar position in Case C-408/95 *Eurotunnel SA v SeaFrance* (1997) finding that the *TWD* principle did not apply where the contested provisions were contained in a directive and where, as a result, it was not obvious that an annulment action would have been admissible.

Article 232 (ex Article 175) EC

Introduction

11.38 Article 232 provides for judicial review of failures to act by Community institutions and so serves to compel an institution to act when it has a legal duty to take a particular action. It acts as a complement, and is similar in structure, to Article 230. Indeed, the ECJ examined the relationship between the two remedies in Case 15/70 *Chevalley v Commission* (1970) finding that the two articles 'merely prescribe one and the same method of recourse'. In Case 302/87 *Parliament v Council*, however, the ECJ seemed to dissociate itself, in part at least, from this approach to Article 230 and Article 232, known as the 'unity principle'. The court was adamant in that case that, even though Parliament could seek review under Article 232, it did not necessarily follow that it should have standing under Article 230. This perspective is, perhaps, less a reflection of the relationship between Article 230 and Article 232 and more an expression of the ECJ's view, at that time, of the institutional balance of power in the Community.

Under Article 232, Parliament, the Council, the Commission and the European Central Bank may be sued for a failure to act. Both Parliament and the European Central Bank were added to the institutions expressly subject to review under Article 232 by the Maastricht Treaty. Before an omission by one of these institutions is treated as reviewable, the failure to act must amount to a breach of a Treaty obligation. Article 232 therefore covers all failures to act where there is legal duty under Community law to take action. In Case 13/83 *European Parliament v Council* (1985) Parliament brought an action with respect to the alleged failure by the Council to establish a framework for a common transport policy as required under the then Article 74 (now Article 70 EC). The ECJ found that the obligation to introduce a common transport policy Article 74 was not sufficiently precise to the extent that a failure to further pursue a common transport policy amounted to a breach of the Treaty. The court found that an applicant under Article 232 must specify the measures which the erring institution has failed to take and so allow for remedial action. Parliament had not specified the measures necessary in order to achieve a common transport policy and so could not succeed under Article 232. Parliament was successful in one respect, however. It had requested the Council to take specific action under the then Article 75(1)(a) and (b) (now Article 71(1)(a) and (b) EC) with respect to international transport and non-resident carriers. This failure to act was a breach of a specific obligation under the Treaty.

11.39 It is clear from Article 232(2) that an action will only be admissible if the relevant institution 'has first been called on to act'. The Treaty does not specify when this approach to the relevant institution should be made, but in Case 59/70 *Netherlands v Commission* (1971) the ECJ, in the context of the equivalent ECSC Treaty provision, found that such an approach should be made within a reasonable period of time. Once the institution has been called on to act and has defined its position concerning the alleged failure to act within a two-month time period, Case 48/65 *Lütticke v Commission* (1966) provides that the action cannot go any further. This definition of position is then an act which could, subject to the usual requirements as to standing, be further challenged under Article 230 if necessary. If the institution does not define its position within the two-month time limit, an Article 232 action may be brought within a further period of two months. The definition of position is therefore central to the operation of Article 232, but neither the Treaty nor the ECJ has provided a comprehensive definition of what this involves. In Case 302/87 *Parliament v Council* the ECJ gave some guidance when it found that the response of the Council to the Commission's request to take action with respect to transport did not amount to a definition of position. The Council had replied to Parliament's complaint by stating the current policy and promising that further progress and policies would be undertaken. The court found that this response neither denied nor confirmed the alleged failure to act and, further, did not give any indication of the Council's view as to the measures which it had been requested to take. A further indication of the ECJ's view is set out in Cases 166, 220/ 86 *Irish Cement Ltd v Commission* (1988).

Locus standi

11.40 Article 232 provides that 'the member states and the other institutions of the Community' have standing to bring an action and so the Council, the Commission, the Parliament and the member states are all privileged applicants under Article 232. In Case 13/83 *European Parliament v Council* (see above **11.38**) the ECJ confirmed that Parliament was 'an institution of the Community' and so did have standing.

11.41 Mirroring the position under Article 230, natural and legal persons have limited locus standi. Such a person can only bring an action in connection with a binding act which the institution in question had an obligation to address to him. Despite this apparently restrictive formula, it is clear from the case law of the ECJ that Article 232 is not limited to review of a failure to take a decision actually addressed to the applicant. It also covers measures which, had they been taken, could have been challenged by the applicant under Article 230. In Case 246/81 *Bethell v Commission* (1982) the ECJ held that the omitted act must be an act which the applicant was legally entitled to claim. The applicant had requested the Commission to take action against price fixing between airlines and, unhappy with the Commission's response to his request, took action under Article 175 (now Article 232 EC). The ECJ found that while the applicant had, as a frequent user of airlines, an indirect interest in the proceedings:

> ...he is nevertheless not in the precise legal position of the actual addressee of a decision, which may be declared void under the second paragraph of Article 173, or in that of the potential addressee of a legal measure which the Commission has a duty to adopt with regard to him, as is the position under the third paragraph of Article 175. It follows that the application is inadmissible...

11.42 Further evidence of the difficulties faced by individuals is provided by Case 247/87 *Star Fruit Co v Commission* (1989) where the applicant sought to challenge a refusal by the Commission to take Article 226 enforcement proceedings. The ECJ simply found that:

> ...the Commission is not bound to commence the proceedings...but in this regard has a discretion which excludes the right for individuals to require that institution to adopt a specific position.

See also Case T-277/94 *AITEC v Commission* (1997) on review of failures to act in the state aid sector under Article 86. Under Article 233(1), if the action succeeds, the institution is required to take the necessary measures to comply with the judgment of the ECJ.

The plea of illegality under Article 241 (ex Article 184) EC

11.43 Like Article 230 and Article 232, this article provides for challenges to certain acts of Community institutions but it differs in that it only allows acts of the institutions to be challenged indirectly. It is not a separate form of action. The plea of illegality may only be raised in the context of proceedings which have already been initiated on other grounds (Cases 31 and 33/62 *Wöhrmann v EEC Commission* (1962)).

11.44 The use of Article 241 to challenge Community measures indirectly can perhaps be best illustrated by its incidental application in Article 230 proceedings. As we have seen, legal and natural persons face significant difficulties in bringing an Article 230 action against a regulation owing to its general nature. An individual may, however, challenge a specific decision addressed to him under Article 230 on the grounds that the original regulation on which the decision is based is illegal (provided, of course, that the conditions of Article 230 are met), and may challenge the regulation from which the decision is derived or which the decision is implementing by raising a plea of illegality under Article 241. The challenge to the regulation is therefore made under Article 241 in an incidental manner to the main annulment proceedings concerning the contested decision. The challenge to the regulation may be taken on this indirect basis under Article 241 in the course of the larger Article 230 proceedings, even where a direct challenge to the regulation under Article 230 is time-barred and so Article 241 may be therefore be usefully used to circumvent time bars.

11.45 Article 241 provides that a plea of illegality may be raised in proceedings 'in which a regulation adopted jointly by the European Parliament and the Council, or a regulation of the Council, of the Commission, or of the ECB is at issue'. The action thus appears only to cover regulations and to be limited in scope. It is clear, however, from Case 92/78 *Simmenthal v Commission* (1979) that the action also covers acts of the institutions which produce similar effects to regulations but which do not take the form of regulations. The ECJ also found in *Simmenthal* that Article 241 must be given a wide interpretation in order to:

> ....provide those persons who are precluded by the second paragraph of Article 173 from instituting proceedings directly in respect of general acts with the benefit of judicial review of them at the time when they are affected by implementing decisions which are of direct and individual concern to them.

If the Article 241 plea succeeds, the regulation is 'inapplicable' and may not stand as the basis for the contested decision which will, as a result, be void. The regulation itself will not be annulled.

Contractual and tortious liability of the Community—actions for damages may be contractual, quasi-contractual, or tortious

Contractual liability of the Community (Article 288(1) (ex Article 215(1)) EC)

11.46 The first paragraph of Article 288 deals with the contractual liability of Community institutions and compensation actions. It provides that liability shall be governed by the law applicable to the contract. The Community's contracts will normally contain a choice of law clause. There is no specific procedure for compensation. The jurisdiction of the Court over contractual arbitration clauses is governed by Article 238 (ex Article 181) EC.

11.47 Quasi-contractual liability, ie actions based on unjust enrichment, are not provided for specifically, but the Court has found in staff cases that there is Community liability based on the general principle of unjust enrichment recognised by most member states. This was so, for example, in Case 18/63 *Wollast v Commission* (1964) where a Commission employee was found to have been unjustly enriched by receiving full pay during a period when she had not worked because she had been dismissed. The dismissal had been annulled by the court, and she was thus entitled to payment. However, a deduction was made from the full pay as she had not had certain expenses, eg for child care.

Damages against Community institutions (non-contractual liability) (Articles 235 (ex Article 178) and 288 (ex Article 215) EC)

11.48 Community liability in tort described as 'non-contractual liability', is governed by Articles 235 and 288(2) EC. This liability is not specified and it has been a matter for the court to interpret its ambit. The Community may be liable for both *'fautes de service'*, ie wrongful acts on the part of one of its institutions, and *'fautes personnelles'*, ie wrongful acts on the part of its servants. As long as the wrongful acts are committed in the performance of a Community official's duties, the institution concerned may be sued. These concepts are derived from French law, but are applied by the court in its own way.

In determining liability 'in accordance with the general principles common to the laws of the member states' (Article 288(2) EC), the ECJ has drawn on the common elements governing tortious liability in the member states in order to develop its own specific principles of Community law.

The parties

11.49 There is no limitation on the person bringing the action. Against whom should the action be brought? Article 288(2) states that 'the Community' shall make good any damage. In Cases 63–69/72 *Werhahn v Council and Commission* (1973) the Court ruled that the action should be brought against the institution which is responsible. If two institutions are involved, it is quite correct to bring the action against both. (Where

270

Community liability is involved because of one of its institutions' actions, the Community should be represented before the ECJ by the institution(s) against which the matter giving rise to liability is alleged.)

Time limit

11.50 A time limit of five years is provided, running from the occurrence of the event giving rise to liability (Article 43 of the Statute of the ECJ): see Case 51/81 *De Franceschi* (1982). The limitation period only begins to run from the moment when the damage becomes known: Cases 145/83 and 53/84 *Adams v Commission* (1985). The applicant became aware of the event giving rise to the damage he suffered after the time limit had expired and the Court ruled that the limitation period does not begin to run until the injured party becomes aware of the event giving rise to his claim; Cases 256, 257, 265, 267/80 & 5/81 *Birra Wührer v Council and Commission* (1982): for the purposes of Article 43 of the Statute of the Court the five-year limitation period runs from the time of actual damage, and not from the earliest time the action could have commenced.

Wrongful act

11.51 *Fault* Unlike in the ECSC Treaty, there is no requirement of fault in the EC Treaty. Nevertheless, the ECJ has always required proof of fault. There should be a fault committed by the Community as well as damage suffered by the applicant and a causal link between the fault committed and the damage.

Faute de service includes any failure in the organisation and function of the public authority:

• civil wrongs (ie all sorts of torts);

• abusive application of powers; see Cases 5, 7, 13-24/66 *Kampffmeyer* (1967): improper use of crucial provisions of a regulation is capable of giving rise to liability on the part of the Community;

• non-performance of obligations; see Cases 9 & 12/60 *Vloeberghs v High Authority* (1961);

• inadequate organisation of the administration; see Case 23/59 FERAM (1959); Cases 156/79 & 51/80 *Gratreau* (1980);

- inadequate supervision; see Cases 19, 21/60 and 2–3/61 *Fives Lille Cail* (1961); Cases 29, 31, 36, 39–47, 50, 51/63 *Laminoirs* (1965);

- erroneous information; see Cases 19, 20, 25, 30/69 *Richez-Parise* (1970);

- unlawful termination of staff contracts; see Cases 7/56 & 3–7/57 *Algera* (1957–58);

- insufficient protection of rights of staff members; see Case 110/63 *Willame* (1965);

- breach of internal rules; see Cases 10 and 47/72 *Di Pillo* (1973);

- breach of a superior rule of law; see eg, Case 5/71 *Aktien-Zuckerfabrik Schöppenstedt* (1971) (non-discrimination);

- breaches of the duty of confidentiality and the duty to warn the applicant; see Cases 145/83 and 53/84 *Adams* (1985).

Liability without fault

11.52 In his opinion in Cases 9 and 11/71 *Compagnie d'Approvisionnement v Commission (No 2)* (1972), the Advocate General left open the possibility that the principle of 'equality in the face of public burdens' might be applied in Community law. Under this doctrine the state may be liable in certain circumstances in the absence of fault if it can be demonstrated that measures taken by the state have placed an abnormal and unjustifiably severe burden on certain individuals who have thus been required to make a disproportionate sacrifice in the general interest. However, the Court ruled that no liability arose here, but did not say anything further on the general question of strict liability.

Damages

11.53 The damage must be actual (*réel et certain*). In Cases 5, 7, 13-24/66 *Kampffmeyer* (1967) the ECJ admitted claims for loss of profit; also loss due to currency fluctuations: Case 74/74 *CNTA* (1975).

In staff cases, damages may be claimed for anxiety and injured feelings by a Community employee wrongfully dismissed or unfairly treated: Cases

7/56 and 3–7/57 *Algera* (1957–58). Actual damage must be proved, or at least imminent damage which is foreseeable with sufficient certainty: Cases 56–60/74 *Kampffmeyer* (1976).

The damage must not be too remote: Case 4/69 *Lütticke* (1971); there should a causal link between the damage and the act complained of. Damage may be adjudged to be non-existent where the applicant is able to pass on the loss sustained to his customers: Cases 64, 113/76, 167, 239/78, 27, 28 and 45/79 *Dumortier (Quellmehl & Gritz)* (1979).

Causal link

11.54 The ECJ has accepted the notion of a causal link on a number of occasions without any further elaboration. See eg Case 4/69 *Lütticke* (1971).

In Cases 64, 113/76, 167, 239/78, 27, 28 and 45/79 *Dumortier (Quellmehl & Gritz)* (1979) the ECJ gave a further clarification: in the field of non-contractual liability for legislative measures, there is no obligation for the Community to make good:

> ... every harmful consequence, even a remote one, of unlawful legislation;

the damage alleged must be

> ...a sufficiently direct consequence of the unlawful conduct of the institution concerned.

The burden to prove the causal link between the harmful behaviour of Community institutions and the alleged damage falls on the applicant: Case 40/75 *Bertrand* (1976).

11.55 The causal link may be severed by contributory negligence on behalf of the applicant: C-308/87 *Grifoni* (1990).

In Case 169/73 *Compagnie Continentale* (1975) the court said that in a claim based on misleading information the required causal link will be established only if the information would have caused an error in the mind of a reasonable person. See also the general discussion of causal link in the Advocate General's opinion in this case (at pp 148–154).

11.56 Apportionment is reserved for claims of particular merit: Cases 145/83 and 53/84 *Adams v Commission* (1985). This is one of the few cases in this field where an individual has been awarded substantial damages, but it is a remarkable and tragic one. Mr Adams was employed by the Swiss pharmaceutical company Hoffmann-La Roche and had passed certain confidential documents on to the Commission which contained evidence of violation of the competition law Article 86 (now Article 82 EC) of the Treaty. He had left Switzerland but returned there for a visit and was arrested and imprisoned for having violated Swiss law on commercial secrecy. While he was in prison his wife committed suicide. After his release he sued the Community for damages. The Court held that the Commission had violated its duty of confidentiality by not taking steps to prevent Hoffmann-La Roche from learning the name of the informant. However, Mr Adams's damages were reduced by 50% to take into account his own contribution in failing to protect his own interests.

Distinctive nature of the remedy

11.57 Non-contractual liability under Article 288(2) EC exists as a separate remedy from the remedies for judicial review under Articles 230 and 232 EC. This was not the view taken originally by the ECJ in Case 25/62 *Plaumann* (1963) (see **11.16**). The case was declared inadmissible as Plaumann lacked locus standi. However, the Court declared the action admissible, although it then dismissed the case on its merits. It said that a reviewable act which has not been annulled cannot form the basis of an action for damages. This is an extremely restrictive interpretation which had been rejected by the Court in Cases 9 and 12/60 *Vloeberghs v High Authority* (1961). It had been contended there that Vloeberghs did not have standing to bring an action for review, and therefore could not bring a tort action. The Court had held that review actions and tort actions were separate remedies. Then, in Case 4/69 *Lütticke v Commission* (1971) the Court rejected the *Plaumann* approach and held:

> The action for damages provided for by Article 178 (now Article 235 EC) and the second paragraph of Article 215 (now Article 288 EC) was established as an independent form of action with a particular purpose to fulfil within the system of actions and subject to the conditions for its use, conceived with a view to its specific purpose...

11.58 This was further confirmed in Case 5/71 *Aktien-Zuckerfabrik Schöppenstedt v Council* (1971), which concerned a regulation under which no compensation was payable in case of loss. The company sued for damages and the Council contested admissibility on the grounds that such compensation would nullify the legal effect of the regulation. The Court said again that it concerned two separate types of action. *Schöppenstedt* was also important because it set out for the first time the principles governing Community liability for acts of the institutions (see **11.60**). The language it used in setting out these principles has been echoed in the later judgments of the court concerning liability of member states for violation of Community law (see Chapter 9).

The current practice is, in appropriate cases, to claim in the alternative: see eg Case 112/77 *Töepfer* (1978).

11.59 Article 288(2) EC can be used as a separate remedy from the remedies under Articles 230 and 232 for judicial review to obtain damages for the effects of an unlawful regulation, even though the regulation is of legislative nature and cannot be the subject of an action by a private party under Article 230 EC. See eg Cases 9 and 11/71 *Compagnie d'approvisionnement (No 2)* (1972); Case 4/69 *Lütticke* (1971).

Liability for legislative acts

11.60 Liability extends to acts of a legislative or normative character, such as regulations, provided that there is a 'sufficiently flagrant violation of a superior rule of law for the protection of the individual' ('*Schöppenstedt* formula'): see Case 5/71 *Aktien-Zuckerfabrik Schöppenstedt* (1971); see also Cases 83, 94/76, 4, 15 and 40/77 *HNL* (1978); Cases 197-200, 243, 245 and 247/80 *Ludwigshafener Waltzmühle* (1981); Case 281/84 *Zuckerfabrik Bedburg* (1987) and Cases 194-206/83 *Asteris* (1985).

The *Schöppenstedt* formula contains three requirements:

- *First requirement*: breach of a superior rule of law. See Case 74/74 *CNTA* (1975). The Commission was held liable to pay compensation for losses incurred as a result of regulation which abolished with immediate effect and without warning the application of agricultural export subsidies (MCAs): this was a serious breach of the principle of legitimate expectation;

- *Second requirement*: the breach must be sufficiently serious. See Cases 83, 94/76, 4, 15 and 40/77 *HNL* (1978): the Community may not incur responsibility for damage caused by a legislative act on the sole condition that it has been found illegal or invalid. In a legislative field involving wide discretion, the Community will not be liable unless the institution concerned has 'manifestly and gravely disregarded the limits on the exercise of its powers'. In Cases 64, 113/76, 167, 239/78, 27, 28 and 45/79 *Dumortier (Quellmehl & Gritz)* (1979) the breach of the principle of non-discrimination was held to be sufficiently serious. Quellmehl and Gritz producers were a small, clearly-defined group, and their loss went beyond the risks normally inherent in their business. In recent years, however, the ECJ has been less restrictive in its approach to what constitutes a sufficiently serious breach. In Case C-220/91P *Commission v Stahlwerke Peine-Salzgitter AG* (1993) the ECJ (in the context of a liability action based on a decision of the Court of First Instance) held that arbitrariness in making the decision was not necessary in order to show that there had been a sufficiently serious breach. In addition, the principle evident from cases such as *Dumortier* that damages are likely to be awarded only where there is a small number of potential claimants has now changed. From Cases C-104/89 and C-37/90 *Mulder No 2* (1992), it appears that a damages claim may be successful even where there is a large number of potential claimants.

The above cases seem to show that this requirement has two aspects to it: (a) the degree of harm suffered and the extent to which it is concentrated on a small group of victims; (b) the extent to which the law has been violated (the conduct of the institution concerned must be verging on the arbitrary). The severity of both these requirements has, however, as outlined, been lessened.

- *Third requirement*: the rule of law infringed must be one for the protection of the individual. See Cases 9 and 12/60 *Vloeberghs* (1961): the principle of free movement of goods was not intended for the benefit of coal importers; and Cases 5, 7, 13-24/66 *Kampffmeyer* (1967): a provision in an EC regulation intended at ensuring 'appropriate support for agricultural markets' intended to benefit, inter alia, the interests of individual undertakings such as importers.

From the case law it seems that as long as the rule of law can be construed as designed in part to benefit a particular group of people then the third requirement is met. Moreover, the fact that an individual would not have *locus standi* to challenge the rule under Article 230 EC due to lack of direct and individual concern does not necessarily mean that the provision is not intended to protect his interests.

Not only must the group affected be small and clearly defined but it must also be closed. In Case C-152/88 *Sofrimport* (1990) the ECJ pointed out that undertakings such as the applicants, with goods in transit at the time when the regulations were made, constituted a 'restricted group which could not be extended after the contested measures took effect'.

Limits of Community liability

11.61 *Acts of Community servants* In the case of *faute personnelle*, the Community is liable on the principle of vicarious liability. In Case 9/69 *Sayag v Leduc* (1969) the ECJ held that 'in the performance of their duties' in Article 288(2) means that the Community is only liable for those acts of its servants which, by virtue of an internal relationship, are the necessary extension of the tasks entrusted to the institutions. This is a very restrictive interpretation of Community's vicarious liability. *In casu*, the use of a private car by a Community servant could only be considered as constituting performance of his duties in the case of *force majeure* or exceptional circumstances of such compelling nature that the Community could not otherwise perform its functions. This, therefore, did not cover the use of a servant's private car during the performance of his duties.

11.62 *Concurrent fault on the part of the member states* The ECJ has proceeded by way of the following analysis: (a) is there joint liability on the part both of the Community and the member state? If there is, then (b) is the member state to be considered primarily liable so that it would be reasonable for it rather than the Community to pay compensation? If so, then (c) the applicant must pursue his remedy in the national courts before the ECJ can further entertain his claim: see Cases 5, 7, 13-24/66 *Kampffmeyer* (1967); Case 96/71 *Haegeman* (1972).

But where the real complaint is about the conduct of Community institutions, or where it is clear that national law can provide no remedy, an action under Article 288(2) EC may be admissible: see Case 281/82 *Unifrex* (1984); Case 175/84 *Krohn* (1986).

Further reading

Schermers, Heukels & Mead (eds), *Non-Contractual Liability of the European Communities* (1988) Martinus Nijhoff.

Wyatt, 'The relationship between actions for annulment and references on validity after TWD Deggendorf' in Lonbay and Biondi (eds), *Remedies for Breach of EC Law* (1997) Wiley.

Neuwahl, 'Article 174 paragraph 4 EC: past, present and possible future', [1996] 21 ELR 17.

Hartley, 'The European Court, judicial objectivity and the constitution of the European Union', [1996] 112 LQR 95.

Arnull, 'The European Court and judicial objectivity: a reply to Professor Hartley', [1996] 112 LQR 411.

Arnull, 'Private applicants and the action for annulment under Article 173 of the EC Treaty', [1995] 32 CMLRev 7.

Rasmussen, 'Why is Article 173 interpreted against private plaintiffs', [1980] 5 ELRev 112.

Greaves, '*Locus Standi* under Article 173 EEC when seeking annulment of a regulation', [1986] 11 ELRev 119.

Lysen, 'Three questions on the non-contractual liability of the EEC', [1985/2] LIEI 86.

Wils, 'Concurrent liability of the Community and a member state', [1992] 17 ELRev 191.

Self-test questions

1. How can the European Court of Justice review actions of the Community institutions?

2. What types of Community acts may be reviewed by the Community courts under Article 230 and Article 232?

3. How did the European Court of Justice improve the position of Parliament in bringing actions under Article 230 and Article 232?

4. 'Natural and legal persons face formidable obstacles in challenging an act of a Community institution before the Community courts.' Discuss.

5. What is meant by 'direct concern'?

6. Compare the position of privileged and non-privileged applicants in bringing a direct action against a Community institution.

7(a) Assume that Samson is the sole importer of Indonesian typewriters in the United Kingdom and that such typewriters are not imported into any other member state. In 1998 the United Kingdom Government accuses him of falsely labelling the typewriters as British products but has insufficient evidence to take action. In 2000 the United Kingdom learns that Samson intends to import a further large quota which it suspects he will market under the brand name of a German manufacturer. It requests the Commission to adopt a regulation banning the importation of typewriters from Indonesia for the year 2000. This is done.

Can Samson bring proceedings against the regulation under Article 230 EC?

(b) Assume that in 1998 the Council adopts a regulation giving Community nationals with a law degree from a member state the right to practise in any other member state. Article 7, however, provides that if the degree was obtained before the member state where it was obtained had joined the Community, a special examination in Community law (set by the Commission) must be passed.

Justinian is a Greek who obtained his degree in Greece in 1969. Does he have standing to bring annulment proceedings (against Article 7 only) under Article 230 EC? Would the position be any different if the measure was adopted in the form of a decision addressed to each of the member states?

8. 'There are certain circumstances where neither an action for failure nor an action for annulment are available, and a party may be left without any judicial remedy whatsoever against the conduct of the institutions.' Is this a true description of the situation? Discuss.

CHAPTER TWELVE

Free Movement of Goods: (1) The Abolition of Customs Duties and Internal Taxation

SUMMARY
- Basic concepts
- The customs union – common customs tariff
- Free movement of goods provisions in the Treaty
- Part I: pecuniary charges: Articles 23–29 (ex Articles 9–29) EC, Article 90 (ex Article 95) EC
- Obstacles
- Customs duties and charges having equivalent effect
- Internal taxation: discriminatory and/or protective
- What is the distinction?
- What are similar products?
- What are competing products?
- A charge must be either a customs duty or internal tax
- Can either be justified?
- VAT issues
- Excise duties and duty-free

Introduction

12.1 The European Community is a form of economic integration, combining elements of a customs union, a common market, common economic policies and provisions for economic and monetary union. See

Articles 2, 3 and 4 (ex Articles 2, 3 and 3a) EC. The Community was intended from its inception to be more than a free trade area, an arrangement between states in which they agree to remove customs duties and quotas in trade between them, but where they remain free individually to determine the duties on imports from third countries.

12.2 A *customs union* is a customs area involving various states cordoned off by a single external tariff and within whose boundaries no customs duties or quotas apply to all goods regardless of their origin. Once goods originating in a third country have been admitted anywhere in the customs union, they may circulate freely throughout the member states. The customs union thus presents itself as a single trading block to the outside world.

12.3 A *common market* entails yet closer integration among the participating states. The objective of a common market is to achieve not just free movement of goods, but also free movement of services and of the means of production (labour and capital). It comprises common external regulation for both goods and services as well as for production factors. Thus, a common market encompasses a customs union and in addition needs free movement of labour, ie persons, as labour is a factor of production and a major element in the production of goods.

The Customs Union – common customs tariff (Articles 26 and 27 (ex Articles 18–29) EC

12.4 A central feature of the European Community is the free movement of goods. The 'four freedoms' in the EC Treaty are the free movement of goods, persons, services and capital. The next two chapters are concerned with the free movement of goods. In order for goods to move without obstacle within the Community, it was necessary, first of all, to abolish customs duties and similar charges (Article 25 (ex Article 12) EC), to deal with internal taxation (Article 90 (ex Article 95) EC), and to see to it that non-pecuniary obstacles, such as quantitative restrictions and similar barriers, should not exist without good reasons (Articles 28, 29 and 30 (ex Articles 30, 34 and 36) EC).

The EC Treaty includes two chapters dealing with free movement of goods entitled 'The Customs Union' (Article 25 (ex Articles 12–17) EC) and 'Elimination of Quantitative Restrictions Between Member States' (Articles 28-31 (ex Articles 30–36) EC). Chapter 2 in Title V deals with internal taxation in Articles 90–93 (ex Articles 95–99) EC. A number of articles have been deleted by the Treaty of Amsterdam. These were provisions whose objectives have been achieved and which are thus spent. The old Article 13 (now deleted) provided for the abolition of existing duties within the transitional period, whereas Article 25 (ex Article 12) EC provides for the prohibition of *new* duties; the other articles applied the same for exports. As the distinction between existing and new duties is no longer necessary all the relevant articles have been deleted and replaced by Article 25 in its present form. Article 23 (ex Article 9) EC provides that the Community shall be based on a customs union which will cover all trade in goods, and which will involve the prohibition between member states of customs duties on imports and exports and of all charges having equivalent effect and the adoption of a common customs tariff in their relations with third countries.

In addition to the removal of barriers to trade within the EC itself, a customs union includes the harmonisation of customs regulations on trade with third countries. To this effect, the EC has established, and operates, a common customs tariff (CCT), that is, a single external tariff applied by all EC member states to imports originating in third countries. In addition, Community customs rules must be considered in a wider international context, especially in the light of the arrangements under the World Trade Organisation (WTO) which include the General Agreement on Tariffs and Trade (GATT).

The necessary uniformity of regulation of the external commercial relations of the member states is ensured through the Community Customs Code [OJ 1991 L 187/1], which codifies all the provisions of customs legislation governing the Community's trade with third countries.

Free movement of goods provisions in the Treaty

12.5 The EC Treaty lists the following main obstacles to the free movement of goods in the EC:

- customs duties on imports (and exports): Articles 23 (ex Article 9) and 25 (ex Article 12) EC;

- charges having equivalent effect to customs duties: Articles 23 (ex Article 9) and 25 (ex Article 12) EC;

- discriminatory internal taxation on imported goods: Article 90 (ex Article 95) EC;

- quantitative restrictions on imports: Article 28 (ex Article 30) EC and exports; Article 29 (ex Article 34) EC;

- state monopolies of a commercial character: Article 31 (ex Article 37) EC.

12.6 No definition is given in the EC Treaty of the term 'goods', which is used interchangeably with the term 'products'. See eg Articles 23(2) (ex Article 9(2)) and 24(1) (ex Article 10(1)) EC. However, the Court has stated in Case 7/68 *Commission v Italy* (1968) that:

> ... by goods within the meaning of (Article 23 (ex Article 9) of the Treaty), there must be understood products which can be valued in money and which are capable, as such, of forming the subject of commercial transactions.

Obviously, this definition is very wide and had been held to cover, inter alia, articles of an artistic, historic, archaeological or ethnographic nature: Case 7/68 *Commission v Italy* (1968); gold and silver collectors' coins, provided the coins were not in circulation as legal tender: Case 7/78 *Thompson* (1978); all forms of waste: Case C-2/90 *Commission v Belgium* (1992); as well as electricity: Case C-393/92 *Almelo* (1994).

12.7 This chapter deals with *pecuniary* charges imposed on goods which may constitute an obstacle to the free movement of goods across borders within the Community.

In the original Treaties, fiscal policy and taxation were mainly deemed to fall within the competence of the member states. The EC Treaty is generally only concerned with problems of *indirect* taxation such as customs duties, internal taxation and VAT, whereas direct taxation is not, generally speaking, within the competence of the Community.

It should be noted that, once goods enter the Community at any point of entry, they are in free circulation in the Community and no further obstacles can be put in their way unless they are justified by one of the exceptions provided for by the Treaty.

Customs duties

12.8 In the original EC Treaty, Article 12, which became the first Article to be found to be directly effective by the Court in Case 26/62 *Van Gend en Loos* (see above Chapter 7), prohibited the raising of customs duties or the introduction of new ones. It was known as the 'standstill' provision. Article 25 EC, which replaces Article 12, now simply states that:

✳ Customs duties on imports and exports and charges having equivalent effect shall be prohibited between member states. This prohibition shall also apply to customs duties of a fiscal nature.

The unchanged wording of Article 23 (ex Article 9) EC provides for the prohibition of all customs duties on imports and exports and of charges having equivalent effect and for the establishment of the common customs tariff (CCT) in relation to third countries, ie those which are not member states. The CCT makes goods from within the EC more competitive than those from third countries because third country goods attract duty on entering the EC. In the early years of the Community, attention was concentrated on the CCT and as a result the Tariff was established ahead of schedule. In addition, all customs duties such as those at issue in Case 26/62 *Van Gend en Loos*, ie between member states, were removed in advance of the 1969 deadline for the end of the transitional period. When the ECJ found that Article 12 (now Article 25 EC) had direct effect, this meant that the abolition of customs duties was made more effective, as individuals and companies could turn directly to their national courts in case of difficulties. The articles in the EEC Treaty relating to the abolition of the duties as well as to the establishment of the CCT were therefore removed by the Treaty of Amsterdam. Thus, the EEC was remarkably successful at achieving the customs union, but other barriers to the free movement of goods, ie charges having equivalent effect to customs duties, still remained.

Charges having equivalent effect to a customs duty

12.9 The abolition of customs duties does not necessarily mean that goods will remain free from other charges. There are numerous charges and other compulsory payments that can have the same effect as customs duties, that is, rendering the imported goods more expensive in comparison to domestically-produced goods. In practice, the effect of such charges is no different from that of import or export duties. Consequently, such charges are referred to as 'charges having equivalent effect' or 'equivalent charges to customs duties'. It is not always easy in practice to determine whether a specific charge amounts to a 'charge having equivalent effect'. In Cases 2 and 3/62 *Commission v Luxembourg and Belgium* (1962), the Court defined equivalent charges as:

❋ 〝 ... duties whatever their description or technique, imposed unilaterally, which apply specifically to a product imported by a member state but not to a similar national product and which by altering the price, have the same effect upon the free movement of goods as a customs duty. 〞

The relevant criterion is always the discrepancy in the treatment of imported goods in comparison with domestically-produced goods, to the extent that the discrepancy is disadvantageous to imports. See Case 132/78 *Denkavit* (1979).

12.10 Examples of charges imposed on imported products by reason of the fact that they cross a frontier are, inter alia, statistical levies: Case ✷ 24/68 *Commission v Italy* (1969); charges for health inspections: Case 132/ ✷ 80 *United Foods and Abele v Belgium* (1981), and storage charges prior to the completion of customs formalities: Case 132/82 *Commission v Belgium* (1983). In certain circumstances a charge may be permissible under Community law, such as in the cases where it is levied in respect of a service rendered for the benefit of the importer, if it is specifically required by Community law: Case 18/87 *Commission v Germany* (1988); or international law: Case C-111/89 *Bakker Hillegom* (1990); or if it is a part of a system of internal taxation: Case 78/76 *Steinike und Weinlig* (1977).

12.11 In Cases 2-3/69 *Sociaal Fonds voor de Diamantarbeiders v Brachfeld* (1969), Belgian law required all importers of uncut diamonds to pay a levy into a workers' social benefit fund. The ECJ ruled that the nature of the prohibition on customs duties was general and absolute. The purpose for which any levy was made was of no importance. The prohibition was based, therefore, on the fact that:

〝 ... any pecuniary charge – however small – imposed on goods by reason of the fact that they cross a frontier constitutes an obstacle to the movement of such goods. 〞

Such a charge did not have to be discriminatory or protective in its effect, nor did it matter whether the product on which the charge was imposed was in competition with any domestic product.

12.12 One of the charges most frequently imposed on products entering and leaving a country are those for health inspection. Animal products and plants may still be subjected to such inspections if these are necessary to protect public health. Article 30 (ex Article 36) EC provides for

286

exemptions from the free movement of goods inter alia on grounds of public health and the protection of national treasures. Inspections of imports of slaughtered meat, fruits and vegetables, living animals and plants may, therefore, be necessary, but could the inspection fee charged violate Article 23? This question has given rise to a complex body of case law. The Court has held that inspection fees levied only on imported products violated Article 9 (now Article 23 EC), even though some other inspection fee was levied on similar domestic products: Case 29/72 *SpA Marimex v Italian Finance Administration* (1972). Later, the Court held that a state could not justify a fee on the ground that the inspection is necessary to protect general health, stating that the public should bear the cost and not the importer: Case 87/75 *Bresciani* (1976). However, the Court added that if the same fee is charged for the inspection of imported products and of domestic products, 'applied according to the same criteria and at the same stage of production,' then the fee is not a charge equivalent to a duty, but rather a systematically applied internal tax, which is to be analysed under Article 95 (now Article 90 EC).

[handwritten margin note: Can the M. S justify the fee]

In many sectors, the Community has set up a system of Community-wide health and safety inspections. In Case 46/76 *Bauhuis v Netherlands* (1977), the Court held that a fee for the health inspection of bovine animals, required by a Community agricultural regulation before export to another state, did not constitute an illegal charge equivalent to an export duty, provided the fee covered only the actual cost of the inspection. In Case 77/72 *Capolongo v Maya* (1973), Italy had introduced a charge on imported egg boxes as part of an overall charge on cellulose products, the aim being to finance the production of paper and cardboard in Italy. The charge was imposed on all egg boxes, imported and domestic, but the Court said there was breach of Article 13 (now repealed) which provided for the progressive abolition of customs duties. It was discriminatory if it was intended exclusively to support activities which specifically benefited the domestic product.

12.13 Case 77/76 *Fratelli Cucchi v Avez SpA* (1977) concerned the legality of a levy on imported sugar; domestic sugar was subject to the same levy. The proceeds were to finance the sugar industry, both beet producers and sugar refiners. The Court held:

- if the charge had the *sole* purpose of financing activities for the specific advantage of the domestic product;

- if the taxed domestic product and the domestic product to benefit are the same; and

- the charges imposed on the domestic product are made up in full by the benefit, this would be a charge equivalent to customs duty;

even if the charge gave only partial benefit to the domestic product, it may still breach Article 90 (ex Article 95) EC (see Case 73/79 *Commission v Italy* (1980)).

12.14 The above cases show that it is not always easy to distinguish between acceptable and unacceptable charges. If the UK government imposes conditions on imported beef which reflect the same rigorous animal health conditions and inspections which British beef undergoes and the same charges are made for such inspections for British as for imported beef, this may be justifiable on health grounds, but it would not be acceptable if the intention was to make it more difficult for non-British beef to be sold in the UK than for domestic beef.

12.15 Are there any charges which can be acceptable under EC law? The only exceptions fall within a very limited range and will be interpreted narrowly by the Court:

- charges for services rendered to the importer or exporter;

- charges arising under a provision of Community law (inspection).

Charges for services rendered

12.16 Although the ECJ has stated in a number of cases that charges for services rendered *are* lawful, it has imposed a number of conditions to limit the scope of such charges. It is difficult to convince the Court that any charge is a service. In Case 63/74 *Cadsky v Istituto Nazionale per il Commercio Estero* (1975), an inspection charge was levied by the Italian state for quality control of exported vegetables. Italy argued that such quality controls improved the reputation of Italian produce abroad and were, therefore, of benefit to all exporters. The ECJ considered that such a benefit was too remote from individual exporters and that the charge could not be regarded as an individual service to an exporter. In Case 170/88 *Ford España v Spain* (1989) a flat rate charge was made for customs formalities carried out at the place of destination. Spain argued that this was of benefit to the importer who thus did not to have to carry out these formalities at the border. However, the charge was made on a flat-rate basis and the Court again considered this could not be a specific service to an individual importer. In Case 340/87 *Commission v Italy* certain formalities were carried out for importers outside defined hours and this *was* considered to be a specific service for which an additional charge could be made. However, it was found that the customs posts should have been open anyway during those hours under Community regulations and, therefore, the charge could not be considered to have been imposed for a specific service.

Charges arising under a provision of Community law

12.17 If charges are imposed under Community rules they will not be considered to be charges having an equivalent effect to a customs duty as long as:

- they do not exceed the actual cost of the services rendered;

- they are obligatory and uniform for the product anywhere in the Community;

- they help to promote free movement of goods and, in particular, if they avoid obstacles which may have been raised by unilateral inspection measures instituted under Article 30 (ex Article 36) EC (see further Chapter 13).

In Case 46/76 *Bauhuis v Netherlands* (1977) some of the fees paid for animal health inspections were related to national law requirements, some to Community law requirements under a Community directive. The Court held that the Community law charges promoted the free movement of goods, as they removed obstacles to free movement which national measures under Article 30 would have created. The national inspection charges, however, did constitute an obstacle to free movement and were, therefore, considered to be an equivalent charge.

The same reasoning would also apply to charges for inspections carried out under international agreements, as long as the need for unilateral inspection is again removed.

Discriminatory or protective taxation: Articles 90–93 (ex Articles 95–99) EC

12.18 Articles 90–93 (ex Articles 95–99) EC are located under the 'Tax Provisions' Title VI, Chapter 2 of the Treaty. The intention was clearly, however, to prevent member states from replacing the customs duties they had been obliged to abolish with discriminatory internal taxes. Article 90 has been directly effective since Case 57/65 *Alfons Lütticke GmbH v Hauptzollamt Saarlouis* (1966). This case confirmed that the doctrine of direct effect did not just apply to Treaty articles containing a prohibition or 'stand-still' clause, as was the case in Case 26/62 *Van Gend en Loos* (see Chapter 7).

12.19 Articles 23–25 and 90–93 are complementary but mutually exclusive. The distinction is easy to make: the first set of Articles deals with goods arriving at the frontier, Articles 90–93 deal with taxes imposed internally by the member state. The distinction has its importance. Whereas charges at the border are seldom justified and do not have to be protectionist, internal taxation may be justified as long as it is does not discriminate against imported products. Such discrimination may take the form of direct or indirect discrimination. The first paragraph of Article 90 deals with direct or indirect taxation imposed on similar products; the second paragraph deals with taxation which would afford indirect protection to other products.

12.20 Even if there is little or no domestic production, the tax levied on imported products will still be regarded as internal taxation if the tax is part of a general system of internal taxation applying equally to whole classes of domestic or foreign products (see Case 78/76 *Steinike & Weinlig v Germany* (1977)). In Case 90/79 *Commission v France (the French Reprography case)* (1981) a levy was imposed on reprographic equipment, most of which was imported. The ECJ said that the fact that most of the goods on which the tax was imposed were imported was not in itself sufficient to fall foul of Article 95 (now Article 90 EC). If the levy related to:

> ... a general system of internal dues applied systematically to categories of products in accordance with objective criteria irrespective of the origin of the products. (at para 14)

it would not be caught by Article 95.

12.21 Article 90, unlike other articles on the free movement of goods, is contained in Title VI of the Treaty which deals with tax provisions. On the face of it, this Article would, therefore, not apply to products originating in third countries. According to Article 23(2) only provisions within the first two chapters also apply to products originating in third countries. Article 90 only refers to products 'of other member states'.

However, in Case 193/85 *Co-operativa Co-Frutta* (1987) Article 95 (now Article 90 EC) was interpreted by the Court in parallel to the other rules on the free movement of goods. This case concerned taxation of non-EEC bananas imported into Italy through other member states. The Court referred to the principles of the common customs tariff and the common commercial policy which meant that products, once imported into the Community and in free circulation in the Community, should not be subject to discriminatory or protective internal taxation. Article 90 would not be infringed, however, if the goods are imported directly from a third country into the member state.

12.22 In contrast to Articles 25 and 28, internal taxation only constitutes a breach of Community law under Article 90 if it is discriminatory or has protective effect. Furthermore, it only applies to products imported from other member states. Nevertheless, in Case 142/77 *Statens Kontrol v Larsen* (1978) the court said the aim of the Treaty was to guarantee generally the neutrality of systems of internal taxation. If this meant, therefore, that discriminatory taxation imposed on a product to be *exported* constituted an obstacle to the free movement of goods, such a tax was also incompatible with the Treaty. As the two above cases show, the court again showed its readiness to 'fill the gap' in the terms of a particular Treaty provision in order to attain the objectives of the Treaty.

Discriminatory taxation

12.23 The first paragraph of Article 90 prohibits member states from imposing internal taxation, both directly and indirectly, on products from other member states which is in excess of that imposed on similar domestic products. Even if the rate of tax applied to both foreign and domestic products is the same, it is the effect of the tax which should be considered. Thus, even if the same products are charged the same amount of tax, but the method of collection favours the domestic product, this would constitute discrimination (see Case 55/79 *Commission v Ireland* (1980), where importers were required to pay the charge immediately, whereas domestic producers were allowed a longer time to pay).

12.24 Indirect discrimination, although more difficult to determine, is clearly also outlawed. In Case 112/84 *Humblot v Directeur des Services Fiscaux* (1985) cars with a power rating of below 16 CV were taxed on a progressive, gradual scale. Above this rating, all more powerful cars were taxed at a much higher, flat rate of Frs 5,000. Traditionally, French cars are smaller than, for example, German cars and there was no French car produced which had a power rating of more than 16 CV. Humblot successfully challenged the much higher tax. The Court said that this tax was liable to cancel out any advantages imported cars might have in terms of maintenance, comfort, etc. It offended against the principle of neutrality with which domestic taxation must comply. The French subsequently amended the system of taxation. However, this, too, was declared by the Court to be incompatible with the Treaty in Case 433/85 *Feldain v Directeur des Services Fiscaux* (1987), because the amended system modified the discrimination, but did not eliminate it and still favoured the smaller French cars. These cases are in contrast to Case 200/85 *Commission v Italy* (1986) which concerned higher taxation of diesel-engined cars with a cubic capacity above a certain threshold. Although this meant that the higher tax only applied to imports, the Court held that this in itself was not necessarily discriminatory and was capable of objective justification. The Court did, however, indicate that the Commission's arguments and economic analysis were insufficient as they had omitted to look at the car market as a whole rather than that for diesel-engined cars. In Case 127/75 *Bobie v Hauptzollamt Aachen-Nord* (1976) the German system of taxation of beer was scrutinised. The system was designed to benefit small producers by imposing lower taxes on lower volumes of production. For imported products, however, a uniform rate applied which was mid-way between the two rates imposed on German beer producers. This, therefore, had an adverse effect on Bobie, a small Belgian brewery which would have paid less if it had been a small German brewery. The Court ruled that this was discriminatory. If it was not possible administratively to apply different rates to imports as it was difficult to obtain production figures from foreign breweries, the lowest rate should be applied to imports. This may well result in reverse discrimination by treating importers more favourably, but reverse discrimination is not outlawed by the Treaty. It applies, in fact, in the field of goods as well as persons (see Chapter 18).

Although discrimination, either direct or indirect, is not allowed, it is possible to defend such discrimination if the member state has an objective justification for its conduct. Thus these rules are less harsh than those regarding discrimination as to nationality or even direct sex discrimination, where there is no objective justification accepted by the court.

Similar products

12.25 There are products which have similar characteristics and which meet the same needs of consumers. Even if the facts do not always bear this out, this may be because consumer habits have changed due to excessive taxation of one product as against another. In Case 106/84 *Commission v Denmark* (1986) and Case 243/84 *John Walker & Sons Ltd v Minister for Skatter og Afgifter* (1986) the Court accepted that wine made from grapes and wine made from other fruit were similar, although the alcohol content was achieved in different ways. Both came from the same basic product and both were fermented. Thus, they could satisfy the same needs of consumers, although this was to be assessed by the potential development of consumer habits rather than by the existing situation. However, Scotch whisky and liqueur made from fruit were not similar: they were made from different basic products, cereal as against fruit, and obtained by different methods, distillation as against fermentation. Moreover, their respective alcohol content differed significantly. Different spirits are not necessarily always similar if they have sufficiently pronounced different characteristics. Some spirits have relatively specific uses, whereas others are used more widely and may be consumed neat, mixed or diluted (see Cases 168, 169 and 171/78 *Commission v France, Italy and Denmark* (1980)).

Protective taxation

12.26 The second paragraph of Article 90 applies if taxation on imported products is set so that it affords protection to domestic products. Such protection does not have to be proved in reality; it is sufficient if the tax mechanism is likely to achieve such a result. The protective effect has to be assessed by looking at the overall position. Protection may exist even where the domestic product is similarly subjected to unfavourable treatment, if the proportion of domestic product so treated is minimal. The reverse also applies if only a small percentage of the imported product is given favourable treatment. As long as imports are treated unfavourably in comparison to domestic products, protection probably exists.

Competing products

12.27 How does the Court determine whether products are in competition with each other? Would wine and beer, for example, be in competition so that they should not receive different internal tax treatment? In Case 170/78 *Commission v United Kingdom* (1980) the Commission maintained that they were competing products as there was some actual, and also potential, substitution of one product for another.

The UK government pointed to the differences in manufacture, basic product, price structure and alcohol content. Consumers would consume beer in pubs and in connection with work, whereas wine consumption was more unusual and special and part of a different social custom. The Court rejected the view that the degree of substitutability should be tested against one country or one region as consumer habits could not be considered as fixed. It accepted the Commission's argument that both drinks are capable of meeting identical needs: they may be used a thirst-quenching drinks or to accompany meals. Consumer habits should not be crystallised by giving advantages to one drink over another. Nevertheless, the Court qualified this by finding a competitive relationship only between beer and the cheaper wines with lower alcoholic strength. Twenty years later, it would seem that the Commission's view has been vindicated. It is quite clear that consumer habits in the UK *have* changed and that much more wine is consumed, both in pubs and privately, than was the case 20 years ago.

In Case 184/85 *Commission v Italy* (1987) and in Case 193/85 *Co-operativa Co-Frutta v Amministrazione delle Finanze dello Stato* (1987) the Court regarded bananas and table fruit typically produced in Italy as being in partial competition because they were alternative choices for the consumer. The banana production in Italy was so small as to be negligible and a tax imposed on both domestic and imported bananas was therefore regarded as giving indirect protection to Italian table fruit. Even if this case concerned a charge on a product from another member state when there is little or no similar or identical domestic production, it does not constitute a charge equivalent to a customs duty, but an internal tax under Article 90 if it relates to a general system of internal dues applied systematically to categories of products in accordance with objective criteria irrespective of the origin of the product. If we contrast this case with Case 27/76 *United Brands Co v Commission* (1978) we see a different approach by the Court in a slightly different context. Although in the Article 90 cases the Court considered the degree of substitutability sufficient to constitute partial competition which could justify a finding of fiscal protection, in an Article 82 (ex Article 86) EC case such substitutability was not sufficient to conclude that bananas did not form a market distinct from other fruit markets (see further **14.20**).

Value added tax (VAT)

12.28 When the Treaty of Rome was first signed, all member states, with the exception of France, applied cumulative taxes on firms' turnovers.

Their disadvantage was that they were cumulative from one stage to the next, making it impossible to determine the amount of tax included in the price of a product. The amount of tax depended on the number of stages in the production chain. Articles 90 and 91 (ex Articles 95 and 96) EC stipulate, on the one hand, that imported products may not be taxed more highly than similar domestic products and, on the other, that any repayment of tax on export may not exceed the taxes actually paid on the product concerned. Under the system of Value Added Tax, which is being progressively harmonised in the Community, the export of goods from one member state to another is exempt from VAT, whereas the importation of goods into a member state is subject to the payment of VAT in that member state. The Sixth VAT Directive (Council Directive 77/388, OJ 1977 L 145/1) established a uniform VAT base, but there is not yet a uniform VAT rate in the Community; there is a band with lower and upper limits, but the upper limit is not fixed whereas a lower limit is only permitted under special, limited exceptions (see Directives 92/77 [OJ 1992 L316/1] and 92/111 [OJ 1992 L384/47]). Zero rating (eg for books and children's clothes in the UK) still remains permissible.

The reason for the adoption of a uniform VAT base was, in fact, unrelated to tax. The reason was the adoption by the Council of Ministers of a decision to finance the Community budget through its own resources, part of which was to be made up of a given percentage of the common VAT base. Own resources are not calculated on the basis of national VAT receipts, but on the VAT base which, therefore, had to be the same in all member states if each were to make an equitable contribution to the Community budget.

The eventual goal is to switch VAT payments from the state of destination to the state of origin. This means that the seller in the state of origin, selling to someone from another member state, would charge VAT on the purchase which the buyer would then claim back in his own home state. It is proving difficult to achieve this and, meanwhile, a transitional system stays in place. An example of difficulties which arise under the present system is given below.

12.29 As importation is always a chargeable event, irrespective of whether the importer is commercial or a private person, VAT may be levied where goods were not originally intended for export or when the goods were acquired second-hand. This was the subject of the dispute in Case 15/81 *Schul v Inspecteur der Invoerrechten* (1982), which involved a boat imported into the Netherlands, thus attracting VAT, which was purchased second-hand in France. The value of the boat was higher than its original value on which VAT had been paid in France. No VAT would have been payable in the Netherlands on such a second-hand sale.

12.30 This may appear to be a breach of Article 90, but was correct under the VAT Directive. The Court's approach was as follows: the second-hand price of a boat sold within the Netherlands would reflect the fact that VAT had been paid on the boat when new, and Community law should, therefore, be interpreted in such a way that the sale of a boat purchased in another member state would also reflect such an element. In calculating the value of the boat for tax purposes on importation, the French VAT element in the original price should be taken into account and deducted. It was suggested that this should be the same proportion of the second-hand price as the original VAT had been of the new price, but could not exceed the VAT actually paid. Dutch VAT on importation should then be calculated on the second-hand price minus the French VAT. The residual French VAT (not exceeding the amount actually paid) should then be deducted from the Dutch VAT due. The overall effect should be that the same tax would be payable on the boat as on one bought in the Netherlands. Thus, Article 90 would have been complied with as there was no discrimination against the imported product. Taxation in the country of origin, the ultimate objective, would do away with the need for such complex considerations.

Excise duties and duty-free

12.31 Market integration can never be complete and distortions continue to be caused by the absence of harmonisation of excise duties, such as those imposed in the UK on petrol, alcohol and cigarettes. These duties are much lower or absent in other member states, such as France, and this continues to cause distortions in the market.

These duties have on the whole been regarded very much as within the competence of the member states. In Case C-296/95 *R v Customs and Excise Comr, ex p EMU Tabac* (1998), a company, acting as agent on behalf of individuals in the UK, acquired cigarettes and tobacco in Luxembourg from another company for consumption by those individuals. The first company also arranged for the goods to be transported. It was paid for its services. The ECJ ruled that the UK were entitled to charge excise duty on these products.

Until July 1999 it had been possible to buy certain products 'duty-free', ie not subject to tax and duty, on ships travelling between member states and in airports and on aircraft travelling between member states. This then came to an end and 'duty-free' is now confined to travel beyond the external borders of the Community. The situation since has highlighted the different policies of member states in respect of the raising of excise duties, as large cross-border movements of shoppers are to be noted for example from France to Italy and from the UK to France to purchase goods such as alcoholic drink and tobacco products.

Further reading

For more detailed basic definitions see Willem Molle, *The Economics of European Integration: Theory, Practice, Policy* (1997), part I.

Annull, Dashwood, Ross and Wyatt, *European Union Law* (4th edn, 2000) Sweet and Maxwell, Chapter 12.

Weatherill and Beaumont, *EC Law* (3rd edn, 1999) Penguin, Chapters 13 and 14.

Oliver, *Free Movement of Goods in the EEC* (3rd edn, 1996) Sweet & Maxwell, Chapters 1–4.

Easson, 'Fiscal discrimination: new perspectives on Article 95', [1981] CML Rev 521.

Self-test questions

1. Describe the difference between a customs duty or charge having an equivalent effect, and internal taxation.

2. Do both types of charges have the same effect; can either type ever be justified?

3. Can a charge be both a customs charge and internal taxation?

4. Gaston, a French farmer, sells a lorryload of beef to Kevin, a retail butcher in Folkestone. When the consignment arrives in Dover, Customs stop the load and inform Kevin there have been recent outbreaks of BSE in France and it is, therefore, necessary to subject the meat to a thorough health check. This will cost a considerable amount as the check

has to be carried out by qualified BSE experts, of whom there are only a few in the UK. Under EC law, are the authorities entitled to do this? If so, who should pay for such a check?

CHAPTER THIRTEEN

Free Movement of Goods: (II) Quantitative Restrictions and Measures having Equivalent Effect

SUMMARY

- **Prohibition of quantitative restrictions and measures having equivalent effect: Articles 28 and 29 (ex Articles 30-35) EC**
- **Distinctly and indistinctly applicable measures**
- **Derogations (Article 30 (ex Article 36) EC)**
- **The rule of reason**
- **The principles of mutual recognition and equivalence**
- **Special cases**
- **The ruling in *Keck* and its aftermath**
- **Article 29 (ex Article 34) EC**

Prohibition of quantitative restrictions and measures having equivalent effect

13.1 The abolition of customs duties and charges having equivalent effect alone (see Chapter 12) would not have been sufficient to guarantee the free movement of goods within the single market. In addition to pecuniary restrictions there are other barriers on trade of a non-pecuniary nature, usually in the form of administrative rules and practices, protectionist or otherwise, equally capable of hindering the free flow of goods from one member state to another. Articles 28 and 29 (ex Articles 30–35) EC are designed to eliminate these barriers and cover a much wider range of measures than Articles 23 (ex Article 9) and 25 (ex Articles

299

12–16) EC, but unlike for these latter Articles provision is made for derogation under Article 30 (ex Article 36) EC.

13.2 All of the above Treaty provisions are addressed to, and relate to measures taken by, member states. However, 'measures taken by member states' has been interpreted in the widest sense to include the activities of any public body, legislative, executive or judicial, or even a semi-public body, such as a quango, exercising powers derived from public law. In Case 222/82 *Apple and Pear Development Council v K J Lewis Ltd* (1983) a body set up under a statutory instrument and funded by levies paid by private individuals under a statutory obligation was held by the ECJ to be subject to Article 28.

Nor need the 'measures' concerned be binding measures: Case 249/81 *Commission v Ireland (Buy Irish Campaign)* (1982). In 1978 Ireland launched a programme to promote Irish products. An action was brought by the European Commission under Article 169 (now Article 226 EC) of the Treaty to put a stop to this. Certain activities of the Irish Goods Council, a government-sponsored body charged with the promotion of Irish goods, principally through advertising and a 'Guaranteed Irish' symbol (ie non-binding acts) were held to be in breach of Article 28 EC. Even though no binding measures were involved, the Council's actions were *capable* of influencing the behaviour of traders and thereby frustrating the aims of the Community in relation to the free movement of goods. The campaign was a reflection of the Irish government's considered intention to substitute domestic products for imported products on the Irish market and therefore to check the flow of imports from other member states. Therefore, although the Irish government was not setting a limit on the number of imported goods (indeed the proportion of sales of Irish goods in relation to all goods fell), and although the advertising campaign was a non-binding measure (ie it was not adopted formally by the Irish government), the campaign still fell within the ambit of Article 28. The Court said:

> (para 27)... the potential effect of the campaign on imports from other member states is comparable to that resulting from government measures of a binding nature.

A 'measure' may also be insufficient action by a member state. In Case C-265/95 *Commission v France* (1997) the Court found in an Article 226 action that France had omitted to take sufficient action to allow the importation and free movement of agricultural produce from other member states. For decades, the police had been inactive in the face of violent protests by the French farmers.

300

13.3 Although Articles 28 and 29 EC are addressed to member states, this does not mean that Community institutions or individuals are free to act in breach of these provisions. However, Community institutions may derogate from them where they are expressly authorised to do so by other provisions of the Treaty, for example, in implementing the common agricultural policy as contained in Articles 32–38 (ex Articles 38–46) EC: Case 37/83 *Rewe-Zentral* (1984).

13.4 The prohibition, as between member states, of quantitative restrictions covers both quantitative restrictions as such (quotas) and measures having equivalent effect to quantitative restrictions (MEQRs). In Case 2/73 *Geddo* (1973), the Court said that any measures which amount to a total or partial restraint on imports, exports or goods in transit constitute quantitative restrictions within the meaning of Article 28 EC. The concept of measures having equivalent effect to quantitative restrictions has been interpreted very widely by both the Commission and the Court.

13.5 To offer member states some guidance as to the meaning and scope of these measures, the Commission issued Directive 70/50 (OJ, English Special Edition, 1970 (1), p 17). Although the directive was issued under Article 33(7) EEC (now repealed) and therefore applicable only to measures to be abolished during the transitional period, it has been suggested that it may still serve to provide non-binding guidelines to the interpretation of Article 28 EC. The directive provides a non-exhaustive list of measures capable of having equivalent effect to a quantitative restriction. The guidelines fall into two parts. Article 2 of Directive 70/50 covers 'measures, other than those applicable equally to domestic or imported products'. This category of measures is known as '*distinctly applicable measures*', meaning that imports are identified specifically in them and placed at a disadvantage. Article 3 relates to measures which cover equally domestic and imported goods of particular types: '*indistinctly applicable*' measures. It covers measures affecting the marketing of goods. The reason for prohibiting this kind of measure was that goods which complied with what was acceptable in one member state might not comply in another. This would mean for example that manufacturers would need to operate two or more lines of production or accept that the second member state's market was closed to them. As we shall see, the judicial interpretation of Article 28 has gone well beyond the directive.

13.6 The Court, in Case 8/74 *Procureur du Roi v Dassonville* (1974) introduced its own definition of measures having equivalent effect to quantitative restrictions. A dealer in Belgium had bought Scotch whisky in France. This had been imported from the UK which, at the time, was not yet a member of the Community. The whisky was, therefore, in free circulation in the Community. Belgian law required that this product had to be accompanied by a certificate of origin, in order to prevent fraud, but there was no certificate and it would have been very difficult to obtain one as the whisky was in free circulation. Dassonville made up his own certificate. As a result, he was prosecuted for forgery. On a reference from the Belgian court to the Court of Justice under Article 177 (now Article 234 EC), the ECJ held that the requirement of a certificate, as it would be more difficult to obtain by the importer for a product already in free circulation in another member state than for a product coming directly from the country of origin, constituted a MEQR. The Court gave its definition of a MEQR, which is now known as the 'Dassonville formula', and which has since been applied consistently, almost verbatim, by the court. According to this formula it concerned:

> All trading rules enacted by member states which are capable of hindering, directly or indirectly, actually or potentially, intra-Community trade are to be considered as measures having an effect equivalent to quantitative restrictions.

Thus, it is not necessary to show an actual effect on trade between member states, as long as the measures are capable of such effects. In the 'Buy Irish' case (see 13.2) the campaign did not increase sales of Irish goods, but it was nevertheless capable of falling within Article 30. The Court does not appear to recognise a de minimis rule in relation to Article 28 (see for comparison 14.13 and 14.14).

Dassonville was a case where discrimination against the imported product was clear. A like product was being treated differently according to its origins. The Court has concluded that, even if domestic and imported products are treated in the same way, but because of certain circumstances the result disadvantages the imported product, such a practice may also fall under Article 28. In Case 82/77 Openbaar Ministerie v van Tiggele (1978) fixing minimum prices was held to fall within the scope of Article 28 if this meant that the price was set so high that an importer could not take advantage of the fact that his product was much cheaper because of lower production costs and thus lost his competitive advantage. There may be indirect discrimination, as the Court found in Case 207/83 Commission v United Kingdom (re Origin Marking) (1985). Although all goods were required to be origin-marked, this made it possible for the British consumer to exercise a prejudice against imported goods.

Although such origin marking may be acceptable in the case of a typically regional or local product, the Court interpreted the practice restrictively in Case 113/80 *Commission v Ireland (Irish Souvenirs)* (1981) where, although the souvenirs depicted typically Irish symbols such as shamrock or wolfhounds, it still fell foul of Article 28 as the place of manufacture of the product was not relevant. The measure was discriminatory without justification. It may be possible to justify such rules if, in fact they constitute only discrimination in form, not in fact. In Case 13/63 *Italy v Commission* (1963) the Court considered that a French ban on imported electrical goods from Italy only was justified as it was particularly the dramatic increase in Italian imports which had created problems for French industry.

> 'the different treatment of non-comparable situations does not lead automatically to the conclusion that there is discrimination. An appearance of discrimination in form may therefore correspond in fact to an absence of discrimination in substance. Discrimination in substance would consist in treating either similar situations differently or different situations identically.' (para 4)

The same reasoning applied in more recent waste cases, where a ban on cross-border movement of waste was justified for reasons of environmental health: Case C-2/90 *Commission v Belgium (Walloon Waste)* (1992) and Case C-203/96 *Chemische Afvalstoffen Dusseldorp et al v Ministerie van VROM (Dusseldorp)* (1998) (but see further **13.31**).

Derogations under Article 30 (ex Article 36) EC

13.7 The principal provision for derogation from Articles 28 and 29 (ex Articles 30-34) EC contained in the Treaty is Article 30 (ex Article 36) EC. It provides that Articles 28 and 29 EC shall not preclude prohibitions or restrictions on imports, exports or goods in transit justified on grounds of:

• public morality, public policy or public security: Case 72/83 *Campus Oil* (1984) (see **13.9**); Case 34/79 *Henn and Darby* (1979) concerned a ban on the importation of pornographic literature. The Court found this ban was contrary to Article 28. However, although the importation of such material was prohibited, there was a limited tolerance in the UK of the dissemination of such material, which varied between different regions. The Court accepted that the general purpose of the UK policy was to restrict trade in those articles and therefore accepted the import ban was justified. This is to be contrasted with Case 121/85 *Conegate* (1986), where a similar import ban on inflatable 'love love dolls' could not be upheld as the domestic rules could not be seen as a sufficient restriction or prohibition;

- the protection of health and life of humans, animals or plants: Case 238/82 *Duphar* (1984); Case 124/81 *Commission v United Kingdom* (1983) (UHT milk);

- the protection of national treasures possessing artistic, historic or archaeological value: Case 7/68 *Commission v Italy* (1968) (art treasures); or

- the protection of industrial and commercial property: Case 38/70 *Deutsche Grammophon* (1971) (see **15.4**).

According to the second paragraph of Article 30 such prohibitions or restrictions will not be upheld if they constitute means of arbitrary discrimination or disguised restriction on trade between member states.

13.8 The question whether a measure can be justified is separate from the question as to whether it amounts to arbitrary discrimination against intra-Community trade. Under Article 30 EC, first sentence, the justification has to be made out; the second sentence is concerned with the use and effects of the measure under consideration to ensure that the justification invoked is not misused (Case 97/83 *Melkunie* (1984)). National measures which member states seek to justify under Article 30 EC must not only be justified but also be proportionate to their purpose (Case 7/68 *Commission v Italy* (1968) (art treasures); Case 124/81 *Commission v United Kingdom* (1983) (UHT milk)).

13.9 Although the grounds listed in Article 30 EC appear extensive, they have been narrowly construed. Case 40/82 *Commission v United Kingdom* (1982) shows the reluctance of the Court to exceed the narrow interpretation of Article 30. A UK ban on the importation of poultry meat and eggs allegedly because of an outbreak of the highly contagious Newcastle disease, particularly in France, was held by the Court not to be justified. The motives for the ban were suspect, little or no consultation with either Community institutions or member states had taken place and the ban was imposed just in time before Christmas to prevent the importation of turkeys into the UK. French turkey producers subsequently brought a claim against the UK government which was struck out in the Court of Appeal as no tort could be identified. Nevertheless, the UK government paid compensation. See *Bourgoin v MAFF* (1986).

The list of exceptions contained in Article 30 is exhaustive. The Court has continually insisted that Article 30 EC only covers justifications of a non-economic nature: Case 95/81 *Commission v Italy* (1982). Thus, the concept of public policy in Article 30 EC, for instance, does not include the economic policy or system of the member states and economic legislation adopted for its implementation or proper functioning. That is not to say, though, that justified measures are incapable of having economic effects in certain respects. In Case 72/83 *Campus Oil* (1984) the Court accepted that under certain limited circumstances the public security argument could be respected. There was a requirement under Irish law that importers of petrol in Ireland had to buy 35% of their requirements from the state-owned oil refinery, where prices were determined by the government. As the supply of oil, as a vital energy source, was of fundamental importance to a member state, the exception was allowed here, as long as it served the interest the Article was intended to protect and the measure was not disproportionate. This should be contrasted with Case C-347/88 *Commission v Greece* (1990) where the state's rights to exclusive marketing of oil products were not held to be proportionate. The Court has held on many occasions that the purpose of Article 30 EC is not to reserve certain matters to the exclusive jurisdiction of the member states. It merely allows national legislation to derogate from the principle of the free movement of goods to the extent to which this is and remains justified in order to achieve the objectives set out in that Article: Case 153/78 *Commission v Germany* (1979): the risk to health of meat products would not increase if fresh meat used in its manufacture had been imported from another member state, as this would not in itself increase the risk of contamination.

13.10 Yet another restriction on national measures, even in cases which fall within the categories referred to in the first sentence of Article 30 EC, is contained in its second sentence. If a measure is in principle justified on any grounds enumerated in Article 30 EC, it will cease to be so once it is established that it offends against the second sentence of this provision by being a means of arbitrary discrimination or a disguised restriction on trade between member states. The Court has indicated that the principle of proportionality constitutes the basis of the second sentence of Article 30 EC: Case 227/82 *Van Bennekom* (1983). It is for the national court to show, for example, that a risk to health exists and that the national rules are necessary to give effective health protection. Thus, the second sentence is designed to ensure that the justifications permitted in the first sentence of Article 30 EC are not abused: in Case 53/80 *Officier van Justitie v Koninklijke Kaasfabriek Eyssen* (1981) a Dutch ban on the use of nisin, a preservative considered harmful by the Dutch authorities, was acceptable as a state is entitled to protect the public from substances the safety of which is the subject of genuine scientific doubt (but see Case 40/82 *Commission v United Kingdom* (1982) (see above **13.9**)). In relation to the first sentence of Article 30 EC, the second sentence operates as a further 'notwithstanding' provision, an overriding requirement: Case 102/77 *Hoffmann-La Roche* (1978).

The rule of reason

13.11 In view of the very wide definition of measures having equivalent effect to quantitative restrictions, which was given in *Dassonville* (see **13.6**) and to a large extent repeated in subsequent cases, it is not surprising that the court sooner or later would have accepted the need to restrict the effect of that definition in some way. In *Dassonville* the Court indicated that if, in the absence of Community measures, a member state takes measures to prevent unfair practices such measures should be reasonable and should not constitute a hindrance to trade. The Court made plain that such a 'rule of reason' is subject to the condition of the second sentence of Article 30 EC, ie that the prohibition or restriction may not constitute a means of arbitrary discrimination or a disguised restriction on trade between member states. In any event it is now established that the rule of reason will only be available to justify measures which apply equally to domestic as well as imported products, ie *only to indistinctly applicable measures*: Case 113/80 *Commission v Ireland* (1981) (Irish souvenirs). Thus, the rule cannot save a distinctly applicable measure such as the one in *Dassonville*.

Indistinctly applicable measures

13.12 In Case 120/78 *Rewe-Zentral AG v Bundesmonopolverwaltung für Branntwein (Cassis de Dijon)* (1979), the German authorities refused the importation of a French liqueur, Cassis de Dijon, which had a lower alcohol content (by between 15% and 20%) than the equivalent German products. The plaintiffs attacked the rule as a MEQR. The German authorities advanced arguments of public health and consumer protection: (a) the marketing of drinks with a lower alcohol content might more easily induce a tolerance towards alcohol than drinks with a higher alcohol content; and (b) the fixing of a lower limit for the alcohol content of certain liqueurs was designed to protect the consumer against unfair practices on the part of producers and distributors of alcoholic beverages. Liqueurs with a lower alcohol content would have an unfair competitive advantage as alcohol was by far the most expensive ingredient in the drink. The Court ruled that the measure did fall within Article 30 (now Article 28 EC) and thus the fixing of minimum alcohol levels for beverages imported from another member state was prohibited under the Article. After referring to the *Dassonville* formula, the court added, however, that:

Rule of Reason:

> Obstacles to movement within the Community resulting from disparities between the national laws relating to the marketing of the products in question must be accepted in so far as those provisions may be recognised as being necessary in order to satisfy mandatory requirements relating *in particular* to the effectiveness of fiscal supervision, the protection of public health, the fairness of commercial transactions and the defence of the consumer.

The expression 'mandatory requirements' is a somewhat misleading term, which is much more clearly expressed in the French: 'exigences impératives' or the German: 'zwingende Erfordernisse', perhaps better translated (as Weatherill also suggests) as: compelling needs or requirements. However, the term has become so generally accepted and used that I shall continue to use it.

13.13 Prior to *Cassis*, it was assumed that any measure falling within the *Dassonville* formula would breach Article 28 EC and could only be justified on the grounds provided for by Article 30 EC. Since *Cassis*, at least where indistinctly applicable measures are concerned, courts may apply the rule of reason to Article 28 EC. If the measure is necessary to protect mandatory requirements, it will not breach Article 28 EC at all. Distinctly applicable measures on the other hand, will normally breach Article 28 EC but, as we have seen (**13.1–13.10**), may be justified under Article 30 EC. The distinction is significant, since the mandatory requirements permitted under *Cassis* are wider than the grounds provided under Article 30 EC and, unlike the latter, are non-exhaustive. This use of the rule of reason is a recognition by the Court of the need, pending action at Community level, to allow member states to act in order to ensure that certain interests or values are guaranteed in the general interest.

Measures coming under the rule of reason must be applicable to domestic and imported products alike, and be reasonable and proportionate.

13.14 So far, the court has accepted only non-economic justifications as falling within the rule of reason. It is, nevertheless, remarkable how few of the member states' arguments have been accepted on the facts. In Case 286/81 *Oosthoek's Uitgeversmaatschappij BV* (1982) national rules prohibiting the offer of free gifts to buyers of encyclopaedias fell within the scope of Article 28. Legislation restricting certain forms of advertising and sales promotion might limit intra-Community trade; even if the scheme was indistinctly applicable it might force a producer to adopt different schemes or to discontinue a scheme which was thought to be particularly effective. However, the Court accepted that the system of offering free gifts might mislead consumers as to the real prices of certain products, thus distorting competition. Therefore, legislation restricting or even prohibiting such practices was capable of contributing to the mandatory requirement of consumer protection and fair trading. Case 382/87 *Buet and Business Educational Services v Ministère Public* (1989) is another of the very few cases in which a justification based on the rule of reason has been upheld by the Court. The protection of the consumer from door-step selling techniques was held by the Court as being capable of justification. In Case C-368/95 *Familiapress v Bauer Verlag* (1997) Austrian legislation directed against misleading sales promotion which prohibited publishers from including prize crossword puzzles in their papers was held by the Court to be caught by Article 28. The Court accepted, however, that there could be a justification based on the need for diversity in the media. This was a matter for the national court to determine. In the overwhelming majority of cases the Court has indicated that certain justifications are admissible but has then gone on to find that the national measures involved were unreasonable, disproportionate or even protectionist (albeit disguised).

The principles of mutual recognition and equivalence

13.15 In *Cassis* the Court also set out the connected principles of mutual recognition and equivalence. It said (at para 14):

> There is therefore no valid reason why, provided that they have been lawfully produced and marketed in one of the member states, alcoholic beverages should not be introduced into any other member state; the sale of such products may not be subject to a legal

prohibition on the marketing of beverages with an alcohol content lower than the limit set by the national rules.

While the basic principle in *Dassonville* has a very wide scope, it proceeds from a negative standpoint, that is, a prohibition. In *Cassis* the Court attempts to force the member states to adopt a more positive approach to the principle of the free movement of goods, that of the mutual acceptance of goods. Since *Cassis*, the key to the Commission's policy, contained in Commission Communication OJ 1980 256/2 giving its interpretation of the *Cassis* judgment, and especially also in the 1985 White Paper on completing the internal market (COM (85) 310) and in the Court's case law in the field of the free movement of goods (and more recently services) has been the *principle of equivalence*, whereby national measures are regarded as unlawful restrictions on the free movement of goods if they are merely 'equivalent' to those of another member state, or covered by mutual regulations, where the objectives and methods of achieving them are reasonably similar.

13.16 The Commission took action against France in Case C-184/96 *Commission v* France (1998). France had issued a decree regulating trade descriptions for foie gras and other, similar, products. The decree specified a minimum content of foie gras and other ingredients for these products. However, the decree failed to include a mutual recognition clause allowing similar products which did not entirely conform with these minimum requirements to be marketed in France. France claimed justification on the grounds of consumer protection and the prevention of false descriptions. The ECJ ruled that the absence of a mutual recognition clause was disproportionate. Although France was entitled to ensure that goods from other member states which were markedly different should not be sold under the name foie gras, this should not apply to products which were very close, but not wholly in conformity with the the product. Generally, as in *Cassis*, the Court has expressed the idea of equivalence in terms of a member state being obliged to accept goods lawfully produced and/or marketed in another member state. This was also declared expressly in Case 27/80 *Fietje* (1980). In that case the Court held that the obligation to use a certain name on a label could make it more difficult to market goods from another member state and the rule would therefore have to be justified on grounds of consumer protection. If the label was such that it provided information on the nature of the product, that could be justified, unless the same information could be read from the original label on the product from the other member state. It was for the national court to decide whether this was so. In other words, the principle of equivalence gives rise to a presumption that goods which have been lawfully marketed in another member state will comply with the 'mandatory requirements' of the importing member state. This can be rebutted by evidence that further measures are necessary to protect the interest concerned. This presumption will, however, be hard to rebut; the Court has applied the principle of proportionality rigorously excluding all measures that go beyond what is strictly necessary to achieve the desired end. In Case 261/81 *Rau v De Smedt PvbA* (1982), Belgian legislation required margarine to be packaged in square packets to distinguish it from butter. Thus, the importation of margarine packaged in any other form was prohibited. The Court held that, although the measure was aimed at the protection of consumers, the measure was disproportionate and was, therefore, caught by Article 28 EC. However, in Case 188/84 *Commission v France* (1986) woodworking machines imported from Germany, which did not afford the same level of protection to their users as machines manufactured under French legislation, which was designed to protect users of the machines against their own mistakes, could be refused entry.

13.17 Until now, the Court has recognised a number of mandatory requirements:

- the *protection of consumers*: in Case 94/82 *De Kikvorsch Groothandel-Import-Export BV* (1983), Dutch legislation prevented the importation of German beer because of rules concerning the level of acidity and because of alleged confusion from information contained on the label concerning the strength of the original wort used in the production of beer, creating confusion in respect of the indication of alcoholic strength; a particularly striking example is Case 178/84 *Commission v Germany* (1987), the '*German Beer Case*', where the German beer purity laws prevented importation of other beers which had additives. In both cases the court denied that the mandatory requirement of consumer protection justified such a prohibition;

- the prevention of unfair commercial practices: Case 6/81 *Beele* (1982), and

- the need to protect the environment: Case 302/86 *Commission v Denmark* (1988) (the *Danish Bottles Case*),

- the effectiveness of fiscal supervision: Case 823/79 *Carciatti* (1980),

- the promotion of culture (the cinematographic industry): Cases 60 and 61/84 *Cinéthèque SA v Fédération Nationale des Cinémas Français* (1985), and

- the diversity of the press: Case C-368/95 *Familiapress v Bauer Verlag* (1997).

13.18 Since indistinctly applicable measures restricting imports will be subject to the rule of reason under *Cassis de Dijon*, it will normally only be necessary to apply Article 30 EC to distinctly applicable measures in breach of Articles 28 or 29 EC. However, where indistinctly applicable measures are clearly discriminatory in their effects on imports the court may still insist on justification under Article 30 EC. In Case 124/81 *Commission v United Kingdom* (1983) (UHT milk) the court considered UK rules requiring French UHT milk to be subjected to licensing requirements could not be justified by the public health argument. The treatment in other member states should be accepted as sufficient on the basis of mutual recognition. Distinctly applicable measures, on the other hand, can never be justified under the rule of reason. In Case 113/ 80 *Commission v Ireland* (1981) (Irish souvenirs) a requirement that souvenirs should be origin-marked was discriminatory and could not be justified on the basis of consumer protection and fairness of commercial transactions which are not mentioned in Article 30 (see **13.6**).

Barriers in the form of technical standards

13.19 In Case C-226/97 *Lemmens* (1998) the Court explained the scope of its judgment in Case C-194/94 *CIA Security International v Signalson and Securitel* (1996), concerning Directive 83/189/EEC (which is now the consolidated Directive 98/34), which provides for preventive checks, at Community level, of national technical standards and regulations. The requirement of notification of such standards is in order to avoid the creation of new obstacles to trade in goods between member states. The Court had held in that judgment that breach by a member state of its obligation to notify the Commission in advance of its technical standards constituted a substantive procedural defect such as to render the technical regulations in question inapplicable, and thus unenforceable against individuals. In *Lemmens*, the court stated that, while failure to notify renders technical regulations inapplicable inasmuch as they hinder the use and marketing of a product which is not in conformity with them, failure to notify does not have the effect of rendering unlawful any use of a product which is in conformity with the unnotified regulations. The same applies where such a product is used by the public authorities in proceedings against an individual, provided that the use is not liable to create an obstacle to trade which could have been avoided if the notification procedure had been followed. In the case before the national court which referred the case to the ECJ, that meant, in practice, that breach of the obligation to notify a technical regulation on breath-analysis apparatus did not have the effect of rendering evidence obtained by means of such apparatus, authorised in accordance with regulations which had not been notified, unusable against an individual charged with driving while under the influence of alcohol.

The scope of Article 28 and some difficult cases

13.20 There were special difficulties in a series of cases in which the Court had not specifically stated that the contested measure fell within or beyond the scope of Article 28 EC, but left it up to the national courts to assess the measure in the light of its objective and the necessity and proportionality of that objective: Cases 60 and 61/84 *Cinéthéque v Fédération Nationale des Cinémas Français* (1985).

In a series of cases the Court found that the national provisions in question had no intra-Community effect and as such fell outside Article 28. In Case 155/80 *Oebel* (1981) the Court so decided where the rule related to a prohibition on baking and selling bread at night. Case 75/81 *Belgium v Blesgen* (1982) concerned a limitation on selling spirits in public places, while Case C-23/89 *Quietlynn & Richards v Southend Borough Council* (1990) related to a limitation on pornographic material. It was also suggested by Slynn AG in *Cinéthèque* that a French rule banning the sale or hire of videotapes of films during the first year after their release should fall outside the ambit of Article 28. He said:

> ... in an area in which there are no common Community standards or rules, where a national measure is not specifically directed at imports, does not discriminate against imports, does not make it any more difficult for an importer to sell his products than it is for a domestic producer, and gives no protection to domestic producers, then in my view *prima facie*, the measure does not fall within Article 30 [now Article 28], even if it does in fact lead to a restriction or reduction in imports.

However, the ECJ did not follow the Advocate General but ruled that the measure did fall within Article 28 EC, but could be objectively justified as long as it was proportionate.

13.21 It is against this background that one should view the Sunday Trading cases which ultimately led the ECJ to reconsider its case law on Article 28 in *Keck and Mithouard* (1993).

In Case C-145/88 *Torfaen Borough Council v B&Q plc* (1989) in the UK, the sale of certain goods was banned on a Sunday. The law was challenged throughout the UK by, amongst others, B&Q, a large DIY chain. B&Q became involved in a series of county court actions in the UK. In a bid to justify its actions, B&Q alleged that the ban on Sunday trading infringed Article 28 EC in the sense that it was a measure that could actually or potentially, directly or indirectly, hinder intra-Community trade. Surprisingly, the Court found that the ban fell within the ambit of Article 28 and it was thus for the UK government to justify the measure under the public policy exception in Article 30 EC. The Court introduced a two-stage test for the application of Article 28 EC. First, the Court held, it was necessary to decide whether the national rule pursued an aim which was objectively justifiable under Community law. Whether such justification existed, said the ECJ, was a question of fact for the national court to decide. This was surprising since there is no real difference between a ban on trading on Sunday and a ban on selling bread at night. Some statistical evidence was offered in this case, but not in others and it may be that there is a greater effect on the volume of trade in the Sunday Trading cases, but, as many commentators opined, Article 28 had become a *carte blanche* for traders to trade rather than a means of ensuring market access to non-domestic goods in the context of the internal market.

The Court was prepared to accept that shop opening hours 'reflect certain political and economic choices' which were at present a matter for the member states. The second limb of the test required an assessment of whether the effects of the rule exceeded what was necessary to achieve the desired end. The Court felt that this was a matter of fact and therefore up to the national courts. The Court concluded its remarkably brief judgment by ruling that Article 28:

> ... does not apply to national rules prohibiting retailers from opening their premises on Sunday where the restrictive effects on Community trade which may result therefrom do not exceed the effects intrinsic to rules of that kind.

13.22 In Case C-312/89 *Conforama* (1991) and Case C-332/89 *Marchandise* (1991), the Court simply stated – without seeking to support its statement by any reasoning – that the restrictive effects on imports of legislation banning employment in shops on Sundays were proportionate to the end pursued. Accordingly, it held quite generally that legislation prohibiting the employment of staff on Sunday was compatible with Article 28, without in any way limiting this ruling to employment in shops.

13.23 In Case C-169/91 *Stoke-on-Trent and Norwich City Council v B&Q plc* (1992), the Court said that account had to be taken of whether the restrictive effects of the national measure on intra-Community trade were 'direct, indirect or purely speculative and whether those effects do not impede the marketing of imported products more than the marketing of national products'. If this was so, although the measure could be caught by Article 28, if it was proportionate there would be no breach of Article 28.

This ruling prompted suggestions that the Court was developing a new category of measure – measures which apply equally in law and in fact (see Weatherill and Beaumont, *EC Law* (1999) pp 610 ff). Whereas dual burden measures affect domestic and imported goods in unequal measure either in fact, such as those concerning the composition of goods, or in law, in the case of indistinctly applicable measures such as those in *Cassis*, these measures apply equally to domestic and imported goods both in fact and in law and produce an equal burden on domestic and imported products. However, the Court took a different turn in its ruling in *Keck and Mithouard* (see below **13.24**).

There was also the difficulty that the ECJ, by applying *Dassonville* too literally, was giving traders an excessive tactical advantage over the member state authorities. Once *Dassonville* can be satisfied so easily it becomes incumbent on the member state to justify its actions. This in itself is not an easy task and does not guarantee uniformity. Indeed, while some county courts in the UK found the ban on Sunday trading justified, others did not – a reflection that the test of proportionality required to justify a measure falling within Article 28 is, to a significant extent, based on a value judgment.

The prospect that such national rules, with no real link to market penetration, would fall so easily inside Article 28 with such a varying response from the national courts was not a course the Court was willing to countenance.

As Weatherill observes: two decades of case law in the vein of *Cassis* had been characterised by a collapse of a simple divide between the

Community's interest in promoting integration and the member states' responsibility to citizens to select appropriate levels of social and economic regulation. A change or even reversal of the Court's previous stance had become inevitable.

The significance of the ruling in Keck

13.24 Case C-267, 268/91 *Keck and Mithouard* (1993) concerned the criminal prosecution in France of the applicants for selling (French) coffee and beer at a loss contrary to French law. The applicants invoked Article 28 as a defence arguing that the French rule hindered the free movement of goods within the meaning of the *Dassonville* formula. The Court first noted that the aim of the national legislation was not to regulate trade in goods between member states and that although the measure might have an effect on the volume of trade, that was not determinative of whether a national rule should be caught by Article 28. The ECJ then stated that the increasing tendency of traders to invoke Article 28 where the rules were not aimed at products from other member states led it to 're-examine and clarify its case law'.

The Court said that the mutual recognition principle and the mandatory requirements principle, as laid down by *Cassis*, continued to apply to requirements to be met by goods 'such as requirements as to designation, form, size, weight, packaging, labelling and presentation'. The Court then declared:

> However, contrary to what has previously been decided Article 30 (now Article 28) will not be infringed by national rules relating to certain selling arrangements that apply in the same manner, both in law and in fact, to all traders within the national territory.

For indistinctly applicable measures, the choice was between 'rules that lay down requirements as to designation, form ...(etc) to be met by goods' where one simply applied *Cassis* and 'certain selling arrangements...' In the latter scenario the rule fell outside Article 28 altogether and thus did not need to be justified.

Keck, even at first sight, narrows the scope of Article 28. The Court's failure to list the cases it overruled and the ambiguity of 'certain selling arrangements' does not, with respect, make for absolute clarity. Although Oliver and other commentators helpfully differentiate between requirements to be met by goods and selling arrangements on the basis that the former relate to factors intrinsic to a product while the latter describes elements extrinsic to a product, it has been through the preliminary reference procedure under Article 234 that this distinction has been clarified – at least to an appreciable extent. However, in some cases this distinction is not easily drawn, eg in Case C-368/95 *Familiapress v Bauer Verlag* (1997) a prohibition in Austria on the sale of periodicals containing prize competitions, although directed against a method of sales promotion, in fact had a bearing on the actual content of the product and thus, in principle, fell within Article 28. However, the measure could be justified by the mandatory requirement of press diversity (see 13.17). In Case C-315/92 *Verband Sozialer Wettbewerb eV v Clinique Laboratories* (1994) there was a German prohibition on the use of the name Clinique for cosmetics as this might mislead consumers into believing the product had medicinal properties. The German word Klinik means hospital. The Court concluded that consumers in other member states were apparently not susceptible to such confusion as they had much less restrictive rules. After all, the word for hospital resembles the name Clinique in other Community languages too. These cases were thus decided in line with the *Cassis* principles.

13.25 In Case C-292/92 *Hünermund v Landesapothekerkammer Baden-Württemberg* (1993), decided a month after *Keck*, the Court ruled that the German regulation in question fulfilled the test in *Keck* and thus fell outside Article 28. The rule related to a prohibition on excessive advertising for non-medical products sold legally in pharmacies. In Case C-412/93 *Leclerc-Siplec v TF1 Publicité and M6 Publicité* (1995), the ECJ ruled to the same effect as regards a French ban on advertising certain products on TV. The rationale for this rule was to maintain the income of newspapers (especially the local papers) from advertising. It thus had no link with market access. Similarly, in Cases C-69 and 258/93 *Punto Casa SpA v Sindaco del Commune di Capena* (1994) an Italian law regulating business opening hours for retail sales provided for the total closure of shops on Sundays and public holidays. The plaintiffs operated shops that frequently opened on Sundays. The Court concluded that such regulations fell within the definition of selling arrangements and that Article 28 did not apply 'to national legislation on the closure of shops which applies to all traders operating within the national territory and which affects in the same manner, in law and in fact, the marketing of domestic products and of those from other member states'. In Cases C-401 and 402/92 *Criminal Proceedings against Tankstation't Heuske and J B E Boermans* (1994) rules relating to restrictions on Sunday trading were also held to pass the test in *Keck* and thus fall outside the scope of Article 28. The Court ruled to the same effect in Case C-391/92 *EC Commission v Greece* (1995) in relation to a requirement that processed milk for infants could only be sold in pharmacies. The rule was a mere limitation on the means of distribution of a good without affecting its composition. It applied equally to all products irrespective of origin and to all traders. In Cases C-34, 35 and 36/95 *KO v de Agostini and TV-Shop* (1997) measures against a TV advertiser broadcasting from another member state would not fall within Article 28 as long as they affected product marketing in the same way. It was a selling arrangement (televised advertising) which applied to all traders within the national territory. Whether the ban affected in the same manner the marketing of domestic products and of those from other member states was a matter for the national court to determine. However, the Court did point out that a total ban would deprive the applicant of its most effective (or, as the applicant said, its only) weapon to penetrate the Swedish market and that national courts should look at the question of proportionality. The Court interpreted the rules concerning the freedom to provide services in much the same way. In that respect the court said there was also an obstacle to that freedom, when taking account of the international nature of the advertising market.

13.26 These cases clearly demonstrate the purpose of the *Keck* judgment: to prevent the Community system from being clogged up with issues not relating to market access: the Court did not want to extend Article 28 in such a way as to become embroiled in what are essentially questions of social policy.

These cases also reveal that selling arrangements relate to measures determining *when* or *how* goods may be sold. Furthermore, the *Greece* case shows that selling arrangements include by whom and where products are sold. Therefore, Case C-369/88 *Delattre* (1991) and Case C-271/92 *Laboratoires de Prothèses Oculaires v Union Nationale des Syndicats d'Opticiens de France* (1993) can no longer be considered good law. In the first case an indistinctly applicable measure granting to dispensing pharmacies the exclusive right to sell medicinal products was held to fall within Article 28. In the latter, the Court ruled to the opposite effect as regards a rule that only qualified opticians could sell contact lenses.

13.27 However, there are problems with *Keck*. Although the cases so far cited fit in well with the formula of certain selling arrangements that do not discriminate in law or in fact, this may not always be the case. First, the criterion of selling arrangements ignores the fact that products are often distributed in a marketing mix where appearance and content (governed by *Cassis*) are inseparable from its advertising (a selling arrangement – *how* a product is sold). Moreover, as Jacobs AG observed in his opinion in the *Leclerc-Siplec* case, advertising is crucial for market access – without doubt the ability to launch and sustain a Community-wide advertising campaign of the producers' choice (subject to Article 30 EC or the mandatory requirements) is one way of aiding the free movement of goods. Second, Jacobs AG in the same opinion has criticised the requirement of discrimination in law or in fact:

> If an obstacle to free movement exists, it does not cease to exist simply because an identical obstacle affects domestic trade.

13.28 Case C-470/93 *Verein gegen Unwesen in Handel und Gewerbe Köln eV v Mars GmbH* (1995) is an example of the sort of problems which may arise in spite of *Keck*. This case is very much on the borderline between *Keck* and *Cassis* and could have been decided either way. Thus, there has been a fair amount of controversy over this case.

As part of a Europe-wide publicity campaign ice-cream bars were offered in wrappers marked '+ 10%', while the quantity of each product had in fact been increased by 10% exactly. The German association for combating unfair competition brought proceedings against Mars GmbH under German unfair competition law arguing that consumers could be misled in two ways. Firstly, one could assume that the 10% increase in quantity was granted without any price increase and secondly the actual increase in quantity was considerably smaller than the coloured marking on the wrapping, which itself occupied much more than 10% of the surface of the wrapper, suggested. The German court referred the case to the ECJ asking whether the prohibition in question is compatible with the principles of the free movement of goods. The problem in this case is that advertising measures such as the one Mars introduced are of a dual nature. On the one hand they are a mere selling promotion, on the other hand they affect the product – here its packaging – itself. This explains why this case is on the boundary between *Keck* and *Cassis* and why the *Keck*-formula has been criticised as being too rigid and formalist. Had Mars started a similar campaign without changing the product packaging, eg by using posters with the same message, this campaign would have been regarded as being a mere selling arrangement, thus staying outside the scope of Article 28. However, both the Court and the Advocate General concluded in this case that Article 28 was applicable because

> 'a prohibition [...] which relates to the marketing in a member state of products bearing the same publicity markings as those lawfully used in other member states, is by nature such as to hinder intra-Community trade' (para 13 of the judgment).

Consumer protection was not accepted as a justification for the prohibition, as the price had not been increased and a 'reasonably circumspect consumer' is aware of the fact that there is not necessarily a link between the size of markings and the size of the increase in the product. Article 28 therefore precluded the German prohibition in this case.

13.29 In Case C-405/98 *Konsumentenombudsmannen v Gourmet International Products* (2001), the Court ruled that the case law laid down in joined Cases C-267/91 and C-268/91 *Keck and Mithouard* (1993) was not applicable here. Treaty provisions relating to the free movement of goods and the freedom to provide services did not preclude a prohibition, imposed by Swedish legislation, on the advertising of alcoholic beverages in periodicals, unless it is apparent that the protection of public health against the harmful effects of alcohol can be ensured by measures having less effect on intra-Community trade. The Court held that, in the case of products like alcoholic beverages, the consumption of which is linked to traditional social practices and to local habits and customs, a prohibition of all advertising directed at consumers in the form of advertisements in the press is liable to impede access to the market by products from other member states more than it impedes access by domestic products. Such a ban would not have that much effect on the sales of local alcohols which already had an established market, but it would make it much more difficult for foreign alcohols to enter the market.

In Case C-254/98 *Schutzverband gegen unlauteren Wettbewerb v TK Heimdienst Sass GmbH* (2000) only local Austrians were given licences to sell groceries from vans in the administrative district where they were based. This could have been justified as it intended to promote sales by local shopkeepers. However, this disadvantaged a German shopkeeper, no more than five miles away, based just across the border, who could not obtain a licence, whereas an Austrian shopkeeper, based no nearer, could. Although the rule did not intend to discriminate as to nationality, in fact the effect on goods of different origin was different.

13.30 On the whole it can be said that the Court has been consistent in its post-*Keck* case law. There are a number of straightforward *Keck* cases such as *Hünermund*, *Leclerq-Siplec* etc. By consistently following the approach set out in *Keck* the court has restored legal certainty after a period of incoherent case law. By introducing a fairly straightforward formula such as the *Keck* standard without many details, conditions and exceptions, the Court has made sure that there is room for a later refinement if needed. Not all post-*Keck* cases, however, are entirely predictable, as in the case of *Mars*.

13.31 In Case C-379/98 *PreussenElektra* (2001) German legislation obliged electricity supply undertakings to purchase the electricity produced in their area of supply from renewable energy sources and to pay for it in accordance with a statutory minimum price. Although the Court ruled that the German legislation constituted, at least potentially, an obstacle to intra-Community trade, it then stated that account should be taken of the aim of the provision and of the particular features of the electricity market (para 72). The provision was designed to protect the environment and the health and life of humans, animals and plants. The Court observed that the nature of electricity makes it difficult to determine its origin and in particular the source of energy from which it was produced. Furthermore, there was a proposed directive in which the Commission had taken the view that the implementation in each member state of a system of certificates of origin for electricity produced from renewable sources capable of being the subject of mutual recognition was essential in order to make trade in that type of electricity both reliable and possible in practice. Therefore, the Court concluded that, 'in the current state of Community law concerning the electricity market', the German legislation was not incompatible with Article 28 EC (para 81). Advocate General Jacobs questioned whether this was a case for relaxation of the rule that the list of exceptions in Article 30 (ex Article 36) EC was exhaustive, and that environmental protection should be a justification of a rule even if it was discriminatory. However, the Court allowed the justification on the grounds of environmental protection, a *Cassis* type justification, but said the legislation was not incompatible with Article 30. (See further argument in Craig and de Burca (3rd edn, pp 659–661) in favour of doing away with the distinction between Article 30 justifications and *Cassis*-type mandatory requirements.)

13.32 The problem of reverse discrimination (see also Chapter 18) also arises in the case of goods. A member state may well continue to impose stricter rules on its domestic product than on the foreign product. This was clearly the case in the *German Beer* case (Case 178/84 *Commission v Germany* (1987)) (see **13.17**). In Case C 321-324/94 *Pistre* (1997) the designation of French '*jambon de montagne*' (mountain ham) was reserved for ham from pigs living on particular high mountain slopes in France. This meant that ham from other pigs, even if living the same type of life, could not bear that designation. In fact, foreign producers did call their product mountain ham without encountering problems. The problem arose with a French producer who used the designation without being entitled to do so. He was prosecuted and claimed this was a breach of Article 28. The French government claimed it was a purely internal situation. The Court said that just because the situation was confined to one member state, that did not mean Article 28 could not apply. If the effect of the measure was to facilitate the marketing of domestic goods to the detriment of foreign goods this meant there could be at least a potential hindrance to intra-Community trade. The same sort of issue arose in Case C-448/98 *Guimont* (2000). A French rule allowing only cheese with a rind to be sold as Emmenthal (hardly a typically French designation) again did not hinder imports in practice. The Court said this rule was potentially an obstacle to trade, but there was no Community reason why the rule could not be applied to French producers. This is different to *Pistre* of course, where no foreign product could ever achieve the standard set by the French rule, whereas in the simpler *Guimont* and *Cassis* cases there was no reason why a foreign producer could not reach that standard.

As we shall see later (eg in **18.14** and **18.15** in *Bosman*) the court may apply the same principles to the different freedoms, for example to the free movement of goods and services, although there are differences in treatment as well as similarities.

Article 29 (ex Article 34) EC

13.33 Article 29 (ex Article 34) EC contains the same prohibition of quantitative restrictions and MEQRs on export restrictions, such as those in Case 53/76 *Bouhelier* (1977), which concerned a quality inspection of watches exported from France, whereas no such inspection was required for domestic watches. This was held by the Court to be a MEQR. However, in contrast to Article 28, Article 29 will only apply if there is discrimination and thus indistinctly applicable measures will not fall under Article 29. In Case 15/79 *Groenveld BV v Produktschap voor Vee en Vlees* (1979) domestic producers of meat products were prohibited from stocking or processing horsemeat. Horsemeat cannot be easily detected in meat products and this was to avoid the risk of horsemeat being present in products being sold to countries where the consumption of such meat is forbidden, although this was not the case in the Netherlands. The Court said that this was not a discriminatory measure as it applied equally to domestic products and exports and it was therefore permitted. For a measure to fall under Article 29, there must be discrimination, in contrast to what we have seen for Article 28. Thus the *Cassis* justifications cannot apply.

13.34 In a rare example of Treaty infringement proceedings brought under Article 227 (ex Article 170) EC by one member state against another, Belgium brought proceedings against Spain in Case C-388/95 *Belgium v Spain* for maintaining in force national legislation providing that, in order for wine to be able to use its designation of origin (Rioja) it had to be bottled in that region. In an earlier case, C-47/90 *Delhaize* (1992) the Court had held that measures limiting the quantity of wine which could be exported in bulk whilst allowing such sales in bulk within the region were in breach of Article 29. In this case, however the Court said that new evidence had since been gathered demonstrating an underlying justification of such measures and that the obligation of bottling wine in the region was compatible with Community law as a necessary and proportionate means of the objective pursued in the absence of any less restrictive alternative measures. The Court therefore dismissed the action.

Further reading

Mortelmans, 'Towards convergence in the application of the rules on free movement and on competition' (2001) 38 CMLRev 613

Maduro, *We the Court: the European Court of Justice and the European Constitution: A critical reading of Article 30 of the EC Treaty*, Hart Publishing 1998.

S Weatherill, 'Recent case law concerning the free movement of goods: mapping the frontiers of market deregulation', [1999] CMLRev36, pp 51–85L.

Gormley, 'Reasoning renounced? The temarkable judgment in *Keck v Mithouard*', [1994] EBLR 63.

W P J Wils, 'The search for the rule in Article 30 EEC: much ado about nothing?', [1993] 18 ELRev 475.

N Reich, 'The "November Revolution" of the European Court of Justice: *Keck, Meng* and *Audi* revisited', [1994] 31 CMLRev 459.

Stephen Weatherill, 'After *Keck*: some thoughts on how to clarify the situation,' [1996] CMLRev 885-906.

Lawrence Gormley, *Prohibiting Restrictions on Trade within the EEC* (1985), North Holland, p 54.

J Steiner, 'Drawing the line: uses and abuses of Article 30 EEC', [1992] 29 CMLRev 749.

A Biondi, 'The merchant, the thief and the citizen: the circulation of works of art within the European Union', [1997] 34 CMLRev 1173.

Self-test questions

1. What are measures having an equivalent effect to a quantitative restriction (MEQR)?

2. Do the cases of *Keck* and those following it represent a change in the attitude of the ECJ towards defining what is a MEQR?

3. Are the mandatory requirements recognised in *Cassis de Dijon* to be understood as exceptions to Article 28 (thus extending Article 30) or as taking measures out of the ambit of Article 28 altogether?

CHAPTER FOURTEEN

Competition Policy

SUMMARY

- **The EC competition rules**
- **Article 81 (ex Article 85) EC: the general structure**
- **The *de minimis* principle**
- **Conditions for exemption**
- **Decentralization of the application of Article 81(3)**
- **The new Regulation 1/2003**
- **Negative clearance and 'comfort letters'**
- **Block exemptions**
- **Block exemption Regulation 2790/99**
- **Article 82 (ex Article 86) EC : abuse of a dominant position**
- **The relevant market**
- **The meaning of abuse**
- **Merger control**
- **The Merger Regulation (Regulation 4064/89)**
- **Enforcement of EC competition rules**
- **The role of the national courts**
- **National competition law**

Introduction

14.1 The purpose of competition law is to ensure that the economic actors, in pursuing their activities, do not prevent, distort or restrict competition or abuse their position in the market to the detriment of competitors and/or consumers.

Competition policy has now become one of the most developed policies of the Community. This policy is based on the fundamental principle set out in Article 3(1)(g) EC whereby the Treaty requires 'a system ensuring that competition in the Common Market is not distorted'. A set of analytical provisions is devoted to that principle. Articles 81–89 (ex Articles 85–94) of the Treaty as well as secondary legislation (in particular the Merger Regulation) aim at ensuring that private or public undertakings, under the pressures of increasing costs, do not resort to concerted practices, or to strengthening or abusing their dominant position resulting in distortive effects on the common market.

Competition policy in the EC must also ensure market integration and ensure that the barriers to intra-Community trade that are removed by legislative measures are not replaced de facto by other types of market partitioning.

Finally, the Community's competition policy aims at reconciling the traditional aims of competition law and the integration of the Common Market with the competitiveness of Community industries (Article 157 (ex Article 130) EC) in the global market.

In this chapter we shall concentrate on the provisions dealing with the actions of private undertakings. However, the Treaty also deals with the distortive effect on competition arising from the granting of special and exclusive rights to public undertakings or undertakings entrusted with public services (Article 86 (ex Article 90) EC), anti-dumping rules and rules on state aids (Articles 87–89 (ex Articles 92–94) EC).

Article 81: the general structure

14.2 Article 81(1) prohibits all agreements between undertakings, decisions by associations of undertakings and concerted practices which may affect trade between member states and which have as their object or effect the prevention, restriction or distortion of competition within the Common Market.

The Article itself provides a non-exhaustive list of examples of agreements which fall within the provision. Article 81(2) provides that any agreement or decision in breach of Article 81(1) shall be automatically void. Under Article 81(3), Article 81(1) may be declared inapplicable when the agreements which potentially fall within the provision fulfil a number of specified requirements.

14.3 Article 81(1) contains three essential elements:

- some form of collusion in the form of an agreement between undertakings, or a decision by an association of undertakings, or a concerted practice;

- which may affect trade between member states; and

- which must have as its object or effect the prevention, restriction or distortion of competition within the Common Market.

Article 81: collusion between undertakings

Undertakings

14.4 In the absence of a legislative definition, the Commission and the court have interpreted the term 'undertaking' to include any legal or natural person engaged in some form of economic or commercial activity involving the provision of goods or services. Examples of undertakings for the purposes of EC competition law include limited companies, partnerships, trade associations, agricultural co-operatives, sole traders and state companies engaged in all economic sectors.

A group of companies is treated as a single undertaking and the conduct of a subsidiary is normally attributed to the parent if the subsidiary company has followed the parent's market policy: Cases 6 and 7/73 *Commercial Solvents* (1974).

Undertakings based outside the EC come within the scope of Article 81(1) EC even if the collusion takes place outside the EC, provided that the collusion takes effect within the EC (see Cases 48, 49 and 51–57/69 *ICI* (1972); Cases 89, 104, 114, 116-117, 125–129/85 *Wood Pulp* (1988)).

Agreements

14.5 This term has been interpreted to mean oral or written agreements. A gentleman's agreement enforceable by arbitration has been considered as falling within the definition of Article 81(1): Case 41/69 *ACF Chemiefarma NV v Commission* (1970). Failure to prove existence of an agreement would in any event have little impact given the extension of the prohibition to concerted practices. There must be an agreement between at least two parties: in Case T-41/96 *Bayer/Adalat v Commission* the CFI annulled the Commission's decision (OJ 1996 L 201/1) on the grounds that it had not established that there was an agreement and unilateral behaviour was not suffice to create an agreement under Article

81(1). Bayer had taken measures to deter exports, although the wholesalers had sought to get round these. The Commission held this to constitute an 'agreement' but this was overturned by the CFI. The decision is being appealed by the Commission to the ECJ (Case C-3/01 *Commission v Bayer* pending).

Decisions by associations of undertakings

14.6 Associations of undertakings (such as trade associations) may co-ordinate their activities, and obtain an anti-competitive effect without having recourse to a formal agreement. This explains the rationale for their inclusion in Article 81(1). The phrase 'decisions by associations of undertakings' has been interpreted by the court as including a non-binding recommendation by a trade association to its members in Case 8/72 *Vereeniging van Cementhandelaren v Commission* (1972).

Concerted practices

14.7 In Cases 48, 49 and 51-57/69 *ICI (Dyestuffs)* (1972), the court defined a 'concerted practice' as a form of co-operation between undertakings which without having reached the stage where an agreement properly so called has been concluded, knowingly substituted practical co-operation for the risks of competition. In the light of the case law, concerted practice will be considered to exist where there is positive contact between the parties (eg meetings, discussions, exchanges of information) and such contact has the object of influencing market behaviour and removing in advance the risks of uncertainty by maintaining or altering the conduct of the undertakings and leads to conditions of competition not corresponding to the normal competitive forces of the market. Parallel behaviour (ie undertakings acting identically on the market) does not in itself constitute a concerted practice but it provides strong evidence thereof. Before the conclusion can be drawn that there has been concertation, it has to be ascertained whether there is any other possible explanation for the parallel conduct.

Oligopoly

14.8 Parallel behaviour can also arise in markets which are oligopolistic. A monopolistic market is one where one company dominates and is able to restrict output and thereby set uncompetitive prices. At the other end of the spectrum, in a market with a large number of competing companies (an atomistic or dispersed market), competition will be strong. In between lies the oligopoly. Such a market is characterised by a relatively small number of companies trading in a homogenous product where barriers to entry and price transparency are high. Under such conditions, without any agreement or understanding between them, the companies may follow a strategy of adopting similar behaviour in the market. For example, because it is easy for customers to switch suppliers, a price cut by one must be followed by similar cuts by the others and therefore is uneconomic. The result is 'conscious parallelism' (Whish prefers 'tacit co-ordination') where the companies mirror each other's behaviour. Such behaviour may lead to uncompetitive conditions prevailing on the market as the companies can establish supra-competitive prices or limit output but it is acknowledged to be a rational response to market conditions and is not illegal under Article 81. Therefore, it must be discounted as an explanation for parallel behaviour before a finding of an illegal concerted practice can be sustained. In the *Dyestuffs* case the ECJ made it clear that parallel behaviour by members of an oligopoly arising from rational responses to a competitor's behaviour was legal; in determining that there was indeed a concerted practice the ECJ referred to the large number of producers involved (there were 10, supplying 80% of the market) and concluded that the market therefore could not be oligopolistic. In addition, the division of the relevant market into five national markets with different price levels and structure also made it 'improbable that a spontaneous and equal price increase would occur on all the national markets'. In *Woodpulp*, the Commission's finding of a concerted practice was overturned by the ECJ and the judgment relied, in part, on the fact that the Commission had overlooked 'oligopolistic tendencies of the market' (Cases 89, 104, 114, 116–7, 125–129/85 A *Ahlstrom Oy v Commission*, para 126).

Article 81: effect on trade between member states

14.9 In order to be in breach of Article 81(1) the agreement, decision or concerted practice must affect intra-Community trade. This requirement applies equally to Article 82 and effectively defines the boundaries of the jurisdiction of Community law. The basic test defining the circumstances in which an agreement falls within Article 81(1) EC was first stated by the court in Case 56/65 *Société Technique Minière v Maschinenbau* (1966), as follows:

It must be possible to foresee with a sufficient degree of probability on the basis of a set of objective factors of law or of fact that the agreement in question may have an influence, direct or indirect, actual or potential, on the pattern of trade between member states.

The test is similar to the one applied in *Dassonville* (see **13.6**) with regard to Article 28 (ex Article 30) EC but it is wider in scope as it refers to a mere effect (even potential) and not to the hindrance to trade between member states. An agreement which extends over the national territory of only one member state may nevertheless infringe Article 81(1) as it reinforces the partitioning of the Common Market along national lines. Thus, the Article has consistently been applied to collusions between undertakings in the same State: Case 8/72 *Vereeniging van Cementhandelaren v Commission* (1972).

Article 81: object or effect of the collusion between undertakings

14.10 Article 81(1) provides a non-exhaustive list of restrictions which are prohibited. This list includes agreements or practices which:

(a) directly or indirectly fix purchase or selling prices: Case 123/83 *BNIC v Clair* (1985) or any trading conditions; Case 26/76 *Metro SB-Grossmärkte GmbH v Commission* (1977);

(b) limit or control production: Case 41/69 *ACF Chemiefarma v Commission* (1970); markets: Case 45/69 *Boehringer Mannheim v Commission* (1970); technical development, or investment;

(c) divide markets or sources of supply: Case 44/69 *Bucher & Co v Commission* (1970);

(d) apply dissimilar conditions to equivalent transactions with other trading parties, thereby placing them at a competitive disadvantage: Case 73/74 *Groupement des Fabricants de Papiers Peints de Belgique v Commission* (1975);

(e) make the conclusion of contracts subject to acceptance by the other parties of supplementary obligations which, by their nature or according to commercial usage, have no connection with the subject of such contracts.

The rationale of the Article is to prevent any form of distortion of competition. However, this aim is to be reconciled with that of protecting the internal market. Therefore the principle applies to both vertical and horizontal agreements.

14.11 Vertical agreements are agreements between undertakings at different levels of trade or industry, for example, those between a producer and a distributor. Horizontal agreements are agreements between undertakings at the same level of trade or industry, for instance, between two or more manufacturers, or two or more wholesalers of goods who compete with each other. In some cases in which the parties did compete or could have competed with each other without the agreement, a vertical agreement might be seen as also having horizontal elements.

From an economic perspective vertical agreements usually pose less of a threat to competition and, on the contrary, are often economically beneficial as they improve efficiency to the advantage of consumers. However, the aim of avoiding the fragmentation of the market has led the court and the Commission to be vigilant also on vertical agreements.

In this respect, *Consten and Grundig v Commission* (Cases 56 and 58/64) is a very significant case which decided that vertical agreements are also caught by Article 81. Grundig had agreed with Consten that the latter would be the exclusive dealer for Grundig's products in France. Consten's cumbersome obligations towards Grundig (not dealing with competing brands, promoting the products, minimum purchase requirements, arranging after-sales service, etc) were balanced by the fact that Consten received absolute territorial protection for the products. Furthermore, Consten enjoyed reinforced protection through intellectual property rights on the products in its contract territory. When a third party tried to import products into France which had been bought in Germany, undermining the arrangement between Consten and Grundig, they sued the company on various grounds, including trade mark infringement. The Court upheld the Commission decision that the agreement was in breach of Article 81. The avoidance of market partitioning is still one of the main focuses of the Commission's policy. This is confirmed by the high fine imposed on Volkswagen for the system of restrictions on parallel imports which the company had imposed on its Italian dealers in order to insulate a lower-priced market (Commission Decision, *VW*, OJ 1988 L124/60).

14.12 However, recognition of the beneficial effects of many vertical agreements has led the Commission to issue a number of block exemptions covering various types of vertical agreement. The Commission has adopted a single block exemption replacing many of these block exemptions for different categories of vertical agreement (Commission Regulation No 2790/99; see **14.28**). It also, in 1999, exempted certain vertical agreements from the requirement that they be notified prior to individual exemption (Article 4(2) Council Regulation No 17/62 as amended by Council Regulation No 1216/1999).

The de minimis principle

14.13 It is a well established principle that an agreement which would potentially fall within Article 81(1) is not caught by the prohibition if it does not have an appreciable effect on competition. This principle was first established by the Court of Justice in Case 5/69 Volk (1969). The Court stated that an agreement falls outside the scope of Article 81(1) EC when it has an insignificant (de minimis) effect on the market. In 1997 the Commission issued the *Notice on Agreements of Minor Importance* (OJ 1997 C 372/4) which superseded earlier versions and provided guidance as to when an agreement does not fall within Article 85(1) (now Article 81(1) EC). A Notice is an official document issued by the Commission. Whilst such Notices are not legally binding and provide general guidance rather than definitive principles, they are of significance as they express current Commission policy. A new *Notice on Agreements of Minor Importance which do not Appreciably Restrict Competition under Article 81(1)* was issued by the Commission in 2001 (2001 OJ C368/13).

14.14 The new *de minimis* Notice states that agreements between undertakings 'which are actual or potential competitors' (ie 'horizontal' agreements) where the aggregate share of the undertakings does not exceed 10% of the relevant market will not contravene Article 81(1). In the case of vertical agreements between undertakings which are 'not actual or potential competitors' the threshold of the market share is increased to 15%. Where it is difficult to determine whether the agreement is one between competitors or non-competitors, the 10% threshold will apply.

The new Notice lowers the *de minimis* market share threshold to 5% for both competitors and non-competitors in markets where competition is restricted by the 'cumulative foreclosure effect' of parallel networks of agreements having similar effects on the market. Such an effect is unlikely to exist where less than 30% of the market is covered by such networks of agreements.

Exemption from the application of Article 81(1) does not apply in cases of particularly serious breaches of competition law. The Notice sets out the hard-core restrictions which, if included in the agreement, will make the application of the *de minimis* principle invalid. Examples of when the exemption will not apply are agreements between competitors which have as their object the fixing of prices when selling to third parties or the allocation of markets or customers, and agreements between non-competitors restricting the territory into which the buyer may sell goods or services.

The Notice also states that agreements between small and medium-sized undertakings are rarely capable of appreciably affecting trade between member states and are unlikely to fall within Article 81(1) (see **14.9**).

Individual exemption

14.15 Agreements or decisions which fall within the prohibition of Article 81(1) EC are void: Article 81(2) EC, unless it is possible to sever the offending clause: *Consten & Grundig v Commission*. However, Article 81(3) EC provides for the 'exemption' of agreements which, otherwise, would be void under Article 81(1) provided that certain conditions are met.

Conditions for exemption

14.16 Article 81(3) EC provides for both positive and negative conditions for exemption. The former concern the pro-competitive effects of the agreement, decision of undertakings or concerted practice whilst the latter conditions concern the limited adverse effect on competition caused by the agreement.

The positive conditions are that the agreement, decision of undertakings or concerted practice:

• contributes to the improvement of the production or distribution of goods or to the promotion of technical or economic progress;

• allows consumers to receive a fair share of the resulting benefit.

The negative conditions are that the agreement, decision of undertakings or concerted practice:

• imposes no restrictions on competition that are not indispensable to obtaining the benefit;

- does not create the possibility for the undertakings involved to eliminate competition in respect of a substantial part of the products in question.

Both sets of conditions must be satisfied before exemption can be granted. If that is the case, the Commission will adopt a final decision stating the duration of the exemption. The Commission also has the power (frequently exercised) to attach conditions and obligations to the exempted agreements. In order to supervise the respect of the terms of the decision the parties are often requested to submit periodic reports.

Decentralisation of the application of Article 81(3)

14.17 The system that has been in operation since 1962 is that under Article 4(1) and 9(1) of Regulation 17/62 (OJ Spec Ed 1959–62, 87) the Commission has exclusive competence to grant such exemptions after prior notification. Such an individual exemption could only be granted if the agreement had been notified to the Commission pursuant to Regulation 17/62 which set out the procedure for notification and established the rights of the parties within the procedure.

The notification, which was done by means of a specific form (Form A/B), resulted in an immunity from fines even if the agreement was subsequently found to contravene Article 81(1) EC.

14.18 Reform of the application of Article 81(3) was at the heart of the Commission's programme for modernisation of EC competition law which was set out in the White Paper on Modernisation of the Rules implementing Articles 85 and 86 of the EC Treaty, published in 1999 (Commission Programme 99/27, 28 April 1999 OJ 1999 C132/1).

Regulation 1/2003 on the Implementation of the Rules on Competition laid down in Articles 81 and 82 of the Treaty has now been legislated and will give effect to these reforms. It comes into effect on 1 May 2004.

The central provisions are the abolition of the requirement for prior notification and the decentralisation of the application of Article 81(3). Article 81(3) is to be made directly effective, so that National Competition Authorities and national courts can apply it. At present, Article 81(1) and 81(2) are directly effective (Case 127/73 *BRT v SABAM* (1974)) and can be applied by the national courts, but until the present reform programme comes into effect national courts are precluded, by the terms of Article 4(1) of Regulation 17/62, from giving exemption under Article 81(3). One problem that this causes is that undertakings against whom action is being taken in the national courts, can bring proceedings to a halt by lodging a notification with the Commission for Article 81(3) exemption (para 100 of White Paper). The proposed reform involves the abolition of the notification system and its replacement by an ex-post system where Article 81(3) would be applied by the national authorities and courts without prior decision by the Commission, making Article 81 as a whole directly effective (as is Article 82).

14.19 Centralised control over the exemption system was necessary when Community competition law was developing so that there could be coherent interpretation and uniform application of Article 81(3). The creation of a consistent body of law based on the application of Article 81(3) by the Commission since the inception of the Community now makes it possible to maintain legal certainty despite decentralisation of application of the provision. Decentralisation of the application of the competition rules has become essential to relieve the Commission of part of an ever-increasing work-load, allowing it to concentrate its resources on investigating the most serious infringements of the competition provisions. The problem of the burden on Commission resources will be exacerbated with the projected enlargement of the EU. The new Regulation is due to take effect on 1 May 2004 when ten additional countries join the EU. Central to the new regime is the principle that the Commission and the National Competition Authorities will 'form ... a network of public authorities applying the Community competition rules in close co-operation' (Recital 15 Regulation 1/2003). The result will be to give national authorities greater powers: they are well placed to take action as they are better acquainted with local markets and national operators and are closer to complainants (para 46 of White Paper). The requirement that undertakings wishing to invoke Article 81(3) must notify their restrictive practices to the Commission has placed them under a heavy burden of work and cost. The proposed ex-post system leaves the responsibility for assessing whether an agreement is compatible with the EC competition rules with the undertakings themselves; years of operation of the rules has ensured that undertakings and national courts are well acquainted with the principles governing the application of Articles 81 and 82. Companies will then be able to invoke the direct effect of Article 81(3) as an argument in their defence before the national courts.

The new Regulation

14.20 Article 2 of the Regulation specifies the burden of proof: it is for the party or authority alleging an infringement to prove it; the undertaking or association of undertakings wishing to rely on Article 81(3) has the burden of proving that it has fulfilled the conditions set out in that provision.

The Commission has a power enshrined in Article 10 of the new Regulation to take a decision 'where the Community public interest ... so requires', declaring that Article 81(1) does not apply, either because the conditions of Article 81(1) are not fulfilled or because the conditions of Article 81(3) are satisfied. It may also declare that Article 82 does not apply. This may be used by the Commission where there is uncertainty about the lawfulness of a certain type of agreement (perhaps of a novel nature) to provide guidance to the market.

Article 9 of the Regulation allows the Commission to take 'commitments' from undertakings that they will take action to meet the concerns raised by the Commission; the Commission can make these binding on the undertaking and subsequently will take no action unless there is a change of circumstances or the undertaking does not comply with those commitments. This mirrors the similar practice under the Merger Regulation.

14.21 A number of provisions in the new Regulation 1/2003 facilitate co-operation between the Commission, the National Competition Authorities (NCAs) and the national courts. So it is clearly stated that the Commission and the NCAs will 'apply the Community competition rules in close co-operation'; the Commission must supply the NCAs with the most important documents relating to its decisions as to whether there has been an infringement of the competition provisions, on the granting of interim relief (not specifically mentioned in Regulation 17/62 but included in the new Regulation in terms echoing earlier case-law of the Court) or on accepting commitments. The NCAs must inform the Commission when commencing an investigation; they should also inform the Commission 'not later than 30 days' before the adoption of any decision requiring an infringement to be brought to an end (Article 11(4)), before 'accepting commitments and before withdrawing the benefit of a block exemption (which the NCAs are now able to do). Information is to be shared; NCAs can ask the Commission its opinion in a particular case; NCAs and national courts must not take decisions which conflict with decisions of the Commission. Where the Commission initiates proceedings, the NCAs will no longer have competence to apply Articles 81 and 82. Where the case concerns more than three member states, the Commission will generally take jurisdiction.

The implementation of the new Regulation is an example of the principle of subsidiarity in practice. As a first step in the reform process,

Regulation 1216/99 entered into force on 13 June 1999. This Regulation amends Article 4(2) of Regulation 17/62 to the effect that certain vertical agreements no longer have to be notified to the Commission in advance in order to qualify for individual exemption.

Negative clearance and comfort letters

Negative clearance

14.22 Under the present system of prior notification and exclusive exemption by the Commission, an alternative to seeking individual exemption under Article 81(3) is that the parties may seek 'negative clearance', that is a decision by the Commission that an agreement or a decision does not infringe Article 81(1) at all.

'Comfort letters'

14.23 Again, under the present system, instead of adopting a decision granting formal exemption or issuing negative clearance, the Commission may write a letter to the parties concerned, known as a 'comfort letter'. Such a letter is an informal letter indicating that in the Commission's view there is no need to intervene under applicable competition rules. Indeed, most cases are resolved in this way. The comfort letter may be withdrawn if there is a change in the circumstances. The need for comfort letters arose because of the over-load on the Commission's resources from the notification and exemption procedure. The Commission could only issue a limited number of formal decisions of individual exemption in any year and had recourse to the informal 'comfort letter' as an alternative.

14.24 According to the Court, comfort letters are administrative letters outside the framework of the Treaty and do not bind national courts, nor can they be invoked before the ECJ in annulment proceedings: Cases 253/78 and 1-3/79 *Procureur de la République v Giry and Guerlain* (1980). Comfort letters do not have the status of a decision.

With the abolition of the notification requirement, comfort letters will no longer be issued; negative clearance will no longer be relevant.

Block exemptions

14.25 The mechanism to obtain individual exemptions under Article 81(3) EC has been slow and cumbersome. In many cases, notably those involving vertical agreements which pose no threat for competition and can be economically beneficial, imposing individual notification placed an unnecessary burden on undertakings and created a heavy workload for the Commission.

To address these issues, categories of agreements have been exempted from Article 81(1) EC by means of Regulations, known as block exemptions, which grant class relief. The most important block exemption regulations have been issued in relation to agreements within the following categories:

- specialisation: Regulation 2658/00 OJ 2000 L 304/3 replacing Regulation 417/85;

- research and development: Regulation 2659/00 OJ 2000 L 304/7 replacing Regulation 418/85;

- technology transfer: Regulation 240/96, OJ 1996 L 31/2;

- categories of vertical agreements and concerted practices in the motor vehicle sector: Regulation 1400/2002 OJ 2002 L203/30 replacing Regulation 1475/95;

- categories of vertical agreements and concerted practices: Regulation 2790/99, OJ 1999 L336/21.

Block exemptions contained in Regulations 1983/83 (exclusive distribution agreements), 1984/83 (exclusive purchasing agreements) and 4087/88 (franchise agreements) were repealed as of 31 May 2000 (see Regulation 2790/99, Article 12(1)).

14.26 Each of the block exemptions contains its own individual criteria which must be satisfied in all respects. Block exemption regulations tend to follow a pattern according to which certain clauses are specifically permitted ('permission clauses'). Certain other provisions, which always restrict or distort competition, are expressly forbidden and would take the whole agreement outside the scope of the block exemption ('prohibitive clauses'). Some of the block exemption regulations contain a further category of clauses ('grey clauses') which require the agreement to be notified to the Commission. If the Commission takes no action within six months, then the agreement in question is deemed to have qualified for a block exemption.

14.27 In practice, block exemptions are extremely useful and widely used. An agreement which falls within the terms of a block exemption does not have to be notified to the Commission and there is no danger that the contracting parties will be fined for breach of Article 81 EC. However, there are also some disadvantages in bringing a transaction within the scope of a block exemption and in this system in general. First, the prohibited clause lists are often wide and difficult to apply for the parties. Second, block exemption regulations comprise strict form based requirements. Therefore their outcome is often considered narrowly legalistic in a situation which would benefit from a more economic based approach. Third, the exemption might lead the parties to distort agreements which would make the Common Market more competitive, integrated and efficient in order to fall within the formal terms of the block exemption. Finally there is a real risk that the Commission might exempt agreements that distort competition as block exemptions are form based rather than effect based. The Commission has recently adopted a more economic based approach described in 'Guidelines on Vertical Restraints in EC Competition Policy' (OJ C291 of 30.10.2000). The shift in policy is apparent in the block exemption for Vertical Restraints, Regulation 2790/99.

Block Exemption Regulation 2790/99

14.28 The block exemption on vertical agreements and concerted practices Regulation 2790/99 entered into force on 1 January 2000 but the key provisions applied from 1 June 2000. This Regulation replaces the old block exemptions covering exclusive distribution agreements, exclusive purchasing agreements and franchising agreements. It applies to vertical agreements (including selective distribution agreements) covering both services and goods and it applies to goods supplied for resale and to goods for use.

It was adopted in response to criticism of the treatment of vertical agreements in EC law and represents a more market-orientated, economics-based approach.

Its main objective, according to the Commission, is to allow companies which do not have market power (ie have less than 30% of the market) to benefit from a 'safe haven within which they are no longer obliged to assess the validity of their agreements with Community competition rules'. The 'Guidelines on Vertical Restraints' are long and detailed and are to assist undertakings in carrying out an evaluation of their position in regard to Article 81.

The Regulation

14.29 Article 3 introduces a cap of 30% market share on the availability of the block exemption. This applies to the market share of the supplier except in the case of an exclusive supply obligation as defined in Article 1(c) of the regulation, where it is the buyer's share which is relevant. Over this threshold, an individual exemption can still be applied for.

Article 4 sets out the prohibited list of provisions (hard-core restrictions) which will preclude the block exemption from applying, including the imposition of fixed or minimum resale prices, export bans and restrictions of passive sales.

Article 5 forbids direct or indirect non-compete clauses, although inclusion of such clauses do not make the whole agreement ineligible for exemption.

Other new Regulations

14.30 Regulation 2659/00, a new block exemption for Research and Development agreements, entered into force on 1 January 2001. The Commission recognises the value of Research and Development (R & D) and that there are advantages in small and medium sized companies co-operating on R & D. So the block exemption confers exemption from Article 81(1) for agreements between companies which have agreements to co-operate in R & D provided that:

(1) At the time the agreement is entered into their combined market share is below a market-share threshold of 25% for competing undertakings (Article 4).

(2) The agreements do not contain prohibited hard-core restrictions set out in Article 5 (ie price-fixing, limitation on output or sales, prohibition of passive sales). The inclusion of such clauses invalidates the whole agreement (Article 5).

(3) The block exemption is for three types of R & D agreement in relation to goods and services (Article 1):

— joint R & D of products or processes and joint exploitation of the results;

— joint exploitation of the results of R & D of products or processes consequent to a prior agreement between the parties to carry out such joint exploitation;

— joint R & D but then no joint exploitation of the products or processes produced.

Article 3 sets out the conditions for the application of the block exemption.

Regulation 2658/00 sets out a new block exemption for Specialisation Agreements which came into force on 1 January 2001.

Article 82 (ex Article 86) EC: abuse of a dominant position

The prohibition

14.31 Under Article 82 EC, any abuse by one or more undertakings of a dominant position within the Common Market or in a substantial part of it is prohibited as incompatible with the Common Market in so far as it may affect trade between member states. This prohibition is followed by a number of non-exhaustive examples of abuses.

There are three essential elements in establishing a breach of Article 82 EC:

• determination of what is the relevant market;

• establishing that the company is dominant in that market, a process in which market share is an important but not the only factor; and

• proving that there has been abuse of that position.

It is then necessary to show that the abuse has affected intra-Community trade.

Article 82 EC: the dominant position

14.32 A dominant position was defined in Case 27/76 *United Brands v Commission* (1978) as a:

> ... position of economic strength enjoyed by an undertaking which enables it to prevent effective competition being maintained on the relevant market by giving it the power to behave to an appreciable extent independently of its competitors, customers, and ultimately, of its consumers.

In order to assess dominance within the meaning of Article 82 EC it is necessary to examine the key factors of the relevant product and geographical market.

The relevant market

14.33 Dominance has to be assessed in relation to a particular, defined market. The correct identification of the relevant market is critical, and can be controversial. Determining the relevant market will clarify which producers can be regarded as actual or potential competitors leading to a clear view of the competitive constraints operating upon the allegedly dominant company; thus the market power of the company can be evaluated.

The relevant market has two main parameters: the product market and the geographic market (the temporal market is also of significance and the ECJ has established that dominance must be sustained over a period of time: see Case 6, 7/73 *Commercial Solvents* and Case 27/76 *United Brands*). An important case on the definition of the relevant market under Article 82 is Case 27/76 *United Brands*.

The relevant product market

14.34 The essential concept used by the ECJ to determine the boundaries of a particular product is that of interchangeability: those goods or services which are interchangeable fall within one product market. The definition of this market therefore requires an assessment of the extent to which products may be regarded as substitutes for each other, an analysis of the 'cross-elasticity' of demand or supply.

In Case 27/76 *United Brands* the Commission decision that United Brands was in breach of Article 82 was reviewed by the ECJ and the question of what the relevant product market comprised was an issue. The question raised was whether the relevant product market was the market for bananas, which was the product that United Brands traded, or the whole fresh fruit market, as claimed by the company. The company's share of the latter was relatively small. The Court considered the cross-elasticity of demand between bananas and fresh fruit. An analysis of the market confirmed that consumers' buying habits in regard to bananas were not significantly affected by the price and availability of other fresh fruit, indicating low cross-elasticity of demand: consumers do not substitute other fresh fruit for bananas when the price of that

342

fresh fruit, which varies seasonally, is relatively low compared to that of bananas. Bananas are unaffected by seasonal variations in production. A significant group of consumers was identified by the Court which had a constant need for bananas: the very young, the old and the sick. The ECJ made reference to the physical characteristics of bananas, to their appearance, taste, softness, seedlessness and ease of handling, which distinguishes them from other fruit. This case and subsequent case law therefore establishes a test of cross-elasticity or substitutability of products for identification of the relevant product market, the test to be made with reference to physical characteristics, price and intended use (see *Commercial Solvents*).

In *Continental Can* the Commission's evaluation of what was the relevant product market was overturned by the court. The market here was assessed in relation to cross-elasticity of supply (the extent to which other companies can switch production to the goods in question and thus potentially enter the market as competitors).

The geographic market

14.35 The ECJ defined the geographic market in *United Brands* as 'an area where the objective conditions of competititon applying to the product in question [are] the same for all traders'. Three member states had particular arrangements in regard to trade in bananas with overseas territories or, in the case of the UK, Commonwealth countries, and therefore the Court excluded them from the scope of the relevant geographic market.

14.36 The Commission has issued a Notice on the Definition of Relevant Market (OJ 1997 C 372/3).

In regard to the definition of the relevant product market in relation to cross-elasticity of demand, the test developed by the Commission and set out in the Notice is to ask whether a hypothetical, small (5–10%) permanent price increase would lead consumers to switch to another product. If it would do so to an extent that made the price increase uneconomic, those products are considered to be interchangeable anf therefore part of the same product market: if an increase in price of one product causes a significant switch by consumers to the other then they are part of the same product market.

Supply substitutability comprises an analysis of whether suppliers are able to switch production to manufacture the relevant products and market them in the short term without incurring additional costs or risks.

The test set out in the Notice is similar: if a manufacturer raises the price of a product by a small amount would it be cost-effective for manufacturers of other products to compete by switching production to make that product? If so, then the goods or services they produce are part of the same product market.

The relevant geographic market comprises the area in which the undertakings concerned are involved in the supply of products or services and where the conditions of competition are sufficiently homogenous to be distinguished from neighbouring areas because the conditions of competition are appreciably different in those areas.

Dominance

14.37 Once the relevant market has been identified, the question of whether the undrtaking is dominant in that market can be considered. The first and most important factor is that of market share.

In Case 6/72 *Continental Can* v *Commission* (1973), the share of the German market held by Continental Can was 70–80%. In *United Brands* the company was held to be dominant with a market share in the relevant market of only 40–45%, but a significant factor was that its share was several times larger than that held by the next largest competitor. This is often a relevant factor in determining market power. In Case C-62/86 *AKZO* (1991) the Court considered that a stable market share of 50% or more raises a presumption of dominance. In *Virgin/British Airways* (2000) the Commission found British Airways to be dominant in the market for air travel agency services where it had a share of 39.7%. The Commission took into account the fact that the nearest rival, Virgin, had only 5.5%. British Airways is seeking review of the Commission's decision.

Barriers to entry

14.38 In assessing the dominance of an undertaking the issue of potential competition must be taken into account. This requires assessment of the prevailing barriers to entry for potential competitors which might enter the market; whether the barriers to entry of the particular market are high or low affects the constraints on the dominant company and will determine the ambit of its autonomy.

Examples of barriers to entry which have been taken into account by the Court in determining dominance are: legal provisions: Case 333/94P *Tetra Pak Int SA v Commission* (1996); superior technology: *United*

Brands, Case 322/81 *Michelin v Commission* (1983), Case 85/76 *Hoffman-La Roche* (1979); deep pocket: *United Brands*, Case 6/72 *Continental Can*; economies of scale, vertical integration and well-developed distribution systems: *United Brands*; a well developed sales network: *Hoffman-La Roche*; product differentiation: *United Brands*, advertising had established a high profile brand image for the Chiquita banana.

A firm's behaviour may provide evidence of dominance, eg a discriminatory rebate system as in *United Brands*.

One further requirement for a finding of a breach under Article 82 is that the dominance must be in a 'substantial part' of the common market. The ECJ found that Southern Germany is sufficient to fulfil this requirement, which could be considered to operate as a *de minimis* threshold: see Cases 40–48, 50, 54–56, 111 & 113–114/73 *Suiker Unie* (1975).

Joint/collective dominance exists when two or more undertakings are linked in such a way that they adopt the same conduct in the market (Cases T-68, 77, 78/89 *Italian Flat Glass* (1992). In this case the concept was mentioned by the CFI, but not applied) (see further 14.51 and 14.52). Case C-395–396/96P *Compagnie Maritimes Belge* (2000) was the first case in which the ECJ applied the principle of collective dominance under Article 82.

The meaning of abuse

14.39 Article 82 EC does not prohibit dominance. It is the abuse of a dominant position which is illegal under Article 82 EC. The Article provides an illustrative and non-exhaustive list of examples of abuses which includes imposing directly or indirectly unfair pricing, limiting production, discrimination in contractual terms and the imposition of supplementary obligations.

14.40 The Court of Justice held that abuse is an objective concept: Case 85/76 *Hoffmann-La Roche* (1979). Article 82 has been defined as covering practices which are likely to affect the structure of a market where, as a result of the presence of a dominant undertaking, competition has been weakened and which, by having recourse to methods different from those governing normal competition on the basis of performance, have the effect of hindering the maintenance or development of the level of competition still existing on the market: *United Brands* and Case 322/81 *Michelin* (1983).

14.41 Article 82 prohibits practices which may be allowed in normal competitive circumstances but are not permissible because of the dominance of an undertaking. A dominant undertaking is effectively entrusted with a 'special responsibility' not to harm competition in general. However, a claim of abuse can be rebutted by providing 'objective justifications'. This was confirmed in, for example, Case T-30/89 *Hilti* (1991), (but rejected on the facts, CFI judgement upheld on appeal Case C-53/92P).

14.42 The definition of abuse provided above which focuses on reduction of competition is based on the fundamental principle of undistorted competition set out in Article 3(1)(g) of the Treaty. However, Article 82 also applies to cases in which the structure of the market has not been affected unfavourably. The provision has therefore been interpreted as penalising various forms of unfair competition.

In summary, two main categories of abuses can been identified: those relating to reduction of competition and those concerning unfair competition. In some cases they overlap and are difficult to distinguish.

Reduction of competition

14.43 Since *Continental Can* the court has construed Article 82 as prohibiting conduct which substantially reduces competition. The main forms of this type of abuse are:

- predatory pricing whereby a company seeks to eliminate a competitor by setting its prices at a particularly low level: Case C-62/86 *AZKO* (1991); Case T-83/91 *Tetra Pak* (1994);

- tying-in, which is the last type of abuse listed in Article 82 and refers to making the conclusions of contracts subject to acceptance by the other parties of supplementary obligations which by their nature or according to commercial usage have no connection with the subject of such contracts: Case 53/92 *Hilti*; Case 85/76 *Hoffmann-La Roche* (1979); Case 311/84 *Telemarketing* (1985); and finally

- refusal to supply which, however, can also be seen as a form of unfair competition.

Unfair competition

14.44 This form of exploitative abuses occurs where the dominant undertaking takes advantage of its position by imposing unfair trading conditions. The most common examples of these exploitative abuses include:

- unfair prices and unfair trading conditions; this type of abuse is referred to in Article 82(a). Unfair pricing may be either low or high pricing. The test for unfair pricing is controversial and there have been few cases under this heading;

- *ad hoc* discrimination; this consists of not treating like cases alike. This conduct is expressly prohibited by Article 82(c) which prohibits applying dissimilar conditions to equivalent transactions: *United Brands, AZKO*; and

- refusal to supply; this form of abuse, which is not explicitly prohibited by Article 82 has been nevertheless thoroughly analysed in the European Courts' and the Commission's case law. Where a dominant company is found to have abused its position by a refusal to supply, it would have to show objective justification.

14.45 The prohibition was originally applied in cases in which the refusal was addressed to previous customers (*Commercial Solvents, United Brands*). In *Magill TV Guide* (Case T-69, 70, 76–77 & 91/89 1991) it was, controversially, applied in a situation where there was no previous commercial relationship between the parties. The principle in this case developed into what is known as the 'essential facilities doctrine' (see *Sea-link/B & I - Holyhead*: interim measures 1992). This is where a dominant company controls and uses an essential facility and other companies are unable to compete without access to this facility. Where the dominant company then refuses access, it will be in breach of Article 82 unless there is objective justification. This can also apply where a company owns an essential facility and uses its power on that market to strengthen its position in another related market. So in *Sea-link* itself, the complaint was that Sealink which owned the Holyhead port in North Wales from which it operated a ferry service, allocated inconvenient sailing slots to its rival ferry operator, B & I. In C-7/97 *Oscar Bronner* (1998) a reference was made to the ECJ which ruled that for a breach of Article 82, access to the essential facility must be 'indispensable', and lack of access should have the effect of eliminating all competition in the market. This was not the case in *Bronner* itself.

It should be noted that Article 82 EC does not provide for any possibility of exemption.

Enforcement of EC competition law

14.46 Regulation 17/62 and now the new Regulation 1/2003 give the Commission wide powers of investigation and enforcement of Articles 81 and 82 EC. Complaints to the Commission about alleged breaches of EC competition rules may be submitted both by member states and indivuduals. The Commission may also initiate an investigation on its own initiative.

Under Article 14 of Regulation 17/62 the Commission has had extensive powers to require information to be supplied as well as to search premises and take copies or extracts of records: see also Cases 46/87 and 227/88 *Hoechst AG v Commission* (1989). These powers are extended in the new Regulation to include the right to search the homes of directors, managers and other members of staff where a reasonable suspicion exists that books or other business records which might be relevant to an investigation are stored there. This power is subject to review by the ECJ. Officials of the NCAs are obliged actively to assist the Commission in carrying out searches; the decision by the Commission to undertake such a search will be taken after consulting the NCA in whose country the search is being carried out. NCAs can also carry out inspections on their own behalf or at the request of anothr NCA. NCAs can also carry out inspections on their own behalf or at the request of another NCA. These provisions affirm the duty of member states under Article 85 (ex Article 89) EC to afford assistance to the Commission in the exercise of its functions under the Treaty.

14.47 The right of access to the file, subject to the interests of undertakings in the interest of protection of business secrets and requirements of confidentiality, is now guaranteed in the Regulation itself, reflecting earlier case law of the European Courts: Case T-7/89 *SA Hercules v Commission*, T-30/91 *Solvay v Commission* (equality of arms) and see Commission 'Notice on the Internal Rules for Processing Requests for Access to the File' (OJ 1997 C 23/3).

14.48 As under Regulation 17/62, the new Regulation empowers the Commission to impose fines of up to 10% of the total turnover in the previous business year of each of the undertakings involved in an infringement of the competition rules. Such a fine may also be imposed for failure to comply with commitments or an order for interim relief. The periodic penalty payment which can be imposed to compel undertakings to terminate such breaches have been increased to a maximum of 5% of the average daily turnover in the previous business year; the maximum fine for supplying incorrect or misleading information and other procedural offences has also been increased, to 1% of the total turnover in the preceding business year.

14.49 All Commission decisions, including enforcement decisions and decisions to investigate, fine or otherwise penalise companies must be published and are subject to judicial review by the Court of First Instance: Case 60/81 *IBM v Commission* (1981) and Case T-64/89 *Automec v Commission* (1990). Record fines of 855.22 million euros were imposed on eight companies in November 2001 for the 'vitamin' cartel offences—constituting eight distinct market-sharing and price-fixing cartels operating between September 1989 and February 1999. Thirteen companies, both European and non-European, participated; five were not fined because the cartels of which they were part came to an end more than five years before the Commission launched its investigation. Hoffman-La Roche, which was the instigator and participated in all the cartels, was fined a cumulative fine of 462 million euros.

Leniency notice

14.50 In 1996 the Commission adopted a 'leniency notice' which gave immunity or reduced fines to companies which came forward with information about cartels. This followed on from the successes of the United States in adopting such a policy and, according to a press release (ip/02/247) issued by the Commission, the 1996 leniency notice 'greatly contributed to the adoption in 2001 of 10 cartel decisions in which 56 companies were fined a total of 1,836,000,000 euros', which was a greater amount than that levied in fines in total between 1957 and 2000.

Aventis (formerly Rhone-Poulenc) was the first company to be given a 100% reduction in fines imposed for its participation in the vitamin cartels for Vitamin A and D because it was the first company to co-operate with the Commission (however, it was fined for its participation in another cartel where it provided no information). Subsequently other companies were also given 100% immunity.

14.51 On 30 October 2002 the Commission found that Christie's and Sotheby's had colluded in a price-fixing cartel. Christie's came forward with information and was given total immunity from fines. Although the date of the finding was after the revised leniency notices took effect, the immunity was based on the 1996 regime because the application for leniency was in 2000.

Christie's benefited from full immunity because it provided 'decisive proof' of the cartel at a time when the Commission had no investigation open; the requirement for 'decisive proof' under the 1996 regime has been changed to encourage companies to come forward. The revised leniency notice came into effect on 14 February 2002 and is aimed at making 'whistle-blowing' more attractive to companies.

14.52 Complete immunity from fines will be given (i) to the first member of a cartel which informs the Commission about an undetected cartel, giving sufficient information for the Commission to launch an inspection of premises of the implicated companies and (ii) to the first member of a cartel to provide the Commission with the necessary evidence to establish an infringement where the Commission has had sufficient information to launch an inspection but not enough evidence for a successful prosecution. This immunity can only be granted where no undertaking has qualified for immunity under (i).

Other companies which provide evidence which contributes 'significant added value' to the information which the Commission holds, and which end their involvement in the cartel, will be given reduced fines on a sliding scale (downwards) as further companies come forward.

The 2002 leniency notice brings the European regime closer to that established in the United States.

Merger control

14.53 The EC Treaty does not contain express provisions regulating mergers. There is Court of Justice case law both under Article 86 (now Article 82 EC) and Article 85 (now Article 81 EC) depending on the circumstances: see respectively Case 6/72 *Continental Can v Commission* (1973) and Cases 142 and 156/84 *BAT Co Ltd – R J Reynolds Industries Inc v Commission* (1987).

The Merger Regulation (Regulation 4064/89)

14.54 On 21 December 1989 the Council adopted a long-standing Commission proposal for a Regulation on the control of concentrations of undertakings: Regulation 4064/89, OJ L 1989 L 395/1. The Regulation has subsequently been amended (see, most recently, Regulation 1310/ 97 OJ 1997 L 180/1). The Regulation, which came into force on 21

September 1990, requires compulsory notification for concentrations with a Community dimension.

The concept of concentration encompasses mergers, acquisitions and 'full function' joint ventures (but see below). A transaction amounts to a concentration when it involves the a change in control of an undertaking. The Commission has adopted a Notice on the concept of concentration (OJ 1998 C 66/02) which sets out in detail the means by which control is deemed to be acquired for the purposes of the Regulation.

14.55 A joint venture is considered 'full function' when it performs on a long lasting basis all the functions of an autonomous economic entity. This concept is explained in more detail in the Commission Notice on the concept of full function joint ventures (OJ 1998 C 66/01).

A concentration will have a Community dimension when the participating undertakings meet specified thresholds of turnover. The original thresholds were set very high, so relatively few concentrations came within their scope. In 1997 an additional, lower, set of thresholds was added in an attempt to bring more concentrations within the scope of application of control by the Community.

14.56 The Regulation is inspired by the principle of the 'one-stop shop' whereby concentrations falling within the Regulation requirements must be notified to the Commission only. However, if the concentration does not meet the Community dimension national rules apply. The Regulation provides for mechanisms to send back to member states concentrations which have a prevailing national relevance (Article 9) and conversely to submit to the Commission concentrations which would not otherwise fall within the Commission's jurisdiction (Article 22).

14.57 The Commission has now issued a proposal for extensive amendment of the Merger Regulation, in particular to address the continuing problem of multiple filing in cases which do not fall under the criteria set out above. Rather than further lowering the thresholds to catch more proposed mergers, the Commission has taken the approach of simplifying the procedures under which the investigation of mergers can be transferred to the Commission from the member states and vice versa under Articles 9 and 22; these can now also be applied at a pre-notification stage: the notifying parties are given the opportunity to make a reasoned request for a referral in either direction. The Commission will also have exclusive jurisdiction in cases where all the member states concerned, or a minimum of three such member states, agree to the case being referred to the Commission under Article 22. Notification may take place prior to the conclusion of a binding agreement by the parties and, where they do notify post agreement, the deadline of one week after the conclusion of a binding agreement for notification is abolished. In the revised Regulation, a concentration is defined as arising from 'a change of control on a lasting basis', reflecting criteria which are already applied in practice. If adopted, the Regulation is scheduled to take effect by 1 May 2004.

14.58 In Cases C-68/94 and C-30/95 *France v Commission (Kali & Salz)* the ECJ established that joint dominant positions fall within the scope of the Merger Regulation even though the Regulation does not explicitly say so. In Case T-102/96 *Gencor v Commission* (the first Commission decision actually proscribing a merger on the grounds that it would create a joint dominant position), the CFI clarified that a position of collective dominance could be held by undertakings in an oligopoly.

14.59 Between 1990 and 2002 the Commission gave outright prohibitions on 18 transactions, amounting to less than 1% of notified cases. Between June and October 2002, three Commission decisions prohibiting mergers were overturned by the CFI on review giving rise to unprecedented criticism of the Commission. In the first of these decisions, the Commission prohibited a merger between Airtours and First Choice on the ground that the merger would create a collective dominant position (Commission Decision in Case No IV/M, 1524 *Airtours/First Choice*). This was reversed by the CFI in an important judgment which sets out criteria which must all be met for a finding of collective dominace: T-342/99 *Airtours plc v Commission*.

14.60 First, each member of the oligopoly must know how the other members are behaving in order to monitor whether or not they are adopting the common policy. Second, there must be adequate deterrents to ensure that members of the oligopoly do not depart from the common policy, and, thirdly, it is necessary to establish that the reactions of 'current and future competitors' as well as consumers do not put the common policy at risk: para 62. Applying these criteria to the position after the proposed merger, the CFI held that the Commission had failed to establish that a collective dominant position would be created; the decision, was 'vitiated by a series of errors of assessment as to factors fundamental to any assessment of whether a collective dominant position might be created': para 294.

14.61 The other two judgments, Case T-5/02 and Case T-80/02 *Tetra Laval BV v Commission* and Cases T-310/01 and T-77/02 *Schneider Electric SA v Commission* were delivered by the expedited procedure. The Commission is appealing the *Tetra Laval* judgment to the ECJ on the grounds, inter alia, that the CFI imposed a disproportionate standard for proof in merger prohibitions and has therefore exceeded its jurisdiction, which is limited to review for errors of fact or reasoning and does not give it competence to substitute its view for that of the Commission. However, it has now cleared the acquisition of Sidel by Tetra Laval (Decision of 13 January 2003).

14.62 The revised Merger Regulation sets out a definition of dominance which makes it clear that oligopolies are covered by the Regulation: one or more undertakings shall be deemed to be in a dominant position if, *with or without co-ordinating,* they hold the economic power to influence appreciably and sustainably, the parameters of competition...' (Article 2, italics added). Recital 21 makes it clear that Article 2 covers situations of oligopoly.

The Commission has now also issued a draft Notice on the Appraisal of Horizontal Mergers. In order to improve decision-making in merger cases in particular, the Commission has now created a post of chief Competition Economist who will, with his team, participate in merger and other competition investigations.

14.63 In the cases notified under the Merger Regulation, the Commission has one month (in the new Regulation, 25 working days) to announce to the undertakings and the member states concerned that it will be conducting an inquiry. Thereafter, the Commission has four months (ninety working days as amended) to rule in favour of or against the proposed merger. Recognising the pressure that these time limits have created, there is now the possibility of a twenty day extension where the case is a complex one, at the request of, or with the agreement of, the parties. The test applied to clear a concentration involves an evaluation of whether it creates or strengthens a dominant position as a result of which effective competition would be impeded in the Common Market or a substantial part of it.

The role of the national courts

14.64 *At present* In Case C-234/89 (1991) *Delimitis* the court expressed some of the governing principles which were subsequently incorporated in the Commission's Notice on Co-operation between National Courts and the Commission in Applying Articles 85 and 86 (now Articles 81 and 82 EC) (OJ 1993 C 39/6). The Court clarified that the Commission 'is responsible for the implementation and orientation of Community competition policy', and reaffirmed its exclusive competence (now only relevant pending the adoption of Regulation 1/2003: see above) to adopt decisions in implementation of Article 85(3) (now Article 81(3) EC).

14.65 Articles 81(1) and 81(2) and 82 EC are directly effective (see above) and they give rise to rights and obligations on the part of individuals and national courts have a duty to protect and enforce these rights. Indeed, under the doctrine of supremacy of Community law, EC competition rules may also be relied upon to challenge contradictory national rules.

14.66 In particular Article 81(2) renders the offending agreements (or parts thereof) null and void. Since this is a directly effective provision, national courts will normally hold the offending clauses void. In cases of doubt as to the correct interpretation of EC competition rules, national courts can avail themselves of the guidance of the Court of Justice under Article 234 (ex Article 177) EC.

14.67 It is the Commission's policy expressed in the Notice that, in line with the principle of subsidiarity, it will only take enforcement action with regard to complaints concerning alleged breaches of Articles 81 and 82 EC where there is a 'Community interest'. In deciding when there is such an interest, the Commission will consider, inter alia, if there are suitable remedies available at the national level. In cases where the Commission takes the view that there is no 'Community interest' in proceedings, it will take no further action and the complainant will be expected to take action before the national courts: Case T-24/90 *Automec v Commission* (1992).

After implementation of Regulation 1/2003

14.68 The role of the national courts will become much more important as the shift in the enforcement on EC competition law to the national level takes effect. In Case C-453/99 *Courage Ltd v Crehan* the ECJ decided, in an Article 234 reference from the Court of Appeal, that Article 81 precludes the application of the English rule that a party to an illegal contract cannot recover damages from the other party. The party seeking damages must, however, not have significant responsibility for the breach of Article 81. This judgment should encourage actions for damages under Article 81 in the national courts.

National competition law

14.69 In 1998 the UK Competition Act was adopted (Competition Act 1998). It repeals the Restrictive Trade Practices Acts 1976 and 1977, the Resale Prices Act 1976, the Restrictive Practices Court Act 1976, and those parts of the Competition Act 1980 dealing with anti-competitive conduct. A prohibition based on Article 81 (ex Article 85) EC (Chapter I) and a prohibition based on Article 82 (ex Article 86) EC (Chapter II) were introduced. The Act aims at facilitating business by aligning domestic law with Community law. In this respect s 60 of the Competition Act 1998 provides that questions arising under the Act in relation to competition within the UK are to be dealt with in a manner which is consistent with the treatment of corresponding questions under Community law, principles and case law.

14.70 The Enterprise Act 2002 came into force in June 2003. It establishes the Office of Fair Trade as a corporate body replacing the office of the Director of Fair Trading. Its provisions are 'largely complementary to those of the Competition Act 1998'; in regard to competition law, its object is to ensure more transparent and accountable decision-making by the competition authorities, including provisions requiring consultation and reasons to be given for significant decisions. The Act introduces a criminal penalty of up to five years' imprisonment for those who operate hard-core cartels and a new power to disqualify directors found to have committed serious breaches of competition law. The Act also contains provisions intended to facilitate the bringing of actions for damages for breach of competition law in the courts.

The Enterprise Act also covers mergers. Before the Act, the Secretary of State for Trade and Industry had the power to clear mergers or to refer them to the Competition Commission. Under the Act, it is the Office of Fair Trade (OFT) which decides whether to clear a merger or refer it. Where the OFT has a reasonable belief that a merger will lead to a substantial lessening of competition within any market or markets in the UK for goods or services, it must refer the merger to the Competition Commission.

Further reading

Korah, *EC Competition Law and Practice* (7th edn, 2001) Hart Publishing.

Whish, *Competition Law* (4th edn, 2001) Butterworths (5th edn due October 2003).

Korah, *Cases and Materials on EC Competition Law* (2nd edn, 2001) Hart Publishing.

Jones and Sufrin, *EC Competition Law: Text, Cases and Materials* (2001) OUP

Furse, *Competition Law of the UK & EC* (3rd edn, 2002), OUP (4th edn due August 2003).

Rivas and Horspool, *Modernisation and Decentralisation of Competition Law* (2000) Kluwer.

Whish, 'The enforcement of EC competition law in the domestic courts of member states', [1994] ECLRev 60.

Soames, 'An analysis of the principles of concerted practice and collective dominance: A distinction without a difference?', [1996] ECLRev 24.

Whish, 'Regulation 2790/99: The Commission's new style block exemption for vertical agreements' [2000] 37 CMLRev 887–924.

Ehlermann, 'The modernization of EC antitrust policy: a legal and cultural revolution?', [2000] CMLRev 537–590.

Griffiths, 'A glorification of de minimim—the regulation on vertical agreements', [2000] ECLRev 241.

Carle J, 'The new leniency notice', [2002] 6 ECLRev 265–272.

Klimisch, 'Decentralized application of EC competition law', [1999] ELRev 463.

Al-Dabbah, 'Conduct, dominance and abuse in market relationships', [2000] ECLRev 45.

Baker and Wu, 'Applying the market definition guidelines of the EC Commission', [1998] ECLRev 273.

Jones, 'Woodpulp: concerted practice and/or conscious parallelism?', [1993] ECLRev 273.

Monti G, 'The scope of collective dominance under Article 82', [2001] 38 CMLRev 131.

Ysewyn and Caffarra, 'Two's company, three's a crowd: the future of collective dominance after the *Kali & Salz* judgement', [1998] ECLRev 468.

Self-test questions

1. What is a block exemption?

2. What are the key factors to define a relevant market?

3. What is a comfort letter?

4. What elements have to be proved in order to establish a breach of Article 81? Cite appropriate cases.

5. What routes are open to a company which believes that a competitor/supplier is breaching EC competition law?

6. What will be the main change in procedure under Article 81 and application of the articles when Regulation 1/2003 comes into effect? What are the benefits of this change?

CHAPTER FIFTEEN

Intellectual Property

SUMMARY
- **Property rights and the Treaty**
- **The free movement of goods**
- **The doctrine of exhaustion**
- **Common origin**
- **Anti-competitive agreements**
- **Abuse of a dominant position**
- **Harmonisation**

Property rights and the Treaty

15.1 Article 295 (ex Article 222) EC says that 'This Treaty shall in no way prejudice the rules in member states governing the system of property ownership'. Article 295 could be read as a 'ring-fencing' provision, designed to take national property rights outside the reach of Community law.

However, if Article 295 were to be interpreted in this way, it would undermine the effectiveness of Community law. As the discussion in this chapter will show, firms and individuals can exercise their property rights in a way that frustrates Community objectives. It would be surprising if the draftsmen of the Treaty intended to give national property law immunity from Community law.

15.2 The European Court of Justice (ECJ) has responded to this problem by distinguishing between the *existence* of a property right and its *exercise*. In the absence of Community harmonisation of property law (see **15.26** below), defining when a property right *exists* is a matter for national law: however, under certain circumstances, Community law can intervene in the way that a property right is *exercised*. As a result, Community law has been applied to a range of property rights, including real property and different forms of personal property.

The conceptual foundations of the existence/exercise distinction may be shaky: it is hard to see how Community law can curtail the exercise of a property right without making incursions into its fundamental subject matter. Nevertheless, the distinction has been of great practical use to the Community. This is true particularly in relation to intellectual property ('IP') rights. IP rights – such as copyrights, design rights, origin marks, patents and trade marks – can be exercised in ways that lead to the territorial partitioning of Community markets, and restrictions on competition between firms.

As a result, national IP rights may be vulnerable to challenge under the Treaty's rules on free movement of goods (Articles 28–30 (ex Articles 30–36) EC), and the Treaty's competition rules (Article 81 (ex Article 85) and Article 82 (ex Article 86) EC). The free movement rules, in combination with competition rules, are capable of having a deregulatory effect: that is, they may result in striking down parts of national law that are in conflict with them. Member states, faced with *ad hoc* deregulation of this sort, have two options. On the one hand, they can continue to regulate IP rights at a national level, while accepting that, on occasions, Community law will override national law. One the other hand, they may feel that it is more effective to regulate IP rights at a Community level. This can mean harmonising national IP rules on the basis of Community norms or, alternatively, establishing new types of pan-Community IP rights.

15.3 Before going to the main part of the discussion, an introductory point should be made. IP rights protect a variety of things, ranging across designs, software, forms of expression, technical innovations, rights in living things (such as plants) and brand identity. As this chapter is only an introduction to the subject, the emphasis here is on identifying common principles that apply to all IP rights. However, when reading the chapter, it would be useful to bear in mind that, before Community law can be applied, it is necessary to identify the legitimate scope of a given IP right. The legitimate scope of an IP right will vary considerably depending on the commercial role it plays, and the interest it protects. In practice, therefore, the common principles described in this chapter will be applied in a way that is sensitive to these variations. This is clear, for example, in relation to copyright which, although a single form of IP right, is used in quite different commercial and technological contexts.

Article 28

15.4 This chapter will start by looking at the rules on the free movement of goods. Two examples show how IP rights can be exercised in a way that prevents imports.

Case 78/70 *Deutsche Grammophon* (1971) concerned the copyright to the Polydor record label, which was owned in Germany by Deutsche Grammophon (DG), and in France by a subsidiary of DG. Polydor records were more expensive in Germany than in France. As a result, a firm called Metro bought Polydor records in France, and imported them into Germany for resale. However, resale of the imports involved an infringement of DG's German copyright. In effect, German copyright law, by giving DG the exclusive right to market Polydor records in that member state, allowed DG to put up a barrier between national markets, and prevent lower priced imports of Polydor records. The ECJ held that it would breach Article 30 (now Article 28 EC) to allow DG to assert its copyright in this way.

Case 15/74 *Centrafarm v Sterling Drug* (1974) concerned drugs manufactured by Sterling Drug Inc and patented by them in different member states. The drugs were more expensive in the Netherlands than in the UK and Germany. Centrafarm bought supplies of the drugs in the UK and Germany, and imported them into the Netherlands. Sterling Drug Inc invoked the Dutch patent to the drugs to prevent resale of the imports. The ECJ held that exercising the Dutch patent in this way infringed Article 30 (now Article 28 EC).

15.5 If a practice breaches Article 28, it may be possible to justify it relying on one the derogations contained in Article 30. Article 30 says that restrictions on the free movement of goods can be justified 'on grounds of the protection of industrial or commercial property', provided that the restrictions 'shall not, however, constitute a means of arbitrary discrimination or a disguised restriction on trade between member states'. When the Treaty was drafted in the mid-1950s, the phrase 'intellectual property' was not in widespread use: however, in round-about terms, the notion of 'industrial or commercial property' means the same thing.

15.6 The ECJ has made it clear that the reference to 'industrial and commercial property' in Article 30 does not mean that all restrictions on imports resulting from the exercise of national IP rights can be justified. The Court has used the following technique for determining the extent to which the exercise of an IP right is justified under Article 30.

15.7 First, it is necessary to identify the *purpose* of the IP right. For example, the Court has held that the purpose of a patent is to 'recompense the creative effort of the inventor' (*Centrafarm v Sterling Drug*); similarly, it has held that the purpose of a trade mark registration is to protect the goodwill (ie the consumer loyalty) associated with a brand and also to reassure consumers that a product bearing the trade mark derives from the same commercial source (Case 16/74 *Centrafarm v Winthrop* (1974)).

15.8 The subject-matter of an IP right is the ability to exploit the right in a way that is consistent with, and proportionate to, its purpose. In essence, this means that the owner of an IP right is allowed to put a product protected by that right into circulation in the internal market for the first time (because of the free movement provisions contained in the European Economic Area (EEA) Agreement, the internal market is treated as covering the whole of the EEA). If, for example, I consent to goods being sold in Belgium, I cannot then prevent the goods being resold in Austria, by means of relying on an IP right conferred by Austrian law. By agreeing to have the goods sold in Belgium, I have exhausted my Austrian IP rights, along with my IP rights throughout the EEA: in effect, I have consented to the goods being in free circulation.

15.9 The principle of exhaustion sometimes comes as a shock to owners of IP rights. For example, the owner of a brand will want to keep tight control over the after-market for branded goods. If the brand owner wishes to price-discriminate, ie to charge different prices for the same brand in different member states, it will be necessary to use national IP laws to prevent 'leakage' of goods from low price to high price countries. However, the ability to do this is lost by exhaustion.

15.10 The role played by the consent of the owner of an IP right must be underlined. Exhaustion happens when the owner has consented to a product being marketed.

The pivotal role played by consent means that a right is not exhausted when a product protected by an IP right in one member state is imported from another member state in which the product cannot be protected by IP law (for example, because it is not patentable there), and the product has been manufactured in the second member state without the consent of the owner of the IP right. In contrast, if an IP right owner consents to a protected product being marketed in a member state in which no national IP protection is available, this consent does exhaust the right (Case 187/80 *Merck v Stephar* (1981)).

If two undertakings are legally and economically independent of each other, one undertaking can rely on a national IP right to block imports by the other. This is because, in this situation, the imports are not taking place with the consent of the IP right owner. In contrast, if one undertaking licenses another undertaking to produce or distribute a product, or if the two undertakings are members of the same group (as in a parent-subsidiary relationship, for example), then they are not legally and economically independent of each other: sales by one are made with the consent of the other, leading to exhaustion.

If an IP right is the subject of a compulsory licence (ie a licence granted by the operation of law rather than through the consent of the IP right owner) the right is not exhausted when the licensee sells the protected product (Case 19/84 *Pharmon v Hoechst* (1985)): again, here, consent is absent. Finally, assignment of an IP right is not treated as involving consent to free circulation. If I, for example, assign a trade mark to an independent undertaking in France, but retain ownership of the same mark in Germany, I can use my German trade mark to prevent imports into Germany of goods bearing the French mark (Case C-9/93 *Ideal Standard* (1994)). The assignor and I remain independent of each other. Moreover, each trade mark has acquired an independent function, indicating a different origin for the marked goods, depending on the territory of sale (see also the discussion of *Hag II* below). To prevent the application of national trade mark law would lead to confusion amongst consumers, who would not be certain about the true origin of the marked goods.

15.11 If an IP owner sells protected goods outside the EEA, does this exhaust the IP right within the EEA? As Community law stands at the moment, the answer appears to be no. The First Trade Mark Directive (Directive 89/104/EEC) gives legislative effect to the principle of exhaustion. In Case C-355/96 *Silhouette* (1998) the ECJ held that the directive did not envisage international exhaustion, but only internal exhaustion. The result is that a trade mark owner can sell goods at a lower price outside the EEA than within it, and then use national IP laws within the EEA to prevent leakage of lower-priced goods from non-EEA sources. In addition, the court held that the directive prevented member states from providing for international exhaustion in national law. The directive was an act of complete harmonisation of national trade mark rules: this point is returned to below in the discussion of harmonisation.

15.12 Unfortunately, although the ECJ confirmed that the directive did not envisage international exhaustion, it failed to address the meaning of 'consent' as set out in Article 7 of the directive. Article 7 states that a trade mark owner cannot prohibit the further marketing of goods in the EU when he has put those goods on the market in the EU or has consented to their sale. This has led to further cases on the subject of consent. Case C-173/98 Sebago v GB-Unic (1999) concerned the parallel importation of genuine Sebago shoes from outside the EU into Belgium. In Sebago the ECJ stated that for there to be consent within the meaning of Article 7 such consent had to relate to each individual item of the product in respect of which exhaustion was pleaded. GB-Unic, a Belgian company which had imported Sebago shoes identical in style to the range sold by authorised distributors in Belgium, claimed that there was implied consent to the sale of identical shoes imported from outside the EU. It attempted to distinguish Silhouette on the basis that the spectacle frames in that case were of an old style currently not on sale in the EU. The Sebago decision caused widespread criticism throughout the EU particularly from importers and retailers who argue that such a rule allows brand owners to artificially maintain higher prices within the EU than outside.

15.13 The issue of consent was revisited in two recent English High Court cases which were referred to the ECJ. The first case, Levi Strauss v Tesco Stores Ltd (2000) related to whether or not express consent needed to be given by a brand owner to the importation of his branded goods into the EU from outside, or whether consent is implied if there is no express prohibition to importation and subsequent re-sale. Secondly, in the case of Zino Davidoff SA v Imports Ltd (2000), Davidoff authorised the sale of its perfumes in Singapore with a prohibition on the distributor against re-sale outside Singapore. There was no requirement, however, that the Singapore distributor impose a similar restriction on subsequent purchasers and re-sellers. The English High Court held that it was arguable that re-sellers down the chain were free to market wherever they wanted, including the EU.

In the joined cases C-414/99, C-415/99 and C-416/99, Zino Davidoff v A & G Imports' Levi Strauss & Co v Tesco Stores (2002) the ECJ held that the proprietor's consent to the resale of goods inside the EEA which had been put on the market with his consent outside may indeed be implied depending upon the circumstances of the original placement. However, it added that a national court must be persuaded that the proprietor unequivocally renounced his right to oppose such resale. In particular, the ECJ held that consent could not be inferred by the fact that the proprietor did not tell all subsequent purchasers of the goods outside of the EEA of his opposition to resale within the EEA; nor could it be inferred even if the goods carried no warning of a prohibition against resale inside the EEA; and it could not be inferred from the fact that the proprietor sold the goods without imposing any contractual prohibition on resale, even if, according to the law governing the contract, the sale included an unlimited right of resale, or at least a right to market the goods in the EEA. Finally, for those wishing to prove consent, the Court held that it is irrelevant that the importer of the goods was unaware that the proprietor objected to their sale in the EEA; nor is it relevant that authorised dealers in the goods did not impose contractual restrictions on purchasers alerting them to the proprietor's opposition, even if they were aware of it. This judgment has been generally welcomed by brand owners. Certainly, following the judgment, it may prove extremely difficult for a reseller to persuade a national court that the brand owner has impliedly renounced his opposition to the resale of his goods in the EEA.

15.14 The doctrine of exhaustion which operates within the EEA does not mean that there is a total loss of control over the after-market for the protected goods. The extent of any control depends on the exact subject-matter of the right concerned. This can be seen in Case 102/77 *Hoffmann-La Roche v Centrafarm* (1978), a case involving the drug Valium. The drug was sold by Hoffmann-La Roche in Germany, and by a Hoffmann-La Roche subsidiary in the UK. It was more expensive in Germany than in the UK. Centrafarm bought supplies of the drug in the UK, and repackaged it for sale in Germany. Although it was made clear on the new packs that they were being sold by Centrafarm, the packs still had the Hoffmann-La Roche trademark on them. Repackaging and importing the drugs infringed Hoffmann-La Roche's trademark in Germany. In this case, the ECJ accepted it would be compatible with Community law for a trade mark owner to prevent imports of marked goods that had been repackaged, if the repackaging affected the original condition of the product. This conclusion followed from the purpose of a trademark: if consumers were to not be confused about the origin of a product, and were to be guaranteed that it had not been interfered with in a way that affected its condition, then it was legitimate for the trade mark owner to take action to prevent repackaged imports. By the same token, if a way of repackaging could be found that did not interfere with the original condition of the product, then it would not be permissible for the owner of an IP right to rely on Article 30 (now Article 28 EC) as a way of preventing imports of the repackaged product. The ECJ held that in these circumstances importation of repackaged goods could not be prevented, provided (a) that the importer gave notice to the trade mark owner of the intention to repackage, and (b) the fact that repackaging had taken place and the identity of the repackager were clear to consumers.

15.15 Therefore, in determining whether a trademark can be used against an importer that has repackaged goods, it is necessary to ask whether the firm opposing imports has a legitimate reason for not wishing to see the goods commercialised in a different form. A legitimate reason is one related to the purpose of the trade mark as a guarantee to consumers of the origin of marked goods. On the other hand, it may be that opposition to repackaging is simply an unjustified attempt to deflect imports: reliance on national law in this situation will be treated as a disguised restriction on inter-state trade. The distinction between legitimate opposition to repackaging and opposition that constitutes a disguised restriction on trade has received legislative recognition in Article 7 of the First Trade Mark Directive: it has been developed also in a series of cases (see eg Cases C-427, 429 and 436/93 *Bristol-Myers Squibb v Paranova* (1996)). The decision of the ECJ in Case C-379/97 *Pharmacia and Upjohn v Paranova* (1999) shifted the balance in re-packaging situations slightly towards the brand owner. Although the ECJ confirmed that a parallel importer was not required to prove an intention on the part of a trade mark owner to partition markets within the EU, the replacement of the trade mark by the parallel importer had to be objectively necessary if the proprietor was to be prevented from opposing it. This condition of necessity was satisfied if the prohibition on the importer against replacing the trade mark prevented or hindered effective access to the market in the importing member state, eg if a rule of law in the importing state prevented use of the mark in that state which was allowed in the exporting state. The condition of necessity would not be satisfied, however, if the replacement of the trade mark was an attempt by the parallel importer solely to secure a commercial advantage.

Trade mark proprietors can also object to the resale of goods if their 'mental' condition, that is to say, their brand image, is likely to be damaged. In Case C-337/95 *Parfums Christian Dior v Evora* (1997), a chain of cut-price chemists in the Netherlands sought to sell Dior perfume imported from France. As a matter of policy, Dior France sold its perfume only through exclusive outlets. The ECJ held that Dior could object to the resale of its goods if it was done in such a manner as to endanger its mark's advertising function, in this case its prestigious image. In *Davidoff* too, in the High Court, it was argued that there were legitimate reasons for opposing the further commercialisation of the goods under Article 7(2) of the directive because product codes had been removed. However, the Court disagreed on the basis that the evidence did not indicate that the removal of such codes would impair the condition of the goods or their recall (see also 15.13).

Common origin

15.16 A brief account should be given of the common origin saga: it shows the ECJ applying the free movement rules in a way that is fairly hostile to IP rights, but then changing its mind and being more careful to ensure that IP rights are not interfered with.

Case 192/73 *Van Zuylen Frères v Hag AG (Hag I)* (1974) involved a trade mark which had been registered in Germany, Belgium and Luxembourg. Originally, Hag AG, a German firm, owned the trade mark in each of the three countries. At a later date, ownership of the marks in Belgium and Luxembourg was transferred to another company, VZF, leaving Hag AG with the German trade mark. This splitting of the trade mark was not a voluntary act on the part of Hag AG, but resulted from sequestration of the assets of German companies after the Second World War.

VZF tried to prevent Hag AG from selling its branded coffee in Luxembourg, arguing that this would infringe its ownership of the 'Hag' mark there. The ECJ held that relying on trade-mark ownership in one country to prevent imports of marked goods from another country could not be justified under Article 30 *where the mark in question had a common origin.*

A problem with *Hag I* was that the court did not explain why the fact that a trade mark had a common origin led to this conclusion. The two brand owners in this case were quite distinct companies, not linked legally or commercially. VZF had not consented to Hag AG marketing 'Hag' coffee. Another problem raised by *Hag I* was whether the principle set down in it was intended to apply to forms of IP right other than trade marks.

15.17 The doctrine of common origin was criticised heavily as having no basis in principle. In Case 119/75 *Terrapin v Terranova* (1976) the court made it clear that the doctrine did not prevent one firm from opposing use of a similar trade mark by another firm from which it was legally and economically independent: for example, if firm A owned a trade mark in the UK, it could use UK IP law to oppose imports of a product bearing a confusingly similar trade mark owned by a firm in a different member state. Nevertheless, in *Terrapin*, the ECJ did defend the doctrine, explaining it as response to one of the purposes of a trade mark. The Court held that splitting a trademark undermined its function which, according to the Court, was to reassure consumers that the marked goods had the same origin. Once the protective function of the trademark had been undermined, there was no basis on which the owner of part of the mark could prevent the owner of another part from selling marked products.

However, in *Hag II* (Case C-10/89 (1990)) the court overruled *Hag I*. In *Hag II*, the Court held that splitting of the trade mark without consent had led to each of the new marks acquiring a separate function: each mark indicated a new and quite different origin for the branded goods. As such, it was acceptable for each owner to take action to protect the new mark within the territory to which it applied.

The Treaty's competition rules

15.18 Agreements and concerted practices relating to the use of IP rights, such as licenses, are capable of infringing Article 81(1). However, if an agreement infringes Article 81(1) it may qualify for exemption under Article 81(3). An important distinction between Article 30 and Article 81(3) can be noted. If the exercise of an IP right goes beyond the protection of the subject-matter of the right, it cannot be justified on the basis of Article 28. However, the exercise of an IP right that goes further than is necessary to protect its subject-matter can benefit from an Article 81(3) exemption. This follows from the fact that for the exercise of an IP right to have infringed Article 81(1) (and hence be in need of an Article 81(3) exemption) it must have been exercised in a manner which goes beyond the boundaries of its subject-matter.

Relationships between direct competitors

15.19 Agreements between undertakings competing directly in the same market are capable of restricting competition between them. Imagine, for example, that the owners of two different trade marks enter into a delimitation agreement, under which each owner agrees not to use its own mark in a particular territory, or in relation to particular products. An agreement of this sort may be perfectly legitimate: if the trademarks are similar enough to cause confusion to consumers, a delimitation agreement may be the best way to avoid confusion. However, the restrictions in the delimitation agreement must go no further than is necessary to achieve its legitimate object: any unnecessary restriction on use of the marks may infringe Article 81(1). In addition, not all delimitation agreements are entered into in order to avoid confusion.

Two direct competitors could use a delimitation agreement as a form of cartel, in which they allocate customers or territories between them. If so, provided that there is more than a *de minimis* market effect, Article 81(1) will apply.

Other forms of IP agreement between direct competitors may infringe Article 81(1). For example, if two pharmaceutical firms form a co-operative joint venture in order to carry out a research and development ('R&D') project, it may involve cross-licensing or pooling of IP rights. By sharing their IP rights, the firms are limiting the possibility of independent competition between them. However, at the same time, they are creating the possibility of advances in R&D, and the stimulation to competition that could result from this: as a result, an Article 81(3) exemption might be available (see **15.23** below).

Assignments

15.20 Can the assignment of an IP right be caught by Article 81(1)? It is generally accepted that a straightforward transfer of assets falls outside Article 81(1), even if the transfer is the result of an agreement, and has an anti-competitive effect. As such, an IP assignment on its own cannot be caught by Article 81(1). However, if an assignment agreement contains restrictions on the future competitive behaviour of the assignor or assignee, these restrictions may infringe Article 81(1).

What happens if an assignment agreement does not contain any explicit restrictions on the future behaviour of the parties, but the assignor and assignee co-ordinate their competitive behaviour after the assignment has taken place? The Court of Justice has negotiated its way round this difficulty by holding that if an assignment has taken place, Article 81(1) may still apply *if the assignment agreement continues to produce effects even after it has been performed.* Such an effect will be found only if the market behaviour of assignor and assignee after assignment appears to have the elements of co-ordination or a concerted practice, and this outcome is 'peculiar to the agreement and producing the same result as that envisaged by the agreement' (Case 341/87 *EMI* (1989)). What the ECJ appears to have had in mind here is a co-ordination of behaviour that, although not provided for explicitly in an assignment agreement, would not have taken place but for the assignment.

Licences

15.21 The majority of the Article 81(1) decisions relating to IP rights concern licensing. Of significance in this area is the control of vertical agreements, ie agreements not between direct competitors, but between firms at different levels of the market, such as a manufacturer and a distributor.

The licensing of an IP right allows its exploitation in return for payment by the licensee. As well as dealing with payment (for example, in the form of royalties) an IP licence may contain provisions that restrict the competitive behaviour of the parties.

Such restrictions do not infringe Article 81(1) automatically. For example, some restrictions on competitive behaviour may be necessary if an IP licence is to be a commercial success: restrictions which are directly related and necessary to a legitimate commercial transaction are described as ancillary restrictions, and fall outside Article 81(1). Case 258/78 *Nungesser v Commission (Maize Seeds)* (1982) involved a licence of plant breeders' rights, which gave the licensee a degree of protection from competition within Germany. The ECJ held that an obligation on the licensor not to license the rights to other undertakings within Germany, and not to compete with the licensee directly, did not infringe Article 85(1) (now Article 81(1) EC). This conclusion was justified by the need to give the licensor an incentive to invest in a potentially risky business, and to introduce new products into Germany. On the other hand, the Court held that absolute territorial protection for the licensee, in effect sealing off the German market from competition totally, would infringe Article 85(1): the licensor would not be allowed to accept an obligation to prevent licensees in other territories from selling into Germany.

Care should be taken when reviewing restrictions in order to determine whether they fall within Article 81(1). It is necessary to distinguish between different commercial situations: the reward for risk-taking argument used in *Maize Seeds* may not apply in relation to licences for other sorts of IP rights.

15.22 While exclusivity clauses giving a degree of protection from competition within a territory are obvious targets for Article 81(1), many other aspects of IP licences such as terms dealing with duration, royalty payments and tie-ins (eg where the licensee is required to buy certain goods from the licensor, or is tied to the licensor even after the licensed IP right has run its course) and challenges to the validity of an IP right are capable of restricting competition and hence infringing Article 81(1) (see eg *Campari* OJ 1978 L 70/69; Case 262/81 *Coditel v Cine Vog Films* (1982); Case 193/83 *Windsurfing International* (1986); *Moosehead/ Whitbread* (OJ 1990 L 100/32).

Article 81(3)

15.23 Article 81(3) exemptions are of two kinds: individual exemptions and block exemptions. Individual exemptions are needed only when block exemptions do not apply. Applications for individual exemptions have recently been discouraged in practice, but historically exemptions have been granted to a variety of different agreements involving IP rights. The block exemption on vertical agreements (Regulation 2790/99) contains provisions exempting restrictions on the exploitation of IP rights. However, the most important block exemption dealing with IP rights is the Technology Transfer Block Exemption (Regulation 240/96). This covers patent and know-how licenses, and mixed agreements (relating to both patents and know-how). The Technology Transfer Block Exemption also covers patent and know-how agreements containing ancillary provisions relating to other kinds of IP rights, such as trade marks (see further **14.16**).

Article 82

15.24 Article 82 prohibits the abuse of a dominant position. If an undertaking is dominant, the way in which it exercises its IP rights may come under scrutiny. The fact that a dominant undertaking merely owns intellectual property does not, of itself, constitute abuse: *Case 24/67 Parke, Davis & Co v Probel* (1968). The same is true, according to the UK courts, when a dominant undertaking asserts its intellectual property rights against infringers: *Pitney Bowles Inc v Francotyp-Postalia GmbH* (1991). However, there are exceptional circumstances which may justify a finding of abuse. An example is found in the *Magill* case (Cases C-241 and 242/91 P (1995)), involving three TV companies, each with copyright over weekly schedules for its own programmes. Magill, an independent publisher, planned to produce a multi-channel TV listings magazine: however, the TV companies concerned would not license copyright to Magill for this purpose. The Commission held that this refusal was abusive. The Court of First Instance and the ECJ upheld this decision on appeal.

Magill caused alarm amongst IP lawyers. In many sectors, IP rights form the most valuable assets owned by a business. Did *Magill* mean that dominant undertakings would be forced, on a routine basis, to license their IP rights to competitors? In fact, compulsory licensing will only be required when the dominant undertaking is seeking to exercise an IP right in a way that goes beyond protection of its subject-matter. In *Magill*, for example, the refusal of the TV companies to grant copyright licences was an act of product-suppression: the TV companies had not planned to publish a multi-channel listings magazine, but simply wished to prevent anybody else from doing so. In Case C-97 *Oscar Bronner v Mediaprint* (1999), it was held that there were three necessary factors for a finding of abuse. First, would a refusal, in this case to include a newspaper in a national home delivery service, be likely to eliminate competition in the 'downstream' market? Second, was the refusal incapable of objective justification? Third, was its inclusion essential to potential competitors, in that there was no substitute for it available? Although not, itself, concerned with IP rights, the *Oscar Bronner* judgment has been followed by the courts when dealing with IP rights in the area of compulsory licensing, such as, for example, in Case T184/01 *IMS Health Inc v Commission of the European Communities* (2002). In this recent case, the President of the ECJ confirmed, following *Magill*, that the exercise of intellectual property rights may be subjected to restrictions imposed under Article 82 only in exceptional circumstances. Interestingly, he also went on to assert that the primary consideration was to safeguard the interests of consumers rather than to protect the position of particular competitors.

15.25 In addition to providing a basis for claims for compulsory licensing of IP rights, Article 82 may be used to change the terms of IP licences. The *Microsoft case* (Commission's 23rd Annual Report on Competition Policy) involved licences for MS-DOS and Windows software. Certain aspects of the licences were challenged under Article 82. For example, Microsoft calculated its licence fees on the basis of the number of PCs sold by the licensee. This meant that even if the licensee sold a PC that did not contain MS-DOS or Windows, it would still have to pay Microsoft a royalty. Article 82 was used to prevent Microsoft from extracting royalties on this basis.

IP harmonisation

15.26 The introduction to this chapter referred to the fact that member states, instead of maintaining separate systems of IP law, can choose to develop a common IP system within the framework of Community law. Member states may agree to harmonise national IP laws. However, as the *Silhouette* case shows, harmonisation may be treated as exhaustive, preventing member states from adopting unilateral standards that diverge from Community norms. An alternative approach is to create new forms of pan-Community IP rights. In relation to industrial designs and trade marks, the chosen approach has been both to harmonise national laws and to create a pan-Community IP right.

15.27 The First Council Directive 89/104 (OJ 1989 L 40/1) deals with approximation of national trade mark laws. However, the directive does not create a Community trade mark as such. Creation of a Community trade mark is achieved by the Community Trade Mark Regulation (Regulation 40/94 OJ 1994 L 11/1). A trade mark valid throughout the Community can now be registered: it is then subject to a single set of Community rules. Under the Regulation, member states have to designate certain national courts as Community Trade Mark Courts to deal with disputes over exercise, such as infringement proceedings. In all important respects, the law relating to national trade marks and the Community trade mark is the same. The Office for the Harmonization of the Internal Market (OHIM) in Alicante, Spain administers the system.

15.28 The OHIM will also administer the newly introduced Registered Community Design and the Unregistered Community Design, which relate to the protection of industrial designs. From 2003, the Registered Community Design may be obtained through an application to the OHIM and will be effective throughout the EU, as will the Unregistered Community Design. National law relating to registered designs has also been harmonised through the adoption of Directive 98/71/EC. In the UK, harmonisation of the laws relating to registered designs has been achieved through substantial amendment of the Registered Designs Act 1949.

15.29 While a substantial amount of UK copyright law conforms to a variety of international conventions, there has been no overall attempt to harmonise copyright protection across the EU. Instead, a number of EU directives have concerned themselves with particular aspects of copyright law, most often and not surprisingly, in the area of new technology, such as computer programs, semi-conductor chips and electronic databases. Perhaps the most important directive in this area to date is the Information Society Directive (Directive 2001/129/EC). The directive, which is due to be implemented in the UK during 2003, harmonises basic rights to copyright protection in relation to new means of reproductive technology, most notably digital broadcasting, 'on demand' services and the internet. Although implementation of the directive will mean few substantial changes to already existing copyright law in the UK, it has been criticised for circumventing the exceptions to protection available to more traditional forms of copyright work, such as the exception which allows use of a copyright work for private study without payment to the copyright holder.

15.30 The EC has had less success in its attempts to introduce a Community patent. The Community Patent Convention (OJ 1976 L 17/1) was adopted with the goal of introducing a Community patent, not governed by national law. The Convention has been amended by the Agreement relating to Community Patents (15 December 1989), which also added a number of protocols to the Convention. Implementation of the Convention has been hampered by a lack of agreement on the part of member states. Under the Convention, Community patents would sit side-by-side with national patents: in relation to a particular invention, a potential patentee would be able to apply for national patents or a Community patent.

15.31 Finally, the international context should be mentioned. The World Intellectual Property Organization (WIPO), a UN organisation, administers a number of international conventions concerned with intellectual property rights, for instance the Berne, Paris and Rome Conventions. WIPO also oversees an arbitration centre, particularly useful in disputes over internet domain names which can cut across national boundaries. All the member states are signatories to these conventions and they play an active role in WIPO. Equally important to the protection of intellectual property rights is the Trade-Related Aspects of IP Rights (TRIPS) Agreement (MTN/FA II-AIC, 2659 Rev (1995)) which was negotiated through and is overseen by the World Trade Organisation (WTO). The TRIPS agreement sets down minimum standards of protection which should be given to intellectual property and WTO plays an active role in determining disputes that arise under this agreement.

Further reading

WR Cornish, *Intellectual Property* (5th edn, 2003) Sweet & Maxwell.

Guy Triton, *Intellectual Property in Europe*, (2nd edn, 2002) Sweet & Maxwell.

Paul Taylor, *EC and UK Competition Law and Compliance*, (1999) Sweet & Maxwell.

R Whish, *Competition Law* (4th edn, 2000) Butterworths.

Stephen Weatherill, 'Recent Case Law Concerning the Free Movement of Goods: Mapping the Frontiers of Market Deregulation', [1999] CMLR 51–85.

Self-test questions

1. Can the existence/exercise distinction be justified as an example of purposive interpretation? Could Article 295 be interpreted differently?

2. When can the owner of a national IP right rely on that right to oppose imports?

3. Why should the Court of Justice treat types of IP right in different ways, depending on the commercial role played by the right?

4. When can a restriction on competitive behaviour contained in an IP licence or other agreement be lawful?

5. Does the application of Article 82 create great uncertainty for IP right owners with a dominant market position?

CHAPTER SIXTEEN

Free Movement of Persons: (I) Workers' Rights

SUMMARY

This chapter deals with the first part of the Free Movement of Persons: Workers: Articles 39–42 (ex Articles 48–51) EC.

• **What is a worker?**
• **Independent rights**
• **Rights for workers' families**

Introduction

16.1 In the Treaty of Rome (1957), the abolition of obstacles to the free movement of persons was included as one of the main objectives of the achievement of a common market, now renamed an internal market (Article 3(c) EC). Together with the abolition of obstacles to the free movement of goods, services and capital, these became known as the 'Four Freedoms'.

To achieve the objectives contained in Articles 2 and 3(c) EC of an increased standard of living and economic expansion, and to be able to achieve one capital market where goods could move freely, it was necessary to have the fullest possible mobility of the economically active part of the population in order to achieve one single labour market. These aspirations are embodied in the original Treaty in the articles concerning free movement of workers (Articles 39–42 (ex Articles 48–51) EC), self-employed persons (Articles 43–48 (ex Articles 52–58) EC) and the provision of services (Articles 49–55 (ex Articles 59–66) EC).

16.2 However, with the development of the Community into something more than an economic unit, with the growing realisation that there should be an integration of all the peoples of Europe, not just its economically active population, the free movement articles were interpreted expansively by the European Court of Justice and in secondary legislation. This trend culminated in the adoption of directives on the rights of residence for employees and self-employed persons who had 'ceased their occupational activity' (Council Directive 90/365 EEC of 28 June 1990 OJ 1990 L 180/28), those who are self-supporting (Council Directive 90/364 EEC of 28 June 1990 OJ 1990 L 180/26) and students (Council Directive 93/96 EEC of 29 October 1993 OJ 1993 L 317/59, formerly Directive 90/366 EEC which was annulled by the Court of Justice as it was adopted on the wrong legal base (Article 308 (ex Article 235) EC)). This effectively left only a relatively small group of people not entitled to general free movement in Europe: those who are or could be economically active but who fell under the exceptions to the free movement rules and those who are incapable of supporting themselves.

16.3 However, the Maastricht TEU added a Part Two on Citizenship of the Union in Articles 17–22 (ex Articles 8, 8a–8e) EC. Although there was initially doubt as to what, if anything, the scant content of these articles had added to the existing free movement provisions, it was always in principle a dynamic article evidencing a recognition that a union of peoples should involve all of the people, and indicated the beginnings of a truly meaningful European citizenship (see Chapter 18).

The ECJ has emphasised many times that the three Chapters under Title III of the Treaty on Workers, Establishment and Services should be treated equally in respect of entry, stay and non-discrimination. It has given a parallel interpretation of the similar articles contained in the three chapters. Articles 39 (ex Article 48), 43 (ex Article 52) and 49 (ex Article 59) EC all have direct effect and do not depend on subsequent implementation by the Community legislator. The rights guaranteed under the three chapters have been further detailed in directives, many of which also have direct effect. These rights cannot be applied without restriction and member states retain the possibility to limit the rights for reasons of public policy, public security or public health, or because the activity is connected with the exercise of public authority. Such restrictions must, however, be proportionate to the aim pursued.

Free movement of workers

16.4 The first and largest group of the economically active are the employed. The Treaty refers to this group as 'workers' and over the years, with the help of the European Court of Justice, a Community definition of 'worker' has been established.

16.5 Treaty Articles 39–42 are the provisions for the free movement of workers. Article 39 lays down the principles and Article 40 provides details of implementation. Free movement means that there shall be no discrimination as to nationality, that those in search of employment are to be entitled to do so, that those who have moved to another member state for the purpose of employment should be allowed to remain there when they fall ill or retire, and that they should be allowed to take their families with them and have the same social security benefits as a member state's own nationals. These provisions are subject to exceptions, narrowly interpreted by the court, in respect of public policy, public security and public health (Article 39(3) EC), and in respect of employment in the public service (Article 39(4) EC).

16.6 Regulation (EEC) 1612/68 of 15 October 1968, as amended by Regulation 312/76 (OJ Sp Ed 1968 L 257/2, p 475), puts migrant workers' rights into greater detail: Eligibility for Employment (Title I Articles 1-6), Equality of Treatment (with nationals of the host member state), (Title II) and Rights for Workers' Families (Articles 10-12). For a more complete text of the Regulation, see older editions of Blackstone's *EC Legislation* (6th edn and earlier). Regulation (EEC) 1251/70 of 29 June 1970 (OJ Sp Ed 1970 L 142/74, p 402) on 'the right of workers to remain in the territory of the member state after having been employed in that member state' is the logical extension of the previous regulation. It contains the provisions which apply to workers who must be allowed to remain in the host member state after they have ceased their working activity. Regulation 1408/71 of 14 June 1971 as amended and updated by Regulations (EEC) 2001/83, (EEC) 1945/93 and (EC) 1606/98 deals with social security rights for workers as well as for the self-employed (see below **16.20**).

Who is a worker?

16.7 The definition of the concept of 'worker' is not found in Community law texts. Regulation 1408/71 defines the concept of 'employed person' but only for the purposes of social security. The concept of worker was gradually established by the ECJ. It is a concept of Community law, which is not dependent for its meaning on the laws of the member states. The test was laid down by the court in Case 75/63 *Hoekstra (née Unger)* (1964),

in Case 53/81 *Levin v Staatssecretaris van Justitie* (1982) and in Case 66/
85 *Lawrie-Blum v Land Baden-Württemberg* (1986). Mrs Hoekstra was
resident in the Netherlands and had worked there, but was not now in
employment. She incurred medical expenses while visiting her parents
in Germany and claimed from Dutch social security. The entitlement to
payment depended on her status as a worker. The Council Regulation
concerned referred to a 'wage earner or assimilated worker'. The ECJ
explained that Articles 48–51 (now Articles 39–42 EC) of the Treaty,
by the very fact of establishing freedom of movement for workers, had
given Community scope to the term worker. If the definition of the term
were a matter within the competence of national law, it would therefore
be possible for each member state to modify the meaning of the concept
and to eliminate at will the protection of the Treaty given to certain
categories of person. Nothing in the Treaty articles leads to the conclusion
that these provisions have left the definition of the term 'worker' to
national legislation. On the contrary, the fact that Article 48(2) mentioned
certain elements of the concept of 'workers', such as employment and
remuneration, showed that the Treaty attributes a Community meaning
to that concept. The articles would be deprived of all effect if the meaning
could be modified by national law. The concept did not, therefore, relate
to national law, but to Community law. The Dutch court then asked the
ECJ to define the word, in the event it were to find a Community meaning.
It should be recalled that under Article 234 (ex Article 177) EC the court
may always be asked to give a ruling if this is necessary to decide the
case in the national court. In this case it was necessary in order to
determine whether entitlement to social security sickness payments
would exist in similar cases. The court said that a 'worker' is not
exclusively someone who is currently employed. The term also applied
to persons 'likely to remain in the territory of a member state after having
been employed in that state'.

16.8 Case 53/81 *Levin v Staatssecretaris van Justitie* (1982) is the most
often quoted for a precise definition of what exactly constitutes a worker.
Mrs Levin was a British national residing in the Netherlands, married to
a non-Community national. She had part-time employment as a
chambermaid, and earned a wage which was below the minimum
considered necessary for subsistence in the Netherlands. The Dutch
government argued that a worker had to work at least the minimum
number of hours considered normally to constitute full-time employment
or to reach at least subsistence level. The court rejected this as referring
to national legislation and thus not binding, as the term should be
regarded as a Community concept. As it so often does, the court gave a

contextual interpretation and looked at Articles 2 and 3 of the Treaty which speak of improvement of standards of living and a harmonious development of economic activities. Part-time work, although it may provide an income lower than the minimum subsistence wage in the country concerned, constituted for a large number of people an effective means of improving their living conditions. The effectiveness of Community law would be impaired and the achievement of the objectives of the Treaty would be jeopardised, if only those were considered to be workers who worked full-time and attained at least the minimum wage for subsistence.

16.9 A worker is an individual who performs services for and under the direction of another, for remuneration. While part-time employment was *[Kempf; work must be effective + genuine not marginal + ancillary]* not excluded from the field of application of the rules, the work must, however, be effective and genuine and not purely 'marginal and ancillary'. It includes, as in *Levin*, those who receive less than the minimum wage and those who receive supplementary benefits, as in Case 139/85 *Kempf v Staatssecretaris van Justitie* (1986). Mr Kempf was a part-time music teacher who gave lessons for twelve hours a week. The court made it clear that, as long as the aforementioned criteria are satisfied, the motives which may have prompted the worker to seek employment in another member state are of no account and must not be taken into consideration. In Case 66/85 *Lawrie-Blum v Land Baden-Württemberg* (1986) *[worker defined.]* the question came up again. At the same time, the question was posed as to employment in the public service, of which more later. The court emphasised again that the term 'worker' is a Community concept, that *[services 1, direction 2, remuneration 3]* it means a person who performs services for and under the direction of another person in return for which he receives remuneration. This applies to trainee teachers who work under supervision and receive remuneration for giving lessons to pupils.

16.10 The work itself must be an economic activity. This was considered *[must be an economic activity. cf]* to be so in Case 196/87 *Steymann v Staatssecretaris van Justitie* (1988). Mr Steymann received no remuneration for his work in a religious community but was looked after by the community in return for his work, and this the court considered to be sufficient. However, in Case 344/87 ✱ *Bettray v Staatssecretaris van Justitie* (1989) someone working under a *[not social]* compulsory social rehabilitation scheme to help him get rid of his drug addiction fell on the other side of the line. This was not an economic activity. The scheme had as its primary purpose the reintegration of potential workers into the labour market. Its objectives were social, not economic. In more recent cases, the court has clarified the concept further, applying objective criteria to the test of 'effective and genuine' work. This could include someone in occupational training if there was proof that the trainee had worked long enough to become fully acquainted with the job performed (see Case C-3/90 *Bernini v Minister van Onderwijs en Wetenschappen* (1992)). Here, as in Case C-357/89 *Raulin v Minister van Onderwijs en Wetenschappen* (1992) which concerned someone working under a contract with no fixed hours, the court emphasised that it was ultimately a matter for the national court to decide if such a person has the status of worker. Students on sandwich courses which require practical experience in another member state may also be regarded as workers (see Case C-27/91 *URSAFF v Hostellerie le Manoir* (1991)). This clarifies the type of situation with which Case 197/86 *Brown v Secretary of State for Scotland* (1980) was concerned (see **16.15**). A student who undertakes casual work in a country in which (s)he intends to study may be regarded as a worker. It seems now that this will depend on the person's intention as evidenced by the duration of the work and the extent to which the person has acquired the necessary skills. Thus, Mr Brown could not claim the full status of worker as he had acquired it solely on the basis of having been admitted to university whereas in Case 39/86 *Lair v Universität Hannover* (1988) Lair could claim to be a worker as her work was connected with her wish to enter university, but not undertaken solely in preparation for her course (see further **18.29**).

16.11 The court stated in Case C-350/96 *Clean Car Autoservice GmbH v Landeshauptmann von Wien* (1998) that the right of workers to be engaged and employed without discrimination necessarily entails as a corollary the employer's entitlement to engage them in accordance with the rules governing freedom of movement for workers. Thus, an employer can rely on these rules as much as the workers themselves; a rule providing that at least one manager of an undertaking has to be an Austrian resident constituted indirect discrimination.

Independent rights

Right of residence

16.12 The corollary of the right to enter and to work is the right to remain for a reasonable time while looking for a job. Article 39(3) of the Treaty provides for this right, but refers to the right of free movement only 'to accept offers of employment actually made' (Article 39(3)(a) (ex Article 48(3)(a)) EC). The court has interpreted this provision

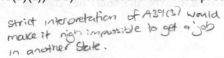

strict interpretation of A39(3) would make it nigh impossible to get a job in another State.

382

---

expansively, as in Case C-292/89 *R v Immigration Appeal Tribunal, ex p Antonissen* (1991), pointing out that 'a strict interpretation of Article 48(3) (now Article 39(3) EC) would jeopardise the actual chances that a national of a member state who is seeking employment will find it in another member state and would, as a result, make that provision ineffective'. The Article therefore had to be interpreted as giving a non-exhaustive list of rights for nationals of member states in the context of free movement, including the right to move and stay within the territory of the member state for the purposes of seeking employment.

16.13 Council Directive 68/360 EEC of 15 October 1968 on the abolition of restrictions on free movement and residence within the Community for workers of member states and their families (OJ Sp Ed [1968] (II) p 485) deals extensively with the provision of residence documents to those who are entitled to residence, ie workers and their dependants. However, a residence permit is simply evidence of the Community right of residence and failure to obtain one is not sufficient reason to expel a Community national. The possession of a residence permit is only declaratory and constitutive of the right itself. In Case 48/75 *Royer* (1976) the court had said explicitly that the right of nationals to enter the territory of another member state and reside there for the purposes intended by the Treaty – in particular to look for or pursue an occupation or activities as employed or self-employed persons, or to rejoin their spouse or family – is a right directly conferred by the Treaty and acquired independently of the issue of a residence permit by the competent authority of the member state. There is a reference (in Article 7 of the Directive) to those who are involuntarily unemployed, from whom a valid residence permit may not be withdrawn, but this would not seem to cover the case eg of Mr Vitale (see below, **18.36**). The simple production of a passport or identity card upon entry suffices and visas may not be required. In Case 157/79 *R v Pieck* (1980) the court stated that failure to comply with the national requirements for obtaining a residence permit should not lead to disproportionate penalties, such as imprisonment or deportation. See also Case 48/75 *Royer* (1976) and Case 118/75 *Watson and Belmann* (1976) (see also **17.24** and **18.5**, below).

16.14 Why and for how long will someone be considered to be a jobseeker? In *Antonissen* the court said that it was not contrary to Community law to require an individual to leave a member state's territory if he had not found work for six months, unless he could show that he was continuing to seek work and had a genuine chance of finding it. The six-month limit which applied to a jobseeker in the UK was

6 month limit can be invoked if
unlikely to find work.

acceptable, but both Darmon AG and the court refused to state a clear time limit. The court refused to accept an argument referring to a three-month period noted in the minutes of a Council meeting during which Directive 68/360 was adopted. The time granted must be reasonable. It was possible a further extension was acceptable if evidence of a genuine chance of employment could be shown after expiry of the six-month period. If we look at the case of *R v Secretary of State for the Home Department, ex p Vittorio Vitale* (1996) (see further **18.36**) we see that such time limits can be used to good effect by those who claim to be jobseekers and/or students. The right of residence is a Community right which should be distinguished from social rights which do not always extend as far.

16.15 Voluntary unemployment is only mentioned in Article 7(1) of Regulation 1612/68 and in Article 7 of Directive 68/360 of 15 October 1968 (OJ Sp Ed 1968 L 257/13, p 485). Article 7(2) of Regulation 1612/68 provides there shall be no discrimination in respect of 'social advantages' and this has been interpreted by the court as also capable of applying to access to education. Someone leaving his employment in order to become a student on a vocational course may still retain his status as a worker, even if he left employment voluntarily, if there was an evident link between the employment and the course of study (see Case C-357/89 *Raulin v Minister van Onderwijs & Wetenschappen* (1992) and Case C-3/90 *Bernini v Minister van Onderwijs en Wetenschappen* (1992); also see **16.10**). However a difficulty arose in Case 197/86 *Brown v Secretary of State for Scotland* (1988). Mr Brown was a student with dual British and French nationality who had gone to school in France. He had been accepted by the University of Cambridge for a course in electrical engineering, and decided to gain some work experience by taking up a position in Scotland for eight months. The job he had been offered was only available to students who had been offered a university place. The court had decided in *Lair* (see **18.29**) that Article 7(2) of Regulation 1612/68 could apply to maintenance grants. However, it ruled that if the immigrant obtained the employment solely by virtue of the fact that he had already been offered a university place, he will not be entitled to the grant as the employment was merely incidental to the university course. Although Brown was engaged on a full-time occupational activity in order to prepare for his university studies, the court ruled that although the work he did was clearly of a genuine and non-ancillary nature and thus fulfilled all the 'worker' criteria as set out in *Levin*, he could nevertheless not benefit from all the social advantages granted to Community workers, as the work had been undertaken after he had been accepted for his electrical engineering degree at Cambridge and in preparation for those studies without being a preparation for further employment. This meant, therefore, that he could not claim a full maintenance grant. The court clearly took the purpose for which the work was undertaken into account, although it had said in *Levin* that the purpose of the work was immaterial. However, the purpose seemed to be relevant in the decision as to the extent of the benefits which would be granted. It seems to be clear that, although students can claim certain advantages, these advantages are not as extensive as those which are available for workers. (But see further Case C-184/99 *Grzelczyk Centre public d'aide sociale d'Ottignies-Louvain-la-Neuve* (2001) at **18.33**.) The rights of dependants of workers, too, are not as extensive as those for workers themselves: in Case 316/85 *Centre public d'aide sociale de Courcelles v Lebon* (1987) the adult child of a worker was no longer entitled to benefits which were of no advantage to the worker himself. This also applies to jobseekers, as in the case of *Antonissen* where the court said that the rights of jobseekers would not necessarily be same as those for workers (see **16.12**). However, Case C-413/99 *Baumbast and R v Secretary of State for the Home Department* (2002) appears to have moved the goalposts to a considerable extent. The Court said, not only should children of migrant workers be allowed to continue their education in the host member state under any circumstances, even if their parent who was the primary carer was in danger of losing their residence either because they were divorced from the migrant worker or because the migrant worker had ceased to work there, but also the primary carer him-or herself should be allowed to reside in the member state as the child's primary carer. The Court cited Article 12 of Regulation 1612/68, but also Article 8 of the European Convention on Human Rights, which contains the requirement of respect for family life (see further **18.49–18.53**).

Rights for workers' families

16.16 Regulations 1612/68 and 1408/71 have been interpreted widely by the ECJ. This has extended the material and personal scope of the regulations to include such elements as income support, old-age benefits and disability allowances as regards migrant workers themselves (see Case C-326/90 *Commission v Belgium* (1992)). The personal scope of the regulations has also been extended, as the aim of the legislation was the full integration of the migrant workers into the host state which, therefore, had to include his family and those dependent on him. Article 10 of

Regulation 1612/68 provides that the members of a migrant worker's family have the right to install themselves with him. This does not mean that the family member must live permanently with the worker, simply that the accommodation available to the worker must be such as to be considered normal for the purpose of accommodating his family. This is a one-off requirement which cannot be repeated: Case 249/86 *Commission v Germany* (1989). It does not imply that the family must live under the same roof permanently. As in Case 267/83 *Diatta v Land Berlin* (1985), a separated, albeit not divorced, wife of a worker living separately cannot, therefore, be denied a right of residence. This right of residence, however, is not an independent right, but is derived from that of the worker. As *R v Secretary of State for the Home Department, ex p Sandhu* (1982) shows, this matter is not entirely clear-cut. Mr Sandhu was an Indian national whose German wife had returned to Germany with their child when the marriage had broken down. After a visit to Germany Mr Sandhu was refused entry into the UK and the Court of Appeal and House of Lords considered his rights had come to an end when his wife returned to Germany. As the situation was different from that of *Diatta* it is not immediately obvious that this should have been considered as 'acte clair' (see **5.22**) and that the obligation for the House of Lords to make a reference under Article 234 EC did not arise.

16.17 The interpretation of the term 'spouse' in Article 10 of Regulation 1612/68 was clarified by the court in Case 59/85 *Netherlands v Reed* (1986) where a British national who went to the Netherlands to live in an unmarried relationship with her British partner, who was working there, was denied right of residence by the Dutch authorities. The court ruled that the term 'spouse' could only refer to a married person and that a general widening of the term would be unjustifiable in view of the lack of 'general social development' in all the member states towards treating unmarried couples in the same way as married ones. However, in this case, the Dutch government treated an unmarried companion in a stable relationship with a Dutch national as a spouse. Therefore:

> It must be recognised that the possibility for a migrant worker of obtaining permission for his unmarried companion to reside with him, where that companion is not a national of the host member state, can assist his integration in the host State and thus contribute to the freedom of movement of workers. Consequently, that possibility must also be regarded as falling within the concept of a social advantage for the purpose of Article 7(2) of Regulation 1612/68.

16.18 'Social advantages' for the migrant worker as required by Article 7(2) of Regulation 1612/68 are, as the court said in Case 207/78 *Even* (1979):

> ...advantages, linked to a contract of employment or not, generally granted to migrant workers primarily because of their objective status as workers or by virtue of the mere fact of their residence on the national territory ...

These advantages include an entitlement to reduction cards for rail travel for large families in France (in Case 32/75 *Cristini v SNCF* (1975) this entitlement continued even for M Cristini's widow after his death), and the right to speak German in proceedings conducted in Belgium where such a right is available to Belgian nationals. In Case 137/84 *Mutsch* (1985) a German national was held to be entitled to speak German in proceedings before a Belgian court. It should be noted, however, that Belgian nationals of certain 'Communes' in Belgium which are German-speaking, also have this right and that German is one of Belgium's three official languages. In Case 152/73 *Sotgiu v Deutsche Bundespost* (1974) Mr Sotgiu, a migrant worker, received a lower separation allowance for working in Germany away from his place of residence than those whose place of residence was in Germany when they were first employed. Mr Sotgiu had come from Italy and allowances paid to those engaged from abroad were lower. This was, therefore, an indistinctly applicable measure which was nevertheless discriminatory as it affected migrant workers more. In Case 15/69 *Württembergische Milchverwertung-Südmilch AG v Salvatore Ugliola* (1970), Mr Ugliola was held to be entitled to have his period of military service in Italy taken into account in Germany in calculating the length of his employment. The rule that only military service in the German Army (the *Bundeswehr*) counted was, again, an indistinctly applicable measure which nevertheless was discriminatory. In Case 235/87 *Matteucci v Communauté Française de Belgique* (1988) Article 7(2) was held to cover grants under a cultural agreement which were available to nationals and which would enable an EC worker to study abroad. A refusal to pay compensation upon the termination of employment which a worker would normally receive under national legislation may constitute an obstacle to free movement. In Case C-190/98 *Volker Graf v Filzmoser Maschinenbau GmbH* (2000) an Austrian law provided for such compensation except where the employee leaves without good reason or is responsible for his dismissal. Mr Graf terminated his employment in order to move to Germany to take up employment there. In the event, the court stated that the legislation did not infringe Article 39 as the worker's choice depended on a future and hypothetical event.

16.19 Social advantages should be distinguished from social security benefits, which are regulated by Regulation 1408/71. Social advantages cannot be exported, whereas social security benefits may be exported in many, but not in all cases. In Case 65/81 *Reina v Landeskreditbank Baden-Württemberg* (1982) an interest-free 'childbirth loan' granted under German law to German nationals in order to stimulate the birth rate of the population was held to be a social advantage within Article 7(2). Therefore, an Italian couple in Germany was also entitled to the loan. The argument against this was that this had little to do with encouraging free movement of workers and that this was a political right linked to nationality. The court said this was a measure to ease the financial burden on low-income families and did not address the demographic point. In any event, the demographic point was dismissed in *Cristini*. Cristini was Italian, not French, but his widow was nevertheless entitled to benefits which were part of French demographic policy.

16.20 The Social Security Regulation (EEC) 1408/71 and its updating amendments (see **16.6**) is intended to co-ordinate social security schemes existing in the various member states and does not create a common social security scheme. Article 4(1) lists the categories of benefit covered by the Directive. The ECJ has generally sought to remove unjustified obstacles to freedom of movement resulting from different laws on social security. In Case C-18/95 *Terhoeve v Inspecteur van de Belastingdienst Particulieren/Ondernemingen Buitenland* (1999) it held the payment of higher social security contributions by a worker who had moved from one member state to another, without his being entitled therefore to higher benefits than those who had resided there continuously to be such an obstacle. Case C-360/97 *Nijhuis v Bestuur van het Landelijk Instituut Sociale Verzekeringen* (1999) concerned the entitlement of a Netherlands civil servant to a Netherlands invalidity pension in respect of the period before the entry into force of Regulation (EC) 1606/98 which extends the basic legislation concerning social security for workers to special schemes for civil servants. Although these Regulations were not directly at issue here, the national court inquired whether Articles 39 and 42 EC nevertheless obliged it to apply them by analogy in order to grant invalidity benefit to a worker who had suffered an incapacity for work arising in another member state. If this were not the case, Mr Nijhuis would be in a less favourable position than someone who had worked only in the Netherlands. The Court answered in the negative: the Council enjoyed a wide discretion and to make such an application by analogy mandatory could only be envisaged where the negative consequences of such a situation could be overcome without having recourse to Community co-ordination measures. Such measures appeared, however, to be essential in this case.

16.21 Recently, a number of cases concerning direct taxation have come before the court. In Case C-279/93 *Schumacker* (1995) and Case C-80/94 *Wielockx* (1995) the court interpreted Article 48 (now Article 39 EC) of the Treaty as meaning that a Community national who gained his main income and almost all of his family income in a member state other than his state of residence was discriminated against if his personal and family circumstances were not taken into account for income tax purposes in the first state. Following these judgments German legislation provided that a couple could, under certain circumstances, be treated as being subject to tax in Germany even where they did not reside permanently there, so that they would be entitled to the tax concessions accorded to residents which took account of their personal and family circumstances. In Case C-391/97 *Gschwind v Finanzamt Aachen-Außenstadt* (1999) the court held that the conditions laid down for that purpose by the German legislature are compatible with the Treaty, namely that at least 90% of the total income of the non-resident married couple must be subject to tax in Germany, or, if that percentage is not reached, that their income from foreign sources not subject to German tax must not be above a certain ceiling. The court considered that where those conditions are not satisfied, the State of residence is in a position to take into account the taxpayers' personal and family circumstances, since the tax base is sufficient there to enable that to be done.

Education for members of workers' families

16.22 Article 12 of Regulation 1612/68 provides that children of nationals of one member state who fulfil the worker criteria shall have access to courses of general education, apprenticeship and vocational training under the same conditions as children of nationals. This article has been interpreted very expansively by the court. In Case 76/72 *Michel S v Fonds National de Reclassement des Handicapés* (1973), the disabled son of an Italian worker in Belgium who had died after having lived and worked there, was entitled to Belgian disability benefit. His rights did not just cover access to courses; as Article 12 of Regulation 1612/68 called upon member states to encourage children of migrant workers to attend 'under the best possible conditions' this meant that the list of educational arrangements in the Regulation should also include disability benefit (see also the magnificent Opinion of Mayras AG). Case 9/74 *Casagrande v Landeshauptstadt München* (1974), continuing the reasoning in *Michel S*, said that access for workers' children to education in Article 12 ('admitted to courses...under the best possible conditions') meant that the provision would also cover any 'general measures intended to facilitate educational attendance' including an educational grant for a secondary school in Germany. The right has also been held to cover grants to migrant workers' children to study abroad, even if this is in the country of origin of the parent and child (Case C-308/89 *Di Leo v Land Berlin* (1990)). Education generally is discussed further in Chapter 18.

Recent developments

16.23 The developing case law on citizenship has prompted the Commission to propose a Directive consolidating, simplifying and amending the existing legislation on free movement. This is further discussed in Chapter 18. The Directive aims to delete a large number of existing instruments, in particular Articles 10 and 11 of Regulation 1612/68: Proposal for a European Parliament and Council Directive on the right of citizens of the Union and their family members to move and reside freely within the territory of the member states: COM (2003) 0199 final.

Further reading

G Federico Mancini, 'The Free movement of Workers in the Case law of the European Court of Justice' in D Curtin and D O'Keeffe (eds), *Constitutional Adjudication in European Community and National Law*, (1992) Butterworths Ireland, p 67.

Handoll, 'Article 48(4) EEC and Non-National Access to Public Employment', [1988] 13 ELRev 223.

Esther Johnson and David O'Keeffe, 'From Discrimination to Free Movement: Recent Developments concerning the Free Movement of Workers 1989–1994', [1994] 31 CMLRev 1313.

D O'Keeffe, 'Judicial Interpretation of the Public Service Exception to the Free Movement of Workers' in D Curtin and D O'Keeffe (eds), *Constitutional Adjudication in European Community and National Law*,

(1992) Butterworths Ireland, p 89.

D O'Keeffe, 'Equal Rights for Migrants: the Concept of Social Advantages in Article 7(2) Regulation 1612/68', [1985] YEL 93.

M Moore, 'Freedom of Movement and Migrant Workers' Social Security: an overview of the Court's jurisprudence 1992-1997', [1998] 35 CMLRev 409.

Council Directive 90/365 EEC of 28 June 1990, OJ 1990 L 180/28.

Council Directive 93/96 EEC of 29 October 1993, OJ 1993 L 317/59, formerly Directive 90/366 EEC which was annulled by the Court of Justice as it was adopted on the wrong legal base (Article 235).

Council Directive 90/364 EEC of 28 June 1990, OJ 1990 L 180/26.

Council Directive. 64/221/EEC on the movement and residence of foreign nationals, OJ Sp Ed 1964 L 850/64, p 117.

Council Directive 68/360 EEC of 15 October 1968 on the abolition of restrictions on free movement and residence within the Community for workers of member states and their families, OJ Sp Ed 1968 (II), p 485.

Regulation (EEC) No 1612/68 of 15 October 1968, as amended by Regulation 312/76, OJ Sp Ed 1968 L 257/2, p 475.

Regulation (EEC) No 1251/70 of 29 June 1970 (OJ Sp Ed 1970 L 142/74, p 402) on 'the right of workers to remain in the territory of the member state after having been employed in that member state'.

Regulation 1408/71 of 14 June 1971 as amended and updated by Regulations (EEC) 2001/83, (EEC) 1945/93 and (EC) 1606/98 OJ 1998 L 209, p 1.

Self-test questions

1. How does an individual qualify as a 'worker'?

2. What rights and social advantages do workers enjoy? Are the rights

enjoyed by their families equally extensive?

3. Hans, a German baker, wants to study nutrition in England. He arrives at Heathrow with his partner, Maria, who is Russian. Hans tells the customs authorities he has come to look for work as a baker. He is given a six-month permit to stay, as is Maria as a visitor. Hans finds work immediately. Maria finds part-time work as a waitress in a local restaurant. After about five months, Maria and Hans split up; Hans leaves his job and applies to the local college to be admitted to a course in nutrition and is accepted. He applies to the local authority for a tuition grant and for a maintenance grant. Both are refused. Maria receives a letter from the immigration authorities informing her that her permit is coming to an end and that she will have to leave. Advise both Hans and Maria. Can EC law help them?

CHAPTER SEVENTEEN

Free Movement of Persons: (II) Freedom of Establishment and the Freedom to Provide and Receive Services

SUMMARY

- **Right of establishment: Articles 43–48 (ex Articles 52–58) EC**
- **Right to provide services: Articles 49–55 (ex Articles 59–66) EC**
- **Right to receive services**
- **How to distinguish establishment and services**

Introduction

17.1 People who move to work in another member state are likely to be employees. The greatest movement of persons is, therefore, likely to be that of 'workers'. Nevertheless, there was a clear need to provide for similar rules for the self-employed, those who wish to move in order to carry out certain activities on a temporary basis, to set up in business or to exercise an independent profession in one of the member states. Many of the rules are similar, but there are also special requirements for the self-employed. What happens if a Dutch plumber wants to go and repair someone's central heating in Belgium? Should a French qualified medical specialist be allowed to go to Germany temporarily to exercise his/her profession, or to set up in practice there? Should a lawyer from one member state be allowed to appear before the court of another or to put up his/her plate and practise in that country? What happens if someone conducts an activity in another member state without going there and, therefore, does not cross a border?

17.2 The right of establishment and the freedom to provide services are generally dealt with together, as there are many common features and provisions. Articles 43–48 (ex Articles 52–58) EC deal with the right of establishment; the right to provision of services is covered in Articles 49–55 (ex Articles 59–66) EC. Just as the provisions in Article 39ff deal with the rights of employees, Articles 43–48 and 49–55 provide for employers, businesses and professionals.

17.3 It is not always possible to determine exactly whether an activity falls within Article 43 or Article 49. An engineering business with its headquarters in Holland could either set up a branch in Belgium to service its Belgian customers or offer its services to Belgian clients from its office in Holland. The first case would constitute establishment, the second would merely refer to the provision of services. However, the two articles are often considered together and are interpreted in the light of the object and purpose of the Treaty, which is to provide the fullest possible freedom of movement for self-employed persons wishing to engage in economic activities, regardless of the exact nature and extent of the provision of the service involved. Someone intending to settle in another member state for economic ends and intending to be integrated permanently in the host state's economy would be regarded as claiming the right of establishment. Services, on the other hand, are of a temporary nature: see in particular Case C-55/94 *Gebhard* at **18.22**.

17.4 Provisions on services are possibly the most dynamic in the Treaty because of the width of what they prohibit and the range of activity which they cover. In the former category, they deal with 'restrictions on freedom to provide (cross-border) services' (Article 49 EC). The ECJ has held that this is wider than discrimination on grounds of nationality or residence (see **17.21** *van Binsbergen*). In the second category, they cover not just narrowly 'economic' activities, such as those of craftsmen and the professions, but extend to the fields of literature, arts, music, sport, the press and broadcasting. Services can also be provided without crossing a border altogether. Services questions tend to be looked at by the court as subsidiary to establishment. This does not reflect development in today's technological society, where for example in the UK 60% of the GDP is attributable to services. In fact, it is sometimes difficult to distinguish between services and the movement of goods. If someone sends data down an internet line, that is a service; if someone presses a button and produces the result of such data, that constitutes goods (see further **17.29**).

17.5 Directive 73/148 (OJ 1973 L172/14) deals with the rights of movement and residence for establishment and services. Here a difference is made between establishment and services as regards the right of residence. Article 4(1) provides for the right of permanent residence to those who establish themselves. A residence permit valid for a period of no less than five years, automatically renewable, shall be issued. Article 4(2) provides that the rights of residence for persons providing and receiving services shall be of equal duration to the period during which the service is provided. Directive 75/34 (OJ 1975 L14/10), which has its parallel for workers in Regulation 1251/70, provides for the right of the self-employed to remain in the host member state after they have ceased their self-employed activity. Temporary absences not exceeding a total of three months in a year will not affect this right. This directive had to be adopted on the basis of the general enabling Article 308 (ex Article 235) EC, as no specific power had been provided in the Treaty.

The right of establishment, like the freedom to provide services, rests first of all on the prohibition of discrimination; they are really rights to equal treatment with nationals of the host member state. This may sometimes lead to reverse discrimination, where a national of another member state will be in a more advantageous position than a national who has not left his own country.

Freedom of establishment

17.6 Articles 43–48 EC are the provisions covering freedom of establishment for the self-employed. This includes not just individuals, as in the case of workers, but also legal persons, companies or firms, and any profit-making undertakings (Article 48 EC). See Case 197/84 *Steinhauser v City of Biarritz* (1985), concerning a restriction on the renting of trading premises.

The freedom to exercise a trade or profession is fundamental to the objectives of the Community. The economy cannot develop as it is intended to if there are obstacles to some of the principal production factors such as labour and the transfer of know-how.

The right of establishment is described in Article 43 EC as the right of a natural person or a company to settle in a member state and to pursue an economic activity there. This includes the right to set up and run a company and the right to pursue an occupation in a self-employed capacity. The exceptions to this right contained in Articles 45 and 46 EC therefore also apply to companies. In Case C-213/89 *Factortame (II)* (1991) it was seen that the principle of non-discrimination as to nationality in Article 12 EC also applies to companies. The Merchant Shipping Act 1988 provided that the majority of shareholders in a company owning British ships had to be British. This was ruled by the Court to be incompatible with Article 12. Article 43 is the basic provision on the right of establishment. The right covers individuals as well as 'companies and firms', which are defined in Article 48 as those 'constituted under civil or commercial law', including co-operative societies and other 'legal persons...'; it excludes, however, non-profit-making organisations. Article 48 provides that such 'companies or firms' are treated in the same way as natural persons.

17.7 A more complex example of broader economic scope may be found in Case 270/83 *Commission v France* (1986). In that case the Court found France in breach of its Treaty obligations because it did not grant to branches and agencies in France of insurance companies whose registered office was in another member state the benefit of shareholders' tax credits for dividends paid to such branches or agencies by French companies under the same conditions as were granted to insurance companies registered in France. The Court rejected the French argument relating to the avoidance of double taxation through corporation tax and dividend tax. In Case C-254/97 *Baxter v Premier Ministre* (1999) the court held that Articles 43 and 48 precluded legislation giving tax allowances to companies established in France exploiting proprietary medicinal products which meant they could deduct from a special levy on their pre-tax turnover only expenditure incurred on research carried out in France. Although there were French-based undertakings which incurred expenditure outside the country and foreign undertakings which incurred such expenditure within France, the tax allowance seemed likely to have a more detrimental effect on undertakings having their principal place of business in other member states.

17.8 In Case 81/87 *R v HM Treasury and IRC, ex p Daily Mail and General Trust plc* (1988) the *Daily Mail* challenged the statutory UK requirement that companies transferring their central management abroad must obtain Treasury permission first, as an obstacle to their freedom of establishment. The statutory provision also enabled the Treasury to ask the company to liquidate some of its assets, thus making it liable for capital gains tax, whereas companies resident abroad had no such liability. The Court pointed out that Article 52 (now Article 43 EC) provided for the setting up of agencies, branches or subsidiaries, but that in the present state of Community law, with wide variations in company law, the Treaty could not confer the right on a company to transfer its central management to another member state:

> ...while retaining their status as companies incorporated under the legislation of the first member state.

17.9 Case C-264/96 *ICI v Kenneth Hall Colmer (Her Majesty's Inspector of Taxes)* (1998) concerned discriminatory fiscal treatment in respect of corporation tax. Under UK law, companies belonging to a consortium through which they control a holding company were only entitled to tax relief if the holding company's business consisted wholly or mainly in the holding of shares in subsidiaries established in the UK. This constituted an obstacle to the establishment of a company incorporated in one member state in another member state. The reasons justifying the discrimination submitted by the UK government, based on the risk of tax avoidance and the diminution of tax revenue resulting from the fact that revenue lost through the granting of tax relief on losses incurred by resident subsidiaries could not be offset by tax on the profits on non-resident subsidiaries, were rejected by the Court. The discrimination was not necessary to protect the cohesion of the tax system at issue. A similar decision may be seen in Case C-307/97 *Saint-Gobain v Finanzamt Aachen-Innenstadt* (1999): it is incompatible with the Treaty for a company with its seat in one member state and holding shares in companies established in another member state not to be entitled to certain concessions in relation to the taxation of those foreign shareholdings and of the related dividends on the same conditions as those applicable to companies limited by shares with their seat in Germany. In Case C-200/98 *X AB and Y AB v Riksskatteverket* (1999), Swedish legislation applying different treatment between various types of intra-group transfers on the basis of the criterion of the subsidiaries' seats constituted a similar obstacle for Swedish companies wishing to form subsidiaries in other member states. The Court also held that Greek tax legislation, which meant that companies having their seat in another member state and carrying on business in Greece through a permanent establishment situated there could not benefit from a lower rate of tax on profits, when that possibility was accorded to companies having their seat in Greece and there was no objective difference in the situation between those two categories of companies which could justify such a difference in treatment (Case C-311/97 *Royal Bank of Scotland v Elliniko Dimosio (Greek State)* (1999)) was incompatible with Community law. Even though the two situations were different in that companies having their seat in Greece were taxed there on the basis of their world-wide income, whereas companies carrying on business in that State through a permanent establishment were subject to tax there only on the basis of profits which the permanent establishment earned there, that circumstance was not such as to prevent the two categories of companies from being considered, all other things being equal, to be in a comparable situation as regards the method of determining the taxable base. Could limits be imposed on an undertaking on the ground that it would use the right of establishment to circumvent the law of a member state (Case C-212/97 *Centros v Erhvervs- og Selskabsstyrelsen* (1999))? Danish nationals resident in Denmark formed a company in the UK which did not trade there. The Danish authorities opposed the registration of a branch of that company in Denmark as they considered that the undertaking was in fact seeking to circumvent national rules concerning, in particular, the paying up of a minimum capital. The Court held that such a practice constituted an obstacle to freedom of establishment and that the fact that a national of a member state who wished to set up a company chose to form it in the member state whose rules of company law seemed to him the least restrictive could not, in itself, constitute an abuse of the right of establishment. It could also not be justified as an imperative requirement in the public interest for the protection of creditors. Furthermore, the proportionality principle was not followed as it was possible to adopt measures which were less restrictive or which interfered less with fundamental freedoms. The Court observed that nothing precluded the member state concerned from adopting any appropriate measure for preventing or penalising fraud, in relation to the company or its members, where it had been established that they were in fact attempting to evade their obligations towards creditors established on the territory of the State in question. The refusal to register the company was thus contrary to the Treaty.

17.10 The original Article 54 EEC provided for a general programme for abolition of restrictions. This is now no longer included in Article 44 EC as amended by the Amsterdam Treaty, which has replaced it, but it retains the detailed instructions to the member states to act in order to facilitate establishment. The General Programme for the Abolition of Restrictions on the Freedom of Establishment (18 December 1961, [1962] OJ 36/62, OJ Sp Ed 1974, Second Series IX) pursuant to Article 54 EEC, like that for services, was introduced in 1961. Obstacles to the right of establishment included not only laws prohibiting non-nationals from exercising professional activities, but also eg work permits, merchant or professional cards, and more costly measures, such as deposits and bonds, or provisions subjecting non-nationals to double supervision, or having to establish oneself in order to provide services. The programme also provided for an end to the restrictions on movement and residence, which was achieved in Directive 73/148 which parallels Directive 68/360 for workers. At the time it was thought that Article 43 did not have direct effect but was conditional on the implementation of the programme. However, even after Articles 43 and 49 had been found to have direct effect, it was still necessary to provide for equivalence of professional standards between Community nationals. The Commission therefore embarked on a programme drafting a number of specific directives to put further substance on the articles. In the 1960s and 1970s more than 50 directives were issued in such diverse fields as the medical and para-medical professions, agriculture, architects, crafts, hotel and restaurant business, commercial agents and the film industry. Although it could be thought that medical directives and those for related professions should not pose too many problems, in fact these took a long time to come to fruition. Some examples are: Directives 75/362 and 75/363 (OJ 1975 L 167/1 and 167/14) on the Recognition of Medical Qualifications; Directives 77/452 and 77/453 on Nurses' Qualifications and Nurses' Activities (OJ 1977 L 452/1 and OJ 1977 L 176/8); Directive 78/686 Recognition of Dental Qualifications (OJ 1978 L 233/1); Directive 78/1026 on the Recognition of Veterinary Qualifications (OJ 1978 L 362/1).

Even these specific directives did not eliminate all the problems which arise in respect of recognition of professional training and qualifications. The standards they laid down were minimum standards expressed in general terms.

17.11 However, these directives took considerable time and effort to achieve, regulating each specific profession. Progress was extremely slow. For example a directive for hairdressers, and even the medical directives, took a long time; that for architects took about fifteen years. Amendments to the directives had already become necessary, such as in Directive 93/16 EEC of 5 April 1993 (OJ L165 07/07/1993) providing for a simplified procedure in the recognition of the qualifications of general medical practitioners. The Commission changed its approach to directives towards a preference for a more general directive recognising professional qualifications. The result was Directive 89/48 (OJ 1989 L19/16). It provided for a general system for ensuring equivalence of university diplomas for courses lasting at least three years. In addition, there has to be completion of professional training, where appropriate, in addition to the university diploma. The directive is based on two principles: (1) mutual trust between member states; (2) mutual recognition: the assumption that certificates awarded in the member states should be accepted in good faith. The education must, however, be comparable: if there are significant differences between training periods, for example, additional evidence of professional experience or additional examinations may be required. This directive was followed by Directive 92/51 on the mutual recognition of post-secondary training of shorter duration, such as vocational training courses. Directive 1999/42 of the European Parliament and Council (OJ L201 31/07/99) provided for a third general system for the recognition of professional qualifications which extended the mutual recognition approach to the sectoral directives, based on experience and skills in addition to the possession of qualifications or diplomas.

What rights of establishment are there in the absence of directives?

17.12 In Case 2/74 *Reyners v Belgium* (1974) Mr Reyners, a Dutch national, had passed all the necessary exams and fulfilled all the other requirements to become an '*avocat*' in Belgium. Belgian law at that time required *avocats* to have Belgian nationality and when Mr Reyners applied to be admitted to the Belgian Bar and to be qualified as an '*avocat*' his application was turned down. The Belgian *Conseil d'Etat*, the highest Administrative Court, referred the case to the ECJ, asking whether Article 52 (now Article 43 EC) had direct effect. The Court replied:

> ...in laying down that the freedom of establishment shall be attained at the end of the transitional period, Article 52 thus imposed an obligation to attain a precise result, the fulfilment of which had to be made easier by, but not made dependent on, the implementation of a programme of progressive measures.

It did not matter that the Council had so far failed to issue all the directives necessary for implementation under Article 54 EEC. Individuals could rely directly on Article 43 EC. However, the directives had not lost all interest since they would contribute towards defining the scope of the exercise of freedom of establishment. See *van Binsbergen* at 17.21 for a parallel case involving services.

17.13 Thus, the pressure for the drawing up of directives had been taken off, but it still proved necessary to have the directives, as will be seen, in particular, in the case of lawyers. The aim of the directives arising from

Article 43 EC was to facilitate matters, not to make implementation depend on it.

17.14 In Case 71/76 *Thieffry v Conseil de l'Ordre des Avocats à la Cour de Paris* (1977) a Belgian national, who had obtained a law degree at a Belgian university, which was recognised as equivalent by the University of Paris, proposed to train for the Paris Bar. He was refused on the grounds that he did not possess a French law degree. The ECJ ruled that this was indirect discrimination, prohibited by Article 43 EC. In Case 11/77 *Patrick v Ministère des Affaires Culturelles* (1977) a British architect had obtained a degree in the UK which was recognised by France on the basis of a ministerial decree. Although there was no directive, such a qualification, recognised by authorities of the host member state as equivalent, should be accepted by the member state concerned. So it seems that even in the absence of a directive it is possible to take advantage of the right of establishment, provided some state authority has recognised the diploma as equivalent. The later case C-61/89 *Bouchoucha* (1990) concerned a French national who had obtained a diploma in osteopathy in the UK. Under French law only qualified doctors were allowed to practise as osteopaths and he was prosecuted when he attempted to practise in France. Directives 75/362 and 75/363 concerned harmonisation and mutual recognition of medical qualifications, but did not define the activities of a 'doctor'. The ECJ said:

> ...in the absence of Community legislation on the professional practice of osteopathy, each member state is free to regulate the exercise of that activity within its territory without discriminating between its own nationals and those of the other member states.

17.15 In Case 107/83, *Ordre des Avocats au Barreau de Paris v Klopp* (1984), the Court ruled that the right to set up branches in other member states included the right for a lawyer to set up more than one place of work, subject to professional rules of conduct. There was no directive co-ordinating national provisions governing access to and the exercise of the legal profession. The French rules laid down that a French lawyer could only belong to one local bar. Nevertheless, there was the possibility for a foreign lawyer to have an office in another country. Therefore, even if national rules provide that someone may only have one professional location, this does not preclude a lawyer from another member state from setting up an office in another member state. See below more generally on lawyers and, in particular, Case C-55/94 *Reinhard Gebhard v Consiglio dell'ordine degli Avvocati e Procuratori di Milano* (1995) (see 18.21).

17.16 In Case 39/75 *Coenen v Sociaal Economische Raad* (1975) the Court stated, however, that although the requirement of business residence in the country where a profession is exercised may be justified, the individual could not be required to have his private residence there as well.

17.17 See also Case 115/78 *Knoors v Secretary of State for Economic Affairs* (1979). Mr Knoors, who had Dutch nationality, had been trained as a plumber in Belgium. The requirements for qualifications in the Netherlands were more stringent than those in Belgium. There was a specific directive in this area which provided that where the exercise of the activity in a member state depended on the possession of certain qualifications:

> ...that member state shall accept as sufficient evidence of such knowledge and ability the fact that the activity in question has been pursued in another member state.

Although the Dutch government argued that the free movement measures did not apply to its own nationals, and it concerned a wholly internal situation, the Court pointed out that the detailed provisions of the directive excluded any possibility of a national abusing the free movement rules by gaining easier qualifications in another member state. A national of the member state should, therefore, be entitled to benefit under the directive. *Knoors*, therefore, seems to indicate that reverse discrimination does not obtain if there is a directive in existence. If there is no directive, a national of a member state who has gained a qualification in another member state which is not equivalent to that in his/her own state cannot rely simply on Article 43. This was made clear in the two cases concerning Mr Auer, a French citizen who had acquired a veterinary qualification in Italy and tried to practise in France. As a result, he was prosecuted. In the first case, Case 136/78 *Ministère Public v Auer* (1979) the Court agreed Mr Auer could not rely on Article 43. Then the directives covering veterinary qualifications were passed and after a second prosecution, the Court accepted in Case 271/82 *Auer v Ministère Public (No 2)* (1983) that he could rely on the Directives.

17.18 In Case 222/86 *UNECTEF v Heylens* (1987) Mr Heylens was a Belgian football trainer who was prosecuted by the French football trainers' union. He was practising as a trainer in France without having any qualifications recognised by the French authorities as equivalent. The Court held that in the absence of Community legislation the French system of recognising diplomas nevertheless had to look objectively at the qualifications held by a national of another member state. Its assessment of the equivalence of the foreign diploma:

...must be effected exclusively in the light of the level of knowledge and qualifications which its holder can be assumed to possess in the light of that diploma, having regard to the nature and duration of the studies and practical training which the diploma certifies that he has carried out.

Similarly, in Case C-340/89 *Vlassopoulou v Ministerium für Justiz, Bundes-und Europeaangelegenheiten Baden-Württemberg* (1991). Mrs Vlassopolou was a Greek national with a Greek law degree who had practised German law in Germany for a number of years. Her application for admission to the German Bar was rejected. The Court stated that member states had an obligation under Article 43 to take into consideration a person's qualifications acquired in another member state and make a comparison between those and the national rules. Case C-154/93 *Tawil-Albertini* (1994) concerned a dental qualification obtained in the Lebanon by a French national. Belgium had recognised the qualification as equivalent but France refused. His qualification had also been accepted in two other member states, the UK and Ireland. The ECJ ruled that the sectoral dental directive did not provide for qualifications obtained outside the EC. The directive only contained provisions concerning minimum qualifications and therefore other member states could not be bound by an agreement between another member state and a non member state. However, in Case C-319/92 *Haim v Kassenaertzliche Vereinigung Nordrhein* (1994) the applicant had a non-member state (Turkish) qualification. He had practised in Belgium and was authorised to practise in Germany. However, when he applied to be allowed to practise within the German social security system, he was told he had to undergo two years of training. The ECJ referred to *Vlassopolou*: the period spent practising under a social security scheme in another member state should be taken into account by the German authorities.

Case C-238/98 *Hocsman v Ministre de l'Emploi* (2000) is particularly important. The applicant's basic medical diploma was obtained outside the EU, in Argentina. However, his specialisation (urology) was obtained in Spain, within a member state. Thus, he had practised lawfully as a specialist in a member state. He also worked in France as a specialist in French hospitals. He then applied to be admitted to the French professional medical association. They refused. The ECJ again stated that *Vlassopolou* and *Heylens* applied and that the medical association should consider his application in this light, taking into account all the qualifications obtained and the relevant experience and comparing the specialised knowledge thus acquired with the national requirements.

17.19 All these cases concerned recognised professions. A different difficulty arises in the case of professions which are recognised in one member state, but not in another. Case C-234/97 *Fernandez de Bobadilla v Museo Nacional del Prado* (1999) concerned a Spanish national seeking to practice her profession of art restorer in Spain. She was a holder of a postgraduate degree in the UK and was rejected for a post at the Prado as the collective agreement there did not recognise this qualification. The Court held: a profession regulated by collective agreement if it is the result of a single national policy or even if it resembles other agreements entered into on an individual basis by other public bodies will fall under the directives for the recognition of diplomas and professional education and training. Even if there is non-regulation, ie no general procedure for recognition, it is up to the public body itself to investigate and ascertain equivalence. (See also Case C-164/94 *Arantis v Land Berlin* (1996) concerning the profession of geologist.)

17.20 The general directives referred to above (in **17.11**) as well as the specific directives referred to in **17.10** were amended by Directive 2001/19/EC of the European Parliament and Council of 14 May 2001 (OJ L206, 31/07/2001 p1–51), which has become known as the SLIM (Simplification of Community Legislation) Directive. This introduces the concept of 'regulated education and training', first established in Directive 92/51, into the general system. It emphasises the importance of 'lifelong learning', particularly in the area of medicine. It provides for a right of appeal under national law against rejection requiring member states to give reasons for such a rejection. It also takes account of the ECJ case law in cases such as *Vlassopolou, Heylens, Tamil Albertini, Haim* and *Hocsman* in respect of the recognition of non-member state qualifications and experience in another member state which had already recognised such qualifications. A note at the end of the directive referred to the shared opinion of EP, Council and Commission that it is important to have consolidated versions, easily accessible to everyone, of the legal texts applicable in the field of mutual recognition of professional qualifications. Thus, the Commission intends to further pursue the work done in Council Directive 93/116 EEC (free movement of doctors) and Directive 1999/42 EC of the European Parliament and Council (third general system) for the recognition of professional qualifications in two stages: initially, it plans to integrate the sectoral directives in to a consolidated framework. The Commission will then examine the possibility of consolidating the directives relating to the general system, in order to continue simplifying the legislation and further facilitate the free provision of services with regard to the conclusions of the Lisbon summit. The Commission will also examine developments in the specific training of general practitioners in member states and the extent of the problems which would arise from the differences in duration and training. This has resulted in a Commission proposal for a draft general directive (COM (2002) 119 OJ C 181 E 30/7/2002 p 183–257) which aims at pursuing these objectives, in the field of establishment and of services. This proposal, which is subject to the co-decision procedure and requires unanimity, is at present going through the legislative process.

The freedom to provide services

17.21 In Case 33/74 *van Binsbergen v Bestuur van de Bedrijfsvereniging voor de Metaalnijverheid* (1974) Mr Kortmann, a Dutch national, who practised in his own country as a legal adviser and representative in social security matters, was engaged by Mr van Binsbergen as his legal representative. He had moved his home to Belgium and corresponded from there with a Dutch court, so it seemed as if he was 'established' in Belgium. The court registrar told him he could no longer act, as under Dutch social security procedure legal representation of persons in social security matters could only be furnished by persons established in the Netherlands. Two questions were referred to the Court:

- Did Article 59 (now Article 49 EC) have direct effect?

- Could a state require residence as a condition to perform the services in issue?

The Court said Article 59 (now Article 49 EC) contained a clear cross-border element. It does not apparently require the two persons involved to be of different nationality, merely to be in two different states, so that the service crosses a border. Article 49(1) (ex Article 59(1)) EC speaks of nationals of member states 'who are established in a State of the Community other than that of the person for whom the services are intended'. Article 50 (ex Article 60) EC shows that the provision of services means anything normally done for money, including legal representation. Most submissions, including that of the UK government, accepted that after *Reyners* Articles 59 and 60 could have direct effect at least as regards discrimination on grounds of nationality. The difficulty was that the legal adviser was obviously not suffering from that sort of discrimination. He, his client, the social security court, and the domestic law in question, were all Dutch. The Dutch law did not mention nationality, but simply disqualified any legal adviser of any country who was not established in the Netherlands. The Court said:

> Taking into account the particular nature of the services to be provided, specific requirements imposed on the person providing the service cannot be considered incompatible with the Treaty where they have as their purpose the application of professional rules justified by the general good – in particular rules relating to organisation, qualifications, professional ethics, supervision and liability – which are binding upon any person established in the State in which the service is provided, where the person providing the service would escape from the ambit of those rules being established in another member state.

The requirement to be established within the jurisdiction of certain courts, if it is objectively justified by the requirement of the general good such as the need to ensure observance of professional rules of conduct connected with the administration of justice and respect for professional ethics, was, therefore, not contrary to Articles 59 and 60 (now Articles 49 and 50 EC). Here, however, the administration of justice could be ensured by less restrictive measures and the exercise of the professional activity was unrestricted within the territory of the member state; thus, the requirement of residence was disproportionate.

The requirement of the general good could be compared with the 'rule of reason' and the mandatory requirements in the area of the free movement of goods (see generally Chapter 13). This is a mobile concept, which differs according to which service as at issue.

17.22 In Case 279/80 *Criminal Proceedings against Webb* (1981), the ECJ held that a British-registered agency for the supply of temporary workers could not place people in the Netherlands without also being registered there, because registration fulfilled different functions in the two countries. In the Netherlands it was intended to promote good labour relations and protect the interests of employees: it was apparently thought that permanent workers in an industry might resent the presence of temporary workers. For this reason the use of temporary workers was severely restricted. In certain industries it was entirely forbidden and, even where it was permitted, they could not be paid more than permanent employees. In the UK, on the other hand, registration was simply intended to ensure the suitability of the persons operating the agency. The Court also noted the sensitive nature of temporary employment agencies which are even banned in some countries. Although the freedom of provision of services was one of the fundamental principles of the Treaty and may be restricted only by provisions justified by the general good, here the court held that such justification existed and that, therefore, Webb could not place workers in the Netherlands without being registered there. On the other hand, in Case C-113/89 *Rush Portuguesa v Office National d'Immigration* (1990) Portuguese workers employed by a company providing services in Belgium were required to be in the possession of work permits. The workers were subject to the rules of employment and social security in their own country. The Court ruled that such a rule was incompatible with Article 49. In Joined Cases C-369/96 and C-376/96 *Arblade and Leloup* (1999) the Court was asked about the limits imposed by Community law on the freedom of the member states to regulate the social protection of persons working on their territory. Were social obligations imposed by Belgian law, breach of which was punishable by penalties under Belgian public-order legislation, applicable in respect of workers of an undertaking set up in another member state who were temporarily deployed in Belgium in order to perform a contract? The Court stated first of all that the fact that national rules were categorised as public-order legislation did not mean that they were exempt from compliance with the provisions of the Treaty, as otherwise the primacy and uniform application of Community law would be undermined. If the requirements imposed by the Belgian legislation had a restrictive effect on freedom to provide services, would they be justified by overriding reasons relating to the public interest? If so, was this interest already protected by the rules of the member state in which the service provider was established or could the same result be achieved by less restrictive rules? Provisions guaranteeing a minimum wage were justified but, in order for their infringement to justify the criminal prosecution of an employer established in another member state, they had to be sufficiently precise and accessible for them not to render it impossible or excessively difficult in practice for such an employer to determine the obligations with which he was required to comply. On the other hand, the obligation to pay employer's contributions to the 'timbres-intempéries' (bad weather stamps) and 'timbres-fidélité' (loyalty stamps) schemes could be justified only if, first, the contributions payable gave rise to a social advantage for the workers concerned and, second, those workers did not enjoy in the State of establishment, by virtue of the contributions already paid by the employer in that State, protection which was essentially similar to that afforded by the rules of the member state in which the services were provided. Obligations to draw up certain documents and keep them in certain places and for a certain times would only be compatible with the Treaty if they were necessary in order to enable effective review of compliance with the national legislation and if no comparable obligations existed in the State in which the undertaking was established.

17.23 The insurance sector is an area of great importance in the service industry and considerations of the general good are important in this delicate sector. In a series of cases concerning insurance undertakings in different member states, the Court dealt at great length with the restrictions imposed on insurance companies by the supervisory authorities in the member state in which the services were provided. In Case 205/84 *Commission v Germany* (1986) the Court considered two types of restrictions imposed by the German authorities on insurance companies. Those providing direct insurance services were required to be established in Germany; in cases concerning co-insurance there was also a requirement that the leading co-insurer had to be established in Germany and must be authorised as the sole insurer of the risk. The Court said that such restrictions would be compatible with Articles 59 and 60 (now Articles 49 and 50 EC):

> ... only if it is established that...there are imperative reasons relating to the public interest which justify restrictions on the freedom to provide services...

Such rules should be proportionate. Because of the sensitive nature of insurance services, the Court found that in the interest of the general good, the first requirement was justified and that the authorisation requirements also satisfied the proportionality test. However, as regards establishment for co-insurers, the Court was not convinced, repeating what it had said in *van Binsbergen* that such a requirement had to be 'indispensable for the attainment of the objective pursued'. It had not been shown that the authorities could not carry out their supervisory task satisfactorily without the undertaking being established in Germany.

The freedom to receive services

17.24 The concept of services also extends to recipients of services. Article 49 does not mention recipients of services, but even before the ECJ had ruled that recipients of services, too, fell under the Article, Directive 64/221 on public policy, public security and public health exceptions (in Article 1) and Directive 73/148 on rights of movement and residence (in Article 1(c)) expressly covered recipients as well as providers of services. In Cases 286/82 and 26/83 *Luisi and Carbone v Ministero del Tesoro* (1984) the plaintiffs claimed that they had an entitlement under Article 49 and Directive 73/148 to go to another member state to receive services. There should not be any obstructions, even relating to payments. Tourists, persons receiving medical treatment and persons travelling for the purposes of education or business are to be regarded as recipients of services. Two Italian residents had been fined for purchasing foreign currency for use abroad in an amount exceeding the Italian exchange control regulations, which set a ceiling on amounts to be taken abroad for purposes of tourism, business, education and medical treatment. Was this movement of capital dealt with under Article 67 (now repealed)? Current payments were covered by Article 106 (now Article 107), whereas Article 67 was essentially concerned with the investment of the funds in question rather than remuneration for a service. The physical transfer of banknotes could not, therefore, be classified as a movement of capital where the transfer in question corresponds to an obligation to pay arising from a transaction involving the movement of goods or services. Article 106 must be interpreted as meaning that transfers in connection with tourism or travel for the purposes of business, education or medical treatment constituted payments and not movements of capital, even where they are effected by means of the physical transfer of banknotes.

In a reference to Case 118/75 *Watson and Belmann* (1976), a case concerning Italian law which provided that immigrants had to report their presence within three days, the ECJ said this sort of provision was compatible with the Treaty as long as the time limits were reasonable. The Advocate General said that Article 59 (now Article 49 EC) was concerned as much with recipients of services as with providers.

17.25 Case C-294/97 *Eurowings Luftverkehrs v Finanzamt Dortmund-Unna* (1999) concerned German legislation concerning business tax on capital and earnings. Under German law, when lessees lease goods from a lessor established in another member state the taxable amount for calculation of the tax which they are required to pay is, in the majority of cases, larger (and therefore their treatment for tax purposes less favourable) than if they were to lease such goods from a lessor established in Germany. The Court said the lessee was a recipient of services and that the German legislation gave rise to a difference in treatment based on the place of establishment of the provider of services, which was prohibited by Article 59 (now Article 49 EC). Germany argued that there was a need for a coherent tax system, and said in essence that the advantage in favour of a lessee who dealt with a lessor established in Germany was counterbalanced by the fact that that lessor was himself subject to the tax. The Court rejected that line of argument, since the link was merely indirect: the holder of a German lease was generally exempt solely as a result of the fact that the lessor himself was liable to the tax at issue, while the latter had a number of means of avoiding actually paying the tax. The fact that a lessor established in another member state was subject there to lower taxation could not justify a compensatory tax arrangement, because such an approach would prejudice the very foundations of the single market. This judgment is another indication as to how much freedom of action a member state has in respect of taxation in the absence of Community rules on harmonisation.

17.26 In Case 186/87 *Cowan v Trésor Public* (1989), a French law provided for compensation for injuries to French nationals and residents who are victims of crimes. Mr Cowan was on a visit to Paris and was robbed and injured. The Court answered the question posed that Article 6 (now Article 12) prohibiting discrimination as to nationality must be interpreted as meaning that in respect of those who travel within the Community as recipients of services the award of compensation to a victim of crime could not be made dependent on a residence qualification.

17.27 In Case C-348/96 *Calfa* (1999) Mrs Calfa, an Italian national who had been charged with possession for personal use, and with use of prohibited drugs while staying as a tourist in Crete, appealed on a point of law against the decision of the criminal court ordering her to be expelled for life from Greece. The Court, when asked for a preliminary ruling, examined whether such a penalty was compatible with the Community rules on the freedom to provide services, Mrs Calfa being regarded as a recipient of tourist services. The Court concluded that there was clearly an obstacle to that freedom which could not be justified by the public policy exception relied on by Greece. The national legislation provided for automatic expulsion following a criminal conviction, without any account being taken of the personal conduct of the offender or of the danger which that person represented for the requirements of public policy, contrary to Directive 64/221/EEC (see **18.5**).

17.28 A growing number of cases concerns the receipt of services which fall under social security schemes. Can I go abroad for dental treatment if I cannot receive the equivalent treatment at home? In Case C-158/96 *Kohll v Union des Caisses de Maladie* (1998) the Court asserted that such treatment amounts to economic services. In Case C-157/99 *Geraets-Smits v Stichting Ziekenfonds VGZ* and *Peerbooms v Stichting CZ Groep Zorgverzekeringen* (2001), persons registered with social security sickness insurance in the Netherlands were subject to a requirement of authorisation to receive medical treatment in another member state. The Court said such authorisation, only given on condition that the treatment was 'normal' and 'necessary', should be capable of objective justification, but had to be considered against arguments of findings of medical science and the absence of any delay in obtaining equally effective treatment at home.

17.29 What about people who move to another member state to receive a service which may not be lawful in their own country? There was a suggestion of this in Case C-159/90 *SPUC v Grogan* (1991) (see **6.14**) where abortion services, legal in the UK but illegal in Ireland were advertised in Ireland. However, the Court declined to rule on the issue there in the absence of an element of remuneration. A number of cases concerning such activities as betting and lotteries have come before the court. Case C-275/92 *Customs and Excise v Schindler* (1994) concerned the promotion and sale of lottery tickets by agents of a German company. Schindler was charged in the UK with an offence against under the then UK lotteries legislation. Member states intervening in the case argued that lotteries are mostly subject to strict control, and indeed generally run, by public authorities. However, there was no total prohibition of lotteries, including in the UK (the case dealt with the situation before 1993 when the National Lottery was set up). The Court accepted that the rules could be justified on social and cultural grounds and the concern to prevent fraud which justify them. The judgments delivered in *Läärä* and *Questore di Verona v Zenatti* fall very much within the same line of case-law as *Schindler*. The Court refused to find fault either with Finnish legislation which grants to a single public body exclusive rights to operate slot machines, in view of the public interest objectives justifying that legislation (Case C-124/97 *Läärä v Kihlakunnansyyttäjä (Jyväskylä)* (1999)) or with Italian legislation which reserves to certain bodies the right to take bets on sporting events (Case C-67/98 *Questore di Verona v Zenatti*, (1999)). The Court held in particular that the fact that the games or gambling targeted in the case were not totally prohibited was not enough to show that the national legislation was not in reality intended to achieve the public interest objectives at which it was allegedly aimed. In *Läärä*, the Court gave a very direct ruling, stating that, since it enabled the public interest objectives pursued to be achieved more easily, a decision to grant an exclusive operating right to the licensed public body rather than to regulate the activities of various operators authorised to run such games within the framework of rules of a non-exclusive nature did not appear disproportionate having regard to the aim pursued. On the other hand, in *Zenatti* the Court said that it was for the national court to verify whether, having regard to the specific rules governing its application, the Italian legislation was genuinely directed to realising the objectives which were capable of justifying it and whether the restrictions which it imposed did not appear disproportionate in the light of those objectives. Case C-268/99 *Jany v Staatssecretaris van Justitie* (2001) concerned the provisions of one of the 'Europe Agreements' for a candidate country which had applied to join the European Union. The Court said these provisions should apply in the same way as the Treaty provisions. The Court referred to *Schindler* and *Grogan* in ruling that Polish prostitutes' services in the Netherlands were to be regarded as services provided for remuneration. Prostitution was tolerated or even regulated in most member states. It would appear that services which are not illegal in all member states would be capable of constituting a service within the meaning of the Treaty.

17.30 Case C-384/93 *Alpine Investments BV v Minister van Financiën* (1995) is an example of a service provider who does not cross any borders. This case concerned a Dutch prohibition on 'cold-calling', contacting people by telephone to sell them financial advice. Arguments based on *Keck* (see **13.24**) that this concerned 'selling arrangements', were rejected and the prohibition was found to be an impediment to the provision of services, but justified on grounds of consumer protection

17.31 Do dependants of service providers have derived rights like those of dependants of workers? The ECJ adopted a wide interpretation of the rights under Article 49 in Case C-60/00 *Carpenter v Secretary of State for the Home Department* (2002) where a provider of services established in his home state (as in *Alpine*, see above **17.30**) was entitled to have his non-EU spouse reside with him. The Court relied on the fundamental right to respect for family life enshrined in Article 8 of the ECHR and on the provisions in Community legislation concerning the free movement of workers and their families (Regulation 1612/68 and Directive 68/360 see **16.6** and **16.13**). The decision to deport her was held to not strike a fair balance between the right to respect for Mr Carpenter's family life and the maintenance of public order and security.

Directive 73/148, which covers rights of family members of service providers, only applies where the service provider has moved to another member state. However, in this case, Mr Carpenter could rely on the right respect for his family life enshrined in Article 8 of the ECHR as it was clear 'that the separation of Mr and Mrs Carpenter would be detrimental to their family life and, therefore, to the conditions under which Mr Carpenter exercise[d] a fundamental right.'

Whilst Mrs Carpenter had infringed immigration law in the UK by overstaying her six month leave to stay in the UK, to deport her would be disproportionate to the aim of protecting public order and security.

17.32 In Case C-459/99 *MRAX (Mouvement contre le racisme, l'antisemitisme et la xenophobie) v Belgium* (2002) the ECJ reaffirmed the importance of protecting the family life of nationals of the member states to whom the Community legislation on freedom of movement applied. The ECJ cited the relevant provisions in the secondary legislation (Article 10 of Regulation No 1612/68, Article 1 of Directive 68/360 and Article 1 of Directive 73/148, Article 3(1) of Directive 68/360 and Article 3(1) of Directive 73/148). However, in accordance with Article 3(2) of Directive 68/360 and Article 3(2) of Directive 73/148, when a national of a member state moves within the Community with a view to exercising the rights conferred upon him by the Treaty and those directives, the member states may demand an entry visa or equivalent document from members of his family who are not nationals of a member state. The ECJ ruled that:

> A 'refusal of a residence permit, and a fortiori an expulsion order, based solely on the failure of the person concerned to comply with legal formalities concerning the control of aliens would impair the very substance of the right of residence directly conferred by Community law and would be manifestly disproportionate to the gravity of the infringement' [para 78].

17.33 Culture, too is a service to which Community nationals should have the same access, wherever they are. In Case C-45/93 *Commission v Spain* (1994), tourists had to pay an entrance fee to Spanish museums whereas Spanish nationals and residents did not. This was held to infringe Articles 12 and 49 of the Treaty.

17.34 The lines between establishment, the provision of services, and the free movement of goods, are becoming blurred. We can see this in cases like *Alpine Investments, Keck, Familiapress* and *Bosman* (see also **18.15**). All these cases concern obstacles to access to markets. The Court in each case needs to determine first whether an obstacle exists, followed by an examination of arguments of objective justification. In spite of Jacobs AG's suggestions to introduce a *de minimis* rule, this has not so far been accepted. However, although there are many similarities in treatment as regards the Court's approach to the interpretation of the Articles and their exceptions, there are also differences. Thus, in *Alpine Investments* the court did not accept that the prohibition on cold-calling was analogous to a trading rule in the sense of *Keck and Mithouard*.

Further reading

J Y Art, 'Legislative Lacunae, the Court of Justice and Freedom to provide Services', in D Curtin and D O'Keeffe (eds) *Constitutitonal Adjudication in European Community Law and National Law* (1992) Butterworths Ireland.

D Edward 'Establishment and Services: An Analysis of the Insurance Cases', [1987] 12 ELRev 231.

J Lonbay, 'Picking over the Bones: Rights of Establishment Reviewed', [1991] 16 ELRev 507.

Directive 73/148 (OJ 1973 L172/14).

Directive 75/34 (OJ 1975 L14/10).

Directive 89/48 (OJ 1989 L19/16).

Directives 75/362 and 75/363 (OJ 1975 L 167/1 and 167/14) on the recognition of medical qualifications.

Directives 77/452 and 77/453 on Nurses' Qualifications and Nurses' Activities (OJ 1977 L 145/1 and OJ 1977 L 176/8); Directive 78/686 Recognition of Dental Qualifications (OJ 1978 L 233/1).

Directive 78/1026 on the Recognition of Veterinary Qualifications (OJ 1978 L 362/1).

Self-test questions

1. Why are directives needed if Articles 43 and 49 have been held to have direct effect by the ECJ?

2. The distinction between establishment and services is not always easy to make. What are the distinguishing criteria?

3. Should the same criteria be applied to the free movement of persons and to the free movement of goods in respect of restrictions?

CHAPTER EIGHTEEN

Free Movement of Persons: (III) Towards a People's Europe?

SUMMARY
- Exceptions to the free movement of persons
- Articles 39(3) and (4), 45, 46 and 55 (ex Articles 48(3) and (4), 55, 56 and 66) EC
- Directive 64/221
- Reverse discrimination
- Special problems: sport, lawyers, education
- Citizenship: Articles 17–22 (ex Articles 8, 8a–e) EC

Exceptions

18.1 The right to free movement of workers, as interpreted by the Court of Justice, is an extensive right, which is only limited by the provisions contained in Treaty Articles 39(3) and 39(4) (ex Articles 48(3) and 48(4)) EC. The same limitations apply to establishment: Articles 45 and 46(2) (ex Articles 55 and 56(2)) EC, and services: Article 55 (ex Article 66) EC. These exceptions to the principle of free movement of persons have been construed narrowly by the court from the very beginning. Of course, a state needs to be able to protect itself from having to admit those who can cause real harm to its own citizens; those who are a threat to national security, who are likely to cause real disruption to the order of the state or those who threaten the health or well-being of its citizens. On the other hand, a state should not use these exceptions to keep out or discriminate against those who are genuinely seeking to move for their own benefit and that of their family and who cannot, upon objective examination, constitute a real risk. It is the balancing of these two groups of (sometimes divergent) interests which is often left to the court to establish and in which it is more successful in some cases than in others. The use of the exceptions, if successful, means the exclusion of a person from the state, either by non-admission or by deportation, and it is surely right that such draconian measures should only be taken if absolutely necessary. In the context of the internal market and the abolition of border controls, it is now not entirely clear how useful these provisions are.

Limitations on grounds of public policy, public security, public health

18.2 Directive 64/221/EEC on the movement and residence of foreign nationals (OJ Sp Ed 1964 L 850/64, p 117) puts the exceptions contained in Article 39(3) EC with regard to workers and in Article 46(1) EC for the self-employed and those providing or receiving services into greater detail. The directive does not distinguish between the different groups of workers and the self-employed, and its provisions apply to all groups equally. It was adopted on the basis of Article 46(2) only, but provides in Article 1 that it applies to the employed, the self-employed (which includes establishment *and* services) and to recipients of services, who are not mentioned in the Treaty itself. It co-ordinates the measures which relate to entry to and deportation from a member state's territory and to the issue of residence permits. The exceptions may not be invoked to serve economic ends. However, as we have seen in previous chapters, the court does sometimes allow non-economic exceptions of the 'Cassis de Dijon' type (ie indistinctly applicable measures). See in particular **13.12**, **17.21** and **17.22**.

The procedural provisions of the Directive are clear enough, but the interpretation of the concepts of public policy and, to a lesser extent, public security, has not been straightforward. The court's interpretation has changed over the years.

18.3 In the relatively early case of *van Duyn* (Case 41/74 *van Duyn v Home Office* (1974)) the court held that the member state, in this case the UK, had the ultimate say in whether Miss van Duyn's conduct was contrary to public policy. The court referred to Article 3(1) of Directive 64/221 which provides that:

> ... measures taken on grounds of public policy shall be based exclusively on the personal conduct of the individual concerned.

The court considered that present association (as against past association) with a body or an organisation could in itself constitute personal conduct which may be considered as a voluntary act by that person. The fact that the Scientology organisation was not prohibited, and thus British nationals could work for it, was then considered by the court. The concept of public policy had to be strictly interpreted and was, moreover, subject to control by the Community institutions. Nevertheless, circumstances justifying recourse to the concept of public policy may vary, and thus it was necessary to allow the competent national authorities a certain amount of discretion. This, therefore, still allowed the English court discretion to refuse entry to Miss van Duyn on the basis that her conduct was 'socially harmful', although the Scientology movement by which she was to have been employed was not prohibited in the UK. The court pointed out that the right of residence may be refused to nationals of other member states who wish to take up employment, whereas it could not refuse its own nationals. It should be noted that this was the first UK case to come to the ECJ after that country's accession to the Community in 1973 and the first case to indicate clearly that a directive is capable of having direct effect. The court was clearly anxious to establish the principle of direct effect of directives but may not, under the circumstances, have wanted to go too far in its interpretation of the public policy concept and give it a Community dimension. However, in Cases 115 and 116/81 *Adoui and Cornuaille v Belgium* (1982) the court did not accept that a member state could deport those who were working in a non-prohibited job in Belgium. Two French topless waitresses were ordered to leave Belgium for reasons of public morality. They were allegedly in reality prostitutes, but prostitution as such is not forbidden in Belgium, only connected activities such as pimping and soliciting. The court said that, if a member state did not adopt repressive measures or other genuine and effective measures designed to combat the activity, it could not justify expulsion of other member states' nationals. It would seem that the case of *van Duyn* would not be decided in the same way today. Mancini A-G wrote extra-judicially that the case overruled *van Duyn*. If such cases were now to be decided by a national court, without making a reference, its decision would be likely to follow *Adoui*. See for comparison the *Schindler* line of cases (**17.29**).

18.4 How much discretion does a member state have in restricting a Community national's right of free movement; can it penalise or expel those it considers undesirable? Article 3(1) of Directive 64/221 refers to measures based exclusively on the personal conduct of the individual. Article 3(2) provides that 'previous criminal convictions shall not in themselves constitute grounds...'. Case 67/74 *Bonsignore v Oberstadtdirektor der Stadt Köln* (1975) concerned an Italian worker in Germany who accidentally killed his brother with a pistol for which he had no firearms licence. He was convicted of causing death by negligence but received no punishment. However, he was ordered to be deported. The court ruled that deportation of a general preventive nature, in order to deter others, could not be justified under Article 3 of the Directive. 'Personal conduct' had to be strictly construed as directly linked to the individual's actions. In Case 30/77 *R v Bouchereau* (1977), M Bouchereau, a French worker in the UK, had past convictions for unlawful possession of drugs. The court held that previous criminal convictions alone were relevant only insofar as they 'manifest a present or future intention to act in a manner contrary to public policy or public security'. Previous criminal convictions could, therefore, only be taken into account insofar as personal conduct which led to the convictions still constituted 'a present threat to the requirements of public policy'. It gave a very narrow definition of the type of measures which could be justified under the exceptions set out by the Directive. It was not enough that the measure had been adopted in reaction to 'the disturbance of the social order which any infringement of the law involves'. Public policy is only infringed by 'a sufficiently serious threat...affecting one of the fundamental interests of society'. Long gone are the days when membership of a marginal sect was sufficient to justify refusal of entry to a member state, as in *van Duyn*.

18.5 Case 157/79 *R v Pieck* (1980) concerned Mr Pieck, a worker in Britain who was prosecuted for staying on when his leave of six months had expired (see **16.13**). The court is generally concerned that any penalties on the failure to possess permits, possession of such permits being the only thing expressly provided for under Directive 68/360, ie a valid identity card or passport, should not be disproportionate. See also Case 8/77 *Sagulo, Brenca and Bakhouche* (1977), where the court allowed higher fines for Community nationals for failing to show the necessary documents than it would impose on nationals. In Case 131/79 *R v Secretary of State for Home Affairs, ex p Mario Santillo* (1980) the court repeated that past criminal convictions should only be taken into account insofar as they are a factor in assessing the personal conduct of the person concerned at the time the expulsion order is made. The *present* danger presented by the person concerned, a psychopath in this case, rather than the *past* danger should be assessed. In Case 48/75 *Royer* (1976) a decision to expel someone for not complying with administrative requirements on residence permits was held by the court not to be justified. The exception had to be interpreted strictly and could not, therefore, be regarded as a condition precedent to the acquisition of a residence permit, but 'as providing the possibility, in individual cases where there is sufficient justification, of imposing restrictions on the exercise of a right derived directly from the Treaty'. The procedures for expulsion should be such that the person concerned has a reasonable time to resist the expulsion and such decisions should be taken by an independent administrative authority.

In the case of Mrs Calfa (see **17.26**) the court also concluded that Greek rules on automatic expulsion measures following a criminal conviction, without any account being taken of the personal conduct of the offender or of the danger that person represented for the requirements of public policy, were contrary to Directive 64/221/EEC.

18.6 In the case of *R v Secretary of State for the Home Department, ex p John Gallagher* (1995) Mr Gallagher, who had come to England to look for work, was working when he was arrested and an exclusion order was served on him. In 1993 he had been convicted of unlawful possession of two rifles in Ireland and sentenced to three years' imprisonment. Mr Gallagher relied on Directive 64/221 and the interpretation of Article 9(1), which provides that a decision ordering a person's expulsion may not be taken, save in cases of urgency, until a competent authority in the host country has given an opinion. This authority should be different from the one ordering the expulsion. The court answered that Article 9(1) must be interpreted as meaning that the administrative authority, ie the Secretary of State, cannot take a decision ordering an expulsion before a competent authority has given its opinion. The competent authorities referred to may be appointed by the same administrative authority as that which gives the expulsion order, as long as the former can act in absolute independence. This is for the national court to decide.

In Case 36/75 *Rutili v Ministre de l'Intérieur* (1975) Mr Rutili, an Italian citizen had been prohibited from entering certain regions of France because of his known political activities. The court said that this could only be accepted if such a prohibition could also have been imposed on French citizens under the same conditions. However, internal provisions in France were much more limited than the conditions the French authorities wanted to apply to Mr Rutili and , therefore, Mr Rutili's right to free movement could not be impeded.

A wholly internal situation

What is the scope of the free movement provisions?

18.7 The provisions for the free movement of persons do not, however, ensure complete free movement within the Community for all its citizens. Apart from the limitations contained in the Treaty itself in Article 39(3) and (4) and Articles 45 and 55 EC, other restrictions exist as well. In order to avail oneself of the free movement provisions in the Treaty, there has to be a 'Community element' and a wholly internal situation does not, therefore, fall under the application of Community law, at least not under that of the provisions we have discussed. The citizenship Articles 17-22 (ex Articles 8, 8a-e) EC introduced by the Maastricht TEU have introduced a new element. Article 18 provides that 'every citizen of the Union shall have the right to move and reside freely within the territory of the member states, subject only to the limitations laid down in the EC Treaty'. It could arguably be true that the situation in Case 175/78 *R v Saunders* (1979) although probably not that in Cases 35/82 and 36/82 *Morson and Jhanjan v Netherlands* (1982) might be viewed differently by the court today. Mrs Saunders had been prosecuted in the UK for disobeying a court order to move to Northern Ireland and not to return for three years. The ECJ refused to deal with the question and ruled that this concerned a 'wholly domestic situation'. The same applied in the case of *Morson and Jhanjan*, where the Surinamese parents of Dutch nationals were refused entry to the Netherlands. They sought to enter relying on Article 10 of Regulation 1612/68 which allows relatives in the ascending line of the worker to join him. They had never worked in any other member state and the court considered, therefore, that this also concerned a 'wholly internal situation'. Again, this was confirmed in Cases C-64 and 65/96 *Land Nordrhein-Westfalen v Uecker* and *Jacquet* (1997) when two non-EC nationals with two German spouses residing and working in Germany sought to invoke Article 7 of Regulation 1612/68. The court declined to allow the claim, in spite of the fact that the German referring court had asked the court to consider doing so. However, in Case C-370/90 *R v Immigration Appeal Tribunal and Surinder Singh, ex p Secretary of State for the Home Department* (1992) the Community element was held to be present. An Indian husband and his British wife had worked in Germany. When they returned, the UK government considered that the Indian husband's right of residence depended on the British wife's right of residence as a national. The court ruled that the fact that the spouses had both worked in Germany triggered the Community element and Mrs Singh's husband was therefore entitled to enter as the spouse of a Community national. In *R v Secretary of State for the Home Department, ex p Adams* (1995) there was again a wholly internal situation. We shall look at this case again under the section on citizenship (see **18.54**). In cases such as *Saunders* and *Adams* the citizenship provisions might be considered by the ECJ to have an impact and provide a remedy, whereas in *Morson and Jhanjan* this might be more difficult. The internal market, therefore still appears to have less relevance in 'wholly internal' situations.

The public service exception

18.8 The second restriction on the free movement of workers is contained in Article 39(4): employment in the public service. It is echoed in respect of the self-employed in Article 45 EC and also in Article 55 EC which refers to Article 45, which speaks of the exercise of official authority.

This restriction, like the previous exceptions, has also been interpreted narrowly by the ECJ. The articles themselves do not define the concept of public service or of official authority and the court has pointed out here again that there should be a Community interpretation of the concepts. In Case 152/73 *Sotgiu v Deutsche Bundespost* (1974) the court stated that the exception only applied to certain activities connected with the exercise of official authority. Mr Sotgiu, an Italian working for the German post office, had been discriminated against in that a separation allowance paid to workers living away from home was increased for those living in Germany but not for those who lived abroad at the time of recruitment. Although this applied without distinction to all nationals, it clearly affected foreign workers more than German nationals. The German post office pleaded the public service derogation, but the Court pointed out (at para 4) that this exception should not 'have a scope going beyond the aim in view of which the derogation was included'. The aim was the protection by member states of rights to exercise state sovereignty by restricting access to certain parts of the public service. The provision could not, however, 'justify discriminatory measures with regard to remuneration or other conditions of employment against workers once they have been admitted to the public service'. The position might change, however, if the non-national were promoted to a job where Article 39(4) did apply.

18.9 In Case 149/79 *Commission v Belgium* (1980) the Commission brought proceedings against Belgium for violation of Article 48(4) (now Article 39(4) EC). The Belgian Constitution required that all those working for local authorities or public enterprises in Belgium should possess Belgian nationality. This included nurses, gardeners, railway workers and nightwatchmen. The court stated (at para 11, p 3900):

> ... that provision removes from the ambit of Article 48(1) to (3) a series of posts which involve direct or indirect participation in the exercise of powers conferred by public law and duties designed to safeguard the general interests of the State or other public authorities. Such posts in fact presume on the part of those occupying them the existence of a special relationship of allegiance to the State and reciprocity of rights and duties which form the foundation of the bond of nationality.

These were very broad guidelines laid down by the court. It did not consider that it had sufficient information to assess whether specific posts fell within the definition and it instructed the parties to examine the posts in question on the basis of the guidelines given. However, the parties could not agree and the court, therefore, had to decide in Case 149/79 *Commission v Belgium (No 2)* (1982) on certain specific posts which fell within the scope of Article 48(4) (now Article 39(4) EC), such as architects and supervisors. It focused on the aim of the Article and looked at the two requirements, which appear to be cumulative rather than alternative. However, other posts such as those of garden hands, cleaners, hospital nurses etc clearly did not fall within that definition. Posts which might be within the scope of Article 48(4) (now Article 39(4) EC) were those of technical office supervisors, stock controllers, and possibly nightwatchmen as they may have easy access to the secrets of the public authority concerned.

18.10 The court's case law concerning nurses and teachers clarifies its views, although problems remain.

In Case 66/85 *Lawrie-Blum v Land Baden-Württemberg* (1986) the court stated that the concept of public service has to be interpreted narrowly, as directly involving the exercise of powers conferred by public law and contributing to safeguarding the general interests of the state. The activities of a teacher and *a fortiori* of a trainee teacher do not, however, involve the exercise of powers conferred by public law. Access to posts should not be limited simply by the fact that they had civil servant status. If the application of Article 48(4) (now Article 39(4) EC) were made dependent on the legal nature of the relationship between the employee and the administration this would enable the member state to determine at will what posts should be covered by the exception contained in Article

48(4). As the court had pointed out in Case 149/79 *Commission v Belgium* (see 18.9 above) 'employment in the public service' must be understood as meaning those posts which involve direct or indirect participation in the exercise of powers conferred by public law and in the discharge of functions whose purpose is to safeguard the general interests of the state and of other public authorities, and which therefore require a special relationship of allegiance to the state on the part of persons occupying them and reciprocity of rights and duties which form the foundation of the bond of nationality. The posts excluded are confined to those which, having regard to the tasks and responsibilities involved, are apt to display the characteristics of the specific activities of the public service. Those very strict conditions were not fulfilled in the case of a trainee teacher and his/her employment could not be described as employment in the public service within the meaning of Article 48(4) to which nationals of other member states may be denied access. Case 307/84 *Commission v France* (1986) concerned a French law limiting the appointment of nurses in public hospitals to French nationals. Mancini AG in his Opinion commented on the criticisms of the court's functional approach in the two *Commission v Belgium* cases. Member states were very resistant to leaving any definition of the concept to the court and preferred an 'organic and institutional' approach, rather than the functional one favoured by the court. However, the court did not accept France's arguments, nor the argument, supported by other member states, that posts which initially would not fall under the public service exception, could change and do so later. Again, in Case 33/88 *Allué and Coonan v Università degli Studie di Venezia* (1989) a nationality restriction could not be imposed on foreign language university teachers.

18.11 In Case C-15/96 *Schöning-Kougebetopoulou v Freie und Hansestadt Hamburg* (1998) the court held that a clause contained in a collective agreement which ignored previous periods of employment in the public service of another member state for the purpose of determining promotion was incompatible with Community law. Such a clause clearly disadvantaged migrant workers who had spent part of their careers in the public service of another member state and thus offended against the principle of non-discrimination. Such a clause could not be justified under the exceptions in Article 39(4).

18.12 The public service exception in respect of the self-employed contained in Article 45 (ex Article 54) EC was analysed by the court in Case 2/74 *Reyners v Belgium* (1974). The case established that Article 43 (ex Article 52) EC had direct effect (see 17.12). The Belgian court also asked the ECJ whether the exercise of the profession of '*avocat*' constituted the exercise of public authority and could, thus, be restricted to Belgian nationals. The court considered that a wholesale restriction of the profession was not necessary and would be disproportionate. It was sufficient if the exclusion of non-nationals were limited to 'those activities which, taken on their own, constitute *a direct and specific connection with the exercise of official authority*' [my emphasis]. If in a profession the exercise, even occasionally, of functions pertaining to public authority could not be severed from the other activities of the profession, the exception would apply. If on the other hand, the exercise of official authority is separable from the professional activity, such an extension of the exception would not be possible. The Advocate General in *Reyners* described the exercise of official authority as 'that which arises from the sovereignty and the majesty of the powers of the state'.

A number of specific problems arise in relation to special fields. We shall discuss some of these below, concerned with sport, lawyers and education.

Free movement in the field of professional sport

18.13 In Case 36/74 *Walrave and Koch v Union Cycliste Internationale* (1974) which concerned a dispute with an international sporting association the court held that the abolition of obstacles to the freedom of establishment and to provide services would be compromised if an abolition of national barriers could be hindered by obstacles resulting from the exercise of their legal autonomy on the part of associations or organisations which do not come under public law. Although Articles 49 and 59 (now Articles 40 and 49 EC), 62 (now repealed) and 64 (now Article 53 EC) relate to the abolition of measures by the state, this does not alter the general nature of the terms of Article 59 (now Article 49 EC) which makes no distinction between the sources of the restriction to be abolished. Thus, Article 49 has horizontal direct effect and may be invoked between individuals.

Case 13/76 *Donà v Mantero* (1976) again showed that sport would be subject to the Treaty insofar as it concerned an economic activity. Italian football teams could not be prevented from hiring non-Italian players. Nevertheless, selection rules concerning national teams playing in international competitions, however, could be limited to those of a particular nationality.

18.14 Case C-415/93 *Union Royale Belge des Sociétés de Football Association ASBL v Jean Marc Bosman* (1996) made a considerable contribution towards clarifying the situation concerning professional sport. Whereas movement of persons for the purposes of exercising an economic or professional activity in another country generally in Europe is traditionally less easy to achieve than, for example, in the United States, the case for those involved in sporting activities is different. Sport has taken on a truly international dimension and it is now almost unthinkable for top level professional football teams to operate without at least a number of players from other countries. If we look at examples of top English football clubs, such as Arsenal, the number of foreign players invariably exceeds that of domestic players in a particular match. Some English teams have on occasion fielded foreign players only, Chelsea Football Club being an example of this.

Mr Bosman, a player with the Belgian club RC Liège, had been transfer-listed but was refused a transfer certificate which is needed for any foreign transfer. Mr Bosman was suspended and unable to play for the whole season. Mr Bosman issued proceedings against RC Liège and the Belgian Football Association and UEFA joined as defendants. Mr Bosman argued Articles 48, as well as the competition Articles 85 and 86 EC (now Articles 39, 81 and 82 EC). UEFA claimed their rules had received Commission approval. The rules were:

- the transfer rules: FIFA, UEFA and URBSFA (Belgian Football Association) rules required that when a player's contract had expired, any new club signing him must pay the old club a fee;

- the nationality rules. Under the rules of UEFA and most of the European Associations a club could not field, in official matches, more than three players who were nationals of other member states, plus two other 'assimilated' players (the so-called 3+2 rule).

Lenz AG in his Opinion said that the rules are subject to Article 48 (now Article 39 EC) insofar as they regulated the employment of professional footballers. He referred to Case 36/74 *Walrave and Koch v Union Cycliste Internationale* (1974) and Case 13/76 *Donà v Mantero* (1976) which established that sport is subject to the rules of the EC Treaty in so far as it constitutes an economic activity. He found that the Belgian rules on foreign players were discriminatory. He accepted that the previous rulings meant that selection for national or perhaps regional representative teams might be limited to those of a particular nationality without involving discrimination within the scope of the EC Treaty. This should not, however, be extended to matches in national leagues or European club competitions where player choice was based on economic considerations and not sporting representation.

Article 48 (now Article 39 EC) read together with Article 52 (now Article 43 EC) goes beyond a discrimination rule towards a broader principle which governs restrictions on free movement if they relate to *access* to the employment market rather than the *exercise* of an occupational activity (para 205 of the Opinion). The transfer rules fell within the scope of Article 48 and may only be justified by imperative reasons in the general interest and may not go further than is necessary to attain those objectives (the proportionality principle). The objective was to preserve a balance between financial and sporting interests of clubs, but the Advocate General doubted that the system fulfilled that objective. Other, less restrictive systems could also fulfil the objective, eg a collective wage agreement could limit the salaries paid by the clubs to the players or it would be conceivable to distribute the club's receipts, such as receipts at the gate and fees received for televised matches among the clubs. The argument that the money was necessary to compensate for the cost of training young players, was acceptable in principle, but the same aims could be achieved at least as efficiently by other means which do not impede the freedom of movement for workers. The Advocate General also discussed the application of Article 85 (now Article 81 EC): the transfer system and restrictions on foreign players were horizontal agreements. This aspect was not dealt with by the court. It is, however, of crucial importance in the implementation of the judgment, as the *Bosman* case shows that the Article 39 structure is insufficient and Article 226 (ex Article 169) EC actions cannot be used. Thus, the enforcement relies each time on the individual's actions, unless the Commission takes the view that collective dominance is involved.

The court agreed Article 48 applied. It answered the first two questions posed as follows:

> 1. Article 48 of the EC Treaty precludes the application of the rules laid down by sporting associations, under which a professional footballer who is a national of one member state may not, on the expiry of his contract with a club, be employed by a club of another member state unless the latter club has paid to the former club a transfer, training or development fee.

> 2. Article 48 of the EC Treaty precludes the application of rules laid down by sporting associations under which, in matches in competitions which they organize, football clubs may field only a limited number of professional players who are nationals of other member states.

The court was aware, however, that this would have a major impact on the football transfer system, and consequently limited the temporal effect of the judgment (as in the *Defrenne* and *Barber* cases, see Chapter 19), declaring that the direct effect of Article 48 could not be relied upon in respect of transfer and other fees already paid or payable under an obligation which arose before the date of the judgment, except for those who had already brought proceedings before their national courts. The horizontal effect of Article 48 was confirmed by the court. It applied not just to the action of public authorities but also to:

> ...rules of any other nature aimed at regulating gainful employment in a collective manner (para 82)

thus confirming its judgments in the two earlier sports cases.

18.15 The real significance of the judgment lies in the general principles set out by the court, moving away from the narrower confines of the football industry. The court referred to Case 81/87 *R v HM Treasury and IRC, ex p Daily Mail and General Trust plc* (1988) (see **17.8**) where it had linked Article 48 (now Article 39 EC) with Article 52 (now Article 43 EC) in its concern to establish coherent principles of free movement. This judgment applies only to cases with a 'Community element'. The court confirmed that Article 39 (ex Article 48) EC did not apply to a wholly internal situation. A better basis for analysis would have been Article 81 (ex Article 85) EC, as the problems concern private agreements irrespective of nationality. However, the court stated (at para 103):

> ... it is sufficient to note that, although the rules in issue in the main proceedings apply also to transfers between clubs belonging to different national associations within the same member state and are similar to those governing transfers between clubs belonging to the same national association, they still directly affect players' access to the employment market in other member states and are thus capable of impeding freedom of movement of workers.

The court referred to Joined Cases C-267/91 and C-268/91 *Keck and Mithouard* (1993) (contrasted with Case C-384/93 *Alpine Investments v Minister van Financiën* (1995), which concerned a challenge under Article 59 (now Article 49 EC) to a Dutch prohibition on 'cold calling' as a technique to offer services in the territory of other member states). The court rejected an analogy with *Keck* and highlighted the material distinction between the two situations (see also **17.30**). *Bosman* could not be considered comparable to the rules on selling arrangements for goods which in *Keck* had been held to fall outside the ambit of Article 28 (ex Article 30) of the Treaty.

The court makes reference to Case C-19/92 *Dieter Kraus v Land Baden-Württemberg* (1993) and Case C-55/94 *Reinhard Gebhard v Consiglio dell'ordine degli Avvocati e Procuratori di Milano* (1995) (see **18.22** below) which elaborate principles governing the lawfulness of national measures that restrict the exercise of fundamental Treaty provisions. Such rules should not, however, offend against the principle of proportionality. They should ensure achievement of the aim pursued and not go beyond what is necessary for that purpose.

The ruling establishes a clear link between the rules concerning free movement of goods in Article 28 (ex Article 30) EC and the exemptions under Article 30 (ex Article 36) EC and *Cassis* (see **13.12**) and those governing free movement of persons in Articles 39, 43 and 49 EC (see also **17.29**) although there are clearly differences in the way in which the court applies the rules in regard to the various Treaty Articles.

It is no exaggeration to say that the *Bosman* case caused a revolution in the world of professional football. Four years on after the judgment there has been an explosion in the use of foreign players, but generally clubs appear to have coped well with this and the fear that this would be detrimental to young players and their training does not seem to have materialised.

18.16 In Joined Cases C-51/96 and C-191/97 *Deliège v Ligue Francophone de Judo et Disciplines Associées ASBL* (2000) Judokas needed permission from their federation to take part in an international sports competition which did not involve national teams. The court said that participation in a high-level international competition did fall within the concept of services, even if they are not paid for by those for whom they are intended. However, the rules did not involve nationality questions or those governing access to the market (as in *Bosman*) but simply were necessary selection rules which by their nature did limit the number of participants. Such rules could not be regarded as constituting a restriction on the freedom to provide services.

18.17 Case C-176/96 *Lehtonen* (2000) concerned rules establishing transfer deadlines in the Belgian basketball federation. These deadlines were different for players from the European Union compared to later ones for players from outside the European Union. The court found that Mr Lehtonen was a worker (as in *Bosman*). The rules did constitute an obstacle to free movement. They might be justified by the fact that late transfers could change the sporting strength of a team and affect the competitive element in achieving a championship and it was up to the national court to look at the rules from the perspective of proportionality. Other than in *Bosman* the difference in treatment was between players from inside and from outside the EU so that it was not a question of discrimination under Article 12.

Free movement for lawyers

18.18 All the cases we have looked at so far concerning lawyers (**17.12, 17.14, 17.15, 17.19**) have been about lawyers with qualifications recognised in the host state. *Reyners* was a Dutch national, but educated in Belgium. He had all the requisite Belgian qualifications. This was, therefore, a pure nationality question. In *Thieffry* and *Klopp* both had qualifications recognised by the host country. Thieffry had a Belgian degree recognised by the Paris Bar as being equivalent; in the absence of implementing directives, the demanding of an additional diploma constituted disguised discrimination.

Similarly, in *Klopp*, who was qualified in both Germany and France, and who applied to open chambers in France in addition to those he already had in Düsseldorf, the fact that national French provisions required *avocats* to maintain chambers within a particular geographical area, but put no restriction on a second set of chambers in such a case, meant that under Article 43 a national of another member state could not be denied the right to set up and practise in the first member state solely on the ground that he maintained chambers simultaneously in another member state.

The Directives regulating the legal profession

18.19 There are a number of directives which apply or modify the case law. Directive 77/249, the Services Directive for lawyers, covers temporary services rendered by a lawyer in one member state to a client in another. The lawyers remain established in their own country and make visits to another, appear in court in the host country and generally work together with a local lawyer, unless this is not mandatory for such a case locally. That was made clear in Case 427/85 *Commission v Germany Re Lawyers' Services* (1988) where the court held that, while the Directive allowed Germans to require the visiting lawyer to act in conjunction with a German lawyer where there is a mandatory requirement of representation, this only applies in such circumstances; however, exceptionally, the 'conjunction rule' can apply in all criminal proceedings, even where it is not necessary to be represented by a lawyer. The 'conjunction' arrangements are best worked out between the visiting and the host lawyers themselves; although there was no objection to a statute laying down a general framework, the detailed rules contained in the German implementing act were too restrictive and consequently contrary to Articles 49 (ex Article 59) EC and 50 (ex Article 60) EC and Directive 77/249. However, the monopoly rights of members of specialised (but not local) Bars, such as that attached to the Supreme Court, could validly be maintained against visiting lawyers from another member state.

18.20 The Services Directive could not be used in Case 292/86 *Gullung v Conseils de l'Ordre des Avocats du Barreau de Colmar et de Saverne* (1988). Gullung was of dual nationality, French and German, and a *Rechtsanwalt* in Offenburg. Membership of the French Bar was refused him for reasons of character. He had previously been a *notaire* in France for 20 years, before he resigned following disciplinary measures taken against him by the relevant disciplinary body (Chambre disciplinaire de notaires du Haut-Rhin). He then attempted to be registered on the list of *conseils juridiques* of Marseille and to be admitted as an *avocat* to the Mulhouse Bar. Both were refused on grounds of character. Appeals were turned down on the grounds that he did not offer the safeguards of dignity, integrity and repute necessary to practise as an *avocat*. Mr Gullung tried to rely on the Lawyers' Services Directive. One of the questions before the court was whether the scope of the Directive was subject to the requirements of public policy. The court said someone who had been barred from access to the profession for reasons relating to dignity, good repute and integrity could not rely on the Directive. The court said that in view of this, it was unnecessary to consider the possibility of relying on the public policy concept. It ruled that a person who is a national of two member states and has been admitted to the legal profession in one of them may rely upon the Directive in the other member state. Furthermore, Article 52 (now Article 43) must be interpreted as meaning that a member state whose legislation requires *avocats* to be registered at a Bar may impose the same requirement on *avocats* from other member states who take advantage of the right of establishment.

18.21 European Parliament and Council Directive 98/5 EC to facilitate practice of the profession of lawyer on a permanent basis in a member state other than that in which the qualification was obtained, the Lawyers'

Establishment Directive, was adopted on 16 February 1998. This Directive was drawn up and approved by the CCBE (Comité Consultatif des Barreaux Européens), the European Association of Bar Councils. The date of implementation was 14 March 2000. The Directive enables lawyers qualified in one member state to practise in another under their home qualification. Lawyers may practise in any field of law, but they are subject to the host country's rules on professional conduct. After three years of 'effective and regular' practice in fields involving the law of the host state, including EC law, a lawyer is exempt from any aptitude test in applying for admission to the profession in the host state. At any time they may apply to have their home professional qualification recognised under Directive 89/48. Once admitted they may use both titles. The directive was challenged in an annulment action in Case C-168/98 *Luxembourg v Parliament and Council* (2000). The court rejected the application on the grounds that it did not infringe the principle of equality in Article 43(EC), that it was adopted on the correct legal basis, and that the provisions of the directive were sufficient to ensure consumer protection.

18.22 The difficulty of drawing the line between establishment and services is discussed in Case C-55/94 *Reinhard Gebhard v Consiglio dell'ordine degli Avvocati e Procuratori di Milano* (1995), where the court went a long way towards clarifying the situation.

Gebhard was a German national, qualified in Germany. He first joined a partnership in Milan and then established his own practice there about ten years later. He mainly advised and represented the interests of German-speakers in Italy and of Italian-speakers in Germany and Austria. Mr Gebhard did not himself practise Italian law; he assisted Italian lawyers whose clients were faced with problems of German law. Following a number of complaints by Italian practitioners the Milan Bar Council prohibited the plaintiff from using the title 'avvocato'. The Bar Council started proceedings against him as they alleged he had contravened the Italian law implementing the Lawyers' Services Directive (Directive 77/249) and suspended him for six months. Mr Gebhard appealed to the National Bar Council (the *Consiglio Nazionale Forense*) which referred questions concerning the interpretation of the Directive and of Articles 52 (now Article 43 EC) and 59 (now Article 49 EC) to the court. The questions asked were: (a) whether an Italian law which prohibited the establishment either of chambers or of a principal or branch office was compatible with the Directive; and (b) what were the criteria to assess whether a lawyer's activities were of a temporary nature. In answer to written questions by the court Mr Gebhard stated that although he did not have his own chambers in Germany he was a member of a *Bürogemeinschaft* – an office from which several independent lawyers practise – in Stuttgart and spent 20% of his time in Germany.

18.23 Léger AG stated (at 18) that the right of establishment and the provision of services constituted two separate branches of Community law which are dealt with by two separate chapters of the Treaty and do not overlap. He pointed out that establishment means integration into a national economy, whereas the principle of freedom to provide services merely enables a self-employed person established in a member state in which he is integrated to exercise his activity in another member state. He added that establishment and the provision of services are mutually *exclusive*. He therefore distinguished the rules governing the two types of activity. Services are covered by the Lawyers' Services Directive which provides for lawyers to be able to practise under their original professional qualification, whereas the establishment of lawyers was still governed by Articles 52ff (now Article 43 EC) of the Treaty. This would now be different with the coming into force of the Lawyers' Establishment Directive (Directive 98/5) (see **18.21**). The conditions imposed on establishment are, of course, much stricter that those imposed on the mere provision of services. The two criteria to distinguish the two situations were: (a) the temporal criterion – services were 'episodic' or irregular; (b) the geographic criterion – an established person in a member state is principally dealing with the market of that state where he concentrates his activity, whereas the provider of a service would only exercise his activity in that place on an ancillary basis. In Case 33/74 *van Binsbergen v Bestuur van de Bedrijfsvereniging voor de Metaalnijverheid* (1974) (see **17.21**) the court had held that if a person provided services almost entirely in the other member state for the purposes of avoiding the professional rules of conduct which would apply to him if he were established there:

> ... such a situation may be subject to judicial control under the provisions of the chapter relating to the right of establishment and not of that on the provision of services.

The lawyer who establishes himself in a member state must conform to local rules as long as they are not discriminatory. The AG's conclusion was that the host member state could prohibit a lawyer providing services from opening *chambers* in that state. This does not mean, however, that a rule absolutely prohibiting the opening of an office in the host member state is acceptable.

The location of the lawyer's principal centre of activity and the duration and frequency of the services provided in the host member state are appropriate criteria for establishing a demarcation line between the activity of a lawyer which comes under the provision of services and that which comes under the heading of establishment.

The court agreed with the Advocate General that Gebhard was established. It reaffirmed the right of professionals to establish a second professional base (see *Klopp*). The exercise of the right and the conditions for its exercise depended on what activities the migrant intended to pursue.

18.24 It is now clear that providers of services can maintain an office or other 'local infrastructure' as long as they can show its necessity for the provision of their service. The rule in Case 205/84 *Commission v Germany* (1986) where the court indicated that a 'permanent presence' would of necessity indicate establishment, is thus modified. So the assumption that full compliance with local rules was necessary no longer applies. The court says that 'in principle' one should conform to local rules – but this raises the question of the scope of such rules. The court's emphasis on *Vlassopoulou* serves to facilitate access by migrants by applying the principle of mutual recognition. The Establishment Directive 98/5 now effectively allows home title establishment and sets out the conditions for doing so (see **18.21**).

18.25 The court ruled as follows:

- the temporary nature of the provision of services is to be determined in the light of its duration, periodicity and continuity;

- the provider of services may 'equip himself with the infrastructure necessary' for the performance of the service, ie he may open an office;

- however, if someone practises on a stable and continuous basis and holds himself out from an established professional base, this is establishment;

- the possibility of establishment and the conditions for the exercise of the right must be determined in the light of the activities he intends to pursue;

- if there are no rules, the person is free to establish himself and pursue his activity in the host member state. If there are rules and conditions, the national of another member state should in principle comply with them;

- national measures which constitute an obstacle to the exercise of the fundamental freedoms guaranteed by the Treaty must comply with the principles of non-discrimination and proportionality; they must be justified by imperative requirements in the general interest and be suitable for securing the attainment of the objective they pursue;

- member states must take account of the equivalence of diplomas, as had been done in Case 71/76 *Thieffry v Conseil de l'Ordre des Avocats à la Cour de Paris* (1977) (see **17.14**) and, if necessary, proceed to a comparison of the knowledge and qualifications required by their national rules and those of the person concerned. This is what the court did in Case C-340/89 *Vlassopoulou v Ministerium für Justiz, Bundes-und Europeaangelegenheiten Baden-Württemberg* (1991) and again in Case C-234/97 *Fernandez de Bobadilla v Museo Nacional del Prado* (1999) (see **17.19**).

Equal treatment in education

18.26 In the Treaty of Rome there was no reference to non-vocational education. Article 128 (now repealed) only referred to the drawing up of general principles for vocational training. The Maastricht TEU introduced a new Title on Social Policy, Education, Vocational Training and Youth. Chapter 3 of this Title sets out the provisions for education, vocational training and youth. Article 3(q) and Article 149 (ex Article 126) EC refer to the development of quality education and how this should be achieved. Educational programmes had been established earlier, such as Erasmus (Dec 87/327; (1987) OJ L 166/20), Commett (Dec 86/365, (1986) OJ L22/17 and 89/27, (1989) OJ L13/28), Lingua (Dec 89/489, (1989) OJ L239). The Tempus programme was developed to promote education concerning the European Union in Central and Eastern Europe (Dec 90/233), and Socrates and Leonardo da Vinci ((1994) OJ C244) are programmes designed to replace and supplement the others.

18.27 At the beginning, educational rights mainly arose from the connection of the recipient with a worker. The most extensive rights were enjoyed by children of workers. In order to achieve freedom of movement for workers and, therefore, allow them to bring their family, their children obviously must enjoy full educational rights. Educational rights for workers and for children and dependants of workers, are established by the secondary legislation. A third category of rights has been developed by the court for students in general. The Erasmus (now Socrates (1994) OJ C244)) programme on educational exchanges was introduced on the basis of Article 128 of the 1957 Treaty of Rome (now deleted) and of Article 235 (now Article 308 EC). In Case 242/87 *Commission v Council* (1989) the Commission contested the adoption of the programme on that legal basis, which implied unanimous voting, and maintained that Article 128 alone would have been sufficient. The court, however, rejected this as that article alone would not have been sufficient; some of the programme involved scientific research and, therefore, Article 235 (now Article 308 EC) needed to be used in addition.

Existing educational rights of children of workers and of workers themselves

18.28 The most extensive educational rights are enjoyed by children of workers. These rights are based on Article 12 of Regulation 1612/68 (discussed at **16.6**). Children residing in the same host member state as their parents enjoy the same educational rights as nationals of that state, including connected rights such as grants. Workers themselves have rights under Article 7(3) of Regulation 1612/68 which provides for equal access to vocational training.

18.29 In Case 39/86 *Lair v Universität Hannover* (1988) the court ruled that a person does not cease to be an immigrant Community worker just because (s)he gives up work in order to become a full-time student; nevertheless, in order to retain worker status there must be a connection between the course of study and the immigrant's previous career. The vocational training, therefore, must be relevant to the worker's previous occupation. This would not apply, however, if the worker became involuntarily unemployed and had to retrain in another occupational activity in order to obtain another job. Vocational training was narrowly defined by the court and had to be alternate to or be closely linked to an occupational activity, particularly during apprenticeship. This would, therefore, not cover universities. However, a maintenance grant, with which this case was concerned, could be considered a social advantage under Article 7(2) of the Directive and could, therefore, be claimed.

18.30 However, in Case 197/86 Brown v Secretary of State for Scotland (1988), Mr Brown was a student with dual British and French nationality who had gone to school in France. He was accepted at Cambridge for a course in electrical engineering. Prior to going to Cambridge he went to Scotland for eight months to gain previous work experience. The work placement was only available to students who had been offered a university place. The court had decided in Lair that Article 7(2) of Regulation 1612/68 could apply to maintenance grants. However, here it ruled that if the immigrant obtained the employment solely by virtue of the fact that he had already been offered a university place, he would not be entitled to the grant as a worker as the employment was merely incidental to the university course (see 16.15).

Educational rights for students

18.31 More restricted, but more widely available now are rights of free movement for students which include rights to equal treatment and thus the right not to have to pay additional fees. In Case 152/82 Forcheri v Belgium (1983) the wife of a Commission official wanted to attend a non-university course in Belgium. She was required to pay an enrolment fee, a 'minerval', which did not have to be paid by Belgian students. The ECJ based its arguments on Article 7 (now Article 12 EC) read in conjunction with Article 128 (now repealed) and ruled that Mrs Forcheri could not be discriminated against under the nationality rule. Case 293/83 Gravier v Liège (1985) concerned a French national whose parents lived in France and who came to Belgium to do a four-year course on strip cartoons. She was required to pay the 'minerval' payable by all non-nationals. This enrolment fee was not based on residence, since, although resident non-nationals were excused the fee, no Belgian citizen, wherever resident, was required to pay it. The legal issues were: did Article 7 EEC (now Article 12) have direct effect? The Treaty was concerned with an 'economic' Community. Does this cover education in general? The ECJ distinguished educational policy (what subjects are to be taught etc) which is outside the Treaty, from questions of access to the educational system. The general principles to be drawn up for vocational training under Article 128 facilitated free movement and conditions for access to such training fell, therefore, within the scope of the Treaty. The imposition of the 'minerval' in this context constituted discrimination on grounds of nationality. Vocational training was considered by the court to be any form of education which prepares for a particular profession or trade. Case 24/86 Blaizot v University of Liège (1988) extended the

438

concept further. Blaizot and the other plaintiffs were all French veterinary students who had paid the *minerval* in Belgium. The court considered that veterinary studies fell within the meaning of the term 'vocational training' even though they were pursued at a university. Neither the provisions of the Treaty nor its objectives gave any indication that the term should be restricted so as to exclude all university education. There were significant variations in the way university studies are treated in the different member states and, indeed in the studies available. An exclusion of university education from the definition of the term 'vocational training' would thus result in unequal application of the Treaty in different member states. University courses which prepare for a career rather than just increase general knowledge were covered, even if the acquisition of that knowledge is not required by law, regulation or administrative provision. The second part of the veterinary course was vocational, the first part was not, but as, according to the court, access to the second part presupposed the successful conclusion of the first, they therefore must be considered as a whole. However, the court refused to allow retrospective application of the judgment.

Different rights concerning tuition fees and maintenance grants

18.32 General rights for students thus include rights in respect of tuition fees, but the right to maintenance grants will depend on the individual's status as a worker. Directive 93/96/EEC of 29 October 1993 (OJ 1993, L 317/59) (which replaces Directive 90/366 of 28 June 1990 (OJ L 186/30) which was annulled because it had been adopted on the wrong legal base (see **16.2**) provides for a right of residence in any member state for any Community national who does not otherwise enjoy this right, during the period of enrolment in a vocational training course at 'any recognised educational establishment' (Article 1). This right also extends to the student's spouse and children.

18.33 The following cases constitute a major advancement in the approach of the court in the light of the above directive and the additions to the Maastricht Treaty.

Case C-184/99 *Rudy Grzelczyk v Centre public d'aide sociale d'Ottignies-Louvain-la-Neuve* (2001) concerned a French national who was studying in Belgium and had obtained entitlement to the 'minimex' (a minimum subsistence allowance paid by the Belgian State). Payment of that allowance to him was stopped because under Belgian legislation this grant was only paid to those nationals of other member states who came within the scope of Regulation (EEC) No 1612/68. This condition, however, did not apply to Belgian nationals and the Belgian tribunal therefore asked the court whether Articles 12 and 18 EC, relating to the principles of non-discrimination and of citizenship of the Union respectively, precluded such disparity in treatment.

The court found first of all that the treatment accorded to Mr Grzelczyk constituted discrimination solely on the ground of nationality because the only bar to grant of the minimex was the fact that he was not a Belgian national. The court then continued as follows:

> 'Within the sphere of application of the Treaty, such discrimination is, in principle, prohibited by Article 12 EC. In the present case, Article 12 EC must be read in conjunction with the provisions of the Treaty concerning citizenship of the Union in order to determine its sphere of application' (para 30)...'

In Case 197/86 *Brown* (1983) the court had said that maintenance grants fell outside the scope of the Treaty. However, the introduction into the Maastricht Treaty of the Citizenship articles, of a chapter devoted to education, and the adoption of Students' Residence Directive 93/96/EEC, meant that there is no longer anything

> 'to suggest that students who are citizens of the Union, when they move to another member state to study there, lose the rights which the Treaty confers on citizens of the Union' (para 35).

The court considered that the conditions in the Directive did allow a member state to withdraw the residence permit or not to renew it if the student had recourse to social assistance and no longer fulfilled the residence conditions. This should not, however, mean that this should be an automatic consequence. If one's resources diminish unexpectedly rapidly, as was the case for Mr Grzelczyk, he could not be discriminated against as long as he was resident in the country. Thus, the fundamental principle of citizenship seemed to determine the scope of his rights.

> 'Union citizenship is destined to be the fundamental status of nationals of the Member States, enabling those who find themselves in the same situation to enjoy the same treatment in law irrespective of their nationality, subject to such exceptions as are expressly provided for.' (at para 31)

18.34 The court's ruling in this case was soon followed by another, in which it reasserted its views. Case C-224/98 *D'Hoop v Office national de l'emploi* (2002) concerned a Belgian national who had completed her secondary education in France, returned to Belgium to study at university and then applied for grant of unemployment benefit known as 'tideover allowance' granted to young people who have just completed their studies and are seeking their first employment. This was refused as she did not fulfill the conditions imposed by the Belgian legislation adopted to comply with Community law, and which required all the education to have taken place in Belgium. The court referred to *Grzelczyk* and again to the Citizenship provisions. The inequality of treatment of certain Belgian nationals who had exercised their freedom to move to pursue education in another member state was 'contrary to the principles which underpin the status of citizen of the Union'. The condition at issue could only be justified on objective considerations independent of the nationality of the persons concerned and were proportionate to its legitimate aim. This was not the case here, with such a general and exclusive condition.

Citizenship of the European Union

18.35 Having considered various categories of economically related free movement of persons, what could Articles 17–22 (ex Articles 8, 8a–e) EC, added to the EC Treaty by the Maastricht Treaty on European Union, contribute further? Could one imagine the court attributing direct effect to Article 18, giving *all* Community citizens a right to move freely within the Community, including those who have no jobs and are no longer jobseekers, and those disadvantaged by a 'purely internal situation'. Indeed, Article 18 states that citizenship of the Union confers these rights subject to the limitations and conditions laid down in this Treaty and by the measures adopted to give it effect. These are the limitations and conditions contained in Article 39(3) and (4) and the equivalent Articles concerning establishment and services, as well as in Directive 64/221.

18.36 The case of Mr Vitale in *R v Secretary of State for the Home Department, ex p Vittorio Vitale and Do Amaral* (1996) was one of the first cases which explored citizenship. Mr Vitale, an Italian citizen, entered the UK in 1993 as a job seeker but never found work, having admitted he was looking for part-time work only in a very limited area of London and only between 10.00am and 4.00pm as a part-time chef or guitar player. He challenged the decision by the Home Office withdrawing his benefit and asking him to leave.

The case reached the Court of Appeal which first considered the question of the possible direct effect of Article 8a (now Article 18 EC).

The court reviewed the relevant Community legislation on rights of residence (Article 48 (now Article 39 EC), Regulation 1612/68 and Directive 68/360) and relevant case law (*R v Immigration Appeal Tribunal, ex p Antonissen* (1991)) (see **16.12** and Directive 90/364) which provides that the right of residence depends on the applicant having sufficient resources to avoid becoming a burden on the social assistance system of the host member state.

18.37 If Article 8a (now Article 18 EC) had intended to sweep aside the limitations upheld in *Antonissen* and to confer an unfettered right of residence, leaving in place only the limitations in Article 48(3) (now Article 39(3) EC) the court found that it would have been necessary to have made that explicit by amendment of Article 48. Equally, Article 8a could not be taken to have replaced the three directives referred to earlier (see **16.2**). These directives all contain the limitation on the right of residence that the visiting national should not become a burden on the social assistance system of the host member state. Nothing in the wording of Article 8a (now Article 18 EC), which makes the right of residence 'subject to the limitations and conditions laid down in this treaty' seemed to indicate anything else. On the other hand, under the directives, but not in the Treaty, there is the right for the national of another member state to be joined by his family and there are other provisions of Articles 48 to 62 (now Articles 39 to 51 EC) which would not be redundant even if the limitations on right of residence no longer existed.

18.38 The court dealt at length with the Council's treatment of the Students' Right of Residence Directive (Directive 90/366 EEC annulled and replaced by Directive 93/96 EEC). It would seem unlikely that the new Directive would have been enacted two days before the Maastricht TEU came into force on 1 November 1993 if its provisions had conflicted with those of the TEU. The implementation of the Directive would have become 'ultra vires' if it conflicted with an unqualified right under Article 8a. It may be true, of course, as counsel for the plaintiff suggested, that the draftsman of the Directive was not 'immediately concerned' with the provisions of the TEU. Is it believable that the right hand did not know what the left hand was doing?

The two Commission reports on the effects of the citizenship provisions were also cited (Com/93/702 final, 21 December 1993 and SEC(95) 731 final, 10 May 1995). The first report states that the general right of nationals of one member state to reside in another has now been placed on a new conceptual basis by enshrining it in the Treaty itself and is thus to be construed broadly. The second Commission report is more specific and states that the freedom of movement of union citizens must be seen in the context of the establishment of the 'area without internal frontiers....' which has not yet been completely achieved, in particular as regards persons. In the view of the Commission, therefore, in practice the Maastricht Treaty has not made any improvement on what went before.

The court attributed due weight to these statements while acknowledging that it was the European Court, not the Commission, which should be the arbiter of what the Treaty means.

18.39 The Court of Appeal was asked to refer the question of construction of Article 8a to the ECJ. Under the *CILFIT* rules (Case 283/81 *CILFIT v Ministry of Health* (1982); see **5.22**) the court was free to refer the matter even if the case was clear. However it did not, and the court dismissed the appeal.

There seem to be good arguments for reference. Admittedly, the Court of Appeal's analysis of Article 8a (now Article 18 EC) was supported by the views of the Commission and of most academic writers. A literal interpretation of the wording of the article may support the conclusion that it cannot have direct effect. It is expressly made dependent on further implementation in Article 8a(2) (now Article 18(2) EC). However, the European Court, applying a different style of interpretation, looking at Treaty articles, in the light of the objectives of the Treaty as a whole, taking into account the place of the article in the general scheme of the Treaty (see Case 43/75 *Defrenne v Sabena* (1976)) has found direct effect in other Treaty articles where this would not be obvious from the wording of the article.

18.40 Another reason why reference would have been desirable was that the cases of *Vitale* and *Do Amaral* had been brought as test cases and that the outcome would affect a large number of similar cases. Moreover, the Court of Appeal pointed out that the Article does create a general right to reside in another member state, presumably over and above that obtainable under Articles 39-49 and Directives 90/364/365/366. It is noteworthy that, although Mr Vitale was informed by the Home Office that he should make arrangements to leave the UK, it was also made clear that there was no intention to deport the plaintiff. It appears to be general Home Office policy not to deport EU citizens, even if their benefits are being withdrawn. Does this not amount to *de facto* acceptance of a general right of residence for all EU citizens? What would be the Home Office policy if Mr Vitale had committed an offence, however minor?

18.41 The arguments in the cases highlighed the growing awareness in the English courts of the increasing contrast between the EC as an 'economic' entity, and the political and constitutional developments represented by the EU, and if correct, they would have had dramatic and far-reaching consequences. The Court of Appeal emphasised, however, that it was the responsibility of Parliament, not the court, to decide on the consistency of EU developments with the national interests of the UK. There should be informed debate before such developments were embodied in a Treaty and 'the national interest as perceived by Parliament must continue to be protected by assent only to Treaty provisions which are clear and unequivocal'.

18.42 A similar problem arose again in *R v Westminster City Council, ex p Castelli; R v Westminster City Council, ex p Tristán-Garcia* (1996), although the circumstances of the plaintiffs were quite different. This case concerned an Italian and a Spanish national, who had entered the UK looking for work, but had contracted AIDS and could not find work, nor support themselves. The judge below had ruled they were not entitled to temporary accommodation as they were unlawfully present in the UK. The Court of Appeal decided that, simply by staying on after a limited leave to stay, the appellants had not become unlawfully resident in the UK. Indeed, in the case of Mr Tristán-Garcia, the Home Office had written to him stating as follows: 'The Secretary of State is...not satisfied that you are lawfully resident here under EC law' but it then added that no steps would be taken to enforce his departure from the UK.

18.43 This case does not mention EC law directly, nor does it refer to any Treaty articles. This judgment raises more questions than it solves. As in the *Vitale* case, the Home Office makes it quite clear that it will not deport an EU citizen who no longer seems to be covered by any of the free movement provisions of the Treaty. On the other hand, the benefit of temporary accommodation was granted in the instant case, but any benefits which Mr Vitale received were withdrawn. This case is not clear as the motives for allowing the plaintiffs to stay in the UK may well have been humanitarian. However, here again the Home Office made it clear that it will not deport an EU citizen who is no longer covered by any of the free movement provisions under the Treaty. This view does not affect a decision to withdraw any benefits. It appears the Home Office policy, if it is one, is a double-edged sword. If healthy, unemployed EU nationals who cannot support themselves are not forced to leave, but have any benefits which they would need to be housed, or to live, withdrawn, this could have unfortunate consequences. It is one thing to *allow* a person to stay, but another to *enable* a person to stay.

18.44 *Secretary of State for Social Security v Remilien; Chief Adjudication Officer v Wolke* (1998) concerned a French and a Dutch single mother. The mothers were deprived of income support in the UK and received the standard Home Office letter sent to jobless EU citizens claiming benefits who were deemed to have become 'a drain on the British taxpayer's money'. The High Court ruled that a person in that position did not become unlawfully present in the UK until (s)he is informed (s)he has to leave and steps are taken to carry out that decision. The Home Office letter alone did not make them unlawfully present. The Court of Appeal allowed the appeals by the Chief Adjudication Officer on the grounds that the letters from the Home Office constituted a requirement to leave the UK which ended their entitlement to income support. On appeal to the House of Lords the decision of the Court of Appeal was reversed. The House of Lords held (Lord Slynn of Hadley dissenting) that since the letters in question did not impose a legal obligation to leave, the appellants, therefore, had not been 'required to leave' so as to end their entitlement to income support.

18.45 Case C-85/96 *Martínez Sala v Freistaat Bayern* (1998) was the first case where the ECJ had to consider the meaning and scope of citizenship of the Union. This case concerned a reference under Article 234 by a German court which dealt with the situation of a Community national residing in Germany who was refused a social security benefit on the ground that she had no residence permit; she only had a certificate stating she had applied for one. The Court held that, compared with the treatment granted to nationals, her treatment entailed discrimination prohibited by Article 6 (now Article 12 EC). However, the German Government submitted, inter alia, that as the claimant was neither a worker nor a jobseeker she did not fall within the scope *ratione personae* of the Treaty so that she could not rely on Article 6. The court held, however, that even if the claimant did not have the status of a worker within the meaning of Community law, her situation was such that, as a national of a member state lawfully residing in the territory of another member state, she nonetheless came within the scope *ratione personae* of the Treaty provisions on European citizenship. Since Article 8(2) (now Article 17(2) EC) of the EC Treaty attached to the status of citizen of the Union the rights and duties laid down by the Treaty, such a citizen lawfully resident in the territory of the host member state could therefore rely on Article 6 of the Treaty in all situations which fell within the scope *ratione materiae* of Community law. The court saw no reason to consider, however, whether Article 18 has direct effect.

18.46 The court refused to follow Jacobs AG, however, in Case C-168/91 *Konstantinidis* (see **6.13**) where he suggested the citizenship rules might be used to constitute a fundamental right for Mr Konstantinidis to move freely anywhere in the Union and this would include the right to the correct transcription of his name. A similarly restrictive interpretation was given by the court in Case C-192/99 *R v Secretary of State for the Home Department, ex p Kaur* (2001), which involved an interpretation of the concept of nationality. The court ruled that a Declaration on the definition of the term 'nationals', annexed to the UK Treaty of Accession 1972, did not have the effect of depriving any person who did not satisfy the definition of any rights under Community law but rather had the consequence that such rights never arose in the first place for such a person (para 25 of the judgment).

18.47 Case C-274/96 *Bickel and Franz* (1998), although mainly concerned with the application of Article 12, mentioned Article 18 without discussing the issue further. The case arose under an Article 234 reference inquiring about the compatibility with Community law of national legislation intended to protect a linguistic minority in Italy. The question referred was whether it was compatible with Community law to refuse to allow rules on the equal use of German with Italian, in particular in criminal proceedings, to be applied in favour of German-speaking Community nationals travelling and staying in *Bolzano*. The court replied that Article 6 (now Article 12 EC) of the Treaty precludes any such refusal, since it would constitute discrimination, at least indirect discrimination, on the grounds of nationality, against recipients or potential recipients of services (see Case 186/87 *Cowan v Trésor Public* (1989) at **17.26**). The discrimination also did not appear to be justified with regard to the objective pursued, since there was no evidence that the objective of protecting the ethno-cultural minority would be undermined if the rules in issue were extended to cover German-speaking nationals of other member states exercising their right to freedom of movement.

18.48 In Case C-378/97 *Criminal Proceedings against Wijsenbeek* (1999) criminal proceedings had been instituted against Mr Wijsenbeek, a Dutch MEP, who had refused to show his passport and establish his nationality when requested to do so upon re-entering the Netherlands. The court asked upon an Article 234 reference whether Articles 7a and 8a (now

Articles 14 and 18 EC) had direct effect. The ECJ did not answer, but simply stated that

> even if, under Article 7a or 8a of the Treaty, nationals have the unconditional right to move freely within the territory of the member states, the member states retain the right to carry out identity checks at the internal frontiers of the Community ...

Penalties could be imposed as long as they were proportionate and comparable to those imposed for similar domestic offences.

18.49 Recent cases, such as *Grzelczyk, D'Hoop* (see **18.33**) and, in particular, *Baumbast* have developed the concept of citizenship very much further and, in *Baumbast*, affirmed that Article 18 (1) is capable of having direct effect. Case C-413/99 *Baumbast, R v Secretary of State for the Home Department* (2002) concerned Mr Baumbast, a German national resident in the UK, married a Colombian who had a daughter with Colombian nationality. They then had another daughter with dual German and Colombian nationality. Mr Baumbast was first employed in the UK and then ran his own company. He had now left. Mr and Mrs Baumbast owned a house in the UK, their children attended school there and did not receive any social security benefits. Mrs Baumbast applied for indefinite leave to remain for herself and her family in October 1995. This was refused by the Secretary of State who then refused to renew Mr and Mrs Baumbast's resident permits.

18.50 R was a United States citizen married to a French national who had moved to the UK to work. R was granted leave to remain in the UK until October 1995 as the spouse of a migrant worker. They had two children with dual French and United States nationality. The couple divorced and R continued to live in the UK. The father continued to live and work in the UK. The divorce settlement left the children in the care of their mother who bought a house and started an interior design business in the UK. She subsequently married a UK national. R applied in 1995 for indefinite leave to remain in the UK for herself and her daughters. This was granted for her daughters as the children of a migrant worker, but Mrs R's application was refused.

The ECJ held that the children of Mr and Mrs Baumbast had the right to continue their education in the UK. Article 12 of Regulation 1612/68 required the best possible conditions for the integration of the migrant worker's family and preventing children from completing their education in the host state would be a disincentive to the migrant worker to exercise his rights of free movement and would therefore 'create an obstacle to the effective exercise of the freedom guaranteed by the Treaty'. The nationality of the children of the migrant worker was immaterial and the rights of children of the 'worker and his spouse' in Regulation 1612/68 must be taken to include children of the spouse who was not an EU national.

Therefore the court held, in regard to the children:

> 'Children of a citizen of the European Union who have installed themselves in a member state during the exercise by their parent of rights of residence as a migrant worker in that member state are entitled to reside there in order to attend general educational courses there, pursuant to Article 12 of Regulation 1612/68.
>
> The fact that the parents of the children concerned have meanwhile divorced, the fact that only one parent is a citizen of the Union and that parent has ceased to be a migrant worker in the host member state and the fact that the children are not themselves citizens of the Union are irrelevant in this regard'.

18.51 The court then considered the situations of the mothers who were the primary carers for the children, who had been refused leave to remain in the UK because one was now divorced from the migrant worker and the other was married to an EU national who was no longer a migrant worker.

The court first referred to the rights of the children, as the removal of their parents who were their primary carers during the period of their education would deprive them of the right to continue that education in the host state. Regulation 1612/68:

> 'must be interpreted in the light of the requirement of respect for family life laid down in Article 8 of the European Convention. That requirement is one of the fundamental rights which, according to settled case-law, are recognised by Community law.
>
> The right conferred by Article 12 of Regulation No 1612/68 on the child of a migrant worker to pursue, under the best possible conditions, his education in the host member state necessarily implies that that child has the right to be accompanied by the person who is his primary carer and, accordingly, that that person is able to reside with him in that member state during his studies. To refuse to grant permission to remain to a parent who is the primary carer of the child exercising his right to pursue his studies in the host member state infringes that right' [paras 72 and 73].

In answer to the second question the court concluded that:

' Where children have the right to reside in a host member state in order to attend general educational courses pursuant to Article 12 of Regulation No 1612/68, that provision must be interpreted as entitling the parent who is the primary carer of those children, irrespective of his nationality, to reside with them in order to facilitate the exercise of that right notwithstanding the fact that the parents have meanwhile divorced or that the parent who has the status of citizen of the European Union has ceased to be a migrant worker in the host member state'.

18.52 The final question concerned Mr Baumbast who was no longer a migrant worker. The court referred to his right as a citizen under Article 18 EC to reside in another member state. This right is subject to the limitations and conditions laid down in the Treaty and secondary legislation. The conditions that were relevant in Mr Baumbast's case were those under Article 1 of Directive 90/364, which requires that EU nationals wishing to live in another member state must have sufficient resources to avoid being a burden on the social assistance system and must be covered by sickness insurance. Mr Baumbast and his family had not used the social assistance system of the UK. They had medical insurance in Germany where they received medical treatment. The objection of the UK authorities was that Mr Baumbast's medical insurance would not cover emergency treatment received in the UK.

The conditions in the Directive were intended to prevent beneficiaries of the right of residence becoming an 'unreasonable' burden on the public finances of the host member state. But such limitations and condition must be applied in accordance with the principle of proportionality. The court therefore held that

'To refuse to allow Mr Baumbast to exercise the right of residence which is conferred on him by Article 18(1) EC by virtue of the application of the provisions of Directive 90/364 on the ground that his sickness insurance does not cover the emergency treatment given in the host member state would amount to a disproportionate interference with the exercise of that right' (para 93)....

18.53 The answer to the third question was therefore given as follows:

'A citizen of the European Union who no longer enjoys a right of residence as a migrant worker in the host member state can, as a citizen of the Union, enjoy there a right of residence *by direct application of Article 18(1) EC*. The exercise of that right is subject to the limitations and conditions referred to in that provision, but the competent authorities and, where necessary, the national courts must ensure that those limitations and conditions are applied in compliance with the general principles of Community law and, in particular, the principle of proportionality'. (my italics)

The case of *Sala* heralded a change compared to the previous case law, as was borne out in the later cases described above. The development of the case law has now been followed by a proposed directive (see below at **18.55**).

18.54 The citizenship articles have not yet had the same effect in regard to cases of 'internal exile' which the ECJ outlawed in the case of *Rutili*. In that case the court said that Mr Rutili could not be prevented from moving freely anywhere in France, but he was relying on his Community right to free movement as an Italian citizen in another member state. This right could previously not be claimed by Community citizens in respect of their own state, but it is arguable that there could now be such a right in cases such as those of *Adams* which concerned restrictions on the free movement of a UK citizen within the United Kingdom. In *R v Secretary of State for the Home Department, ex p Adams* (1995) an exclusion order had been made against Mr Adams under the Prevention of Terrorism (Temporary Provisions) Act 1989 prohibiting his entry into the UK for three years because of his alleged terrorist activities in Northern Ireland. He raised a number of points before the English court, inter alia, that Article 8a (now Article 18 EC) had direct effect and he could, therefore, rely on it before a national court, and that the fact that this was a matter internal to the UK did not take away his Community right to free movement under Article 8a. The Court of Appeal referred these questions to the ECJ, but pointed out that it would be 'astonishing' if there was no national security derogation under Article 8a(1). However, the *Adams* case was taken off the register of the ECJ after political circumstances had changed and Mr Adams's exclusion order had been lifted. It may be at least arguable that in cases such as *Saunders* and *Adams* the citizenship provisions might be considered by the ECJ to have an impact, whereas this would probably not be the case in *Morson and Jhanjan* (see **18.7**).

18.55 A proposed Directive on the Right of Citizens of the Union and their Family Members to Move and Reside Freely within the Territory of the Member States (COM/2003/0199 final) aims at replacing the mass of existing legislation discussed above with a single piece of legislation.

Articles 10 and 11 of Regulation 1612/68, and Directives 64/221EEC, 68/360EEC, 72/194EEC, 75/34EEC, 75/35EEC, 90/364EEC, 90/365EEC and 93/96 EEC are to be replaced by much simplified legislation which takes a new approach in view of the development of European citizenship and of the progress made in the case law. In particular, it specifically takes into account the situation of family members of Union citizens. The date of implementation is 1 July 2005.

Further reading

Weatherill, Case Note on *Bosman*, [1996] 33 CMLRev 991.

Case note by Julian Lonbay on Case C-55/94 *Reinhard Gebhard v Consiglio dell'ordine degli Avvocati e Procuratori di Milano*, [1996] 33 CMLRev 1073.

O'Keeffe, 'Practical difficulties in the Application of Article 48 of the EEC Treaty', [1982] 19 CMLRev 35.

D O'Keeffe and M Horspool, 'European Citizenship and the Free Movement of Persons', The Irish Jurist, (1996), Round Hall, Sweet & Maxwell.

S van den Bogaert, 'Not a wholly internal situation', (2000) ELRev 554

P Cabral, Case C-168/98 *Grand Duchy of Luxembourg v European Parliament and Council of the European Union* (2002) 39 CMLRev 129

Doppelhammer, 'Expulsion: a test case for European Citizenship?', [1999] ELRev 621.

Siofra O'Leary, The Free Movement of Persons and Services, in Craig and de Burca (eds) *The Evolution of EU Law* (1999) OUP.

Catherine Barnard, EC 'Social' Policy, in Craig and de Burca (eds) *The Evolution of EU Law* (1999) OUP.

Jo Shaw, From the Margins to the Centre: Education and Training Law and Policy, in Craig and de Burca (eds) *The Evolution of EU Law* (1999) OUP.

Self-test questions

1. 'Free movement of persons means that any citizen of an EC member state should have the right to travel anywhere in the European Union and live there on equal terms with nationals.' To what extent does this reflect the current position in EC Law?

2. When can a national of a member state rely on the provisions of the EC Treaty on free movement of persons?

3. To what extent does European Community law guarantee a national of an EC member state the right to work in any other EC country?

4. The restriction of the free movement of persons to economic activities is an anachronism and will prevent full integration of the Common Market. Explain, illustrate and criticise.

CHAPTER NINETEEN

Equal Treatment and Sex Discrimination

SUMMARY

- The principle of non-discrimination
- Article 141 (ex Article 119) EC
- What constitutes 'pay'
- Temporal effect of Article 141
- Time limits
- Burden of proof
- Limitations to the equality principle
- The Directives
- Pensions
- Direct and indirect discrimination
- Justification

Introduction

19.1 The principle of non-discrimination is one of the major elements of Community law. As we have seen, discrimination as to nationality is prohibited under Article 12 (ex Article 6) EC, one of the fundamental articles of the Treaty. In the area of free movement of goods, discrimination in favour of domestic products is outlawed by several treaty articles, discriminatory taxation under Articles 23–25 (ex Articles 9–12) EC and 95 (ex Article 90) EC, other forms under Articles 28ff (ex Article 30) EC.

19.2 Other forms of discrimination were not previously addressed by the Treaty, such as discrimination as to race, age, disability, religion and sexual orientation. However, gradually, equality and non-discrimination have achieved the status of general principles of Community law. This has now found its confirmation in the Treaty of Amsterdam which added a new Article 13 to the EC Treaty, providing:

> Without prejudice to the other provisions of this Treaty and within the limits of the powers conferred by it upon the Community, the Council, acting unanimously on a proposal from the Commission and after consulting the European Parliament, may take appropriate action to combat discrimination based on sex, racial or ethnic origin, religion or belief, disability, age or sexual orientation.

This is only an enabling clause, surrounded by all the safeguards limiting Community competence, and providing for the consultation procedure which requires unanimity voting in the Council. It is doubtful if it could have direct effect as it does not seem to fulfil the criteria for direct effect as laid down by the Court (see Chapter 7). Nevertheless, it was a clear indication that the principle of non-discrimination was being confirmed as a general principle of Community law, to cover an extensive array of discrimination, going far beyond the specific forms of economic-based discrimination originally contained in the Treaty.

19.3 Even before the Treaty of Amsterdam came into force Case C-249/96 *Grant v South West Trains* (1998) was referred to the ECJ. It concerned gender discrimination, and some arguments advanced by the plaintiffs referred to the new Article 13. The Court, however, rejected the complaint, based on the state of Community law at the time, which did not provide a legal base to outlaw such discrimination. This appeared to draw back from the Court's ruling in Case C-13/94 *P v S and Cornwall County Council* (1996) where the Court had given a wide interpretation of the principle of sex discrimination in a case concerning transsexuals to include gender discrimination and seemed to point to a general principle of equality. This view was reasserted in Case C-122/99P *D v Council* (2001).

A Swedish employee of the Council was in a same sex relationship which was recognised as a registered partnership in Sweden. D wanted to claim an EU staff household allowance which is granted to employees who are married. The ECJ rejected arguments based on equal treatment, discrimination on the grounds of sex and respect for family life based on Article 8 of the ECHR. The Court stated it could not disregard the views prevailing within the Community as a whole, where same sex partnerships were not considered equivalent to marriage.

19.4 The Commission was quick to propose a number of directives based on Article 13. The first directive to be adopted was Council Directive 2000/43/EC of 29 June 2000 implementing the principle of equal treatment between persons irrespective of racial or ethnic origin. This was followed by Council Directive 2000/78/EC of 27 November 2000 establishing a general framework for equal treatment in employment and occupation. This directive deals with all the remaining forms of discrimination listed under Article 13. It refers to the fundamental rights principles contained in Article 6 of the Treaty on European Union, to the European Human Rights Convention (ECHR) and to general principles which result from 'the constitutional traditions common to the member states'. A number of United Nations instruments are also referred to. It provides that 'the principle of equal treatment' means that 'there shall be no direct or indirect discrimination whatsoever' on the grounds of religion or belief, disability, age or sexual orientation. Indirect discrimination may be objectively justified by a legitimate aim and if it is proportionate. There are a number of exceptions in some fields, eg for the armed forces in respect of age and disability, and in respect of state social security schemes. The Directive also provides that different treatment may not constitute discrimination if by the nature of the particular occupation a certain characteristic is a genuine and determining occupational requirement, so long as the objective is legitimate and the requirement is proportionate (Article 4(1)). In respect of age, difference in treatment may be justified by legitimate aims such as employment policy and labour market and vocational training objectives, so long as the means of achieving such aims are appropriate and necessary. (Article 5). The Directive applies to both private and public sectors. The implementation date is December 2003, and member states then have an additional three-year period to implement the provisions on age and disability. Thus, from the relatively narrow bases of non-discrimination as to nationality (Article 12 (ex Article 6) EC) and the principle of equal pay for men and women (Article 141 (ex Article 119) EC) a far more fundamental and general principle of non-discrimination in the law of the European Union is now clearly established.

In this chapter we shall look in particular at sex discrimination, which, as it developed both in respect of abundant case law and of legislation, has led to the development of the far more general principle of equal treatment.

19.5 Sex discrimination is not specifically contained in the Treaty as a general principle. Article 141 (ex Article 119) EC simply provides that men and women should receive equal pay, thus putting the principle on

455

a purely economic basis. The initial need for sex discrimination legislation was emphasised by France, with relatively advanced social legislation, which feared that through 'social dumping' competition in the Community would be distorted, putting them at a competitive disadvantage. The social aim of the provision may be inferred from the preamble to the Treaty of Rome, which states as an essential objective the improvement of living and working conditions of the peoples of the Community. This combination of economic and social objectives was confirmed by the ECJ in Case 43/75 *Defrenne v Sabena (No 2)* (1976), where it said (at para 12):

> This double aim which is at once economic and social shows that the principle of Equal Pay forms part of the foundations of the Community.

19.6 It is clear that the Court considered the article to be of fundamental importance from the beginning. Furthermore, the expansive interpretation given by the Court of the article, the concept of 'pay' and of the directives adopted pursuant to the article, have led to a far greater development of Community sex discrimination law than was originally anticipated.

19.7 With the development of the case law of the ECJ, giving a wide interpretation, and the addition of much secondary legislation, the Article was extended far beyond its original wording and the Treaty of Amsterdam has now added two more sub-paragraphs, taking account of these developments, but also going beyond them, as in the case of positive discrimination, which read as follows:

> 141(3): The Council...(under the co-decision procedure in Article 251)...shall adopt measures to ensure the application of the principle of equal opportunities and equal treatment of men and women in matters of employment and occupation, including the principle of equal pay for equal work or work of equal value.

> 141(4): Member states are not prevented from taking measures of positive discrimination of the under-represented sex to pursue a vocational activity or to prevent or compensate for disadvantages in professional careers.

19.8 At Amsterdam, the UK 'opt-out' from the Protocol on Social Policy annexed to the Maastricht Treaty had been lifted. This Protocol provided for the conclusion of an Agreement on social policy and the implementation of the 1989 Community Charter on the Fundamental Social Rights of Workers, which (in para 16 concerning equal treatment for men and women) provides that

> action should be intensified to ensure the implementation of the principle of equality for men and women as regards, in particular, access to employment, remuneration, working conditions, social protection, education, vocational training and career development.

The Protocol has now become part of the Treaty in Articles 137–140 and any directives adopted under the Social Protocol as well as new proposals apply to all fifteen member states.

19.9 The addition in Amsterdam to the 'Principles' in Part One of the EC Treaty of the promotion of equality between men and women in Article 2 and a paragraph in Article 3(2) which reads:

> In all the activities referred to in this Article, the Community shall aim to eliminate inequalities, and to promote equality, between men and women' shows that there is now little doubt that the principle of equal treatment between men and women has now been elevated to a general principle of Community law.

The extent of the principle is shown in Council Directive 96/34/EC on Parental Leave (1996 OJ L 145/9) extended to the UK by Directive 97/75 (OJ 1998 L 10/24) after Amsterdam), based on the Social Policy Agreement. This directive extends the principle of equal treatment of men and women to the possibility of reconciling occupational and family obligations. It provides for an individual and non-transferable right for men and women to parental leave on the grounds of birth or adoption of a child for at least three months until a given age up to the age of eight, to be defined by the member states.

What constitutes 'pay'?

19.10 Without resorting to Directive 75/117, the Equal Pay Directive, the court has interpreted 'pay' in Article 141 (ex Article 119) EC to include 'any consideration, whether in cash or in kind, provided by an employer to employees or to retired employees'. In Case 12/81 *Garland v British Rail Engineering Ltd* (1982) the employer granted a benefit in the form of a grant of special travel facilities only to male employees after retirement. This benefit was granted *independently* of any contractual entitlement. The court stated that the legal nature of the benefit was not important for the purpose of Article 119 (now Article 141 EC), provided it was granted *in respect of the applicant's employment*. Therefore, female employees should also receive the grant.

19.11 The definition does not include state pensions, as was made clear in Case 80/70 *Defrenne v Belgium (I)* (1971), the first *Defrenne* case, which Ms Defrenne lost when she claimed that Belgian state social security benefits should come within the definition of 'pay' in Article 141 EC. Directive 79/7 expressly excludes statutory pensions from its provisions. However, occupational pensions are included, ie such pensions which are part of a private social security scheme, even if those benefits are not part of a normal employment contract, but are provided gratuitously by the employer. In Case 170/84 *Bilka-Kaufhaus v Weber von Hartz* (1986) part-time employees, who were mainly female, could only join such a scheme if they had worked for a total of 15 out of 20 years. This scheme was provided by the employer in addition to the existing social security schemes. It was contractual and not statutory in origin. The Court held that this was a benefit which represented consideration paid by the employer to the employee in respect of employment and thus constituted pay. It was discriminatory as a far larger proportion of women than men were part-time employees.

Statutory schemes are in the field of welfare provision, which is not within EC competence. In the past 20 years, more and more moves have been made, particularly in the UK but gradually also in other EU countries, to induce employees to 'contract out' of state pensions in favour of private schemes which fall within the scope of the definition of pay.

What is equal pay for equal work?

19.12 What does equal work mean? Does it cover direct *and* indirect discrimination?

- Direct discrimination would exist in cases where a man would receive more pay than a woman for the reason that she was a woman. The same could apply in reverse.

- Indirect discrimination would occur when part-time workers are paid less than full-time workers, and the part-time workers are predominantly female while the full-time workers are not.

In *Defrenne (No 2)* (see **19.5**), Article 141 EC was held by the Court to be directly effective, but only in respect of *direct* discrimination. The circumstances in which discrimination occurred had to be easily discernible. Since then, the court has moved towards finding that indirect discrimination, too, is covered by Article 141. In Case 170/84 *Bilka-Kaufhaus v Weber von Hartz* (1986) a German department store had an occupational pension scheme which part-time, mainly female, employees could only join if they had worked for a total of 15 out of 20 years. Weber argued that women were more likely to take part-time jobs as they had to look after their families. Bilka responded that the justification for the difference in treatment was that part-time workers were less useful to the store; they were unlikely for example to work evenings or Saturdays.

The Court held that the difference in treatment did constitute indirect discrimination, but provided a three-fold test for measures which might justify such discriminatory measures:

- the measure corresponds to a real need of the enterprise, which might be economic;

- the measure is *appropriate*, ie suitable for attaining the objective pursued by the enterprise; and

- the measure is *necessary*.

These factors together constitute a test of proportionality. The Court found in this case that the test was satisfied and that the discrimination which had occurred was objectively justified on economic grounds.

19.13 This does not necessarily mean that objectively justified grounds other than economic ones would be excluded, such as administrative efficiency, in an enterprise not engaged in commerce or business (see *Rainey v Greater Glasgow Health Board* (1987)).

19.14 *Bilka* confirmed the ECJ judgment in Case 96/80 *Jenkins v Kingsgate (Clothing Production) Ltd* (1981). Kingsgate employed 35 men and 54 women full-time and five women and one man part-time (30 hours a week). The reference from the EAT asked whether the principle of equal pay contained in Article 141 EC and in Directive 75/117 requires that pay for work at time rates shall be the same *irrespective* of the number of hours worked each week. Was there not some commercial benefit for the employer to encourage workers to work the maximum possible number of hours and therefore was it not right to pay a higher rate to such workers? The Court stated that a difference in pay between full-time and part-time workers did not amount to discrimination unless it is merely an indirect way of reducing part-time workers' pay on the ground that the group is composed exclusively or predominantly of women. The onus is on the employer to show the necessity for such a difference in pay.

19.15 In the EOC case (*Equal Opportunities Commission v Secretary of State for Employment* (1994)) the House of Lords considered the proof that was required before objective justification of indirect discrimination was accepted. The UK statute, the Employment Protection (Consolidation) Act 1978, only gave protection to workers in respect of unfair dismissal and redundancy payments if they worked for between 8 and 16 hours for more than five years. Those working more than 16 hours a week would qualify after two years.

The Equal Opportunities Commission brought an action on the grounds that these provisions were contrary to Article 141 EC, and Directives 75/117 and 76/207. The UK government considered that it could objectively justify the discrimination. To impose such burdens on employers would mean that fewer part-timers would be employed. The House of Lords held that the burden of proof was on the government objectively to justify discrimination and this burden had not been discharged. The government, however, had not shown any evidence that the UK had a significantly higher number of part-time workers than other member states. The provisions of the 1978 Act were, therefore, contrary to EC law. Subsequent to this case, the law was changed to deal with the point. The House of Lords' decision was very 'European' and far-reaching. What if the situation with regard to part-timers changed and the UK *did* have more part-timers than other member states? With how many member states would the comparison be relevant? How far back would the government have to look in its statistics?

In Case C-127/92 *Enderby v Frenchay Health Authority and Secretary of State for Health* (1993) the court stated:

> There is a prima facie case of sex discrimination where valid statistics disclose an appreciable difference in pay between two jobs of equal value, one of which is carried out almost exclusively by women and the other predominantly by men. It is for the national court to assess whether the statistics appear to be significant in that they cover enough individuals and do not illustrate purely fortuitous or short-term phenomena.

19.16 Statistics again came to the fore in Case C-167/97 *R v Secretary of State for Employment, ex p Seymour-Smith and Perez* (1999). The case concerned the difference in entitlement to protection against unfair dismissal between full and part-time workers in the UK. The Court held that where a measure adopted by a member state is not based directly on sex, it is necessary to establish that its disparate effect as between men and women differs to such a degree as to amount to discrimination. The national court must verify whether the statistics available indicate that a considerably smaller percentage of women than men is able to fulfil the requirement imposed by the measure. Even if the statistics show a lesser, but persistent and relatively constant, disparity over a long period, this may amount to indirect discrimination. If that is the case, there is in principle indirect sex discrimination which may be justified by objective factors. The onus is on the member state to show that the rule reflects a legitimate aim of its social policy, that that aim is unrelated to any discrimination based on sex, and that it could reasonably consider that the means chosen were suitable for attaining that aim.

In Case C-218/98 *Abdoulaye v Régie Nationale des Usines Renault* (1999) the Court said that it may also be that male and female workers are in different situations, so that the difference in treatment does not constitute discrimination. The Court thus held that the principle of equal pay does not preclude the making of a lump-sum payment exclusively to female workers who take maternity leave where that payment is designed to offset the occupational disadvantages which arise for those workers as a result of their being away from work.

19.17 Similarly, where national legislation grants a termination payment to workers who end their employment relationship prematurely in order to take care of their children owing to a lack of child-care facilities for them, Community law does not preclude that payment being lower than that received, for the same actual period of employment, by workers who give notice of resignation for an important reason related to working conditions in the undertaking or to the employer's conduct. Those payments cannot be compared with one another since the situations covered are different in substance and origin (Case C-249/97 *Gruber v Silhouette International Schmied* (1999)).

19.18 Following similar lines, even if there is a difference in pay between male and female workers, there is no discrimination on grounds of sex if those two categories of workers do not carry out the same work. In this connection, the Court held that work is not the same where the same activities are performed over a considerable length of time by persons the basis of whose qualification to exercise their profession is different (Case C-309/97 *Angestelltenbetriebsrat der Wiener Gebietskranken-kasse v Wiener Gebietskrankenkasse* (1999)).

19.19 The scope of permissible comparisons has been restricted by the Court in Case C-320/00 *Lawrence v Regent Office Care* (2002), the case of the 'dinner ladies'. Female school catering and cleaning staff had changed employers because the local authority they worked for had transferred their jobs to a private company, which paid them less. This meant that they were paid less than their male comparators who were still working for the local authority and whose work had been rated by a job evaluation study to be of equal value. In fact, they had won their case at the time claiming equal pay with them. The Court said that Article 141 EC did not limit its applicability to employees working for the same employer. Nevertheless, in the present case there was no single body which was responsible for the inequality and thus nobody could bring about equal treatment. It was, therefore, not possible to make a proper comparison and Article 141(1) did not apply. The AG's Opinion (April 2003) in Case C-256/01 *Allonby v Acrrington & Rossendale College* repeated the argument that where the work could not be attributed to a single source Article 141 could not apply. In this case, someone was working for the same person, but now in a self-employed capacity via an intermediary company.

Does Article 141 have direct effect?

19.20 In *Defrenne (No 2)* (see **19.5**) Ms Defrenne, a retired flight attendant, sued the Belgian airline Sabena for damages to compensate her for lower pay she had received during her period of employment than was paid to comparable male flight attendants. She based her claim on Article 141 (ex Article 119) EC as there was no provision in Belgian law which could help her.

The Court held that the article was sufficiently precise and unconditional, at least in part, that it could be given direct effect in national courts. It limited this effect to 'direct and overt discrimination which may be identified solely with the aid of criteria based on equal work and equal pay'. It drew a distinction, however, between this and, at para 18:

> ...indirect and disguised discrimination which can only be identified by reference to the more explicit implementing provisions of a Community or national character.

See also Case 129/79 *Macarthys v Smith* (1979).

19.21 Subsequently the ECJ ruled in Case 69/80 *Worringham and Humphreys v Lloyds Bank* (1981) that Article 141 had direct effect in respect of 'all forms of discrimination which may be identified solely with the aid of the criteria of equal work and equal pay'. This included claims based on indirect discrimination and it was confirmed by the Court on several subsequent occasions that such claims could have direct effect (see Case 170/84 *Bilka-Kaufhaus v Weber von Hartz* (1986)). In Case C-33/89 *Kowalska v Freie und Hansestadt Hamburg* (1990) direct effect was found to apply to collective agreements, as was the case in Case C-184/89 *Nimz* (1991).

19.22 Article 141 would now seem to have direct effect in most circumstances, although perhaps the situation is still doubtful in cases of equal pay for equal value (see Case 157/86 *Murphy v Bord Telecom Eireann* (1988)). Furthermore, the direct effect is available horizontally, ie against a private employer such as Sabena. Some Treaty articles, such as Article 28 (ex Article 30) EC have been held by the Court not to have horizontal direct effect, ie as against a private employer.

Temporal effect of Article 141

19.23 In *Defrenne (No 2)* the Court held that the direct effect of Article 119 (now Article 141 EC) could not be relied upon in order to support claims in respect of pay periods prior to the date of the judgment (8 April 1976). The only exception applied to workers who had already instituted a claim at that time. In Case C-262/88 *Barber v Guardian Royal Exchange* (1990) the Court stipulated that the direct effect of Article 141 could not be relied upon in order to claim entitlement to a pension with effect from a date prior to that of the judgment in this case (17 May 1990) except in the case of those who have before that date instituted legal proceedings or raised an equivalent claim under the applicable national law.

Time limits

19.24 A directive can only have direct effect after the expiry of the time-limit for implementation (see Case 148/78 *Pubblico Ministero v Tullio Ratti* (1979) and Chapter 7). In Case C-208/90 *Emmott v Minister for Social Welfare* (1991) the Court stated that a defaulting member state may not rely on an individual's delay in initiating proceedings against it in order

463

to protect rights conferred upon him by the directive, and that national time cannot begin to run before the time such proceedings are started. However, this ruling was qualified in Case C-338/91 *Steenhorst-Neerings v Bestuur van de Bedrijfsvereniging voor Detailhandel, Ambachten en Huisvrouwen* (1993). Mrs Steenhorst-Neerings had claimed sex discrimination in respect of disability benefits payable to her. A national rule limited the retroactive effect of such a claim to 12 months. The Court drew a distinction between this rule and the time limit in *Emmott*. This rule served simply to ensure sound administration, in that it enabled a date prior to that of the judgment in this case (17 May 1990) to be excluded, except in the case of those who had before that date instituted legal proceedings or raised an equivalent claim under the applicable authorities to ascertain the degree of disability and whether conditions of eligibility were satisfied.

19.25 A distinction with *Emmott* was also made in Case C-410/92 *Johnson v Chief Adjudication Officer (No 2)* (1994), where the Court confirmed the distinction made in *Steenhorst-Neerings* between a time bar which had the result of depriving the applicant of any opportunity whatever to rely on her right to equal treatment under the directive, which was the case in *Emmott*, and a rule which 'merely limited to one year the retroactive effect of claims for benefits for incapacity for work' (at para 35). In Case C-188/95 *Fantask A/S v Industrieministeriet (Erhvervsministeriet)* (1998) (see **7.9**), the Court confirmed that *Emmott* was justified by the special circumstances of the case, where the time limit meant that the applicant was deprived of any opportunity to rely on her right to equal treatment under a Community directive, but that Community law did not prevent a member state which has not properly transposed a directive from relying on a national limitation period which was not less favourable than a Community one and made the exercise of Community law neither virtually impossible nor excessively difficult. Further confirmation came in Case C-78/98 *Preston and Fletcher* (2000). A six month time limit on the bringing of a claim for retroactive membership of an occupational pension scheme for a part-time worker was an application of the principle of legal certainty and complied with the principle of effectiveness as long as the national procedural rule did not make it impossible or excessively difficult to exercise the Community right. However, the principle of effectiveness would preclude a procedural rule which restricted periods of service to be taken into account up to two years prior to the date of claim (see further Chapter 9 on national procedural rules). Thus, it is probably right to say that *Emmott* must be seen as a one-off case.

Burden of proof

19.26 In Case 109/88 *Handels- og Kontorfunktionaerernes Forbund i Danmark v Dansk Arbejdsgiverforening (acting for Danfoss)* (1989) the court said that the Equal Pay Directive had to be interpreted as meaning that when a pay system lacks transparency this shifts the burden of proof on to the employer to show that there is no discrimination. Adjustments to the national rules relating to the burden of proof had to be made in such circumstances in order to ensure the effective application of the principle of equal pay.

In Case C-400/93 *Specialarbejderforbundet i Danmark v Dansk Industri, acting for Royal Copenhagen A/S* (1995) the point about transparency and the burden of proof was made again:

> The mere finding that in a piecework pay scheme the average pay of a group of workers consisting predominantly of women is appreciably lower than the average pay of a group consisting predominantly of men does not suffice to establish discrimination as the difference may be due to differences in individual output.

However, the burden of proof was on the employer when such a scheme totally lacked transparency.

Council Directive 97/80 EC of 15 December 1997 on the burden of proof in cases of discrimination based on sex (OJ L 014, 20/01/1998 p 6–8) amended by Council Directive 98/52 EC of 13 July 1998 (OJ L 205, 22/07/1998, p 66) extending the Directive to the UK after Amsterdam, now provides that when a plaintiff has established discrimination, it shall be for the respondent to prove that there has been no breach of the equal treatment principle. The implementation date of this directive was 1 January 2001. The same conditions for reversal of the burden of proof apply to the general framework discrimination Directive 2000/78/EC of 27 November 2000 (see **19.4**) and to subsequent directives.

Limitations to the equality principle

19.27 In Case C-450/93 *Kalanke v Freie Hansestadt Bremen* (1995) the Court indicated a limit to the interpretation of the equality principle. National rules which guarantee women absolute and unconditional priority for appointment and promotion go beyond promoting equal opportunities and overstep the limits of the exception to the principle of equal treatment in Article 2(4) of the Equal Treatment Directive. The article must be interpreted strictly as promoting measures giving a specific advantage to women with a view to improving their ability to compete on the labour market and to pursue a career on an equal footing with men. The addition of the fourth paragraph to Article 141 by the Treaty of Amsterdam (see **19.7**) which first appeared in Article 6(3) of the Agreement on Social Policy, is consistent with this. *Kalanke* was further clarified by Case C-409/95 *Marschall v Land Nordrhein-Westfalen* (1997) which took the same position, providing that an objective assessment taking account of all the criteria specific to individual candidates had to be made and that if these turned out to favour a male candidate, this would be acceptable as long as the criteria themselves did not discriminate against women.

Secondary legislation

19.28 After the Community had adopted a Social Action Programme in 1974, a number of directives were adopted pursuant to Article 119 (now Article 141 EC). The delay in any action on Article 119 until then had given the ECJ the task of interpreting the provision.

The principal directives are:

• Equal Pay Directive: Directive 75/117 EEC, OJ 1975 L 45/19;

• Equal Treatment Directive: Directive 76/207/EEC, OJ 1976 L 39/ 40;

• Social Security Directive: Directive 79/7/EEC, OJ 1979 L 6/24;

• Directive on Occupational Social Security Schemes: Directive 86/ 378/EEC, as amended by Corrigendum 1986 L 283/27, OJ 1986 L 225/40.

These directives express in much clearer language what Article 141 means to do. It should be noted, however, that, even where these directives have direct effect, this will only be vertical direct effect so that the individual has redress against the state or an emanation of the state (see *Marshall v Southampton Area Health Authority* (1986): Chapter 7) but not against a private employer.

Directive 75/117 on Equal Pay for Equal Work

19.29 The directive on equal pay appears at first sight to widen the principle of equal pay for equal work contained in Article 141 because it refers to equal pay for equal value (see Article 1).

When the directive was in preparation, it was not thought that Article 141 would have direct effect and the directive was intended to implement Article 141. However, the ECJ has stated that Directive 75/117 is merely:

> ...designed to facilitate the practical application of the principle of equal pay outlined in Article 119 of the Treaty.

(Case 96/80 *Jenkins v Kingsgate* (1981)). It does not alter the scope of Article 141.

Article 1 of the directive refers to job classification schemes, but does not make the principle of equal pay reliant upon them. The criteria must be drawn up so as to exclude any discrimination.

The directive contains explicit implementing provisions and instructs member states to take effective measures to ensure compliance with the provisions and to ensure that employees are aware of them.

Directive 76/207, the Equal Treatment Directive

19.30 This directive is not based upon Article 141 EC, but instead on Article 308 (ex Article 235) of the Treaty, the 'catch-all' provision, because its subject – that of *equal treatment* – goes beyond that of Article 141, which is concerned with *pay*. Thus, sex discrimination was widened to include many other factors, such as promotion, vocational training and working conditions (Article 1 of the Directive). The directive refers to both direct and indirect discrimination (Article 2). Although the direct effect of Article 141 EC has been widened by the Court to cases of indirect discrimination (see Case 96/80, *Jenkins v Kingsgate* (1981)) there are instances where the presence of such discrimination and any possible objective justification will be difficult for a national court to decide and direct effect will, therefore, not always be possible. In Case 152/84 *Marshall (No 1)*, Article 5(1) of the directive, which applies to working conditions, including conditions covering dismissal, was held to be directly effective. Subsequently in Case 222/84 *Johnston v Chief Constable of the Royal Ulster Constabulary* (1986), Article 3(1) which prohibits discrimination in conditions of employment and Article 4(1) which prohibits discrimination as regards access to vocational guidance and training, were also held to have direct effect. Article 6 of the directive was also considered in *Johnston* to be directly effective. This article requires member states to introduce appropriate remedies for failure to apply the principle of equal treatment. Mrs Johnston had been dismissed from the Royal Ulster Constabulary because she was considered to be unsuitable for firearms training as she was a woman. The Chief Constable of the RUC, against whom Mrs Johnston had brought a claim for sex discrimination, relied on a statutory provision which provided that a certificate signed by the Secretary of State certifying that an act was done for the purpose of safeguarding national security or protecting public safety or public order, was conclusive evidence of that fact. The Court found that Mrs Johnston could rely on Article 6 and that she otherwise would have no remedy at all, which would be a violation of the Article.

Article 2(2) of the directive allows a derogation on the basis of occupational activities in which 'by reason of their nature or the context in which they are carried out, the sex of the worker constitutes a determining factor'. This could include, for example, midwives. Article 2(3) provides that 'the directive shall be without prejudice to provisions concerning the protection of women, particularly as regards pregnancy and maternity'.

19.31 In Case C-273/97 *Sirdar v The Army Board* (1999) the Court held that the exclusion of women from service in special combat units such as the British Royal Marines may be justified under Article 2(2) of the directive by reason of the nature of the activities in question and the context in which they are carried out. Subject to the principle of proportionality, the competent authorities could exercise discretion as to whether to maintain the exclusion in question in the light of social developments, if this was justified in view of the specific conditions for deployment of those assault units and in particular the rule of interoperability. The Court further defined the scope of such justified exclusions in Case C-285/98 *Kreil* (2000). The applicant claimed before the national court that the Bundeswehr had refused to engage her in its maintenance branch. That refusal was founded on the German constitution, which imposes a general exclusion of women from military posts involving the use of arms and allows them access only to the medical and military-music services. Asked whether such an exclusion is compatible with Directive 76/207/EEC concerning access to employment, vocational training and promotion, and working conditions, the ECJ held that this directive precludes the application of national provisions such as those of German law. The Court acknowledged that it is for the member states to take decisions on the organisation of their armed forces.

It does not follow, however, that such decisions are bound to fall entirely outside the scope of Community law. Some specific cases are covered by certain provisions of the Treaty but the latter does not contain a general exception concerning all measures adopted by a member state to safeguard public security. Any limitation of access by women to military posts must therefore comply with Directive 76/207, which permits the member states to exclude from its scope occupational activities for which, by reason of their nature or the context in which they are carried out, sex constitutes a determining factor; it must also comply with the principle of proportionality inasmuch as a derogation from an individual fight the equal treatment of men and women is involved. In view of its scope, the exclusion at issue, which applied to almost all military posts in the Bundeswehr, could not be regarded as a derogating measure justified by the specific nature of the posts in question or by the particular context in which the activities in question were carried out.

19.32 In Case C-185/97 *Coote v Granada Hospitality Ltd* (1998) Ms Coote had brought an action against Granada Hospitality alleging she had been dismissed because of her pregnancy. The claim was settled and she left. Later, she asked her former employers for a reference, who refused because of the case she had brought against them. The Court held that Article 6 of the Equal Treatment Directive requiring member states to ensure effective judicial protection means that this includes measures to ensure judicial protection for workers whose employer, after the employment relationship has ended, refuses to provide references as a reaction to legal proceedings brought to enforce compliance with the principle of equal treatment. Otherwise, such retaliatory measures on the part of the employer might deter workers who considered themselves the victims of discrimination from pursuing their claims by judicial process, and would consequently be liable seriously to jeopardise implementation of the aim pursued by the directive

19.33 In Case 407/98 *Abrahamsson v Anderson & Fogelqvist* (2000) the Court interpreted Article 141(4) EC for the first time. Swedish legislation provided that positive discrimination could apply in cases where a candidate of the under-represented sex possessed sufficient qualifications, even if a candidate of the opposite sex would normally have been chosen. However, the difference in qualifications should not be so great that such application would breach the requirement of objectivity. This legislation applied to university appointments and, as a result, a professorial appointment at Göteborg University went to the female candidate who was considerably less qualified than the male candidate. The Court ruled that both Directive 76/207 and Article 141(4) EC preclude such national legislation. The directive did not allow such a provision which was so unclear as to scope and application that it resulted in appointment of a candidate from the under-represented sex purely on the basis of **sufficient** qualifications. If, however, a candidate presented 'equivalent or substantially equivalent merits', the appointment might be lawful, subject to an objective assessment. Nor could the appointment in this case be justified by Article 141(4) EC as the selection method appeared on any view to be disproportionate to the aim pursued.

19.34 On the other hand, in Case C-158/97 *Badeck* (2000) the Court ruled in favour of a rule laying down binding targets for an advancement plan for women who were under-represented in posts in the academic service. However, there had to be a guarantee that candidatures were the subject of an objective assessment which took account of the specific personal situations of all candidates. A rule providing that half the training places should go to women and that half the places on representative bodies should go to women, if there were enough candidates, was also compatible with Directive 76/207.

19.35 Subsequent to the Equal Treatment Directive, a number of directives was adopted providing for equal treatment of the self-employed and the protection of self-employed women during pregnancy and motherhood (Council Directive 86/613 EEC of 11 December 1986 on the Application of the Principle of Equal Treatment between Men and Women engaged in an Activity, including Agriculture, in a Self-employed Capacity, and on the Protection of self-employed Women during Pregnancy and Motherhood, OJ 1986 L 359/56), and a directive under the health and safety provisions of the Treaty (Article 138 (ex Article 118a) EC) concerning the health and safety of pregnant women and of those who have recently given birth or are breastfeeding (Council Directive 92/85 EEC of 19 October 1992 on the Introduction of Measures to encourage Improvements in the Safety and Health at Work of pregnant workers and workers who have recently given birth or are breastfeeding, OJ 1992 L 348/1). Does the Equal Treatment Directive cover discrimination on grounds of pregnancy? This is considered at **19.47** to **19.53** below.

Directive 79/7, the Social Security Directive

19.36 The broader concept of equal treatment was further extended by this directive. It covers statutory schemes protecting against risks arising from sickness, invalidity, old age, accidents at work and occupational diseases and unemployment (Article 3(1) of the directive). It does *not*, however, cover survivors' or family benefits and also excludes:

...the determination of pensionable age for the purposes of granting old-age and retirement pensions and the possible consequences thereof for other benefits. [Article 7(1)(a)].

19.37 The exceptions have been interpreted very narrowly by the Court. In Case 150/85 *Drake v Chief Adjudication Officer* (1986) an invalidity allowance payable to a married man but not to a married woman caring for a severely disabled person was found to fall within the directive. The carer would have been part of the working population and thus the benefit was covered by the risk provided for in the directive. In Case 102/88 *Ruzius-Wilbrink* (1989) part-time workers were held to fall within the directive. Invalidity benefits payable to part-time workers were linked to their previous earnings, whereas full-time workers were entitled to a 'minimum subsistence income' irrespective of their previous earnings. This was indirect discrimination, as the percentage of women working part-time in the Netherlands was much higher than that of men. As this was indirect discrimination, it could be justified by objective factors unrelated to sex. In Case C-9/91 *R v Secretary of State for Social Security, ex p Equal Opportunities Commission* (1992), however, the EOC brought an action for a declaration that the Social Security Act 1975 was in breach of the directive. The maintenance of different contribution periods for male and female workers under a state pension scheme was authorised under the derogation. It allowed not only men and women to be treated unequally with respect to the moment at which they become entitled to a pension but also covered other forms of discrimination if they were found to be necessary to achieve the objectives of the directive.

19.38 Clarification was obtained in *Barber v Guardian Royal Exchange Assurance Group* (1990). In this case Mr Barber sought to challenge his employers' *contracted out* pension scheme which operated as a substitute for the statutory social security schemes. The parties in such a scheme exercise statutory rights to replace the state pension scheme with that of a pension paid by the employer. The scheme was payable at different ages for men and women, so that when Mr Barber was made redundant at 52, if he had been a woman, he would have been able to receive a pension. As a man, he had to wait until he was 55. The ECJ said (at 28) that although 'contracted out' and therefore in lieu of a statutory scheme, the scheme nevertheless constituted 'pay' within Article 119 (now Article

141 EC). They reasoned that pensions are 'deferred pay' and were received by reason of the existence of the employment relationship. Thus there must be equality as to the age at which it is received. The fact that the benefits are payable at different ages resulted in an overall difference of pay between men and women. This was contrary to Article 119, even if the difference between the pensionable age for men and women was based on the one provided for by the national statutory scheme.

Barber thus opens up the concept of pay even further to include a pension scheme which is not supplementary to a statutory scheme but actually is in lieu of such a scheme – ie a contracted out scheme. Just because a scheme is in lieu of a statutory scheme will not mean that it will fall outside Article 141. This had the effect of requiring member states to bring statutory schemes into line with occupational schemes which were contracted out.

19.39 Difficulties arose with this judgment. The direct effect of Article 141 with respect to pensions had always been doubted as the matter was too complex. Different life expectancies of men and women and other factors leading to complicated actuarial calculations seemed to point to an absence of the criteria for direct effect. This ruling effectively bypassed the Social Security Directive and was clearly far-reaching in its effect. The economic impact of having to adapt national legislation would clearly be grave and 'for reasons of legal certainty' (at 44) the Court therefore limited the retroactive effect of the ruling. It said:

> In those circumstances, overriding considerations of legal certainty preclude legal situations which have exhausted all their effects in the past from being called in question where that might upset retroactively the financial balance of many contracted-out pension schemes...

> It must therefore be held that the direct effect of Article 119 of the Treaty may not be relied upon in order to claim entitlement to a pension with effect from a date prior to that of this judgment, except in the case of workers or those claiming under them who have before that date initiated legal proceedings or raised an equivalent claim under the applicable national law.

This wording caused confusion. Did the ruling only apply to benefits payable after the judgment or to service periods after the date of judgment? In Case C-109/91 *Ten Oever v Stichting Bedrijfspensioenfonds voor het Glazenwassers-en Schoonmaakbedrijf* (1993) the Court made it clear that the ruling applied to periods of employment after the date of the *Barber* judgment subject to an exception in favour of workers who had initiated proceedings before that date.

The Barber Protocol

19.40 Before *Ten Oever* was heard, the Maastricht Treaty on European Union had been adopted. This Treaty included a Protocol to the EC Treaty, which became known as the '*Barber* Protocol' followed by the Court subsequently in *Ten Oever*, which provided that benefits attributable to periods of employment prior to the date of the *Barber* judgment did not constitute pay, subject to the exception for those who had already started proceedings before 17 May 1990. The *Barber* Protocol only applies to occupational schemes themselves, not to access thereto. In Case C-57/93 *Vroege v NCIV Instituut voor Volkshuisvesting BV* (1994) the Court held that the Protocol did not apply to to the right to join an occupational pension scheme; in Case C-128/93 *Fisscher v Voorhuis Hengelo BV en Stichting Bedrijfspensioenfonds voor de Detailhandel* (1994) national rules relating to time limits for bringing actions under national law may be relied upon against workers who assert their right under Community law to join an occupational pension scheme and in Case C-435/93 *Dietz v Stichting Thuiszorg Rotterdam* (1996) the Court confirmed that it had been clear since *Bilka Kaufhaus* that Article 119 (now Article 141 EC) prohibits discrimination in the award of benefits by an occupational pension scheme which results from discrimination as regards the right to join such a scheme, so that employers and pension schemes could not reasonably have considered such discrimination permissible. (See also Case C-78/98 *Preston v Fletcher* (at **19.25**).)

19.41 Although the distinction between pay and occupational pensions had been eroded by the above cases, Case C-152/91 *Neath v Hugh Steeper Ltd* (1993) and Case C-200/91 *Coloroll Pension Trustees Ltd v James Richard Russell* (1994) drew back somewhat from the broad definition of pay. The Court ruled that employers' contributions to so-called 'defined-benefit' occupational pension schemes did not fall within the concept of pay.

19.42 In Cases C-87-89/90 *Verholen v Sociale Verzekeringsbank Amsterdam* (1991) the Court ruled that a national court could of its own motion raise the question of the applicability of Directive 79/7. The husband claimed discrimination, as he had suffered the effects of discriminatory legislation affecting his wife. The Court held that a national court could examine of its own motion the provisions of the directive. These were not confined to individuals who came within the scope of the directive *ratione personae* (at para 22), but could also be invoked by others who had been affected by the discriminatory provisions.

Directive 86/378

19.43 Directive 79/7 is supplemented by this directive which deals with occupational social security schemes, including pensions.

19.44 There are also non-binding recommendations in the field of positive discrimination and sexual harassment: see Case C-342/93 *Gillespie v Northern Health and Social Services Board* (1996). These are now incorporated in Directive 2002/73 (see **19.55**).

Direct and indirect discrimination

19.45 *Direct* discrimination can never be justified. It is only subject to the derogations contained in the directives implementing Article 141 EC. The Court has never ruled on the point, although some suggestions have from time to time been made, eg van Gerven AG in Case C-132/92 *Birds Eye Walls Ltd v Roberts* (1993) invited the Court to consider that 'such discrimination in a case such as *Webb* might nevertheless be justified having regard to the specific circumstances of the case'. The Court ruled there was no infringement of Article 119 (now Article 141 EC) in this case, thus avoiding the question.

19.46 *Indirect* discrimination may be justified by objective factors unrelated to sex. These objective factors were defined by the Court in *Bilka* (**19.12**). In Case 171/88 *Rinner-Kühn v FWW Spezial-Gebäudereinigung GmbH* (1989) the plaintiff worked as an office cleaner for ten hours a week. German legislation excluded workers who normally worked for no more than ten hours a week from payment of sick pay. The proportion of women working these shorter hours was considerably greater than that of men. The Court held that such a legislative provision which results in practice in discrimination must in principle be regarded as contrary to the aim of Article 119 (now Article 141 EC), but may be objectively justified by objective considerations unrelated to sex. The German government alleged (at paras 13 and 14) that part-time workers such as these were not as integrated in, or as dependent on, the undertaking employing them as other workers. Such considerations, insofar as they were generalisations about certain categories of workers, could not be accepted as objective justification. However, it would be different if the member state could show that the means chosen meet a necessary aim of social policy and that they are suitable and requisite for attaining that aim. In Case C-189/91 *Kirshammer-Hack v Nurhan Sidal* (1993) the Court ruled that in the context of equal treatment, legislation favouring small enterprises which were exempt from applying the general rules on unfair dismissal to part-time workers could constitute objective justification. Objective justification is to be decided by the national court.

In Cases C-399, C-409/92, C-425/92, C-34/93, C-50/93 and C-78/93 *Stadt Lengerich v Helmig* (1994) the Court ruled that there was no indirect discrimination if overtime rates were paid to part-time workers only where normal working hours for full-time workers have been exceeded.

Discrimination on grounds of pregnancy

19.47 Is discrimination on the grounds of pregnancy direct discrimination? The Court has stated in a number of cases that a refusal to employ or a dismissal of a woman because she is pregnant amounts to direct discrimination. There are, however, some limitations. In Case C-177/88 *Dekker v Stichting Vormingscentrum voor Jonge Volwassenen (VJV-Centrum) Plus* (1990) and Case 179/88 *Handels-og Kontorfunktionaerernes Forbund i Danmark (acting for Hertz) v Dansk Arbejdsgiverforening (acting for Aldi Marked K/S)* (1990), two cases decided on the same day, the Court stated the principle.

Mrs Dekker applied for a post as a training instructor with a youth training centre. She was pregnant when she applied and so informed the selection committee. The committee recommended her as the most suitable candidate, but the training centre refused to take her on because their insurers would not reimburse the sickness benefits the centre would have to pay during Mrs Dekker's maternity leave because she was pregnant at the time of the application. Mrs Dekker claimed compensation, arguing that the refusal of employment was contrary to the provisions of the Dutch equal treatment law which implemented the Equal Treatment Directive 76/207. The Dutch courts held that the law had been violated but rejected her claim on the grounds that the employer had raised an acceptable ground for justification under Dutch law. Upon referral by the Dutch Supreme Court to the ECJ under Article 177 EEC (now Article 234 EC) the ECJ ruled as follows:

Whether a refusal to employ results in direct discrimination on
grounds of sex depends on whether the most important reason for
the refusal is a reason which applies without distinction to
employees of both sexes or whether it applies exclusively to one
sex. As employment can only be refused because of pregnancy to
women, such refusal is direct discrimination...

The employer had, therefore acted in breach of Articles 2(1) and 3(1)
of the Equal Treatment Directive and the discrimination could not be
justified by the financial detriment which the employer would suffer during
the woman's maternity leave.

19.48 In *Hertz*, Mrs Hertz had had repeated absences from her work
due to an illness arising out of her pregnancy and confinement but which
appeared after her maternity leave. This resulted in her dismissal on
grounds of absence. The Court held that in this case there was no breach
of the Equal Treatment Directive (Articles 5(1) and 2(1)) as the illness
was treated as such, and the applicant's position was therefore comparable
to that of a man who would have been dismissed under the same
conditions. The Court did, however, state that dismissal of a woman on
grounds of pregnancy constituted direct discrimination in the same way
as a refusal to recruit a pregnant woman. A woman is, therefore, protected
from dismissal because of her absence during maternity leave from which
she benefits under national law.

In Case C-394/96 *Brown v Rentokil Ltd* (1998) the Court stated that
the principle of non-discrimination required protection throughout the
period of pregnancy in addition to the period of maternity leave protected
by the Equal Treatment Directive. The directive therefore precluded
dismissal of a female worker at any time during her pregnancy for
absences due to incapacity for work caused by an illness resulting from
that pregnancy. The Court expressly reversed its decision in Case C-
400/95 *Larsson v Føtex Supermarked* (1997), para 23 and concluded, in
passing, that where a woman is absent owing to illness resulting from
pregnancy or childbirth, and that illness arose during pregnancy and
persisted during and after maternity leave, her absence not only during
maternity leave but also during the period extending from the start of
her pregnancy to the start of her maternity leave cannot be taken into
account for the purpose of computing the period justifying her dismissal
under national law.

19.49 There is no justification for direct discrimination, but there are
circumstances in which direct discrimination will not arise. In Case C-

32/93 *Webb v EMO Cargo (UK) Ltd* (1994) the House of Lords referred to the ECJ the case of a woman who had been hired on an indefinite contract to replace a pregnant worker, who had then herself become pregnant. Although she acted as a temporary replacement it was anticipated that Mrs Webb would stay in employment after the other worker returned. The Employment Appeal Tribunal (EAT) and the Court of Appeal had dismissed her complaint on the grounds that her position should be compared with that of a man with a condition as nearly comparable as possible. The House of Lords took the view that the dismissal would constitute direct discrimination but that the motive for the dismissal should be examined, which was that at the relevant time the applicant was unavailable to do the work she had been recruited specifically to do. It therefore considered the situation of a man in a comparable situation. Upon reference to the ECJ asking for an interpretation of the Equal Treatment Directive the Court stated:

> ...dismissal of a woman on grounds of pregnancy constitutes direct discrimination on grounds of sex. Since pregnancy is not in any way comparable with a pathological condition, and even less so with unavailability for work on non-medical grounds, there can be no question of comparing the situation of a woman who finds herself incapable by reason of pregnancy of performing the task for which she was recruited with that of a man similarly incapable for medical or other reasons...

The Pregnancy Directive (Directive 92/85), which had not yet been in force when the national courts decided the case, had also to be taken into account in considering the need for special protection to be given to pregnant women and those on maternity leave. This case concerned an employment contract for an indefinite term and this was referred to by the court in its ruling; the directive precluded:

> ...the dismissal of an employee who is recruited for an unlimited term with a view, initially, to replacing another employee...

The House of Lords, in its judgment applying the Court's ruling, considered this to be an important factor.

19.50 Although the national courts would now have to decide *Webb* differently after the adoption of the Pregnancy Directive, the principle retains its importance in respect of other types of discrimination, eg in respect of terms and conditions of employment. In Case C-342/93 *Gillespie v Northern Health and Social Services Board* (1996), which was concerned with the Equal Pay Directive, the Court ruled that the Equal Treatment Directive did not apply and that, therefore, there was neither a requirement that women should continue to receive full pay during maternity leave, nor did it lay down any specific criteria for the amount of benefit payable to them during that period.

19.51 Perhaps *Webb* represents the high water mark of the Court's case law in this respect. There is still no clear answer as regards temporary, fixed term contracts and those which concern a specific task. The Pregnancy Directive does not set a qualifying period and the only exception is contained in Article 10(1), which provides that in '...exceptional cases not connected with their condition which are permitted under national legislation and/or practice...' dismissal may be permitted. The employer must cite the grounds for such a dismissal in writing.

19.52 In Case C-421/92 *Habermann-Beltermann v Arbeiterwohlfahrt, Bezirksverband Ndb/Opf e V* (1994) the ECJ found direct discrimination because of the existence of an indefinite contract. The German law for the protection of mothers (*Mutterschutzgesetz*) prohibited pregnant women from carrying out night work. The Court drew a distinction between fixed term and permanent contracts. The national prohibition on night work was only for a limited period and thus it would undermine the effectiveness of the Equal Treatment Directive to allow the employment contract to be found void or invalid. Case C-207/98 *Mahlburg* concerned a refusal to appoint a pregnant woman to an indefinite contract on the basis of a statutory prohibition to employ women from the outset and during pregnancy. The Court ruled that Directive 76/207 precluded such a refusal; its provisions aimed at protecting pregnant women could not result in less favourable treatment in regard to their access to employment.

19.53 Since the adoption of the Pregnancy Directive (Directive 92/85) dismissal of workers during the minimum maternity leave prescribed in the directive (see Article 10) would no longer need to be examined under the Equal Treatment Directive. The situation in *Habermann-Beltermann* would thus no longer need to be objectively justified.

In Case C-411/96 *Boyle v Equal Opportunities Commission* (1998) the Court gave for the first time an interpretation of the Pregnancy Directive with a series of answers relating to the interpretation of Article 119 (now Article 141 EC), of the directive as well as of the Equal Pay and the Equal Treatment Directive. Those replies determine the rights of female workers before, during and after their maternity leave and concern the payments to which they are entitled, the time when they must commence their maternity leave, the accrual of rights to annual leave and pension rights and the relationship between maternity leave and sick leave. The case concerned a clause in a contract of employment for staff of a public body which made the application of a maternity scheme which was more favourable than the statutory scheme conditional on the woman's return to work after the birth of the child, failing which she was required to repay the difference between the contractual maternity pay and the statutory payments in respect of that leave. The Court held this did not constitute discrimination.

19.54 The Part-time Workers' Directive 97/81 based on a framework agreement between the social partners is aimed at eliminating discrimination against part-time workers and to assist the development of opportunities for part-time working on a basis acceptable to both workers and employers.

Clause 4 of the Framework Agreement states that part-time workers should not be treated in a less favourable manner than comparable full-time workers unless this can be objectively justified. An objective justification would allow member states to make access to employment subject to requirements as to period of service, time worked or an earnings threshold.

19.55 A new Directive 2002/73 amending Directive 76/207 is to be implemented by 5 October 2005. This directive updates the older Directive to take account of case law and provisions in other, recent Directives. It defines sexual harassment as follows:

> where any form of unwanted verbal, non-verbal or physical conduct of a sexual nature occurs with the purpose or effect of violating the dignity of a person, in particular when creating an intimidating, hostile, degrading, humiliating or offensive environment.

This constitutes sex discrimination.

19.56 It gives a new definition of indirect discrimination:

> where an apparently neutral provision, criterion or practice would put persons of one sex at a particular disadvantage compared with persons of the other sex, unless that provision, criterion or practice is objectively justified by a legitimate aim, and the means of achieving that aim are appropriate and necessary.

479

It provides safeguards to women returning to work after for maternity leave stating that they will be able to return to their job on terms and conditions which are no less favourable to them than before and incorporates the principle laid down in *Coote* (see 19.32) that judicial and/or administrative procedures should be available for all persons who considered themselves to be wronged by the failure to apply the principle of equal treatment to them, even after the relationship in which the discrimination is alleged to have occurred has ended. Member states should ensure real and effective compensation, including removing any upper limit on compensation and reparation.

UK law and EC law

19.57 There have sometimes been difficulties in the interpretation of sex discrimination law by English courts. The House of Lords gave a *communautaire* interpretation of Community law in the *EOC* case, but in other cases the national court did not always find it possible to construe domestic law in the light of Community law. In *Duke v GEC Reliance* (1988) the House of Lords held that as the Sex Discrimination Act 1975, s 6(4) was intended to preserve discriminatory retirement ages, it was not possible to construe it in a manner which gave effect to EEC Equal Treatment Directive 76/207 as interpreted by the European Court of Justice in the first Marshall decision. In *Finnegan v Clowney Youth Training Programme Ltd* (1990) the exclusion of complaints relating to retirement in Article 8(4) of the Sex Discrimination (Northern Ireland) Order 1976 was indistinguishable from the exclusion in s 6(4) of the Sex Discrimination Act 1975 which the House of Lords, in *Duke v GEC Reliance*, held was not to be construed so as to conform to the Equal Treatment Directive (see further Chapter 8).

Further reading

Gilian More, 'The Principle of Equal Treatment: From Market Unifier to Fundamental Right?', in Craig and de Burca (eds) *The Evolution of EU Law* (1999) OUP.

Hervey and O'Keeffe (eds), *Sex Equality Law in the European Union* (1996) Wiley, Parts I–IV.

D Curtin, 'Scalping the Community Legislator: Occupational Pensions and "Barber"', [1990] CMLRev 475.

Erica Szyszczak, 'Community Law on Pregnancy and Maternity', in Hervey and O'Keeffe (eds), *Sex Equality Law in the European Union* (1996) Wiley, Chapter 4.

Case note on Case C-189/91 *Kirshammer-Hack* by M Horspool in [1994] 31 CMLRev 751.

Self-test questions

1. Following the judgments of the Court of Justice in *Marshall* and *Barber*, is it correct to say that there is equality between men and women with regard to matters of equal treatment and 'pay' in Community law?

2. Some forms of sex discrimination may be objectively justified, others can never be justified. Discuss.

3. 'The case law of the Court of Justice on matters of sex discrimination considerably expanded the scope of Article 141. More recently, in applying the principle of equality, the Court has shown uncharacteristic restraint.' Discuss.

APPENDIX

Tables of equivalences referred to in Article 12 of the Treaty of Amsterdam

A Treaty on European Union

PREVIOUS NUMBERING	NEW NUMBERING
Title I	*Title I*
Article A	Article 1
Article B	Article 2
Article C	Article 3
Article D	Article 4
Article E	Article 5
Article F	Article 6
Article F.1*	Article 7
Title II	*Title II*
Article G	Article 8
Title III	*Title III*
Article H	Article 9
Title IV	*Title IV*
Article I	Article 10
*Title V***	*Title V*
Article J.1	Article 11
Article J.2	Article 12
Article J.3	Article 13
Article J.4	Article 14
Article J.5	Article 15
Article J.6	Article 16

PREVIOUS NUMBERING	NEW NUMBERING
Article J.7	Article 17
Article J.8	Article 18
Article J.9	Article 19
Article J.10	Article 20
Article J.11	Article 21
Article J.12	Article 22
Article J.13	Article 23
Article J.14	Article 24
Article J.15	Article 25
Article J.16	Article 26
Article J.17	Article 27
Article J.18	Article 28
*Title VI***	*Title VI*
Article K.1	Article 29
Article K.2	Article 30
Article K.3	Article 31
Article K.4	Article 32
Article K.5	Article 33
Article K.6	Article 34
Article K.7	Article 35
Article K.8	Article 36
Article K.9	Article 37
Article K.10	Article 38
Article K.11	Article 39
Article K.12	Article 40
Article K.13	Article 41
Article K.14	Article 42
*Title VIa***	*Title VII*
Article K.15*	Article 43
Article K.16*	Article 44
Article K.17*	Article 45
Title VII	*Title VIII*
Article L	Article 46
Article M	Article 47
Article N	Article 48
Article O	Article 49
Article P	Article 50

PREVIOUS NUMBERING	NEW NUMBERING
Article Q	Article 51
Article R	Article 52
Article S	Article 53

B Treaty establishing the European Community

Part One	*Part One*
Article 1	Article 1
Article 2	Article 2
Article 3	Article 3
Article 3a	Article 4
Article 3b	Article 5
Article 3c*	Article 6
Article 4	Article 7
Article 4a	Article 8
Article 4b	Article 9
Article 5	Article 10
Article 5a*	Article 11
Article 6	Article 12
Article 6a*	Article 13
Article 7 (repealed)	—
Article 7a	Article 14
Article 7b (repealed)	—
Article 7c	Article 15
Article 7d*	Article 16
Part Two	*Part Two*
Article 8	Article 17
Article 8a	Article 18
Article 8b	Article 19
Article 8c	Article 20
Article 8d	Article 21
Article 8e	Article 22
Part Three	*Part Three*
Title I	*Title I*
Article 9	Article 23
Article 10	Article 24
Article 11 (repealed)	—

PREVIOUS NUMBERING	NEW NUMBERING
Chapter 1	*Chapter 1*
Section 1 (deleted)	—
Article 12	Article 25
Article 13 (repealed)	—
Article 14 (repealed)	—
Article 15 (repealed)	—
Article 16 (repealed	—
Article 17 (repealed)	—
[Section 2 (deleted)]	—
Article 18 (repealed)	—
Article 19 (repealed)	—
Article 20 (repealed)	—
Article 21 (repealed)	—
Article 22 (repealed)	—
Article 23 (repealed)	—
Article 24 (repealed)	—
Article 25 (repealed)	—
Article 26 (repealed)	—
Article 27 (repealed)	—
Article 28	Article 26
Article 29	Article 27
Chapter 2	*Chapter 2*
Article 30	Article 28
Article 31 (repealed)	—
Article 32 (repealed)	—
Article 33 (repealed)	—
Article 34	Article 29
Article 35 (repealed)	—
Article 36	Article 30
Article 37	Article 31
Title II	*Title II*
Article 38	Article 32
Article 39	Article 33
Article 40	Article 34
Article 41	Article 35
Article 42	Article 36
Article 43	Article 37
Article 44 (repealed)	—

PREVIOUS NUMBERING	NEW NUMBERING
Article 45 (repealed)	—
Article 46	Article 38
Article 47 (repealed)	—
Title III	*Title III*
Chapter I	*Chapter I*
Article 48	Article 39
Article 49	Article 40
Article 50	Article 41
Article 51	Article 42
Chapter 2	*Chapter 2*
Article 52	Article 43
Article 53 (repealed)	—
Article 54	Article 44
Article 55	Article 45
Article 56	Article 46
Article 57	Article 47
Article 58	Article 48
Chapter 3	Chapter 3
Article 59	Article 49
Article 60	Article 50
Article 61	Article 51
Article 62 (repealed)	—
Article 63	Article 52
Article 64	Article 53
Article 65	Article 54
Article 66	Article 55
Chapter 4	*Chapter 4*
Article 67 (repealed)	—
Article 68 (repealed)	—
Article 69 (repealed)	—
Article 70 (repealed)	—
Article 71 (repealed)	—
Article 72 (repealed)	—
Article 73 (repealed)	—
Article 73a (repealed)	—
Article 73b	Article 56
Article 73c	Article 57

PREVIOUS NUMBERING	NEW NUMBERING
Article 73d	Article 58
Article 73e (repealed)	—
Article 73f	Article 59
Article 73g	Article 60
Article 73h (repealed)	—
*Title IIIa***	*Title IV*
Article 73i*	Article 61
Article 73j*	Article 62
Article 73k*	Article 63
Article 73l*	Article 64
Article 73m*	Article 65
Article 73n*	Article 66
Article 73o*	Article 67
Article 73p*	Article 68
Article 73q*	Article 69
Title IV	*Title V*
Article 74	Article 70
Article 75	Article 71
Article 76	Article 72
Article 77	Article 73
Article 78	Article 74
Article 79	Article 75
Article 80	Article 76
Article 81	Article 77
Article 82	Article 78
Article 83	Article 79
Article 84	Article 80
Title V	*Title VI*
Chapter 1	*Chapter 1*
Section 1	Section 1
Article 85	Article 81
Article 86	Article 82
Article 87	Article 83
Article 88	Article 84
Article 89	Article 85
Article 90	Article 86
[Section 2 (deleted)]	—

PREVIOUS NUMBERING	NEW NUMBERING
Article 91 (repealed)	—
Section 3	Section 2
Article 92	Article 87
Article 93	Article 88
Article 94	Article 89
Chapter 2	*Chapter 2*
Article 95	Article 90
Article 96	Article 91
Article 97 (repealed)	—
Article 98	Article 92
Article 99	Article 93
Chapter 3	*Chapter 3*
Article 100	Article 94
Article 100a	Article 95
Article 100b (repealed)	—
Article 100c (repealed)	—
Article 100d (repealed)	—
Article 101	Article 96
Article 102	Article 97
Title VI	*Title VII*
Chapter 1	*Chapter 1*
Article 102a	Article 98
Article 103	Article 99
Article 103a	Article 100
Article 104	Article 101
Article 104a	Article 102
Article 104b	Article 103
Article 104c	Article 104
Chapter 2	*Chapter 2*
Article 105	Article 105
Article 105a	Article 106
Article 106	Article 107
Article 107	Article 108
Article 108	Article 109
Article 108a	Article 110
Article 109	Article 111

PREVIOUS NUMBERING	NEW NUMBERING
Chapter 3	*Chapter 3*
Article 109a	Article 112
Article 109b	Article 113
Article 109c	Article 114
Article 109d	Article 115
Chapter 4	*Chapter 4*
Article 109e	Article 116
Article 109f	Article 117
Article 109g	Article 118
Article 109h	Article 119
Article 109i	Article 120
Article 109j	Article 121
Article 109k	Article 122
Article 109l	Article 123
Article 109m	Article 124
*Title VIa***	*Title VIII*
Article 109n*	Article 125
Article 109o*	Article 126
Article 109p*	Article 127
Article 109q*	Article 128
Article 109r*	Article 129
Article 109s*	Article 130
Title VII	*Title IX*
Article 110	Article 131
Article 111 (repealed)	—
Article 112	Article 132
Article 113	Article 133
Article 114 (repealed)	—
Article 115	Article 134
*Title VIIa***	*Title X*
Article 116*	Article 135
Title VIII	*Title XI*
*Chapter 1****	*Chapter 1*
Article 117	Article 136
Article 118	Article 137
Article 118a	Article 138
Article 118b	Article 139

→ *Table of equivalences* ←

PREVIOUS NUMBERING	NEW NUMBERING
Article 130i	Article 166
Article 130j	Article 167
Article 130k	Article 168
Article 130l	Article 169
Article 130m	Article 170
Article 130n	Article 171
Article 130o	Article 172
Article 130p	Article 173
Article 130q (repealed)	—
Article 130r	Article 174
Article 130s	Article 175
Article 130t	Article 176
Title XVII	*Title XX*
Article 130u	Article 177
Article 130v	Article 178
Article 130w	Article 179
Article 130x	Article 180
Article 130y	Article 181
Part Four	*Part Four*
Article 131	Article 182
Article 132	Article 183
Article 133	Article 184
Article 134	Article 185
Article 135	Article 186
Article 136	Article 187
Article 136a	Article 188
Part Five	*Part Five*
Title I	*Title I*
Chapter I	*Chapter I*
Section I	Section I
Article 137	Article 189
Article 138	Article 190
Article 138a	Article 191
Article 138b	Article 192
Article 138c	Article 193
Article 138d	Article 194
Article 138e	Article 195

→ *Table of equivalences* ←

PREVIOUS NUMBERING	NEW NUMBERING
Article 139	Article 196
Article 140	Article 197
Article 141	Article 198
Article 142	Article 199
Article 143	Article 200
Article 144	Article 201
Section 2	Section 2
Article 145	Article 202
Article 146	Article 203
Article 147	Article 204
Article 148	Article 205
Article 149 (repealed)	—
Article 150	Article 206
Article 151	Article 207
Article 152	Article 208
Article 153	Article 209
Article 154	Article 210
Section 3	Section 3
Article 155	Article 211
Article 156	Article 212
Article 157	Article 213
Article 158	Article 214
Article 159	Article 215
Article 160	Article 216
Article 161	Article 217
Article 162	Article 218
Article 163	Article 219
Section 4	Section 4
Article 164	Article 220
Article 165	Article 221
Article 166	Article 222
Article 167	Article 223
Article 168	Article 224
Article 168a	Article 225
Article 169	Article 226
Article 170	Article 227
Article 171	Article 228

PREVIOUS NUMBERING	NEW NUMBERING
Article 172	Article 229
Article 173	Article 230
Article 174	Article 231
Article 175	Article 232
Article 176	Article 233
Article 177	Article 234
Article 178	Article 235
Article 179	Article 236
Article 180	Article 237
Article 181	Article 238
Article 182	Article 239
Article 183	Article 240
Article 184	Article 241
Article 185	Article 242
Article 186	Article 243
Article 187	Article 244
Article 188	Article 245
Section 5	Section 5
Article 188a	Article 246
Article 188b	Article 247
Article 188c	Article 248
Chapter 2	*Chapter 2*
Article 189	Article 249
Article 189a	Article 250
Article 189b	Article 251
Article 189c	Article 252
Article 190	Article 253
Article 191	Article 254
Article 191a*	Article 255
Article 192	Article 256
Chapter 3	*Chapter 3*
Article 193	Article 257
Article 194	Article 258
Article 195	Article 259
Article 196	Article 260
Article 197	Article 261
Article 198	Article 262

PREVIOUS NUMBERING	NEW NUMBERING
Chapter 4	*Chapter 4*
Article 198a	Article 263
Article 198b	Article 264
Article 198c	Article 265
Chapter 5	*Chapter 5*
Article 198d	Article 266
Article 198e	Article 267
Title II	*Title II*
Article 199	Article 268
Article 200 (repealed)	—
Article 201	Article 269
Article 201a	Article 270
Article 202	Article 272
Article 203	Article 272
Article 204	Article 273
Article 205	Article 274
Article 205a	Article 275
Article 206	Article 276
Article 206a (repealed)	—
Article 207	Article 277
Article 208	Article 278
Article 209	Article 279
Article 209a	Article 280
Part Six	*Part Six*
Article 210	Article 281
Article 211	Article 282
Article 212*	Article 283
Article 213	Article 284
Article 213a*	Article 285
Article 213b*	Article 286
Article 214	Article 287
Article 215	Article 288
Article 216	Article 289
Article 217	Article 290
Article 218*	Article 291
Article 219	Article 292
Article 220	Article 293

PREVIOUS NUMBERING	NEW NUMBERING
Article 221	Article 294
Article 222	Article 295
Article 223	Article 296
Article 224	Article 297
Article 225	Article 298
Article 226 (repealed)	—
Article 227	Article 299
Article 228	Article 300
Article 228a	Article 301
Article 229	Article 302
Article 230	Article 303
Article 231	Article 304
Article 232	Article 305
Article 233	Article 306
Article 234	Article 307
Article 235	Article 308
Article 236*	Article 309
Article 237 (repealed)	—
Article 238	Article 310
Article 239	Article 311
Article 240	Article 312
Article 241 (repealed)	—
Article 242 (repealed)	—
Article 243 (repealed)	—
Article 244 (repealed)	—
Article 245 (repealed)	—
Article 246 (repealed)	—
Final Provisions	*Final Provisions*
Article 247	Article 313
Article 248	Article 314

NOTES
* New Article introduced by the Treaty of Amsterdam.
** New Title introduced by the Treaty of Amsterdam.
*** Title restructured by the Treaty of Amsterdam.

Index